£9.99

The Official America Online Internet Guide

MACINTOSH EDITION

David Peal
Kevin Savetz

Osborne **McGraw-Hill**

Berkeley New York St. Louis San Francisco
Auckland Bogotá Hamburg London Madrid
Mexico City Milan Montreal New Delhi Panama City
Paris São Paulo Singapore Sydney
Tokyo Toronto

Osborne/**McGraw-Hill**
2600 Tenth Street
Berkeley, California 94710
U.S.A.

For information on translations or book distributors outside the U.S.A., or to arrange bulk purchase discounts for sales promotions, premiums, or fundraisers, please contact Osborne/**McGraw-Hill** at the above address.

The Official America Online Internet Guide, Macintosh Edition

Screenshot Credits:

Page 298: Text and artwork copyright 1996 by YAHOO! all rights reserved. YAHOO! and the YAHOO! logo are tradmarks of YAHOO!, Inc.

Pages 310, 312, and 344: Reprinted with permission from CNET: The Computer Network, copyright 1996

Page 285: Reproduced with the permission of Digital Equipment Corporation. AltaVista and the Altavista logo and the Digital Logo are trademarks of Digital Equipment Corporation.

Page 289: Reprinted by permission. Infoseek, Ultrasmark, Ultraseek, iSeek, Quickseek, Imageseek, Ultrashop, "proof of intelligent life on the net," and the Infoseek logos are trademarks of Infoseek Corporation which may be registered in certain jurisdictions. Other trademarks shown are trademarks of their respective owners. Copyright \C 1995-1997 Infoseek Corporation. All rights reserved.

Page 433: © 1996 Nando.net

Page 393: © 1997 Exploratorium; used by permission.

Page 399: Credit for buttons on Carnegie Library site: Mark Friedman & Associates

Page 358: © 1997 Hollywood Online Inc.

1234567890 DOC 9987

ISBN 0-07-882345-5

Publisher Brandon A. Nordin	**Proofreader** Rhonda Holmes, Pat Mannion
Editor-in-Chief Scott Rogers	**Indexer** Valerie Robbins
Acquisitions Editor Megg Bonar	**Computer Designers** Jani Beckwith, Peter F. Hancik
Project Editor Claire Splan	**Illustrator** Leslee Bassin
Associate Project Editors Cynthia Douglas, Heidi Poulin	**Series Design** Roberta Steele
Editorial Assistant Gordon Hurd	**Cover Design** Arlette Crosland
Technical Editors Jenn Thompson, America Online	**Cover Illustration/Design** Doug Keeffe Graphic Design
Copy Editor Johanna Martin	

For Carol, Ella, and Gabriel
—dp

For Peace
—kms

About the Authors

David Peal is the author of the best-selling book *Access the Internet*. As former Editorial Manager of the Internet Connection at America Online, he developed several "personality forums" including AnswerMan, NetGirl, and In Business. He also developed comprehensive Internet Help and Search forums.

Kevin Savetz is AOL's Internet AnswerMan and maintains AOL's Net.Help forum. He was editor of the *1996-97 Microsoft Bookshelf Internet Directory* and *Internet Unleashed 1996*. A Macintosh maven, he is a regular contributor to *NetGuide, Computer Shopper,* and other publications. Kevin lives in Northern California with his wife, their dog, four cats, and four Macs.

CONTENTS AT A GLANCE

CONTENTS

America Online made this book possible in many ways, and we are especially thankful to John Dyn, Brad Schepp, and Judy Karpinski for their support. In the Internet Connection Jenn Thompson read the manuscript beginning to end, and offered countless suggestions for improving it. John Ayers and Nicole Flanagan kept us apprised of Internet goings-on at AOL. Nutty schedules made it impossible for the book to reflect everything that AOL is doing in the Internet "space." But we tried.

David O'Donnell (AOL's Postmaster), Bob Hirsh (AOL's FTP administrator), and Lindlee Jenner (AOL's Newsgroup Project Manager) read specific chapters and offered many recommendations. Beth Wiley read the introductory chapters and offered some trenchant suggestions. For helping us anticipate the next generation of AOL's software, otherwise known as Casablanca, thanks to Adam Bartlett, Tim Barwick, Dominic Stirpe, Reggie Fairchild, and Travis Good.

For doing much hard work on Chapter 11, we'd like to thank Mariva Hannah Aviram and Charlie Armstrong. Few people know AOL as well as Charlie, who for years has been the omnicompotent coordinator of the Internet Connection's cyberjockeys.

Osborne/McGraw-Hill's civility made the publishing process a genuine pleasure. The people there who made the book happen are Brandon Nordin (Publisher) and Scott Rogers (Editor-in-Chief), neither of whom ever relented in supporting the project. Special thanks to Megg Bonar, our day-to-day acquisitions editor and advocate. Her assistant, Gordon Hurd, ably coordinated this book as well as its evil sister, *The Official America Online Internet Guide, Windows Edition*. The following people did an amazing job making the physical book despite a painfully compressed production schedule: Claire Splan, project editor; Cynthia Douglas and Heidi Poulin, associate project editors, Roberta Steele, designer, and Rhonda Holmes and Pat Mannion, proofreaders.

ACKNOWLEDGMENTS

David's debts: I would like to thank my wife Carol for once again putting up with the messy business of writing a computer book. With Gabriel and Ella, she again put everything in perspective, which is why the book is dedicated to them.

Kevin's debts: Thanks to Peace for her humor and never-ending support, to David for launching me on this journey, and to Jenn for her copious behind-the-scenes help.

America Online has created the biggest and easiest-to-use online service in the world. America Online has also done more than any organization to bring easy Internet access to millions of people.

If it's so easy, why do you need this book?

For one thing, there's just so much of the Internet: some 60 million people taking part in 60,000 mailing lists and 20,000 newsgroups, and producing some 100 million World Wide Web pages. *Where do you start?* This book provides both the orientation and the starting points you need.

For another thing, *how* do you start? There are many ways of getting information and meeting people on the Internet—the Web, mailing lists, and newsgroups, to mention just the major Internet services. What's more, AOL's Internet tools for have gotten very powerful in a very short period. The Web "browser" in particular is a major application in itself. How do you learn to use all this stuff? How do you find out what's *worth* learning for a particular purpose? This book provides all the "how-to" you need, in one place.

This book can help you make the Net an integral and fun part of your life.

America Online: A Different Kind of ISP

Many Internet service providers (ISPs) give you some software and a phone number and drop you onto the Net without a life preserver. With most ISPs, you get a dialtone. With AOL, you get a community.

You get a *very big* community, at that—eight million people and counting, including a rapidly growing overseas contingent. You also get many ways to interact with people for both private exchanges (electronic mail and Instant Messages) and small-group conversations (chat rooms and Road Trips). On AOL you even get a customizable Buddy List. We couldn't have written this book without e-mail, IMs, our Buddy Lists, and, of course, our AOL buddies.

On AOL you get a community and communications tools. You also get hundreds of places to meet and hang out with others, including Internet-related forums such as AnswerMan and NetGuide, where you can learn about the Internet directly from other members and from experienced Internauts. No other ISP or service offers all this.

When you're on AOL, you're not on the Internet. But with easy-to-use forums *about* the Internet and easy-to-use communications tools such as e-mail, you are more than half-way there, and Internet services and resources are always at your fingertips. Think of AOL as a comfortable electronic community from which the Net is a click away.

"Click away" is not an exaggeration. If you're a sports fan, in the Sports channel you'll get great AOL forums plus links to Internet resources like ESPNet and SportsZone. In the MusicSpace channel, you'll find Rolling Stone on AOL plus Internet resources like the Internet Underground Music Archive and Virtual Library's Classical Music directory. And in the Computers & Software channel, you get access to 100,000 files *on* AOL, plus you can click to the Web sites of all of the major and most of the minor hardware and software vendors.

AOL's goal is to make Internet access seamless and almost secondary. The premise is that what you want to do and who you want to meet are more important than where content is available or how it's accessed. The Internet is thoroughly integrated into the AOL experience.

Who This Book Was Written For

This book was written for Macintosh users who want to get the most from the Internet and AOL.

If you're new to both AOL and the Internet, this book is definitely for you, beginning with Chapter 1. This book is also for seasoned AOL members who are just getting their bearings on the Internet. If you have experience using the Internet on another ISP, you'll want to use this book to find out how to use the Internet services and resources available on AOL and where to find them. Finally, if you're a more advanced user or even a developer, this book can help you better understand the AOL member experience, which separates AOL from an ordinary ISP.

What You'll Find Inside

The book has eleven chapters, each organized more or less logically, but the book is meant to be used as a reference. Read what you need.

Chapters 1 through 10 provide all the orientation and how-to information you need to use the Internet on AOL. After introducing the Internet (Chapter 1) and America Online (Chapter 2), each of the next six chapters looks at the major Internet services.

In Chapters 3, 4, and 5, you'll learn about AOL's tools for communicating with people on the Internet (mail, mailing lists, newsgroups). Then, in Chapters 6, 7 and 8, you'll find out how to use AOL's "information" tools for browsing the Web, publishing on the Web, and downloading files.

Chapter 9 shows you how to do effective searches on the Internet, whether you're seeking an e-mail address, a newsgroup posting, or a Web page. Chapter 10 shows you how to go beyond AOL's built-in Internet tools using "AOL Link": how to get and use great software like Netscape Navigator, IRCle and NCSA Telnet, and how to find and take part in Internet communities such as Internet Relay Chat and MUDs.

Chapter 11 is a directory of some 300 Internet resources—Web sites and newsgroups, for the most part, arranged by AOL channel, from Computers & Software to Travel. Most of these sites are actually integrated in the various channels. Others are sites we really like and think you may want to know about.

Appendix A is a primer about your basic AOL connection: what you need before you sign on, how to sign on, and where to get help.

Appendix B is a glossary you can turn to if you're ever in the dark about some term you see in the book. And if anything's not in the Glossary, we recommend several additional glossaries you can find online.

Elements

Throughout this book you'll find lots of Tips—shortcuts and easy ways of doing things. You'll also find Notes and Cautions to keep you aware of what's really going on and to prevent you from driving into potholes. Text boxes provide Deep Thoughts, amusing diversions, and everything in between. Wherever appropriate, we'll flag what's unique to AOL with an "Only on AOL" icon.

Feedback

This book will succeed only if it helps you get more out of your Internet experience on AOL. We can improve the book only if you let us know what's not correct, what's missing, and what you'd like to see more (or less) of. Occasional praise is fine, too. Any and all suggestions for improvements are welcome, and we're especially interested in knowing how the Internet has become indispensable in your life. Please send your suggestions in an e-mail message to screen name **inetbook97**. If you've never sent a message, read Chapter 3!

Chapter 1

America Online:
Your Gateway
to the Internet

To newcomers, the Internet can seem difficult, even scary. But folks with even a little experience on the Net have a different story to tell. They experience the Internet not as a network of cables and computers but as a community—actually, a collection of many thousands of small communities. On the Internet, as in any community, it's the people who count. Here you will find people from all over the country and the world who share your hobbies, passions, and preoccupations.

The Internet, or *Net*, is also a staggeringly large source of information, but, unlike other information resources, anyone can access the Internet, and anyone can *contribute* to it.

On America Online it's easy to do both. On your travels you will find that the communities and information resources of AOL and the Net complement each other. What you don't find on one, you're likely to find on the other. And when you have questions about finding information or locating people on the Internet, AOL can help in many ways, as you'll see later in this chapter.

The Internet is an immense enterprise, whether it's measured in the amount of content or the number of people or in the rate of growth of both. America Online makes the Net a manageable and seamless extension of the AOL community. AOL's full-powered Internet software lets you communicate with millions on the Internet. AOL also provides the behind-the-scenes technologies to give you the most reliable and enjoyable experience on the Internet. Finally, AOL, with its large and helpful community, never leaves you alone on the Net. Think of AOL as your home and safe haven on the Internet.

If you want to learn to navigate the Net's rich resources and take part in the creation of new electronic communities, this book is for you! Read it to find out how America Online can make your Internet experience as fun, useful, and easy as possible. This chapter gives you an overview of:

- How the Internet can be indispensable in your daily life
- How America Online differs from other Internet Service Providers
- How the Internet got to be what it is today

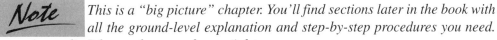 *This is a "big picture" chapter. You'll find sections later in the book with all the ground-level explanation and step-by-step procedures you need. Appendix B has a glossary of essential terms.*

THE INDISPENSABLE INTERNET

I can still recall the excitement of discovering, in early 1994, the "first elementary school with a site on the World Wide Web": Mr. Marshall's fifth grade class in Grand River, Michigan. Recently, I needed the phone numbers and an orientation schedule for my kids' new schools—public elementary schools in Maryland. I didn't think twice about how to get the information; I used America Online to go onto the World Wide Web, the graphical part of the Internet. Within minutes I found just what I needed (Figure 1-1 shows a Web site you can use to access school sites around the world). Even better, I saved the cost of a phone call and avoided the bother of getting put on hold or playing phone tag.

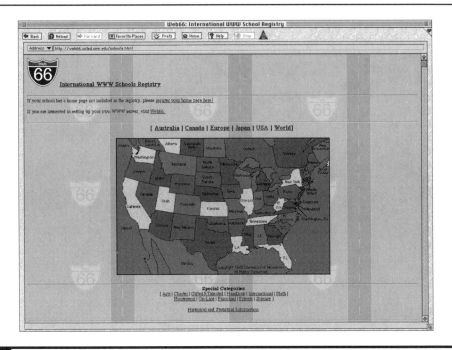

FIGURE 1-1   I found home pages for my kids' Maryland elementary schools using this site

What follows are some other examples of some indispensable Web sites. There's a lot more to the Internet than the Web, but chances are that you'll be spending a good deal of your time on the Internet using great (and fun) sites like these (see "The Web: Just a Part of the Net").

Planning a Vacation?

Last year, while planning a family vacation on the Delaware beach, I used the World Wide Web to find a place to stay. I also located a list of restaurants and found a site called **The Weather Channel**, shown in Figure 1-2, which provides current weather reports and forecasts for any location in the U.S. Another service, **City Net**, can help you plan a trip to just about anywhere. If you need maps, resources on the Internet such as **MapQuest** can provide street maps for any address in the U.S. And you can "zoom out" from any street address to see a larger region so you can plan your car trip.

FIGURE 1-2 The Weather Channel can help you plan that weekend outing, no matter where you live

Note   *Internet addresses for all three of these great trip-planning resources (Weather Channel, MapQuest, and City Net) are listed in Table 1.1, along with other essential resources. Chapter 9 introduces a series of other sites for finding local addresses, street maps, ZIP codes, and other community information.*

Site	Address (URL)
Amazon.com (bookstore)	**http://www.amazon.com/**
Bartlett's Quotations	**http://www.cc.columbia.edu/acis/bartleby/bartlett/**
Career Magazine	**http://www.careermag.com/**
CDNow (compact disc store)	**http://www.cdnow.com/**
City Net	**http://www.city.net/**
Clnet (computer information)	**http://www.cnet.com/**
Disability information	**http://www.webable.com/websites.html**
Excite (to find anything)	**keyword: Excite**
Fedex (to track packages)	**http://www.fedex.com/**
HomeArts Recipe Finder	**http://homearts.com/waisform/recipe.htm**
Internal Revenue Service	**http://www.irs.ustreas.gov/prod/**
Internet Mall	**http://www.internet-mall.com/**
MapQuest (to get a map of any place in the U.S.)	**http://www.mapquest.com/**
ParentSoup	**http://www.parentsoup.com/**
Salon	**http://www.salon1999.com/**
Shakespeare	**http://the-tech.mit.edu/Shakespeare/works.html**
Switchboard (to find anyone)	**keyword: Switchboard**
Virtual Hospital	**http://vh.radiology.uiowa.edu/**
Weather Channel	**http://www.weather.com/**
Web66 (a registry of schools with Web sites)	**http://web66.coled.umn.edu/schools.html**

TABLE 1-1   Twenty essential internet resources

See Chapter 6 for everything you need to know about the Web and Internet addresses, or URLs. See Chapter 11 for 300 more great Internet resources.

The Web: Just a Part of the Net

The Internet used to be a place where all you could do was read. It was inhabited primarily by academics, scientists, and researchers. Things have changed. Think of the World Wide Web as the *graphical* part of the Internet, with more and more sites featuring video, animation, and other multimedia features. (You can read more about the Web in Chapter 6.) The Web consists of perhaps 100 million *pages* with words and pictures (and more) *linked* together in a way that makes it easy to find related information. You'll learn how to make your own using AOL's Personal Publisher service in Chapter 7.

Changing Jobs?

Chances are good that your dream company has a Web site. If not, you can still make an informed career choice using one of the many Web sites, such as **Career.com**, designed for people who are changing jobs. You can also apply for some jobs electronically by sending your resume in an electronic mail (*e-mail*) message. In Chapter 3 you can read all about getting and sending e-mail to people on the Internet.

Too Busy to Shop?

More than a dozen stores, such as **CDNow**, offer electronic storefronts, each offering over 100,000 CDs for sale. You can search for specific CDs, do some comparison shopping, hear sample sound clips, and even purchase CDs. You can't buy a car online yet, but you'll find information about auto insurance as well as details on every make of car on the road. What else can you buy online? Books, chocolate, wine, software, hardware, stocks, you name it. Check out the **Internet Mall**, an Internet institution that lists more than 7,500 electronic stores.

Need Medical Information?

Whether someone in your family has a particularly nasty cold or you want to reduce the risks of a heart attack, you'll find information and knowledgeable people on the Net, as well as sources of online solace and support. I have helped family members find excellent sources of information about Alzheimer's disease and autism on the Net. The **Virtual Hospital** Web site (at the University of Iowa), shown in Figure 1-3, offers a huge amount of information for both patients and clinicians. You'll find some excellent health-related sites in the "Health & Fitness" section in Chapter 11.

No Time to Read the Newspaper?

Hundreds of magazines and newspapers are now available on the Internet, including some that are available *only* on the Net. Computers, music, politics—whatever your interest, it's there. **Clnet**, for example, is a superb information resource for the computer and communications industries. Electronic magazines that exist only on the Web, such as **Salon** and **Urban Desires**, feature some of the best new writing around (Figure 1-4). For daily news of the old-fashioned kind, **U.S. Newspapers on the Net** links you to hundreds of newspapers available in whole or part on the Internet. Clnet, Salon, and Urban Desires are all available as *keywords* on America

FIGURE 1-3 The Virtual Hospital, a world of information for patients and healthcare professionals alike

Keywords

If you're already comfortable getting around AOL, you can use keywords to get anywhere on AOL or the Net. In this book, *keyword: Such-and-such* is shorthand for the following:

1. From the Go To menu, select Keyword to bring up the Keyword window.

2. Type in *Such-and-such* (or **Hecklers** or **Netgirl** or **Nethelp** or **Netguide** or **Answerman** or **Internet** or whatever!) and click Go.

The next chapter has the nitty-gritty details about keywords and navigating AOL.

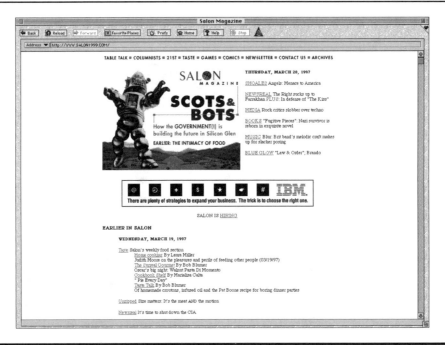

FIGURE 1-4 Salon. It's difficult to *buy* a magazine this good. On the Internet, it's free!

Online; see the previous section "Keywords." For other newspapers on the Net, see "Today's News" in Chapter 11.

Looking for Just the Right Word?

If you ever need an apt quote, don't reach for a reference book. Instead, visit the **Bartlett's Quotations** site on the Web, a searchable list of thousands of notable quotations. Writers and speakers in need of a **Shakespeare** quote in particular will love MIT's searchable archive of the great writer's entire corpus (see Figure 1-5). And if you ever need to find the meaning of TLA, you will probably benefit from one of the Internet's acronym-unscramblers (type in *TLA* and it spits out *Three-Letter Acronym*!). One great acronym dictionary, with 15,000 searchable entries, is discussed in the "Reference" section of Chapter 11. Search and you shall also find thesauruses, dictionaries, and other reference works.

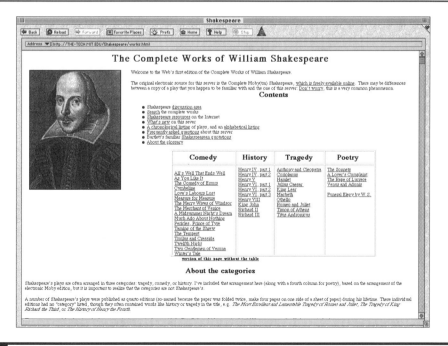

FIGURE 1-5   For pithy and wise words, turn to Shakespeare

AOL's Channels

AOL is organized in *channels*, which you can choose from the Channel menu (see Figure 2-6). Think of a channel as a big community, sometimes with millions of people, whose members have a strong interest and considerable expertise in some general subject such as sports, style, or the day's news. An AOL channel is a much bigger thing than a TV channel. For one thing, it's interactive, which means you help shape the content. If you're new to AOL, choose a channel and settle in! The next chapter takes a closer look at AOL's channels, and Chapter 11 brings you hundreds of Web sites arranged by channel.

Need Help Managing Your Finances?

AOL's Personal Finance channel provides just about everything you need to make an informed investment decision. With this channel's services you can do the following:

- Compare related stocks and funds

- Find summaries of analysts' recommendations

- Get the latest on-target observations of the Motley Fools, AOL's resident financial wizards

- Retrieve up-to-the-moment business news

- Scour Morningstar's reviews of mutual funds or Hoover's Business Resources

On AOL, you can also access the Internet to visit hundreds of personal finance–related Web sites for additional insights. At the **American Express** Web site, for example, you'll find a series of online calculators you can use to figure out how much you're worth, how much you need to save in order to retire in reasonable comfort, how much you have to salt away each year to send a kid to college, and other indispensable information (see "Personal Finance" in Chapter 11). To calculate the penalty of your prosperity, visit the all-too-informative **Internal Revenue Service** Web site.

It's Not *All* Serious!

Most of it's not, in fact. The Internet's roots reached deep into the world of academic research in the 1970s and 1980s, but even then there were games, jokes, and other stuff that wasn't serious. I find myself laughing out loud at the parodies in **the Onion** (**http://www.theonion.com/**), the Web version of a brilliant student newspaper at the University of Wisconsin. On AOL itself, you'll find lots to laugh at in forums such as Hecklers Online (keyword: Hecklers) or Comedy Pub (keyword: Comedy).

HOW AMERICA ONLINE DIFFERS FROM ORDINARY INTERNET SERVICE PROVIDERS

New people are continually joining the Internet community, adding their pages and postings to what is already an ocean of information. If you have plain Internet access from an Internet Service Provider (*ISP*), the Net can seem like some strange city in a foreign country whose language is incomprehensible. In contrast, on AOL you'll get the pleasures of big-city life while avoiding the big-city frustrations of growth, congestion, and the anxieties of feeling lonely and getting lost. On AOL you'll find out what it means to experience the Internet as a community.

Any Internet service provider can give you some software and hook you up to the Net, but you'll find that accessing the Internet through AOL adds layer upon layer of value to the plain Internet connection you can get anywhere else. On AOL you get:

- Community—the tools for communicating with people you know, such as message boards, chat, e-mail, and Instant Messages, and a congenial environment to make new friends

- Context—the integration of the best Internet resources into AOL's forums and channels, simplifying navigation and providing a clear framework for what you do on the Internet

- Value—the best of the Net and the unique AOL experience in a single affordable package

- Speed—the AOL software, servers, network, and compression technologies

- Safety—the tools to keep your kids out of trouble as well as the technologies to buy something securely on the Web

- Openness—the access to just about all Internet software and the ability to go anywhere and do anything on the Internet

- Help—assistance that is available any time, in any way that works for you.

I'm on AOL. Am I on the Internet?

On America Online you are always one mouse click away from the Internet.

America Online is a commercial online service that runs on hundreds of powerful computers in Virginia. AOL provides information from a wide variety of sources (such as magazines and news services) in a wide variety of formats (such as forums and software libraries). More and more of the content is original (AOL produces it). For many people, the best content comes from members themselves, who can express themselves and communicate with each other by e-mail, on message boards, and in chat rooms. Much of what you may like best about AOL—the chat rooms, the Instant Messages, the online versions of magazines such as *NetGuide* and *Newsweek*—is *not* available to people who aren't members.

While AOL is centralized, the Internet is decentralized. No one owns it. No one guarantees the content or is accountable for the quality of the service. It can be difficult to navigate, mostly because there's so much of it.

From AOL, at no additional cost and with no special software, you have full access to the Internet. The result? AOL provides the benefits of both a comfortable environment that's easy to use and the access you want to dynamic, globe-spanning Internet content that's growing by the hour. This access to the Internet is built right into your AOL software.

Still don't know where you are? Here are some ways to tell if you're on the Internet:

- You're using AOL's World Wide Web "browser" (shown in Figures 1-1 through 1-5) to visit a site such as **http://www.whitehouse.gov**.

- You're sending e-mail to, or receiving e-mail from, someone whose address includes an "at" sign (@) and an "address," such as **president@whitehouse.gov**.

- You're reading a newsgroup such as **rec.autos.antique**.

Community

What really sets AOL apart from the myriad Internet Service Providers is community. With eight million members and counting, AOL offers many opportunities for you to meet like-minded people. This also means that on AOL you can always find answers to your questions about the Internet. This is especially important because people on the Internet don't always like to answer newcomers' questions over and over again. You can also find friends on AOL with whom you can swap Internet discoveries.

Community comes in many forms on AOL:

- Communities based on live communication (chat rooms and Instant Messages)

- Communities based on communication that's delayed, such as electronic mail, mailing lists, and message boards

- Cool new communities that combine Web browsing with live chatting

Chat

Chat lets you communicate live with a group of people. You type your comments, press RETURN, and everyone sees your words. Chat is one of those things you'll find only on AOL. Yes, the Internet does have something called IRC (Internet Relay Chat), which you can read about in Chapter 10, but an AOL chat room is like a local deli, soda fountain, or tavern: you'll usually know who you can find there, and you'll likely talk the same "language." (With the creation of AOL's International channel, however, the language may not be English!) You'll find a list of hundreds of chat rooms in the People Connection channel.

Tip   *AOL's Buddy Lists let you know which of your AOL friends are online at the same time you're online. From the Buddy List window, you can send an Instant Message to a friend who's online, or you can invite a group of friends into a private chat room. More information about this feature is available from the AOL Members menu; choose Buddy Lists. If you're unfamiliar with using menus—or haven't installed AOL yet!—Chapter 2 provides all you need to know.*

Instant Messages

Instant Messages allow you to have an electronic "conversation" with other members who are online at the same time. To send an Instant Message, go to the Members menu and select Send an Instant Message. Enter your friend's screen name, type a message and click Send. (AOLers call instant messages *IMs*, and to send someone such a message is to "IM" them.)

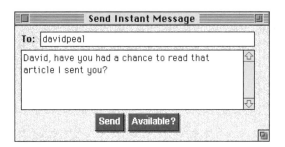

Note   *This book does not cover in detail AOL-only features such as chat rooms, Instant Messages, and message boards. I strongly recommend that you get a copy of Tom Lichty's* Official America Online Tour Guide *for a complete discussion of all the features unique to AOL. Another excellent title is* America Online for Busy People, *by David Einstein (Osborne/McGraw-Hill, 1996). Both books are available in the AOL Marketplace.*

Electronic Mail

Electronic Mail or *e-mail* (or sometimes just *mail*), is hardly unique to AOL, but AOL does offer a uniquely simple-to-use e-mail program. With e-mail you can send letters ("messages") to anyone on AOL or the Internet. Unlike chat and Instant Messages, e-mail does not take place "live." Your mail will arrive in minutes (seconds if your recipient is an AOL member), but the recipient of your missive might be on vacation in Fiji and may not get around to answering you for a couple of weeks. Messages can be composed and refined while you are offline, you can keep a copy of every message you send and receive, and, with messages to AOL members, you can actually change your mind and unsend it if it hasn't been read yet. AOL makes it easy not only to exchange messages with individuals on the Internet but also to exchange files with them and to communicate with *groups* on the Net by e-mail. Chapters 3 and 4 cover mail and mailing lists.

Electronic Newsletters

Electronic newsletters are fairly new in the AOL community, but the technology on which they are based—the mailing list—has been around a long time on the Net. Chapter 4 is devoted to mailing lists. You'll find newsletters for many of your favorite channels and forums, such as: AOL Tip of the Day; AnswerMan; IC-Hilites (Internet Connection); Chatters (People Connection); AOL Live, with schedules of live chat events on AOL; NetGirl, NetGuide, NetNoir, and many more! Newsletters go out to subscribers once a week or so with information about forum or channel events, as well as special tips and member contributions. On AOL you can subscribe to dozens of mailing lists simply by clicking the appropriate button. Just use keyword: Mail to go to the Mail Center and get information about Online Newsletters.

Road Trips

Chat's fine if you want to talk *about* the Internet or if you need help using an Internet tool. But AOL lets you chat with others while you're all visiting a Web site. With Road Trips, AOL makes the Web interactive, giving you an experience that's like going to the movies, but you're allowed to talk—and even heckle.

Road Trips are for members only. In a special window (shown in Figure 1-6) a Web site is displayed in the top *pane*, or part of the window, while a chat pane at the bottom of the screen allows you to share your thoughts about the sites with other members. You can either take a Road Trip created by another member (schedules are posted at keyword: Road trips) or create your own trip.

Context

Unlike what you find on AOL, the information on the Internet follows no standards. That doesn't mean that the Web site about dalmations you just discovered is not reliable; it's just that no one guarantees that it's reliable or accurate or that it's particularly useful for your purposes. If you're changing jobs, writing a paper, researching your competition, or moving to a new city, you don't want to take chances on old or incorrect information.

Here's where AOL offers more value than the garden-variety ISP. AOL gives you clear guideposts as you start your Internet explorations. You'll find the best Internet sites integrated into channels, you'll find the best non-Internet resources, and you'll find lots of opportunities to interact with members via message boards, chat rooms, and e-mail, so you can get help and exchange discoveries about shared interests. All this content—Net sites, AOL resources, and community features—is organized into some 1,500 forums such as AnswerMan, NetGuide, Motley Fools,

FIGURE 1-6   With Road Trips you can visit Web sites with a group—and it's OK to chat or heckle

Hecklers Online, and NetGirl (you can read more about forums in Chapter 2). An AOL forum can provide essential context and vastly simplify your search for people and information on the Internet.

Value

For one reasonable monthly fee you get unlimited access to the entire Internet in addition to all the bounties of AOL's exclusive content and community (see "AOL's Billing Plans"). Other providers offer flat-rate pricing, too, but only on AOL do you get:

- Human contact and the comforts of community

- Exclusive content that provides essential context to the Internet's tools and information resources

- An open platform that puts the whole Internet at your fingertips but keeps it manageable

- Controls that help parents keep their kids safe in cyberspace

- Help resources in every forum—human, fax, e-mail, BBS, and phone

- The sort of fun you'll never have on an ISP!

 For all those questions about how much it all costs, complete information is available at keyword: Billing.

Speed

AOL provides *faster* Internet access than any Internet Service Provider on the market. Independent lab results, from tests of seven configurations of browsers and networks attempting to access 15 popular Web sites, show that AOL's Web access is faster overall than other leading Internet services. Speed is especially important on the World Wide Web, which works by sending words and graphics to your computer; large sites in high demand can be s-l-o-w. Chapter 6 gives you tips for making your Internet connection even faster.

AOL's latest World Wide Web software was built by Microsoft and customized for the AOL service. AOL also has the tremendous resources and technical expertise to run a huge collection of finely tuned Internet computers, or *servers*. Most ISPs these days offer very good browsers, such as Microsoft's Internet Explorer and Netscape's Navigator, but if the computers and Internet connections of these ISPs are working slowly or not at all, even the best software doesn't do you any good. AOL offers great software *and* the blazing connections required to make the Internet work for you. Both the "client" software (on your computer) and the "server" software (on AOL's computers) use a technology called *caching*—a way of storing frequently used data to significantly speed up your access to the World Wide Web.

Here's another reason AOL is so fast: It owns one of the fastest networks in the communications industry, AOLnet, based on the ANS network, which America Online purchased in 1995. (In the late 1980s ANS formed the backbone of the network that predated today's Internet.) AOLnet allows you to connect to AOL (and the Net) using any modem up to 28.8 kbps. Research on faster access, including cable modems, is underway.

Finally, AOL has helped to develop a special *compression* technology created by the Johnson-Grace Company, another company AOL acquired. This technology

AOL's Billing Plans

In 1996, AOL began offering several price plans to fit a variety of needs:

- The $19.95 per month standard plan provides unlimited use of AOL, including access to the Internet. Fondly known as "all you can eat," this plan is available at an even lower rate if you pay ahead of time (see the next two items).

- For $17.95 per month you get unlimited use of AOL, including access to the Internet, if you pay in advance for one year.

- For $14.95 per month you get unlimited use of AOL, including access to the Internet, if you pay in advance for two years.

- The $9.95 per month, "bring your own access" plan provides unlimited access to thousands of unique AOL features, including access to the Internet, if you already have an Internet connection or access through a network on your job or at school. See the section "Using AOL with a Network or Internet Service Provider" in Appendix A.

- The $4.95 per month light-usage plan provides three hours of AOL, including the Internet, with additional time priced at just $2.50 per hour. Members with this plan are notified via a small window when they go back and forth between AOL and Internet content (which traditionally incurs an hourly cost), and "free" areas such as keyword: Help (which traditionally does not incur a cost).

Keyword: Billing has the details about the billing plans, plan switching, your account, your bill, and other good stuff.

reduces the size of the computer files you get over the World Wide Web and AOL, allowing for faster transmission and better image quality.

Safety

Every community has its darker side and shadier characters, so America Online gives parents the tools and the flexibility to assert some control over what their kids see and do on the Internet. What is "unsafe" is a matter of perspective and of personal taste, of course, so AOL's policy is not to censor but to give parents the tools to make such restrictions as they see fit.

AOL gives parents powerful controls to limit kids' access to this material. It makes these controls available in the Parental Controls area, available from the Members menu, as shown in Figure 1-7. One of the choices available allows parents to restrict a child to the Kids Only channel, where it's not possible to freely browse the Web.

With these tools parents can impose one or several (or all) of the following controls:

- Keep kids out of chat rooms and prevent them from receiving Instant Messages.

- Restrict receipt of e-mail—either all e-mail or e-mail from specific e-mail addresses. See Chapter 3 for more information about mail controls.

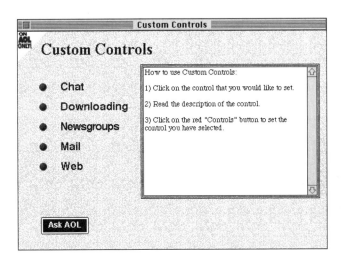

FIGURE 1-7   America Online provides parents with the ability to limit what their kids can see and do on the Net

- Block kids' access to specific newsgroups (or all newsgroups) and prevent them from downloading files from newsgroups. Chapter 5 has the details.

- Restrict kids to the Kids Only channel, where kids' content is concentrated and where the Web-browsing opportunities are limited (see Chapter 6).

- Limit kids to sites approved for children, or a somewhat broader collection of sites approved for teens (see Chapter 6).

Openness

AOL is open in two important ways.

- AOL's Internet access is open in that it is not censored. You can use AOL's built-in software to access any Web site, any mailing list, any newsgroup (with the exception of a very small number of patently illegal ones), and any other site whose address you know. *AOL doesn't censor sites in any way*, but instead gives parents the power to control what their kids do and see on the Net, as spelled out in the "Safety" section.

- AOL's Internet access is also open in that it gives you the choice of using other Internet software with your AOL software. AOL's built-in Internet tools are easy to use and will probably do anything you want them to do. But if you have a yen to use a different World Wide Web browser (such as Netscape Navigator) or a tool that has no built-in counterpart (such as a Telnet or Internet Relay Chat program), you can do it with AOL for Macintosh, as you'll find out in Chapter 10.

Lots of Ways to Get Help

Most Internet Service Providers turn the Internet into one of those holiday toys that "require instruction": you've got to find software, figure out how to use it, stumble around searching for things to do with the software, and waste time on hold trying to get phone help during business hours. Want to find out who else is having the same problem? Good luck.

AOL provides all the Internet help resources you're likely to want. The following Help resources are always at your disposal when you're using America Online.

1

Great Customer Service

At any time while you're on the service, keyword: Help takes you to a huge range of online and offline customer service resources, whether you need help connecting to AOL, using AOL, or finding your way on the Net. You'll find live, interactive help, voluminous help text, information about AOL's fax and BBS-based help, and lots of phone numbers to call any time of the day or night. For technical assistance with AOL for the Mac, you can always call 1-888-265-8007, and at the end of Appendix A you'll find a list of other phone numbers you can use to get help.

Safe Transactions

There's another sense in which AOL provides for your safety. Your commercial transactions on the service have always been transmitted over AOL's private network with a very high degree of security, so you can shop on AOL knowing that your financial transactions are confidential.

You can save time and money by taking advantage of the buying opportunities at the AOL Store in the Marketplace channel and throughout the other channels. On the Internet as well, you can now buy directly from many sites. CDs, chocolates, books—everything can be safely bought today, thanks to the security features and "encryption" standards supported by the latest AOL Web browser, a specially customized version of Microsoft's Internet Explorer browser that's brimming with security features. Industry experts foresee a huge expansion in "electronic commerce" in the years leading up to the turn of the twenty-first century. Chapter 6 has more information about buying stuff on the Web.

Net.help and AnswerMan

For those Internet questions, you'll find help in two closely related forums: Net.help (keyword: Nethelp) and AnswerMan (keyword: Answerman). Figure 1-8 shows what you'll find in the AnswerMan forum. This book was written by two of the people who created these areas. If you like the book, you'll love the forums!

Mail Center

At keyword: E-mail you'll find e-mail tutorials, tips, and general information for making e-mail an indispensable part of your life. At keyword: Mailing lists you'll get the lowdown on lists, plus an AOL-only directory of several thousand of the best

FIGURE 1-8   Help is always a click away on AOL. For all Internet Help, go to keyword: Answerman

mailing lists. Better yet, when you're using the Compose Mail window (see Chapter 3), just click the question mark icon for assistance with any feature.

Browser and WWW Help

Whenever you're using the AOL browser, your "Window to the World Wide Web," just click the Help button for complete help with its functions. At AOL's Web site (keyword: WWW, or just click the Globe icon on the tool bar), click the Help button for pointers to the general best Help resources on AOL.

WHAT KIND OF BEAST IS THE INTERNET?

I've gotten this far without defining the Internet—that's because I'm wary of the common but too simplistic definition of the Internet as a "network of networks." For one thing, the Internet was never intended by some "inventor" to be the globe-spanning, dynamic thing it is today. For another, once you get the hang of the Internet, you will probably experience it as a community, not as as a network of computers and cables. So defining the Internet as a network doesn't really say much about the Internet experience. Understanding three simple facts about the Internet can make for a better experience of the Net community:

- All sorts of computers communicate on the Internet.

- Using the Internet requires different programs to do different things.

- To people who use it, the Internet is not a physical network but a social one.

AOL's Stake in the Net

Across the service, you'll discover that AOL either owns key Internet technologies or has a strategic alliance with the companies that create these technologies. Some of these technologies are available to members for free or at reduced rates, such as PrimeHost (keyword: Primehost), a commercial "hosting" service for businesses and organizations that want someone else to host and maintain their Web sites.

In 1994–95, AOL acquired a series of companies or Internet content, including Navisoft, Booklink, WAIS Inc., ANS, Johnson-Grace, GNN, and Ubique. Many of these companies' products and services, such as Johnson-Grace's compression technology, have been thoroughly integrated into AOL.

Since then, AOL has shifted its strategy from buying cutting-edge companies to making alliances with the companies that lead the Internet industry. America Online's past acquisitions and current alliances with the most important players in the Internet industry—Netscape and Microsoft—ensure that AOL members will always have access to the best technologies in the marketplace. Currently, AOL is working with Bolt Beranek Newman, the consulting company that helped create the Internet some 25 years ago, to improve the performance of AOLnet.

All Sorts of Computers Communicate on the Internet

When you talk on the telephone, you set up what's called a *dedicated connection* between your phone and the phone you're calling. When you send someone electronic mail—or view a Web page or move data on the Internet with other tools—the connection is *not* dedicated. Instead, the message is broken up into *packets*—little pieces of data, all the same size, with information about their sequence, origin, and destination. The packets are sent separately to their destination using the best available path and crossing many separate and autonomously run networks in the process. Packets from the same message might find different routes to their destination, where they're put back together again, as shown in Figure 1-9. Since packets contain information about the whole file and the correct sequence of packets, any errors in reassembling some information cause packets to be re-sent.

What It All Means

In Appendix B you will find a list of essential Internet terms, with short definitions. When you're online, the AnswerMan Glossary (keyword: AM Glossary) has a longer list of Internet terms. Who *is* AnswerMan? Kevin Savetz, co-author of this book.

What goes for a simple e-mail message also applies to more complex things like the World Wide Web. When you visit a Web site, the various files making up the page are separately sent to you and are turned into tiny data packets at the source computer and reassembled at your computer.

Here's the important point: *Any* computer—whether it's based on Windows or the Mac or on bigger systems such as Unix or even a mainframe—can take part in this exchange of packets if it has some software conforming to an Internet standard called TCP/IP, which does the work of making packets, correcting errors, and reassembling files. (See Appendix B for fuller definitions.)

TCP/IP also allows two-way communication. That's what the word "interactive" really means: on the Internet you produce information as well as consume it. On AOL you can produce a Web site, an e-mail message, a newsgroup article, or an FTP file, and you'll find all the Internet applications that allow you to share information with other people everywhere.

What does this all mean for you as an AOL member?

- Packets move at different speeds, over congested networks, and through sluggish servers, which can account for why a Web site visit can be slower than using a forum on AOL. That's the value of AOL's investment in high-performance technology.

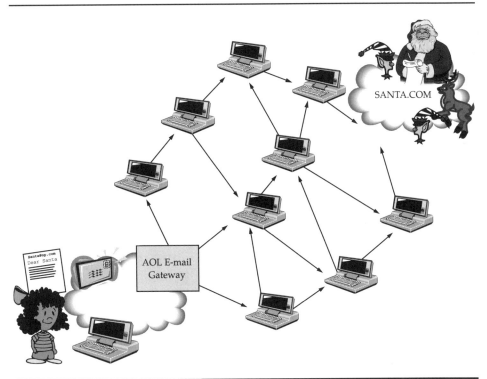

FIGURE 1-9   Packet switching at work. How that message gets to Santa

- The autonomous computers and networks hooked up to this global network are the source of content that's wildly diverse in subject, quality, and appeal. AOL provides the context, parental controls, and search tools you need to find what you and your family want.

DIFFERENT PROGRAMS TO DO DIFFERENT THINGS

Learning the Net means learning to use Net software, which is like learning any software but with two important differences. First, you must learn to use several smaller programs—not one big program—to do several different tasks. Second, the tasks don't take place on a single PC, but on a network. The tasks are not only networked, but most of them enable you to communicate with others.

To use the Internet you need to use several programs:

An e-mail "client"	To send and receive e-mail messages with other individuals on AOL and the Internet. See Chapter 3.
A newsgroup reader	To post messages on any of tens of thousands of international "bulletin boards," each devoted to a specific subject; anyone interested in the subject can read your messages. See Chapter 5.
A World Wide Web "browser"	To browse multimedia creations of words, pictures, and sounds. See Chapter 6.
An FTP (file transfer protocol) "client"	To retrieve software, images, sounds, programs, and other kinds of files from distant Internet computers, and to make these files available to others everywhere. See Chapter 8.

Each of these programs is built into your AOL software. One of them, the World Wide Web browser, is becoming a truly comprehensive application—it's the tool that gives you access to all other tools. On AOL you can use your Web browser to visit FTP sites, to send an e-mail message, and to call up AOL's newsgroup reader.

For now and the near future, however, effective use of e-mail, newsgroups, and FTP requires use of the specific software "clients" built into the AOL software. The browser's great, but it's best suited to browsing the Web.

THE INTERNET AS A SOCIAL NETWORK

America Online differs from other online services in many ways. Most important, AOL is a community. Everyone doesn't know everyone else, but AOL members do have plenty of ways—from IMs to e-mail—to get to know other members safely and reliably. They also have countless places, from chat rooms to forums, to meet people and make friends.

AOL's access to the Internet, unmatched by other online services, puts members in touch with a much larger community as well, a community with its own history, culture, and ways of governing itself. In fact, the Internet community is big enough to be considered a sort of country. Before setting off to explore this new country, it's a good idea to understand something about the sort of place you're about to visit.

A Little History

The Net is the unintended result of many separate dreams and real-world developments. Nobody invented it. First, there were dreamers—early visionaries like Vannevar Bush (in the 1940s), J.C.R. Licklider (in the 1960s), Ted Nelson (since the 1960s), and Tim Berners-Lee (since the late 1980s). Licklider dreamed of a future in which interconnected computing machines would take over people's routine tasks and allow them to spend more time at creative and productive tasks. As a director in the government's Agency for Advanced Research Projects (ARPA) in the early 1960s, Licklider had direct influence on the people who built government networks in the 1960s.

Bush, Nelson, and Berners-Lee were pioneers of a different sort. They imagined new ways of linking related knowledge in a universally available format, laying the groundwork for what is now known as *hypertext* (see Chapter 6). Their work continues to inspire the creators of today's World Wide Web.

Packets and Protocols

In the 1960s, for less-than-visionary reasons, the U.S. Department of Defense wanted to create a network that could operate in the event of war despite possible outages of part of the network. The solution first proposed by Paul Baran at the Rand Institute in California was a packet network, as described earlier in "All Sorts of Computers Communicate on the Internet." Working independently of Baran was Donald Davies, an English engineer who devised a packet-based network that formed the basis of a flexible public network. His motives were anything but military.

Larry Roberts, a computer wizard who came to Washington in 1966 to direct ARPA's networking projects, was influenced by the ideas of pioneers like Davies and Baran and by the sheer technical challenge of enabling different computers to exchange data. In 1969, with ARPA's support, the consulting firm of Beranek, Bolt and Newman in Cambridge, Massachusetts successfully built a packet network, linking four universities on the West Coast, which formed the ARPAnet. New universities were attached to the ARPAnet one at a time in the early 1970s.

One challenge with ARPAnet was that computers could only be added one at a time, through the creation of custom software and hardware *interfaces*—special computers that handled the routing of data between computers. Another challenge was to interconnect different kinds of packet networks, including radio and satellite networks. The big breakthrough in Internet history came in the early 1980s with the development of TCP/IP by Vinton Cerf and several graduate students at UCLA. Cerf is sometimes called the father of the Internet, but he is only the most prominent of a collective effort that involved hundreds of people, some of them visionaries and some not, some envisioning the whole and some focusing on specific parts of the whole.

Birth of the Present

In the 1980s, American research scientists wanted a way to more effectively share information, and they began to demand the same sort of access to networks that, at that time, only computer scientists had. In 1985, the National Science Foundation gave them that access by linking supercomputers at six major American universities, forming the NSFnet, ARPAnet's successor. Each of the nodes became the center of a regional network accessible to all universities, schools, and libraries in the region.

What really fueled the growth of the Net from about 1992 onward was the World Wide Web, an easy-to-use way to access global network resources, which you can read about in Chapter 6. In 1995, the government ended its support of the NSFnet and turned the Internet over to the companies and other organizations that now manage the Internet's rapid expansion.

How Many People Are on the Internet?

In late 1996, approximately 35 million adults *in the United States* were using the Internet, about a quarter of the U.S. adult population and an increase of more than 100% from a year earlier, according to Lou Harris & Associates. (Source: Cyberatlas, **http://www.cyberatlas.com**.)

In January 1997, approximately 57 million people *in the world* used the "consumer Internet" (defined as "users of computers that can *access* information by interactive TCP/IP services such as WWW or FTP"), according to John Quarterman, President of Matrix Information and Directory Services (MIDS) in Austin, Texas. Adding the people in the world who have access only to e-mail makes for a total of some 71 million people. Quarterman also predicts there will be approximately 700 million people using the "consumer Internet" in January 2000, saying "There is to reason to believe that the current rate of Internet growth cannot be sustained for three more years." MIDS's Web site has authoritative information about the size, growth, and definition of the Internet (**http://www.mids.org**).

A Global Community

Chances are very good that most of what you do on the Internet will involve American Internet users and American Internet content. Two thirds of all *hosts* (computers directly on the Internet) are American. However, more than 170 countries have access to the Internet, and on the Internet the information about the rest of the world is overwhelming in scope and quality. Whether you're planning a trip to Fiji, writing a paper about ancient Mesopotomia, studying English gardens, learning about the teas of Sri Lanka, dreaming of a golf trip to Scotland, or trying to find a pen pal in Italy—the Internet can make your job easier, faster, less costly, and more fun.

How to Behave Like a Native

Through e-mail, mailing lists, newsgroups, and Internet Relay Chat, the Internet gives you many ways of communicating with other people around the world. Like any community, the Net has its own guidelines (or *netiquette*), which can be boiled down to two precepts:

- Respect the people who might be reading anything you write and make available on the Net, because you can never predict in whose hands (or mailbox) something will wind up. No one can read your mind or see your body language on the Net, so what you write in jest may be taken seriously. Also, be aware that what you send to one person or place can be forwarded to thousands of people or places. Like your boss, your mom, or a newsgroup with 1,000,000 readers.

- Respect the physical Internet itself by not wasting *bandwidth* and storage space with unsolicited or inappropriate messages, especially commercial postings to uncommercial places.

What happens when you break the "laws" of netiquette? Minor infringements can get you *flamed*—verbally abused in mailing lists and newsgroups. It's not a particularly pleasant experience. Major infringements can get your membership revoked on AOL. In between, you may discover the existence of various blacklists that limit access to some Internet services.

Note   *America Online does not limit members' access to the Internet, but it does expect them to comply with its Rules of the Road guidelines while they're using all Internet services. All networks expect their users to comply with rules when*

they use the network to explore the world; AOL is no different. You'll find more
details about these rules later in this book.

Do unto others, and do unto the network. That pretty much sums up netiquette.
Chapters 4 and 5 give more details about proper behavior on mailing lists and
newsgroups, the two places where netiquette really matters.

How the Net Community Governs Itself

Netiquette goes a long way to explaining how the Internet citizenry control their
own destiny. It's the Net's common law. The closest the Net comes to formal
government is the Internet Society, an international organization made up of
companies, individuals, and government agencies that work to guarantee the
well-being of the Internet as a physical network.

Based in Reston, Virginia, a couple of miles from America Online's new
headquarters in Dulles, the Internet Society helps set the standards with which
tens of thousands of autonomous networks comply, making the Net possible.
It does its work through annual meetings, regular publications, and subgroups
such as the Internet Engineering Task Force and the Internet Architecture
Standards Board. Neither elected by the Internet community nor appointed by
the world's "real" governments, the Internet Society nonetheless effectively
plans the standards required for the Internet's future growth. More and more,
companies such as Microsoft, Netscape, and AOL itself are exerting influence
on the standards-making process, especially the part of the process that relates
to the World Wide Web.

Doing Business in the Net Community

The Internet was built with public money, and "acceptable use policies" kept
businesses and all for-profit activity *off* the NSFnet at first. Since 1991, however,
business has assumed more and more financial and technological responsibilities
for maintaining publicly accessible networks.

What do businesses do on the Internet? Many people and companies see the
Internet as a way to make money, and when they don't immediately succeed at this,
they label the Internet a failure. This is nonsense. Smart businesses know that, for
now, the Net's a great way of cutting costs in every aspect of a business: doing
competitive research, learning about markets, recruiting employees, doing targeted

interactive marketing, selling products, and providing customer support. As security technologies mature, the Net *will* become a place to make money, creating a better experience for consumers as well as companies small and large. AOL's InBusiness forum, led by Dr. Jill Ellsworth, is devoted to the wise business use of the Internet (keyword: Inbusiness).

The Internet has a reputation for being "anti-business." True, there are pockets of hostility to business on the Internet, and there are places where commercial postings are inappropriate. Plus, many small businesses new to the Net are insensitive to the finer points of netiquette. But government made the early Net possible, and it's business that's keeping it going today.

FROM HERE...

This chapter conveys the benefits of the Internet, the benefits of using the Net on AOL, and the *reality* of the Internet on AOL. In the next chapter you learn how to sign onto and get around AOL, and you'll find out exactly *where* the Internet is on AOL.

Chapter 2

Navigating From America Online to Get to the Internet

A s your home on the Net, America Online offers many opportunities to learn about the Internet, get help, and share your Internet experiences with other AOL members. AOL also offers hundreds of links to the best World Wide Web sites and other resources on the Net, and it gives you the freedom to go anywhere you want. This chapter starts with the basics:

- Signing on

- Working with windows, menus, and tool bars

- Finding and navigating AOL forums

- Finding out exactly how to get to the Internet on AOL—the menus, channels, forums, and buttons that take you there

If you're new to AOL, the Macintosh, and computers, you'll want to read or skim this entire chapter. If you're already familiar with AOL you're probably also comfortable using your Mac, so you can skip the early sections and jump straight to *"Where* on AOL is the Internet?"

 This chapter assumes you have installed the AOL software. Appendix A walks you through the process if you haven't yet done so.

GETTING ONLINE

With mouse in hand, you're ready to sign onto AOL. *Signing on*, *connecting*, *logging on*—it's all the same: connecting with AOL in order to read and take part in AOL forums and to use the Internet. To connect with AOL, start your computer (first making sure no one is using the phone and that the modem is on), and follow these steps:

1. With your mouse, double-click the AOL icon in a folder called "America Online 3.0." The AOL program may take a moment or two to display or "load"—it's a big program. When it does display, the Welcome window appears:

2. Type your password in the Enter Password box.

3. Click the Sign On button. AOL now looks for the modem, dials the local phone number you chose during installation (covered in Appendix A), establishes connection with the AOL network, and verifies your password. You're ready to navigate the Internet!

When you successfully sign onto AOL, you'll see two screens: the Channels menu shown in Figure 2-1 and the Welcome screen shown in Figure 2-2. You're online, and you're almost on the Net! (See "Where Am I—Online, Offline, On the Net?")

Where Am I—Online, Offline, On the Net?

You're online from the time you sign onto AOL to the time you sign off. The rest of the time you're...offline. Unlike other Internet providers, AOL gives you many ways to automate routine online tasks, so you can go online only when you have to (or want to). You can do many of your everyday tasks, such as composing e-mail and taking part in newsgroups, while you're offline. The AOL feature that makes this possible, Automatic AOL, is discussed in Chapter 4.

You can visit the Internet while you're signed onto AOL. You don't have to sign off AOL and then sign on somewhere else or use any special software. The

Internet is not "parallel" to AOL but a seamless extension of the AOL experience. You don't have to pay anything extra to use anything on the Internet, unless, of course, you purchase something over the Internet or use one of the very few for-fee subscription services available over the Internet.

Later in this chapter you'll find a directory of the places on AOL from which you can start your explorations of the Internet ("*Where* on AOL is the Internet?").

The Channels menu shown in Figure 2-1 gives you direct access to AOL's *channels*. They're called channels because AOL programs and distributes content, just like the studios and networks of the TV world do. But AOL's channels differ from TV channels in that they are *interactive*. They give you many opportunities to take polls, offer your opinions, share your experiences, and meet other members. Each channel is devoted to a broad subject of interest to members, such as

FIGURE 2-1   The Channels menu lets you access the subjects of most interest to you

entertainment, personal finance, or sports. You'll find access to Internet content throughout AOL's channels in the form of links to great Internet Web sites and newsgroups. (See "The World of AOL Forums.")

The Welcome Screen, shown in Figure 2-2, gives you access to AOL's most popular features, such as e-mail, People Connection, and the Internet, as well as to any new features or live events that are currently going on.

SIGNING OFF

AOL gives you several ways to sign off. Which way you use depends on how you like to do things—with the mouse, from menus, or with the keyboard. These options differ primarily in whether they leave the AOL program open (displayed on your computer monitor) after you sign off. You might want to keep the AOL program open if you'll be signing on again soon with the same screen name, or with a different screen name or *location* (see Appendix A on locations).

FIGURE 2-2   The Welcome Screen takes you to AOL events going on right now, as well as to e-mail, the Internet, and People Connection

To sign off AOL but leave the AOL program open:

■ Move your mouse cursor to the Go To menu at the top of your screen and click your mouse. Then slide the mouse cursor to Sign Off and release the mouse button.

To sign off AOL and close the AOL program, use any of these standard Macintosh techniques for closing a program:

■ Press COMMAND-Q (on your keyboard, hold down the COMMAND (⌘) key. Keeping that key pressed, press Q).

■ Move your mouse to the File menu and click the mouse button. Slide the cursor down to Quit and release the button.

Signing Off from a Network Connection (TCP/IP or an Internet Service Provider)

A new billing plan allows you to access AOL using your local network at work or another Internet Service Provider (ISP). See the "Using AOL with a Network or Internet Service Provider" section of Appendix A for more information. The benefits of this plan are the lower cost and the ready access to AOL via less congested networks. Signing off can be tricky, though. Using any of the methods above to sign off AOL will *not* log you off from your Internet connection. So, if you're signing off AOL, make sure you also log off your other connection to avoid running up your phone bill—unless, of course, you want to continue using your ISP or network account after signing off AOL.

USING YOUR MAC

A window is the box that displays words or pictures. Windows have their own controls, so you can move them, close them, and change their size. Figure 2-3 shows a window that you'll become familiar with: AOL's New Mail window.

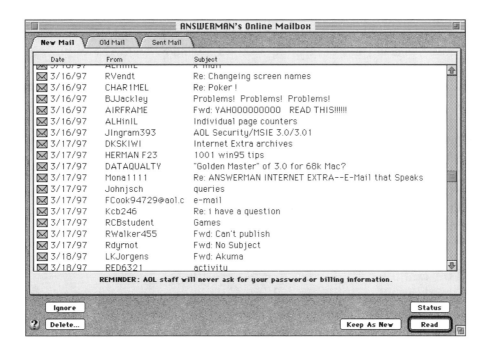

FIGURE 2-3 The New Mail window keeps track of the electronic mail messages you receive.

Window Controls

The windows you use on AOL have the following elements:

- Title bar
- Scroll bar
- Controls for adjusting a window's size

Title Bar

Every window has a title bar—a single line of text at the very top that displays a particular window's name. Figure 2-3 shows a window with ANSWERMAN'S Online Mailbox in its title bar. When you are browsing the World Wide Web and don't know where you are, the title bar will usually give you the site's plain-English name (unless it's French or some other language!).

You can use a title bar to move, or *drag*, a window. Just click on the title bar, keep the mouse button pressed, move the mouse to drag the window to where you want it, and release the mouse to *drop* the window in its new position.

 Sometimes in AOL you'll see a little heart off to the right side of the title bar. Click the heart to save the window in your Favorite Places folder, a list of your favorite sites on both AOL and the Internet. Chapter 6 has more to say about this essential AOL feature.

Scroll Bar

A scroll bar lets you see a document that's too long to fit in a single window. Web sites usually require *vertical* scrolling (see Figure 2-3). From time to time you will see a window so wide that it requires a *horizontal* scroll bar as well; this will appear along the bottom of a window.

You use scroll bars to move by clicking the little square scroll box and dragging it up or down (or right and left). Or, click with your mouse above or below the little box to move up and down a screen at a time (on a horizontal scroll bar, click to the right or left of the square). Or, click on the arrow at either end of the scroll bar to move a little bit at a time for each click. You'll come to rely on scroll bars when you read long e-mail messages, access newsgroup postings, or navigate very long Web pages.

Resizing and Closing Windows

Windows can be adjusted in size so you can easily manage several open windows at the same time. With a simple drag of the mouse you can change a window's size.

You *resize* a standard window by slowly clicking on the Resize tool that's in the lower-right corner of the window. Now drag the border to resize the window as you please.

Note *Some AOL windows cannot be resized, but instead have a fixed rectangular shape. That's because they make heavy use of graphics and are designed to present the most information in the most efficient manner.*

On AOL, almost everything you do causes a new window to open. To keep your screen from getting cluttered, it's a good idea to close windows you are no longer using. You can close any open window by clicking in the close box in the left-hand corner of the window's title bar. You can also close the active window without taking your hands off of the keyboard by typing COMMAND-W.

Inside a Window

Within a window you will find the following elements. They give you a graphical way of finding what you're looking for or doing what you want to do.

Listboxes

In an AOL forum, listboxes contain everything from text articles to links to Internet sites. If the list is too long to fit in the little box, a vertical scroll bar lets you quickly move up and down. (On AOL, if a list is too wide, a horizontal scroll bar *won't* appear!) To open (or go to) an item on the list, double-click it (clicking once merely selects it). Here's a listbox from one of the many topics in AnswerMan's weekly focus area (Keyword: AM Focus).

Drop-Down Lists

Drop-down lists do the work of a listbox but take up less space. The address field in the Web browser includes a drop-down menu for revisiting sites you've been to. (You'll read more about it in Chapter 6.)

Interactive Elements

The Mac has several ways of letting you make a choice or specify a preference.

With a *radio button* you make a single, exclusive choice from a set of options. Simply click with your mouse inside the circle of your choice. Clicking inside another circle selects that button and automatically deselects your first choice.

1. Select a Timeframe: Choose only one

◉ All Dates ○ Past Month ○ Past Week

Check boxes let you choose as many things as you want; click inside any of the boxes as you want (or don't click on any boxes).

2. Select a Category: Choose the categories you wish to search:

☐ Help Desk ☐ Business ☐ Communications

☐ DTP ☐ Development ☐ Education

☐ Games ☐ Graphics ☐ Hardware

☐ Hypercard ☐ Music & Sound ☐ Utilities

A *text box* lets you make a free-form choice by typing some text and providing some information: your address, your name, what you like about a site, what you're searching for, or whatever.

3. Enter a Search Definition: Narrow search by typing in key words.

| games | **SEARCH** |

A clickable *button* performs some action; it takes you to a new place in a new window. In the Welcome screen, for example (Figure 2-2), buttons can fetch your electronic mail and spirit you to live events currently underway on AOL.

 Sometimes it's hard to tell a button from a nonclickable graphic. How do you know for sure whether something is clickable? Pass your mouse over it, and if the mouse pointer turns from an arrow into a pointing finger, you can click.

ORDERING FROM MENUS

A menu gives you a set of related choices. The Mail menu, for example, lets you send a message, see the messages you've sent and received, get information about using e-mail on AOL, edit your Address Book, and more.

Take a moment to explore each of AOL's menus that are lined up horizontally at the top of your screen:

To open a menu so you can see your choices, just move your mouse over the menu and click and hold the mouse button. To make a selection, move the mouse arrow down the menu to the menu selection you want and release the button. If you don't find what you are looking for, just move the mouse cursor away from the menu and let go of the button.

Internet: On Today's Menu

AOL doesn't offer an Internet menu, but it does integrate Internet services into other menus wherever it makes sense. You'll find essential Net or Net-related tools and features in the following places.

Keyboard Alternatives

For some menu items, a keyboard alternative is available. This means that you can go directly to the item using the keyboard instead of selecting from the menu. For example, in the Mail menu, to the right of Compose Mail you'll see ⌘-M. This means that from *anywhere on AOL*, you can compose an e-mail message by holding down the COMMAND (⌘) key and pressing the letter M. Keyboard alternatives are a shortcut to menu items you use all the time.

Here are some useful keyboard alternatives:

- To compose an e-mail message: COMMAND-M

- To open a file: COMMAND-O

- To open the Keyword window: COMMAND-K

- To print something that's displayed: COMMAND-P

- To read your e-mail: COMMAND-R

- To save a file: COMMAND-S

Keyword Window (Go To Menu)

The Keyword Window gives you access to every feature *about* the Internet, as explained in "Your Key(word) to the Internet." Some of the most important keywords for using the Internet are listed in Table 2-1. To enter a keyword, you bring up the Keyword window by either selecting it from the Go To menu or pressing COMMAND-K:

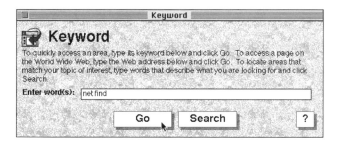

To use the Keyword window, simply type in the keyword (such as one of the keywords listed in Table 2-1), and click Go. If you're not sure of a keyword, type in the subject (such as Internet) and click Search to bring up a list of related AOL areas. Double-click any item to go to an area.

 ## Your Key(word) to the Internet

The easiest way to navigate AOL and the Internet is by using *keywords* (Table 2-1). Think of a keyword as a shortcut. Every AOL forum and many Web destinations have keywords assigned to them—the keyword for the NetGuide forum is **Netguide**, for example.

Here's how to use keywords: First, bring up the Keyword window from the Go To menu, then enter a keyword, and press Go. If you know a URL, or Internet address, such as **http://www.aol.com**, you can enter it in the Keyword field, press Go, and you'll go directly to the Web site. Chapter 6 plumbs the mysteries of URLs.

The most popular Web sites have plain-English keywords, instead of URLs, for example: **Excite**, **Switchboard**, **PathFinder**, and **Disney.com**. A list of such keywords is available at keyword: Web keywords. Keywords can make it easy to get where you going, whether it's on the Net or on AOL. Some of these Web keywords (such as **Excite**) take you directly to the Web, others (such as **Disney**) to an intermediate screen that gives you a set of links to places on both AOL and the Internet.

 Keywords are not case sensitive: ftp, FTP, *and* Ftp *all take you to AOL's File Transfer Protocol area. This book will uppercase the first letter of keywords, but you don't have to follow that practice.*

Keyword	Takes You To
Access	Information about global and domestic AOL access, including a list of numbers
Answerman	AnswerMan forum, with Kevin Savetz, co-author of this book, can answer all your Internet questions and offers a chat room, newsletter, message boards, and more
Billing	Explanation of everything related to your bill, with forms for changing your billing information
Excite	Search the Web and newsgroups (see Chapters 6 and 9)
FTP	Access to thousands of FTP sites (where you can download files) (see Chapter 8)
Gopher	An older Internet service, Gopher still offers many treasures, nicely packaged by AOL for easy access
Http	A Web site whose URL, or Internet address, you know. For instance, type **http://fool.web.aol.com** to go to the Motley Fools Web site
Keyword	A master list of keywords, including Internet-related keywords
Mailing list	A selective, annotated mailing list directory designed for AOL members (see Chapter 4)
Member services	Comprehensive AOL help
Modem	All things modem-related, including configuring, connecting, troubleshooting
Net Find	AOL's own tool for searching the Web . . . for anything!
Netguide	AOL's edition of *NetGuide* magazine, with an abundance of tips, columns, and interactive features
Nethelp	Comprehensive Internet help, a part of the AnswerMan forum
Net highlights	The best of AOL's Internet services, forums, and links

TABLE 2-1   Essential keywords for using the Internet on America Online

2

Keyword	Takes You To
Newsgroups	AOL's tool for exploring 20,000-plus public discussion groups, or newsgroups (see Chapter 5)
PP2	Make your own Web page with Personal Publisher (see Chapter 7)
Quickstart	Tips for new users of AOL and the Net (also Keyword: LearnAOL and Keyword: Discover)
Screen name	Add a screen name or change your existing name
Software	More than 100,000 files to download, including dozens of Internet utilities and thousands of files also available via FTP
Telnet	Telnet Center. Telnet software and tips for accessing remote computers (see Chapter 10)
Web	AOL's Web site
Web keyword	A list of the many dozens of Web sites that can be accessed directly by keyword
Web Diner	Friendly help and useful tools if you're building your own Web page
WWW (same as keyword: Web)	AOL's Web site

TABLE 2-1   Essential keywords for using the Internet on America Online (*continued*)

Favorite Places (Go To Menu)

Gives you a way to keep track of your favorite newsgroups, Web sites, and AOL forums. You can go directly to your Favorite Places folder from the Go To menu. Or, on the tool bar, you can click on the folder with the heart in it. Chapter 6 has the lowdown on Favorite Places.

The Mail Center (Mail Menu)

Takes you to tons of useful information about electronic mail (e-mail), including links to related resources and a long list of electronic newsletters you can receive via e-mail for free. From the Mail menu you can also send a message (by selecting Compose Mail) or get your e-mail (by selecting Read Mail). Both features are available from the tool bar as well.

Preferences (Members Menu)

Takes you to a window that lets you adjust many aspects of your Internet experience, from specifying your home page on the World Wide Web to how you reply to your e-mail messages to whether you save them on your hard disk (see "On Your Own Terms: Setting Preferences for AOL "). Preferences are also available from the tool bar, by clicking the MyAOL button.

On Your Own Terms: Setting Preferences for AOL

America Online offers members many ways to customize the way the service looks and works. You'll find a broad range of choices—*preferences*—and clear online instructions for specifying what you like.

Some of these preferences—called *Parental Controls*—are available only to the master account holder (the person who registered the account) and can be used to set limits on the sorts of things children can do on AOL and the Internet. Parental Controls are all available at keyword: Parental Controls are discussed in Chapters 3, 5, and 6.

Other preferences, which can be used by any screen name within a master account, can be accessed from the Members menu. To do this, select Preferences, then click the appropriate button to adjust your preferences on, for example, AOL's Web browser (click Web), e-mail services (click Mail), or file downloading on the service (click Download). The browser preferences can be set within the browser, too, by clicking the Prefs button.

Tip *Throughout this book, specific preferences are mentioned as they're relevant to the use of specific Internet services, such as e-mail, newsgroups, and the World Wide Web.*

Parental Control (Members Menu)

Allows parents to restrict the activities of their children while they're on the Internet with separate and easy-to-use controls for e-mail, newsgroups, and the Web. Chapters 3, 5, and 6 have the details.

2

The Help(?) Menu

For general AOL help, including using windows, connecting, troubleshooting, and billing. This valuable comprehensive help resource is available even when you're not signed on.

THE AOL TOOL BAR

The AOL *tool bar* is the row of *icons,* or small clickable buttons, that you see at the top of your AOL window, just below the menu bar. The tool bar icons are listed in Table 2-2. Tools vary in purpose: some of these tools let you do something (like the Printer icon, which lets you print). Others take you to a place, such as your Favorite Places folder. Menu commands will do the same things and take you to the same places, but they're tucked away and less intuitive.

THE WORLD OF AOL FORUMS

On the Internet they're called *sites,* on AOL they're called *areas* or *forums.* In either case, think of them as places to go—the reason you go online in the first place. In both sites and forums, you'll find a lot of variations in the ways you get around. Figure 2-4 shows NetGuide, one of the best new AOL forums and one of the most useful if you need general help getting around the Internet.

Elements of an AOL Forum

Forums draw people who share a specific interest—health, investing, relationships, parenting, humor, you name it. In a forum you'll find gobs of information about a specific subject gathered up in one place for easy access. Forums take you to the best Internet sites, too, so you don't have to go searching for them on your own.

Some forums have leaders; others don't. The most important part of any forum is the people who frequent it. There are many ways forums can support their communities. Some have dedicated chat rooms. Others have regular "events" in which the forum leader or a guest chats with members about a specific topic. In many, you'll find automated e-mail, which makes it easy to ask the forum leader a question or to subscribe to an e-mail newsletter. Others take polls and share the results with members. And most forums have message boards, so members can communicate directly with each other.

> A forum makes information available through *buttons, images, listboxes,* and more, which often let you go directly to related sites on either the Internet or AOL. Sometimes you'll find listboxes with files to download, and you'll often find text to read—*lots* of text to read. More and more sites are providing an index and search feature to make it easier to get around.

Read your e-mail messages

Compose an e-mail message

Go to the Channels window (Figure 2-2)

Find out what's hot on AOL and the Web

Go to a chat room in People Connection

Find a file

Get a stock quote or see how your portfolio's doing

Check the latest news

TABLE 2-2 The tool bar gives you quick access to the most commonly used AOL and Internet features

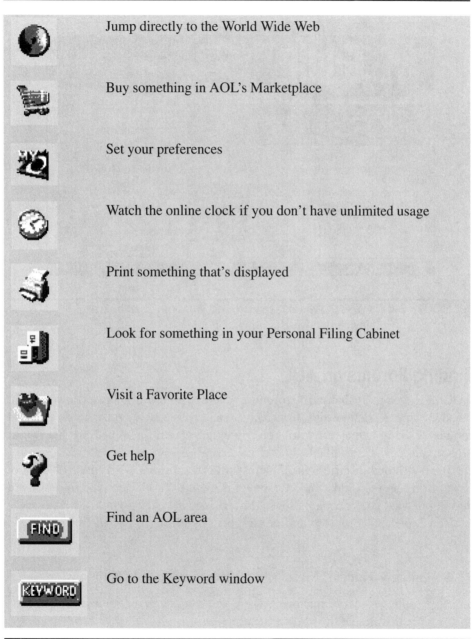

Jump directly to the World Wide Web

Buy something in AOL's Marketplace

Set your preferences

Watch the online clock if you don't have unlimited usage

Print something that's displayed

Look for something in your Personal Filing Cabinet

Visit a Favorite Place

Get help

Find an AOL area

Go to the Keyword window

TABLE 2-2   The tool bar gives you quick access to the most commonly used AOL and Internet features (*continued*)

■ **FIGURE 2-4** Informative text, links to the Web, message boards, a
newsletter—NetGuide has it all

Finding Forums on AOL

AOL offers you more than 1,500 forums to choose from, with subjects ranging from
woodworking to relationships, from Mars to alternative medicine. How do you find
forums of likely interest to you? You can either search for something specific or
browse to see what's available.

To *search* for a specific area of interest on AOL, click the Find button on the tool
bar to bring up the Find window (shown in Figure 2-5). Then type in any word
describing what you're looking for in the text box and click Search.

You *browse* for content and community by clicking one of the following
three tabs:

- ■ **Places & Things**   A channel-by-channel listing of AOL forums

- ■ **People**   A set of directories where you can search for someone's e-mail
  or real-world address

- ■ **Events**   A current schedule of AOL's live events, where you can interact
  with members and celebrities

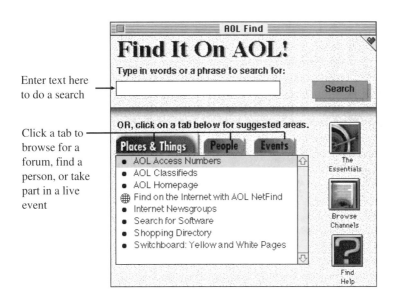

Enter text here to do a search

Click a tab to browse for a forum, find a person, or take part in a live event

FIGURE 2-5 The Find window lets you search for a specific area or browse through all of AOL's offerings

Tip *Whenever you find a place you like, make sure to note its keyword, so you can return there directly in the future. Even better, click on the little heart in the forum's title bar to store it in your Favorite Places folder, so your favorite places are also a click (or double-click) away (see Chapter 6 for more about Favorite Places).*

Another way to find forums that match your interests is to use keyword: Quick Start. Click Match Your Interests to bring up a list of topics, such as "Computers and Internet" and "Reference and Research." Click any topic to find a handful of the best, exclusively AOL resources on that topic (see Figure 2-6).

WHERE ON AOL IS THE INTERNET?

On AOL you're a click away from the Internet. You can get to the Net from the tool bar, from menus, and throughout AOL's channels and forums. Figure 2-7 shows the

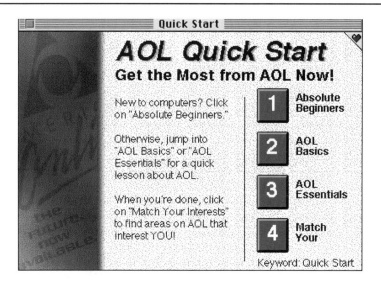

FIGURE 2-6   If you're new, Quick Start helps you find your way around
              AOL and identify forums that match your interests

most visible points of access to the Internet from AOL, but in time you'll blaze your
own paths to the Net. The best Net services and resources on AOL are available in
Net Highlights.

Where Is AOL's Web Site?

From the main AOL window, click the little globe on the AOL tool bar to go directly
to the America Online Web site, shown in Figure 2-8. Keyword: WWW and
keyword: Web do the same thing. In Chapter 6 you'll find out more about this site
and learn how to adjust your Web preferences so that a different Web page comes
up when you click the globe or use those keywords.

How Do I Get to a Web Page Other Than AOL's?

The Keyword window (available on the tool bar, from the Go To menu, or by
pressing COMMAND-K) lets you go directly to any Web site whose address you know.
Just enter the full address (for example, **http://www.apple.com**). If you have a
browser window open, enter the URL (Web address) in the box at the top of the
browser and press RETURN. See "Your Key(word) to the Internet."

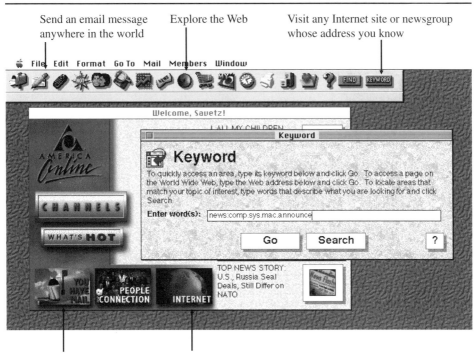

FIGURE 2-7   The Internet is everywhere when you're on AOL. Here are some menus, icons, and keywords to start your exploration

Where Do I Go to Create My Own Web Page?

At keyword: Personal Publisher (or simply PP2) you will find everything you need to create your own "personal page" on the World Wide Web. Making your own page is a breeze on AOL, as you'll see in Chapter 7.

Where Do I Go to Send or Receive E-mail?

Let your mom or your accountant or your elected representative hear from you! E-mail is always a click away on AOL because you can read your mail and send a message from the tool bar. (Figure 2-3 shows the New Mail window, where you read your e-mail). Chapters 3 and 4 provide all you need to know to become a Great Communicator.

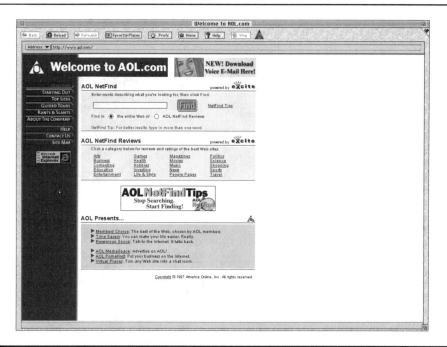

FIGURE 2-8 The America Online World Wide Web site is one of the most frequented on the Internet—and one of the best places to start exploring the Net

Where Do I Go to Take Part in a Global Bulletin Board (Newsgroup)?

Newsgroups are like bulletin boards devoted to topics ranging from scuba diving to vegetarian cooking. You can read postings from the more than 20,000 newsgroups carried by AOL, or you can write newsgroup postings for millions of people to see. Keyword: Newsgroups takes you to the Newsgroups window. In Chapter 5 you'll get the complete scoop on newsgroups.

Where Do I Go to Get Internet Software?

You don't have to go onto the Internet to get the best Internet software. AOL's software library at keyword: Software has a huge archive for you to choose from—and the programs are virus-free! If you need additional files or want to download files from the Internet, you can use FTP, the Net's File Transfer Protocol, which is always available at keyword: FTP. Chapter 8 provides everything you need to know about getting files from either AOL or the Internet.

DOING SEVERAL THINGS AT ONCE ON AOL

The Internet is made up of lots of different types of information which you can access with different types of programs (an e-mail reader, Web browser, and newsgroup reader, for example). You can easily use several Internet programs at the same time while also taking part in exclusive AOL activities such as chatting, sending Instant Messages, and exploring forums. You can open one window to read your e-mail, another to browse the Web, and yet another to make a confession to NetGirl or do stock research.

Of course, with two hands and limited time, you can really only *do* one thing at a time, but, with several windows open at the same time, you can easily transfer data between windows. You can, for instance, copy a URL (Internet address) from the browser or a newsgroup article into an e-mail message and send it to someone else. In Chapter 3 you'll learn to *hyperlink* the address so that another AOL member can go directly to the Web site by clicking the hyperlink in your e-mail message.

How do you do this? First use the mouse to select what you want to copy. Then press COMMAND-C (C is short for copy). Then switch to the window into which you want to "paste" the text and press COMMAND-V to paste it (put it somewhere else).

How do you switch between open windows? Clicking any part of a window brings that window to the top of the pile of open windows. Or, choose the name of the window you want from the Window menu.

USING AOL WITH OTHER MAC APPLICATIONS

Working with multiple applications is easy–you can switch between AOL and other running applications by using the application icon in the right corner of the tool bar.

Why would you want to do this? For one thing, anything you *download* (copy to your computer) will likely require another program to use: a word-processing document will require a program such as Word, for example, and a spreadsheet will require a program such as Excel.

FROM HERE....

The road from here can go any direction you want. Personally, I think it's best to get familiar with all of AOL's Internet capabilities, even if (for example) you're most interested in e-mail and the Web. It's worth having a sense of what's possible if only because on AOL so *much* is possible.

The next three chapters of this book are devoted to human communications on the Internet: mail and mailing lists in Chapters 3 and 4 and newsgroups in Chapter 5.

Chapter 3

Communicating
with E-mail

For millions of people around the world, *electronic mail*, or *e-mail*, or just *mail*, has become a necessity as routine and universal as the telephone and toothbrush. This chapter provides the essential information you need to use e-mail to communicate with people on AOL and the Internet. It covers:

■ Addresses and the elements of a message

■ Sending and receiving messages

■ Sending *effective* messages

■ Managing your incoming and outgoing mail

■ Sending and receiving files attached to messages

The next chapter is all about the Internet's thousands of e-mail-based communities, also known as mailing lists.

Where Is E-mail on AOL?

On AOL you have a choice of ways of writing and reading e-mail messages:

■ You can write e-mail by clicking the Compose icon (showing a pencil) on the tool bar, by selecting Compose Mail from the Mail menu, or by using the keyboard shortcut COMMAND-M.

■ You can read your new e-mail from the Welcome screen by clicking the big You Have Mail button, clicking the New Mail icon (showing a mailbox) on the tool bar, or selecting Read Mail from the Mail menu.

The Mail Center, available from the Mail menu, is loaded with advice, tips, and troubleshooting hints.

IT'S ALL IN THE MESSAGE

Think of an e-mail message in terms of the letters you get via the post office. Both have a sender and a recipient, and both contain a *message* that one person wants to share with another.

However, e-mail differs in many ways from paper mail, and the differences are what make e-mail a better medium in some ways:

- The same e-mail message can go, at no extra cost, to many people at the same time.

- E-mail messages allow for a subject line that states, in the sender's words, what the e-mail message is about, such as "Urgent request" or "History of lemurs." The subject line is a courtesy to the person receiving the message. When you receive e-mail on AOL, the Subject line can help you figure out which messages to read first. Subject lines can also help you keep track of old messages.

Note   *AOL does not require you to supply a subject, but it is a good idea to get in the habit of always putting descriptive subject lines on the messages that you send.*

- E-mail messages can have useful files attached to them—anything from a Word document or an electronic newsletter to a MIDI sound file. It's easier to get files via e-mail than via FTP or the Web (discussed in Chapters 6 and 8), and there's no extra charge.

WHAT IS AN E-MAIL ADDRESS?

How does your message get to someone else's computer? That's the purpose of the e-mail address you include when you send the message. Your e-mail address is typical of any Internet address. It has two simple parts, the user name and the domain name, separated by the "at" sign (@). Think of the *user name* as a person and the *domain name* as the computer attached to the Internet through which the person gets access.

What Is Your Internet E-Mail Address?

Anyone sending you an e-mail message over the Internet must know your e-mail address. There is a very simple formula for figuring out your e-mail address on the Internet. Just take your screen name and add an "at" sign (@) and **aol.com**. If your screen name is SteveCase, anyone with Internet access, anywhere in the world, can send a message to you by addressing it to **stevecase@aol.com**. It doesn't matter whether you use uppercase or lowercase letters, although lowercase is the norm. If there is a space in your screen name, the space is not included in your e-mail address.

Don't know your screen name or the screen name you're currently using? Just check out the title bar of the Welcome screen (Figure 2-2 in Chapter 2 shows mine).

Who You Are on the Internet: User Name

A *user name* on the Internet is the same thing as a *screen name* on AOL: it's the bit of text that identifies individual people on a specific network. On AOL, for example, other members can get mail to you just by using your screen name.

Usually, user names and screen names clearly refer to an actual person or are chosen so that they can be easily remembered. On the Net, it's common to use some combination of first and last names to create a user name. On AOL, there is a stronger tendency to choose personas and amusing names.

Tip *If you're going to get and receive much Internet mail, you might want to create a special screen name that clearly reflects who you are, especially if you plan to take an active part in mailing lists (Chapter 4).*

Where You Are on the Internet: Domain Name

People use *domain names* to identify and communicate with computers connected to the Internet. Every domain name is unique. A domain name has two or more parts, proceeding from specific to general and separated by periods, pronounced "dots" when spoken. Your domain name, **aol.com**, is pronounced "a-o-l dot c-o-m."

The last part of a domain name (*com* or *gov*, for example) is considered the "top-level domain," the most general part. Domains outside the U.S. *usually* have two-character top-level domains: *fi* for Finland, *dk* for Denmark, *ca* for Canada, *uk* for the United Kingdom, and so on. In the U.S., top-level domains *usually* have one of the three-letter names shown in Table 3-1.

Domain	Example	Description
com	**aol.com**	commercial domains (a huge group and the fastest-growing category)
edu	**rtfm.mit.edu**	non-profit educational institutions
net	**commerce.net**	a large group, usually networks
mil	**dscc.dla.mil**	domains operated by a branch of the U.S. armed services
gov	**helix.nih.gov**	non-military domains owned and operated by the U.S. government
org	**eff.org**	non-profit organizations

TABLE 3-1 Top-level three-letter domains

The system works well but isn't always predictable. Many American schools, for example, belong to the Departments of Education of their states and not to an *edu* domain. My kids' schools have the domain name of **mcps.k12.md.us** (Montgomery County Public Schools, grades K through 12, in the state of Maryland, USA). In using a two-letter top-level domain, this particular domain name is consistent with the international practice of using two-letter country codes to indicate a country. Some foreign domain names have top-level names that indicate both domain type *and* country. In the United Kingdom, for example, university (*ac*ademic) domain names sometimes end in **ac.uk** and commercial domain names in **co.uk**. In the near future the system is likely to be dramatically expanded through the creation of new top-level domains, some with more than three letters. A few of the new domains under consideration are *web*, *info*, and *firm*.

 *This system, called the Domain Name System, is used throughout the Internet and is the basis of Internet addressing—not just e-mail addresses. Chapter 6 goes into Internet addresses, commonly known as URLs.*

COMPOSING AND SENDING AN E-MAIL MESSAGE

To compose a new message from scratch, click the Compose icon on your tool bar:

Every message you compose on AOL uses the window you see in Figure 3-1. It doesn't matter whether you're composing a brand-new message or replying to or forwarding a message you've received from someone else. In each case, you use the same window.

With AOL's mail program you must provide the following pieces of information every time you start writing a new message:

■ The **recipient's e-mail address** goes in the Address To field. If the recipient is on AOL, all you have to do is fill in the screen name; you can omit **@aol.com**. Recipients on the Net require full e-mail addresses—user names plus domain names.

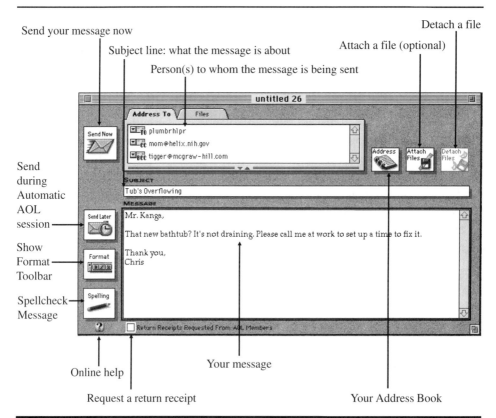

FIGURE 3-1 Compose your messages here, whether they're going to AOL or the Internet. Don't forget to fill in the Address To and Subject boxes!

Note   *E-mail addresses must be exact, in contrast to paper mail. While the post office might be able to figure out the sender's intentions if the recipient's address is hard to read or partially incorrect, the mail computers on the Internet need to have everything exactly right. The importance of addresses isn't unique to AOL; it's the way network computers work. Just like regular letters, messages that can't be delivered over the Internet come back—they bounce—and they'll be returned to you with a cryptic error message. On AOL you'll know right away if you attempt to send a message to an AOL screen name that doesn't exist. However, if you misspell an Internet address, your message will be sent and then bounced as undeliverable, because AOL cannot check the accuracy of Internet e-mail addresses. Double-check your Internet addresses before clicking Send!*

- The message's **subject**, in the Subject line, which gives your recipient some idea of what the message is about (not strictly required by AOL, but it's a good idea to always use a subject).

- The **message** itself, in the big box with the scroll bar. A message can be a word or several pages; an entire book could be written about how to write messages. "Putting Your Best Foot Forward," at the end of this chapter, has tips for writing messages that get attention.

Tip   *You can compose e-mail when you're offline. Just run the AOL software, and, without signing on, click the Compose Mail icon on the tool bar. When you're ready to send the message, sign on and click Send Now. Or click Send Later and schedule an Automatic AOL session.*

Sending E-Mail to More Than One Recipient

When you're sending mail to more than one person, put each e-mail address on its own line in the Address To field. It doesn't matter whether they're on AOL or not on AOL; you put their addresses in any order, each on its own line. (You can just press RETURN between addresses as you type them.) Notice the small "To" to the left of each address—we'll talk more about that in a moment.

If you find yourself sending messages to the same group of people over and over, you can use AOL's Address Book to create a special distribution list, so that you can send one message automatically to everyone on the list (see "Keeping an Address Book on America Online," later in this chapter).

Differences Between AOL Mail and Internet Mail

In principle, sending e-mail over the Internet seems just like sending it to someone on AOL, but in practice there are some important differences:

- **Address.** On AOL the person to whom you send messages can be addressed by screen name alone. On the Net you must know the domain name as well. This is standard practice, by the way. If you omit the domain name, the Net's mail protocol assumes you're sending the mail to someone on the same domain as you. So if you leave off the domain in that message to **kevin@northcoast.com**, the kevin whose domain is **@aol.com** will get your message. This is one error that AOL is not going to catch!

- **File size.** You cannot send or receive file attachments greater than about 2 Mb over the Internet. On AOL-to-AOL mail, however, the limit is higher—about 16 Mb. See "Working with Files: Getting and Sending Attachments."

- **Ability to unsend.** Once a message has left AOL and gone on to someone on the Internet, AOL knows nothing of its whereabouts. Thus, you can't change your mind and unsend it, as you can with a message sent over AOL to someone on AOL.

- **Availability of status.** Likewise, the status of a message sent over the Internet is not available: You can't tell if it's been read. See "If You Change Your Mind: Unsending a Message," later in this chapter.

CCing and BCCing

You'll often want others to be apprised of messages you send. For example, in a company setting, you may want to notify your boss if you're sending a message to her boss or someone outside the department. With AOL you can send a *carbon copy* (also known as a *courtesy copy*) to people who should know of your message but aren't its main recipients.

Finding Mail Help on AOL

Several areas on AOL provide online help and information as you use e-mail. The Mail Center, available from the Mail menu, offers a tutorial, FAQs (compilations of answers to frequently asked questions), links to e-mail resources, and message boards. The focus of the Mail Center is on e-mail sent from one member to another. (By the way, if you've been on AOL for awhile, you'll know that the Mail Center used to be called the Post Office.)

A comprehensive overview of AOL's Internet mail capabilities is available in the Net.help area (keyword: Nethelp).

Tip *If a message to many primary (To) and secondary (CC) recipients turns into a two-way discussion or becomes personal in any way, it's a good idea to prune the list of participants. This way you can turn a potential free-for-all into a true tête-à-tête. To do this, edit the To and CC fields when you make replies (covered later in this chapter).*

To CC someone, enter his or her e-mail address as you normally would, then double-click on the tiny To envelope to the left of the e-mail address. In the window that appears, select the CC radio box and click OK.

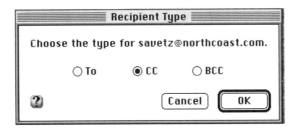

Alternatively, you can click and hold the mouse on the little arrow to the left of the To arrow. Drag the mouse down to CC and release the button.

You can use either method, and you can CC any number of people using either one.

A BCC, short for *blind carbon copy*, is an even subtler and riskier proposition. Unlike a regular CC, BCCs, as the name suggests, are carbon copies that the To and CC recipients won't be aware of.

There's a downside here, too. Imagine that you *receive* a BCC but neglect to notice that the sender wanted to keep the BCC secret from the direct recipients. Suppose you decide to reply to the message and you send your reply to the original sender and all the direct recipients. The "To" recipient(s) may be offended by this botched attempt at secrecy.

An occasion where BCCs do make sense is when you don't want a long list of recipients of the same message to know of each other's existence (or e-mail address). Say you want to send a joke out to both coworkers and family or friends, and you don't want the coworkers to see the addresses of your family or friends, and vice versa.

Sending a BCC is just like sending a CC—either double-click the little envelope or click and drag on the arrow to change the delivery method.

Sending Your Message

With the address(es) typed in, write a short and punchy Subject line to characterize the content of your message. Now type your message in the big box, as shown in Figure 3-1.

Once you've composed a message, you send it on its way by clicking Send Now. Clicking Send Later places your message in a *queue* to be sent during an Automatic AOL session. (The message is available by selecting Read Offline Mail from the Mail menu in the folder called Outgoing Mail.) After you click Send Now, the message closes automatically, and a little window comes up confirming that the message was sent. Click OK.

AOL gives you the choice of *not* closing the message you just sent. (See "Mail Preferences.") Why? It's a good way to double-check your message. If you change your mind about sending the message, AOL gives you a way to *unsend* messages sent to other people on AOL. Keeping a message open is also an alternative to using blind carbon copies (BCCs). For example, after you've sent a message to the direct recipient, you can change the To: and CC: addresses to another address. It's an easy way of sending multiple copies of the same e-mail without rewriting it.

Another reason to keep a message open after you've sent it is to save it as a file to your hard disk—an alternative to using your Personal Filing Cabinet (see the "Saving and Printing Messages" section on that feature). With the message displayed, go to the File menu and select Save As, then provide a filename and folder.

Cancelling a Message Before You Send It

If you decide not to send a message that you've started to compose but haven't sent yet, just click the Close box in the left corner of the message's title bar. If you've entered anything in the message body, you'll be asked whether you want to save the message. Click Don't Save if you want to lose the message forever. Click Save if you want to finish writing the message later, then navigate to a folder where you want to save your message and give it a name. With the message saved, you can later open it, finish writing it, and send it when it's done. You can open it later by simply going to the File menu and choosing Open, then hunting for that message.

Mail Preferences

America Online lets you define several aspects of the way you use e-mail—for example, you can confirm that messages have been sent and you can store your messages in your Personal Filing Cabinet. Some of these aspects will matter to you more than others. Specific preferences are discussed throughout this chapter.

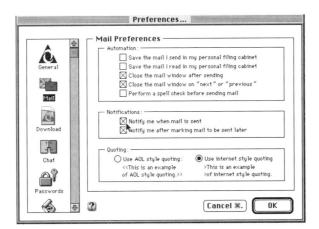

To bring up this window, choose Preferences from your Members menu, then click on Mail. Check or uncheck a preference by clicking inside the little box. Click OK when you're done.

If You Change Your Mind: Unsending a Message

I unsend messages for many reasons: I re-read my message and find I've been intemperate, or that I've made a typo, or that I forgot to attach the file that I meant to attach.

 You can unsend messages to other AOL members but not to people on the Internet.

To reread a message you've sent, go to the Mail menu and select Read Mail. A list of your New Mail will come up—even if you don't have any. Click on the Sent Mail tab and you'll see a list of the messages you have recently sent. Double-click a message's subject line to re-read it. The last message sent will be at the top of the list.

To unsend the message:

1. Select the message from the Sent Mail window, and click the Status button. If the message has been read, the screen name of the recipient will appear alongside the time the message was opened.

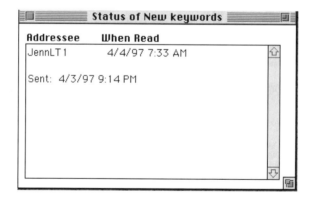

2. If the message wasn't read, click Unsend, and then confirm that you don't want to keep a copy of the message. If the message went to more than one recipient, and if any one of them has read the message, you can't unsend it. If a message goes out to a couple of people and if one of those people is on the Internet, it can't be unsent either.

KEEPING AN ADDRESS BOOK ON AMERICA ONLINE

AOL's Address Book makes it easier for you to keep track of those complex Internet addresses. It can help you create miniature mailing lists, too, so you can routinely send messages to the same group of people. The Address Book can keep your mail from bouncing due to mistyped addresses and vastly simplify your communication with the small groups you're routinely in touch with, especially if group members have messy numerical MCI or CompuServe addresses.

Tip   *You can edit your Address Book while offline, which is useful if you compose offline messages or if you don't want to sign on just to add someone's address.*

To add a person to your Address Book:

1. Bring up the Address Book by selecting Address Book from the Mail menu.

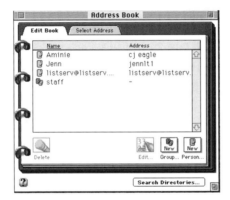

2. Click the New Person button. The New Person window comes up.

The window has four boxes for entering text. In the First and Last Name boxes, type in the name of the individual that you want to see in the Address Book.

In the E-mail Address box, you enter the e-mail address of the person. You can put a short note to yourself about this person in the Notes box.

3. Click OK.

To add a group of people to your Address Book:

1. Bring up the Address Book by selecting Address Book from the Mail menu.

2. Click the New Group button. The New Group window will appear.

3. In the Group Name field enter a name for this group of people—"family" or "staff," for instance.

4. In the Addresses box, type the e-mail addresses of all the people in that group, hitting RETURN to separate each address. Click OK when you're through.

To use your Address Book while composing a message:

1. Click the Address button in the Compose Mail window.

2. From the Address Book, select the name of the person or group to whom you want to send a message. Click the To, CC, or BCC button. The address will automatically be plugged into the field you chose. Close the Address Book window when you're done adding people.

3. Type and send your message.

 Alternatively, you can double-click a person's name to quickly put that name in the To: field of the message.

Using the Address Book is like having your own personal mailing list software. Although less powerful than a mailing list, the Address Book automates the task of sending one message to many people, and it's easy to maintain. Mailing lists are covered in depth in the next chapter.

Finding an Address

The million-dollar question is, "How do you find someone's Internet e-mail address?" A few years ago, the answer was highly involved, requiring a raft of complex programs such as **whois** and **netfind** and other tools devised in the days when Internet users were likely to be researchers or network adminstrators. Today it's a lot easier to find an e-mail address. On AOL, start with the Member Directory (available from the Members menu); on the Internet, start with BigFoot, which is available over the World Wide Web (**http://www.bigfoot.com**). This and other Web services are discussed in Chapter 9.

ADDING PIZZAZZ TO YOUR AOL MAIL

 E-mail is ugly! Black letters against a white background, just like a typewriter. With version 3.0, AOL gives you the ability to make your messages more visually pleasing. However, this neat new feature is available only for your messages to other AOL members, so your creations won't be appreciated on the Internet.

In your member-to-member messages you can now take your text and add flair, color, and outrageous effects:

■ Text color

■ Background color

- Font

- Text size

- Style (bold, italic, underlining)

- Alignment (to align a message with the left or right margin, or to center it)

Applying these features couldn't be easier. In the Compose Mail window, type a message. Click the Format button to bring up the Format tool bar. Use your mouse to select some text. Now click each of the little buttons in the Format tool bar to see what it does (Figure 3-2). Figure 3-3 shows a formatted message.

Formatting gives you some powerful new ways to emphasize words: italics for important words, large bold text for headers, and colors for attention-getting backgrounds, for example. Like all such effects, these mail enhancements can also be distracting, so, unless you're writing ransom notes, only use them when they reinforce your point.

Tip   *In your mail to AOL members, you can even add bullets, those dots you use to list things. To do it, just type OPTION-8. But don't put symbols in your non-AOL mail. They won't make it through AOL's e-mail gateway to the Internet.*

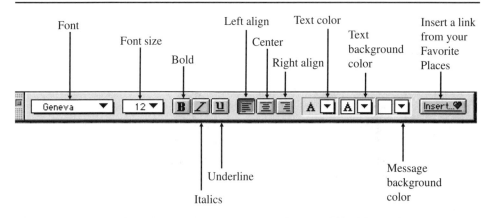

FIGURE 3-2   Formatting your e-mail message is now easy on AOL

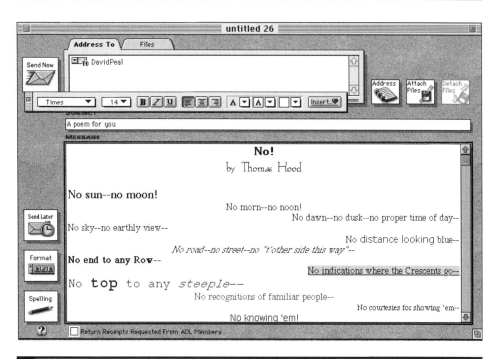

FIGURE 3-3   An awful-looking e-mail message. See if you can do better

Adding Clickable Hyperlinks to Your AOL Mail

Another hot new feature added with Version 3.0 is embedded *hyperlinks*. A hyperlink (or just *link*) is a special kind of text that, when you click it, takes you to a Web site or AOL area (jump ahead to Chapter 6 to find out more about linking). Like formatting, hyperlinks are available only in messages sent to other AOL members. They will *usually* be "stripped out" of messages to people who aren't on AOL.

There are two ways to add hyperlinks:

- *If the site you want to link to is in your Favorite Places folder.* If you want to send a link to an AOL forum, newsgroup, or Web site that you've put in your Favorite Places folder, use this method. Select some text in your message that describes the forum, newsgroup, or site that you're linking to. Click the Insert ♥ button on the Format tool bar to bring up your Favorite Places. Now click and drag the item from Favorite Places onto the selected text of your e-mail message. Then finish the message, and send it. You can add hyperlinks even when you're offline this way.

■ *If you know the Internet address (or URL).* Select some text in a message you're writing in the Compose Mail window. Again, the text should concretely describe the site—it's what gives the recipient the *incentive* to click. Now open the Web site by selecting Keyword from the Go To menu, entering the URL, and clicking Go. Drag the little heart from the Web browser's title bar onto the selected text in the Compose Mail window. That text will become a blue hyperlink. Close the Web browser window, finish writing your message, then send it.

This is what the recipient of the message sees. Clicking the underlined text takes your friend to one of your favorite places on AOL or the Internet:

View this <u>observatory</u> site

BECAUSE SPELLING COUNTS: SPELL-CHECK

Before you send your beautifully formatted message on its way, you can use another groovy feature of AOL mail, the spelling-checker, to make sure it's perfect.

If you've ever used a word processor, you're already familiar with the concept of a spelling-checker. When you're composing e-mail, the spelling-checker is only a click away—whether you're online or offline. After you've written your message, click the Spelling button. The spelling-checker's window will appear as it searches your message for spelling errors, typos, and questionable capitalization.

Select a single word, sentence, or paragraph before you click Spelling to spell-check just that text. If you don't have any text selected when you click Spelling, the message will be checked beginning at the text cursor's current position.

For each word that might be incorrect, the spelling-checker will show you how you spelled it, its best guesses as to how the word really should be spelled, and a field where you can type a correction.

If one of its guesses is correct, simply double-click on the correct word to fix the error in your message. Alternatively, you can click on the correct word and then the Replace button. Or, if you misspelled the word several times in your message, click on the correction and then click Replace All to fix the word throughout the message.

If none of its guesses are correct, you can type the correction yourself in the Replace With field, then click Replace or Replace All.

If you want the spelling-checker to ignore a word for now, click Skip and it will be duly ignored. Clicking Skip All will cause the spelling-checker to ignore that word throughout the message. If you click on Learn, the word will be added to the dictionary permanently, never to bother you again when you use it in future messages.

Finally, the Cancel button will leave the spelling-checker and return you to your e-mail message.

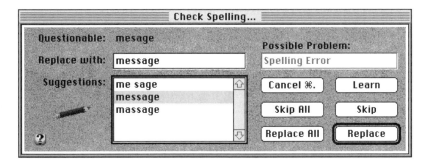

 The spelling-checker will proofread the text in the body of your message, but not the subject line. You'll have to proofread that yourself.

The spelling-checker is rife with preference choices that you can use to customize how it works. Pick Preferences from your Members menu and click on Mail. Notice the check box labeled "Perform a spell-check before sending mail." If you check the box, the spelling-checker will start automatically when you press Send Now or Send Later. The message won't be sent until it is done proofreading the message—clicking the Cancel button will quit the spelling-checker but won't send your message.

There are more preferences to play with: from the Preferences menu, scroll down and click on Spelling. With this menu you can choose what kinds of nits your spelling-checker will pick from your messages: should the first word of each sentence be capitalized? Should it catch doubled words? Should it enforce the old two-spaces-after-punctuation rule? And so on. Customize these to your heart's content, then click OK.

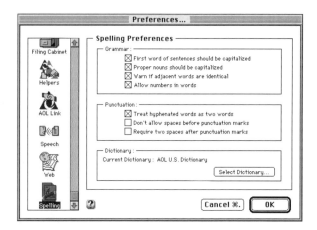

Get into the habit of using the spelling-checker, especially for important messages. But don't let it lull you into a false sense of security: the spelling-checker can't catch bad grammar or typos that happen to spell other words correctly. Proofread your messages yourself, too.

DID THEY GET IT YET? RETURN RECEIPTS

Some messages are so important that you want to know as soon as they have been read. AOL allows you to request a "Return receipt." If you click the Return receipt box at the bottom of your message before you send it, AOL will track the message. When the recipient reads the message, you will receive an e-mail message from AOL (actually, it will appear to be from yourself) notifying you.

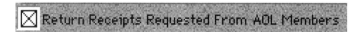

You can use return receipt even if your message is going out to many recipients. Use return receipt to track the most important messages that you send. If you use it with every message, you'll find your mailbox flooded with delivery confirmations.

Message subject: An important message!
When sent: 97-04-06 14:59:12 EDT
Read by: Savetz
When Read: 97-04-06 14:59:27 EDT

Return receipt only works for mail to other AOL members. Due to the way that Internet mail works, it is impossible to tell whether a message to an Internet user has been read. If you should click the Return Receipt button on a message that's going to an Internet user, you'll receive a message from OnlineHost (AOL's computer) reminding you that you will not receive a return receipt for that person.

WORKING WITH FILES: GETTING AND SENDING ATTACHMENTS

Files are everywhere when you use a Mac. You use files when you create documents with your word processor or spreadsheet, when you install AOL, and when you make a Web page. Early in the history of the Internet, it was discovered that files could be attached to e-mail messages and could thus be exchanged almost as easily as simple messages (that was before they invented FTP, the standard way of transferring files, discussed in Chapter 8). On AOL, it's easy to attach files to messages you send. Likewise, you can receive files if they've been attached to messages sent to you. The next section is about attaching files; see also "Retrieving a File from a Message" a little later in this chapter.

Note *As a rule of thumb, you can both send and receive over the Internet any file that's less than 2 Mb. Ordinary word processing documents are rarely greater than 50K (1/40th of 2 Mb). A more realistic limit is 1 Mb, according to David O'Donnell, AOL's Postmaster. Don't know how big your file is? Use the Finder's Get Info command to learn the size of any file on your Macintosh. From the Finder, select the file by clicking on its icon, then select Get Info from the File menu.*

Attaching a File to a Message

AOL makes it easy to attach any file you want to a message. I use this feature daily for sending screen captures (such as the figures used in this book), contracts, chapters, drafts, outlines, and other word-processed documents (files) relating to the writing process. On AOL, you can send files both to other members and over the Net; with multiple To's and CCs you can simultaneously send the *same* attachment to several people on AOL and the Net.

There's one hitch, but it's a small one. AOL's e-mail program adheres to a standard called "MIME," the Multipurpose Internet Mail Extension, which was designed to simplify the transfer of files through the gateways that separate different e-mail systems. To send someone a file attachment over the Internet, your recipient must also be using an e-mail program that supports MIME. Basically, MIME works by converting your *binary* document (a formatted word-processed file, say) into a *text* document, and then telling the recipient's e-mail program how to handle the attached file. Sometimes a MIME document is received as gibberish and has to be *decoded*, but there is plenty of software on AOL that will do this.

To attach a file to your e-mail:

1. With the Compose Mail window open, type in the recipient's address, the subject, and the message, then click the Attach Files button. The Attach File window comes up.

2. Navigate to the place on your hard disk where the file is located, then double-click the file. You'll notice that the file name appears in the Compose Message window where the recipient's name was. You can switch between reviewing the recipients and attachments by clicking on the Address To and File tabs, respectively.

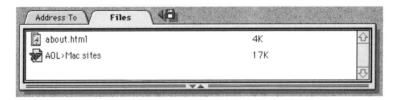

3. Click Send Now. The File Transfer box, with its *thermometer*, now pops up to tell you that your file is being sent; it measures the percentage of the file that's been uploaded from your Mac to AOL's server. A little window tells you when your message has been sent. Click OK.

Note   *You can attach multiple files to one message by clicking the Attach Files button again and picking another file. You can even attach a whole folder of files at once by selecting the folder in the Attach Files window and clicking Attach. When you use either method to attach Multiple Files, the AOL software will automatically compress the files into one file with the extension of .SIT. If the file's recipient is also an AOL user with a Macintosh, the file will automatically be decompressed into its original pieces when it is downloaded. Otherwise, the recipient will need to use a program called StuffIt Expander (on the Mac) or StuffIt Expander for Windows (for Windows users, naturally) to decompress the files. Both utilities are free and are available from the Web site **http://www.aladdinsys.com**.*

If you change your mind before sending a file as an attachment, just click the Files tab, select the file, and click the Detach Files button.

Sending Spam

The Internet term for unsolicited mail is *spam*. Sending spam on the Internet is a taboo, but not because Internet denizens have delicate feelings. Rather, spam wastes space on people's hard disks, wastes network bandwidth, and wastes the time of many, perhaps thousands of people. For most people, it's a nuisance, and for some it's an invasion of privacy.

Sending spam from AOL is a bad idea. Here's the official word from AOL's Community Action Team (CAT):

"If you send unsolicited commercial e-mail messages to individuals on AOL or on the Internet, you run the same risk as in posting such messages to mailing lists. You may receive a TOS warning, and repeated violations may lead to the termination of your AOL account."

See "Avoiding Spam" a little later in this chapter for tips on avoiding junk e-mail.

YOU'VE GOT MAIL! READING YOUR MAIL

You've got mail! You may have heard a voice say this to you when you signed onto AOL. Reading your mail is easy on AOL. Just click the big You Have Mail button

on the Welcome screen. You can read your mail at any point during an AOL session by clicking the Mailbox icon on your main tool bar at the top of the screen.

The New Mail window now comes up. This is the most important mailbox (see Figure 3-4) of three mailboxes. (You've already seen the Sent Mail mailbox, where you check the status of mail you've sent. The final mailbox is for Old mail, messages you have read but which are not "kept as new.") Each mailbox looks similar and can be accessed by clicking on the tabs at the top of the Mail window. All the mailboxes are discussed further in "Managing Your Mailboxes," later in this chapter.

With the New mailbox open, what do you read first? I get a lot of mail and usually start by scanning the subjects and senders. I read personal messages first. Then I read mailing lists; they're not personal, but deal with subjects I care about and contain messages from people whose opinions I want to know. Junk mail usually stands out because of the unknown sender and cheesy subject line:

```
MAKE MONEY EVEN FASTER!
```

Such mail I'm likely to delete instantly, although AOL has a new and useful way to deal with such stuff automatically (see the "Avoiding Spam" box) so it won't even get to your mailbox.

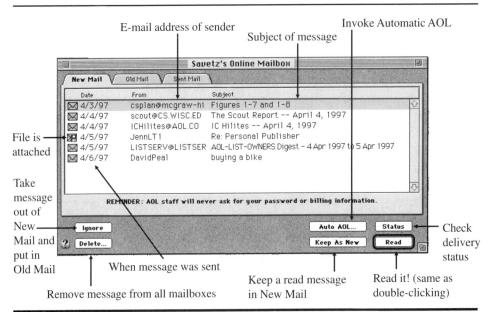

FIGURE 3-4 New mail arrives throughout the day and night on the Internet

You can use Automatic AOL to do most of your mail-reading offline. The technique is especially useful if you have a high volume of mail or subscribe to many mailing lists. You can read about Automatic AOL in Chapter 4.

Each line of your mailbox is devoted to a single message and has four pieces of information (Figure 3-4):

- Whether the message has a file attached to it. If it does, you'll see a little disk icon attached to the ordinary letter icon (see "Retrieving a File from a Message").

- When the message was sent, messages are displayed from most recent to oldest. The date and time a message was sent automatically appears next to the letter icon and serves as a postmark to tell you when the message was sent.

Messages you receive after *opening the New Mail window won't show up. Click the Mailbox icon on the tool bar again to see whether you have new messages.*

- The sender's e-mail address. If the message is from someone on AOL, you'll see just the screen name. If it's from someone on the Net, you'll see the domain name as well. If it's from a mailing list, you'll see the name of the software that sent the message (LISTSERV, for example). Chapter 4 delves further into the mysteries of mailing lists.

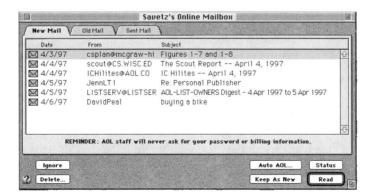

- The message's Subject line, exactly as the sender typed it. If the Subject doesn't fit in the space allotted, it will be cut off.

To open a message, just double-click on it or select the message and click Read.

 If you get a message that you don't want to respond to right away or that you want to keep for future reference, close it, select it in New Mail, then click Keep as New. This will keep the message in New Mail.

Retrieving a File from a Message

You can always tell if someone's sent you a file as an attachment to their message. Ordinarily, a new message sent to you has this little icon in its header:

If there's an attachment, you'll see:

To retrieve a file:

1. To open a message in New Mail window, double-click it. You'll notice a little blue diskette just to the right of the Files tab. Click the Files tab to see a list of the attached files.

2. Click the Download Now button (the button is active only when there's something to download). Click Download Later if you want to download the file later during Automatic AOL. The file will be in your Download Manager (available from the File menu).

3. If you clicked Download Now, a standard File Save dialog box will appear. Confirm the filename (change it, if you want) and navigate to a folder on your hard disk where you want to store it. Click Save to confirm. If a file of the same name already exists, you'll be asked to confirm that you want to get this file and overwrite (delete) the existing one. (This happens all the time with mailing list digests because they usually have the same name. It's unlikely you'll want to save the existing file in this case, but if you do, rename the one you're downloading, and then click Save.) The File Transfer box (just like the one you see when you attach and send a file) tracks the download and tells you when it's done.

Note AOL's Download Manager, available from the File menu even when you're offline, is a wonderful tool for keeping track of files you download, whether you get them from an FTP site, a newsgroup, an e-mail message, or an AOL software library. It conveniently lets you download files in batches, and it helps you keep track of the names of downloaded files and the directories in which you placed them. See Chapter 8 for more information about AOL's Download Manager.

To make use of the file you've downloaded, you'll need a program to view it, play it, run it—in other words, to let it do whatever it does. In some cases, AOL gives you the tools you need. In other cases, you'll need a special application that could be anything from a QuickTime viewer for a video file or a word processor for a **.doc** file. If you've downloaded a program, you will probably need to run it from the Finder.

Some files you download will not be usable with any program you have on your computer because they are either encoded (scrambled, to facilitate transfer as text) or compressed (reduced, for quicker download). The message with the attached file will indicate what kind of file is attached—a MIME file (.MME), UUencoded file (.UUE), or compressed (.ZIP or .SIT) file, for example. In any of these cases, you'll need a special program to decode or decompress the file and make it useful. Two programs I like for decoding or decompressing attached files are StuffIt Expander, which will deal with .SIT, .HQX, .CPT, .ZIP, .UUE, and many other formats; and Decoder, which can decode MME files. Both are available on AOL at keyword: File Search. For more information on decoding MIME files, go to keyword: MIME.

Replying to and Forwarding a Message with an Attachment

If someone sends you an attachment and you reply to it, the attachment won't be included with the reply. If someone sends you an attachment and you forward it to someone else, the attachment *will* be included. You aren't given the option of detaching the file when you forward a message.

USING MAIL CONTROLS TO FILTER INCOMING MAIL

If you're a parent, you may wish to restrict e-mail access for children who have screen names on your master account (the account you registered with). There are strangers on the Internet, just as there are in the real world. If you don't want your children "talking to strangers," you may well want to take advantage of these controls. Here's how:

Managing Your Mailboxes

On AOL every screen name gets three mailboxes on one of AOL's "host" computers. Because we're talking about *AOL's* computers here, you cannot keep unlimited amounts of mail, but AOL is generous in its limits:

- **New** mailbox—messages you haven't yet read or that you have read and decided to keep as new

- **Old** mailbox—messages you've read in the past three to five days and haven't kept as new

- **Sent Mail** mailbox—messages you've sent in the past month (27 days, actually)

If you want to save all your messages, you can do so on *your* computer using one of the techniques described in "Saving and Printing Messages" at the end of this chapter.

Here's how AOL handles your mail from the three mailboxes. Every message you *send* goes into your Sent Mail mailbox (from the New Mail window, choose the Sent Mail tab). This mailbox can hold up to 550 messages, and the oldest messages will get bumped by new ones when you reach this magic number. Also, no outgoing message is available after about a month, no matter how many messages are in the mailbox.

Your Old mailbox holds messages that you've read *but not kept as New*. Your Old mailbox holds only about four days' worth of e-mail, so it's only useful if you've accidentally neglected to keep-as-new a message you recently read. To see your Old mailbox, click the Old Mail tab.

Every message you receive goes into your New mailbox (what you get when you click the big You Have Mail button), which can also hold 550 messages. The 550 figure includes the small number of messages in your Old mailbox.

Sound complicated? Just remember to prune your New mailbox, deleting messages so it never gets full, as explained in the "Managing Your Messages" section. Keep-as-new your most important recent messages. And actively use your Personal Filing Cabinets, so you can keep the mail you've read and sent on your computer, as explained later in "Use Your Personal Filing Cabinet to Save Your Messages."

1. Go to keyword: Parental to go to the Parental Controls area. Click on Custom Controls. In the Custom Controls window, click Mail, then Mail Controls. Finally, select the screen name(s) for which you want to limit incoming mail. The E-mail Parental Controls window, shown in Figure 3-5, comes up.

2. Make *one* of the following choices:

   ■ Allow all mail to the screen name

   ■ Block all mail to the screen name

   ■ Allow e-mail to and from specific people (you must list their addresses at the right side of the screen)

   ■ Block e-mail to and from specific people (you must list their addresses at the right side of the screen)

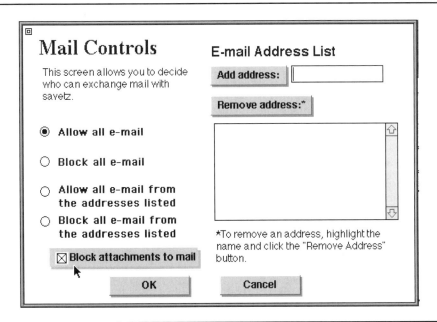

FIGURE 3-5   Decide exactly what kind of e-mail you want a minor to send and receive

If you allow receipt of *any* mail, you can then choose to block all file attachments. If you choose to add or block *specific* e-mail addresses, you must enter the prohibited or allowed addresses one at a time in the Add address field (clicking the "Add address" button after each entry). To remove addresses from the list, just select and click Remove. Click OK when you're done.

 One of the purposes of blocking attachments is to block the exchange of possibly offensive materials.

 ## Avoiding Spam

Junk e-mail—unsolicited commercial mail—is an unpleasant by-product of the commercialization of the Internet. It is usually sent out of ignorance of how the Internet works. As people learn about you or see your screen name on AOL (especially in chat rooms and message boards), you may find yourself the recipient of such unwelcome mail.

AOL offers a unique, free service called Preferred Mail™ (keyword: Preferred mail), which filters out all mail addressed to you from mail addresses known to send unsolicited commercial messages on the Internet. These are the messages that show up from unknown senders with Subject lines that are meant to entice and with messages that usually try to separate you from your money. If you don't mind getting such messages, just click in the "I want mass e-mail solicitations from all these sites!" box. By default, every account is set to use Preferred Mail to block spam.

To receive e-mail from a specific domain on the "blocked list," you can unblock the domain for any screen name at keyword: Mail Controls (Figure 3-5). First, make sure "Allow all mail" is selected on the left. Then, in the E-mail Address list, type in the addresses from which you'd like to receive mail and press RETURN.

Preferred Mail works well, but isn't infallible. It can only block e-mail from sites that are known spammers. If a site has never spammed AOL members before, it won't be in Preferred Mail's blocking list—so the spam messages will get through. You can help assure that the miscreants will be added to the Preferred Mail blacklist. Forward the message to the screen name TOSSPAM. This will allow AOL's Community Action team to be aware of the problem and block the site in the future.

MANAGING YOUR MESSAGES

Every message you get can be handled in several ways. You can:

- Read it and respond (reply) to it
- Read it and forward it to someone else
- Keep it as new
- Delete it
- Ignore it

Tip   *If you receive more than one e-mail message at a time, you can move to the next message simply by clicking the right arrow next to the subject line. To read the previous message, click the left arrow.*

Return Mail: Replying

The easiest way to *send* a message is to reply to a message someone has already sent you. What makes it so easy? When you reply to a message, some or all of the message itself, as well as the address and subject, automatically become part of your new message. All you have to do is write your own message. Usually, you'll want to *quote* the part of the original message to which you want to respond in order to frame and focus your response. If your message elicits a reply, you may be quoted in turn.

Let's say you receive a message, and want to reply to the writer:

1. Use your mouse to select the part of the message to which you want to respond. Select the entire message if there are numerous points you want to reply to. (This is the text that will appear quoted and will be set off by special characters in the recipient's e-mail.) Click either Reply or Reply to All. Replying to All sends your reply to all the recipients of the message, including all the people CCed. If they were CCed on the original message, they'll be CCed on your reply. Reply to: will send a private message just to the person who sent the message.

2. You'll see a Compose Mail window, with the Subject line in the title bar, preceded by the word *Re* and a colon. Edit the To and CC fields by adding and dropping names (either AOL screen names or Net addresses).

3. If you want, select the bit of text that forms the first line:

> In a message dated 97-01-21 16:39:21 EST, you write:

and type in a personal greeting, such as:

> David, in your message you wrote (and I quote):

4. Now type in your actual reply—your comments replying to the original message.

5. When you're done, click Send Now or Send Later.

Replies are tracked in your Sent Mail mailbox, just like any message you send. As with a message you originate from scratch, a reply can be unsent, and you can keep track of its status (whether it's been read). See "If You Change Your Mind: Unsending a Message," earlier in this chapter.

> *Tip*   *On AOL you have a choice in the way you "quote" in your replies. You can place "AOL-style" quote marks at the beginning and end of the quoted passage (<<…>>), or you can place "Internet-style" quotes at the beginning of each quoted line. In the latter, each line begins with the greater-than sign (>). I strongly prefer the Internet style because it makes clear what is being quoted and makes it possible to reply to several different parts of the original message. The downside is that it looks ugly and there's a possibility for weird formatting when the recipient opens the message. To set your preferences, choose Preferences from your Members menu and click Mail.*

Sharing a Message: Forwarding

Forwarding a message means sending it to someone who wasn't a primary (To) or secondary (CC) recipient. As with a reply, you can choose to forward an entire message or a part of it.

To forward a message:

1. With the message displayed, select the exact part of the message to be forwarded and click Forward. Selecting nothing will cause the entire message to be forwarded. A Compose Mail window comes up, with either part of the message quoted or nothing, which is what you see when the whole message is being forwarded.

2. Enter the address(es) of the recipient(s) in the To field, and, if you want, include additional recipients in the CC field.

3. Edit the Subject line if you wish. It will automatically read *Fwd:* plus the Subject line of the forwarded message.

4. Type any comments of your own into the message box; they'll precede the message you're forwarding. Click Send.

Tip   *If you use AOL in any kind of a company or organization, forwarding can be a more effective way of taking part in a group exchange than replying. Why? Because forwarding retains the entire message as-is, without the intrusive quote marks that are used in replies. Plus, it preserves the entire thread of the message. For example, if you send a message requesting information to someone who can't help you, but that person then forwards it to another person who forwards it to yet another person, the ultimate recipient will have a complete record of the exchange. The end recipient will know who wanted the information and why, as well as who has already been approached. You're likely to get better and faster information than you would if you pursued it by phone and wound up playing phone tag with several people.*

Keeping as New

When you read a message and then close it and return to the New Mail window, a check appears through it.

 4/6/97

This tells AOL to remove the message from New Mail when you close New Mail. Next time you open New Mail, the message won't appear, but it will be available for a few days in Old Mail. To keep a message in New Mail, you must select the message and click Keep as New.

Why would you keep a message "new"? It's a good way to keep your most recent mail in one place, especially the personal messages. Why wouldn't you do this? Because it slows down the window's display when you open it, and it is redundant if you're using your Personal Filing Cabinet. The wisely moderate solution is to keep your most important recent messages in your New Mail window and to get into the habit of using your Personal Filing Cabinet (which are always available offline), as explained in the next section.

What if you've read a message and banished it to your Old mailbox (closed the New mailbox after you read it without keeping-as-new)? You can bring it back to your New mailbox by selecting the message from the Old mailbox and clicking Keep as New. It shows up again in the New mailbox next time you open it. See "Managing Your Mailboxes" for an overview of how the different mailboxes work.

Deleting and Ignoring Messages

Of course, you don't have to read, reply to, and forward messages. You can also delete them—even without reading them. Actively deleting messages from your New Mail window is a good idea, because on AOL you can keep only 550 messages in your New and Old mailboxes. While deleting messages makes room for new messages, it doesn't necessarily mean you have to throw away copies of old messages. The next section, "Saving and Printing Messages," offers several techniques for saving messages.

To delete a message that's in your New Mail window, just select the message and click Delete. To delete a bunch of messages that are located right next to each other, hold down the SHIFT key, click on all the messages you want to get rid of, and then click Delete. To delete messages scattered throughout your New mailbox, hold down the COMMAND key, click on each message you want to delete, and then click Delete.

If there's a message or messages you don't want to read (a mailing-list thread you aren't following, for example), select the message(s) and click Ignore. Notice the check mark through the message's icon on the far left. This tells AOL that you have either read or acknowledged a message and don't want to retain it as new. Messages you want to Ignore and that you never open won't ever appear in your Personal Filing Cabinet but will be available in your Old Mail for a few days.

SAVING AND PRINTING MESSAGES

AOL gives you several ways of saving copies of individual e-mail messages that you send and receive. In any organization, you may want to keep a record of all messages for legal and archival purposes. Any particularly important individual messages (to bosses or buddies, for example) are worth archiving as well. In general, saving a message can also save you time and trouble.

Any open message can be easily saved on your hard disk. With the message displayed, go to the File menu and select Save As. Then give the file a name and find a folder to save it in. If you save it with a file type of Mail, all formatting will be retained, but the file will only be readable later by opening it again from the AOL application. If you save it as text only, formatting will be lost, but you'll be able to open the file in your word processor.

Either way, you can later read the message by selecting Open from the File menu and navigating to the place where you've stored the message file.

Tip   *Saving a message as a separate text file is the safest way to keep a copy of your message. You can even copy it to a floppy disk for safekeeping. You* can't *use a word processor to individually access messages kept in your Personal Filing Cabinet, but can access saved messages in this way.*

Use Your Personal Filing Cabinet to Save Your Messages

 On AOL, you get three mailboxes for every screen name and up to five screen names for every account! Because AOL deletes old mail to make room for new mail when your new mailbox is full, it is a good idea to use your Personal Filing Cabinet (Figure 3-6) to keep a copy of *every* message you send and receive on your hard disk—not on AOL's computer.

1. To store mail in your Personal Filing Cabinet, select Preferences from your Members menu and click Mail.

2. Make sure there's a check in the boxes by either or both of the two options: "Retain all mail I send in my Personal Filing Cabinet" and "Retain all mail I read in my Personal Filing Cabinet." Click OK.

 Now messages will automatically be kept on your hard disk and will be available to you when you click the Personal Filing Cabinet icon on the AOL tool bar.

How do you find a message saved in your Personal Filing Cabinet? Clicking the Search button at the bottom of the PFC window gives you a choice of searching messages by their sender or recipient or by their *content*—words used in the actual

Savetz's Filing Cabinet		
Name	Address/Location	Date
▽ 🗄 Incoming Mail	-	-
✉ Checking thru NH	CJ Tripp	4/3/97
✉ File: "ANSWERMAN LIST"	LISTSERV@LISTSERV.AOL.CO...	4/1/97
✉ Fwd: need help with news ser...	ZElston	3/29/97
✉ Meg's Update, April 5 & 6	TalkToMeg4	4/5/97
✉ Protect Your Computer from ...	AOL Tip 4	4/3/97
✉ Re: 021097 – Re: Applicatio...	Try Angular	3/29/97
✉ Re: AnswerMan help	ChChT	3/29/97
✉ Re: AnswerMan stuff	Aminie	3/31/97
✉ Re: IM	JPTierney	4/3/97
✉ Re: MIME & NET HELP LIVE	CJ Eagle	4/3/97
✉ Re: MIME & NET HELP LIVE	CJMezzie	4/4/97

[Auto AOL...] [Find...]

[Delete...]   [New Folder] [Open]

FIGURE 3-6   Use your Personal Filing Cabinet to keep a copy of all the
mail you send and receive

body of old messages you've sent and received. Searching by key word can help
you quickly zero in on specific messages.

To find a message, click on Find from the Personal Filing Cabinet. If you're
looking for a message to or from a specific person, enter that address in the "name
or address field." If you're looking for specific text in a message, enter it in the
"whose contents contain" field. Choose "and" or "or" to restrict or broaden the
search if you use both fields. Clicking the Case Sensitive box will make
capitalization count. When you're ready, click Find.

Tip   *Messages kept in your Personal Filing Cabinet are available to you even
when you're offline. That means you can search, read, and print old
messages without having to sign on first.*

Since your Personal Filing Cabinet is created on your hard disk, you should
manage it to keep it from getting too big. For one thing, a big Personal Filing Cabinet
can take awhile to open and close; it can also slow the AOL program overall. To set
your Filing Cabinet preferences:

1. Choose Preferences from your Members menu. In the list of preference areas, scroll down to Filing Cabinet and click on it.

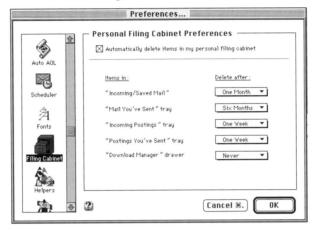

2. Click on "Automatically delete items in my Personal Filing Cabinet."

3. Use the Preferences box to indicate how long to store each type of message on your Mac's hard disk: incoming mail, mail you've sent, incoming and outgoing newsgroup postings, and items that you download.

Printing Messages

The reasons for printing messages are pretty straight-forward: to keep a record of a message in your real filing cabinet, to edit it, to read it at your leisure, and so on.

1. Make sure you have a printer attached to your computer, and make sure it works and is turned on. This book can't help you with printer problems, but AOL's Mac Help Desk (keyword: Mac Help) can.

2. Retrieve the message to print so that it's displayed. It may be in a mailbox or your Personal Filing Cabinet. Or it may even be saved as a text file.

3. Click the Printer icon on the AOL tool bar just to the left of the Personal Filing Cabinet icon (or simply press COMMAND-P):

PUTTING YOUR BEST FOOT FORWARD

Think of an e-mail message in the same way you think of a phone call. In both, you're communicating from a distance. There are plenty of differences between e-mail and a phone call, of course. In e-mail, you can't hear the timbre of someone's voice, and you can't interrupt someone, as you can when they're talking. And e-mail's "asynchronous": you can take as long as you want to respond, since you're not communicating in "real time." Here are some suggestions for communicating as effectively as possible using e-mail.

Cries and Whispers—Don't Do Either in E-mail

A way of showing you really want to get attention is by *shouting*—putting letters in ALL CAPITAL LETTERS. Business spammers, the people who send out unsolicited make-money-fast mail to thousands of people, use the technique all the time. But the attention you get is sure to be negative.

```
GREETINGS FRIEND. HAVE YOU BEEN DREAMING OF BECOMING YOUR OWN
BOSS? DO YOU WANT TO MAKE THOUSANDS OF DOLLARS A WEEK WITHOUT
RISK? WELL...
```

The best way to emphasize individual words in messages you send to someone on AOL is to use italics, as explained in "Adding Pizzazz to Your AOL Mail." To emphasize words in messages sent over the Net, I like to use asterisks on either side of the word (to get some *attention*). Other people use underscores to get _attention_. But, ultimately, the best way to get attention on both AOL and the Net is to write concisely, clearly, and respectfully. Sounds dull, but it's true.

Whispering means using all small letters and no punctuation, and it can be contagious. It looks cool, at first, kind of like an ee cummings poem:

```
hi guys what do you think of that new design have a look at
the comps on the wall and let me know what you think come to
our team meeting today with ideas...
```

Whispering is pleasanter than shouting, but whispered messages can be even harder to read and *parse* (figure out) than shouted messages. Avoiding punctuation can make a message subject to misinterpretation. The alternative? Use well-chosen words and take the time to think through what you want to say.

Take a Deep Breath Before Clicking Send

The powerful features and flexible controls you enjoy on America Online don't always extend to the Internet, which is, after, highly decentralized. In the case of e-mail, for instance, you can't unsend a message after it's been sent. That's just another reason to avoid sending any message you might later regret. It's easy to misunderstand a message you receive because there's no body language to clarify the context, and messages are often hastily typed and sent. Be sure to double-check messages you write so that any emotional freight is clearly marked as such and not subject to misinterpretation. In other words, if you are angry when you write something, count to ten and reread what you've written.

Personalize Your Message

Brevity may be a virtuous way to conserve bandwidth in e-mail, but excessive brevity can sound clipped—insultingly to-the-point and impersonal. Unless this is the message you want to project, it's often a good idea to personalize your messages. Begin with the recipient's name on a separate line, for example. And in replies, make sure to type over the bit that begins

```
In a message dated 96-10-15 04:53:40 EDT, you write:
```

Don't be averse to saying "you" in the body of the message. As in any discussion, if you disagree strongly about something, try to find something positive in your opponent's position or some point of agreement, and phrase your criticisms constructively. In e-mail it is simply too easy to take polar positions on issues that are less than profound. Keeping things personal can defuse an e-mail fight (also known as *flame*). Finally, I like to end messages with a "thanks" and my real name. On mailing lists in particular, nothing is more annoying than not knowing the real person behind a strong opinion.

Quote Aptly

You'll save a recipient's time (multiplied by the number of recipients) if you quote very sparingly in your replies. You do this by selecting the most pertinent word or words in the original message before clicking Reply or Reply to All. Keep your reply to the point and, in general, devote one idea to one message.

Sometimes It's Faster in Person

Not everyone communicates effectively in writing. Some people don't like to write at all or don't answer their mail in a timely manner. If your message matters and your recipient may not be a writer or an e-mailer, talk to the person…in person. If you're messaging many people who work in the same place, the overhead of everyone reading and responding to your message may be greater than the trouble it takes to walk door to door to get a response. A face to face (*F2F*) conversation receives many more replies, counter-replies, and nuances in a minute than an e-mail exchange can in an hour. And it's a good chance to schmooze.

Keep Track of Your Messages

With the volume of e-mail many people receive every day, it is nearly impossible to predict which messages will really matter. Print messages from your boss, your mother, or anyone who matters in your life. And save everything in your Personal Filing Cabinet. Having an e-mail audit trail can save your skin.

Delete Messages Before AOL Deletes Them for You

Because of the limits on the number of pieces of mail you can hold in your various AOL mailboxes (New, Old, and Sent), and because of the volume of e-mail you're likely to receive, especially if you join mailing lists, keep your New mailbox as lean as possible. If you have a total of 550 pieces of mail in your New mailbox, mail sent to you will not be deliverable, and AOL members will get a nice message to this effect; your friends on the Net will get a less-nice message. If you're using your Personal Filing Cabinet, there's no reason to hold any nonessential messages in your New mailbox.

Signal Your Feelings

Words on paper can't convey intention and emotion the way a raised eyebrow or wrinkled nose can. Many *emoticons*—ways of expressing emotion through typewriter characters—were invented in newsgroups. This whole subject will be more fully covered in Chapter 5. For now, it's enough to recommend that you tell people when you're kidding as well as when you're angry. At keyword: Shorthand you'll find a long list of abbreviations to help you signal your feelings (for example, ROFL means "rolling on the floor laughing"). Since many people don't know what these things mean, it can be best to use Smileys. Everyone's familiar with a Smiley face :-) If you're not, turn your head to the left to get the effect.

Rewrite Again and Again, Offline If Necessary

The single most frequent reason why I unsend a message is that I discover a mistake in it. Rereading your messages before sending them can spare you both the negative consequences of an intemperate remark and the flush of embarrassment if you've made a particularly silly error in spelling. The more important the message, the greater the consequences of sending it off prematurely. For my most serious (dullest) messages, I usually draft the message offline, use the built-in spell checker to catch any errors, read it again, log in, and send it. Remember: if a single recipient of your message is on the Net (i.e., does not have an AOL screen name), you will not be able to unsend the message.

Respond to as Much Mail as You Can

As troublesome as it seems to reply to an e-mail message, it is a lot easier than sitting down to write a response, attaching a stamp to an envelope, and mailing it; it's cheaper than the phone; and it's faster than doing it face to face. Everyone gets a lot of mail today, but communication works only if it's two-way. Not answering mail, especially if it's from someone you know and a reply has been requested, may seem rude. It weakens a fabulous communications medium. You don't, of course, have to answer obnoxious unsolicited mail. (Though the temptation to send an obnoxious reply is great, it almost certainly won't be read and does add to bandwidth clutter.) On the other hand, mailing lists (Chapter 4), for all their interactive potential, are pretty passive experiences—only take part if you have something to say.

What's the Point of Your Message?

To make everyone's life easier, it's a good idea to put one idea, or point, in each message (and never send a message without a point). The way to tell whether you have one point in your message is if you can express that point concisely in the Subject line. The reason to avoid multiple points is that they can't easily be replied to, short of quoting the entire message. It's especially maddening if there are multiple recipients, since they will each have varying degrees of interest in the various themes of your message, and the replies may turn into a messy thread. If more than one recipient is involved, the resulting threads can get all tangled up.

Make It Easy on Your Reader

Here are some mechanical devices for making it easier for your reader to read your message. Add a blank line between paragraphs; the white space gives people a chance to breathe. If you want to include items in a list form, keep each item short and make sure it has the same structure as the others. Usually, I use asterisks (*) for unnumbered lists (things whose order has no necessary sequence) and numbers (1,2,3…) for numbered lists (things whose order matters, as in a recipe or any procedure).

FROM HERE...

AOL's e-mail gives you power, flexibility, and ease of use without the bother of having to install and configure complex software. Features like the Personal Filing Cabinet, Spell Checker, Address Book, Automatic AOL, and the informative Mail Center add more value to the mix. The next two chapters look at mailing lists and newsgroups, two different tools that allow you to engage in regular communication with groups of people about a topic of shared interest.

Chapter 4

Discovering Internet Mailing Lists

Welcome to mailing lists—power e-mail. A mailing list, or *list*, lets people anywhere in the world easily share their thoughts with each other about a common interest. The principle is simple. Think of a mailing list as a fancy version of your AOL Address Book. Using the Address Book, you can send one message to many people at the same time by making a single name stand for several individual e-mail addresses. Send an e-mail message to the group address, and the message is delivered to each person's private mailbox.

Mailing lists work a little differently, but the principle is the same. You don't need to understand the workings of the list-management software that makes them possible in order to benefit from the communities that result. There are more than 60,000 mailing lists—triple the number of newsgroups, which are covered in the next chapter.

This chapter does the following:

- Introduces the key distinctions between lists (discussion lists vs. newsletters; moderated vs. unmoderated lists)

- Shows you how to find lists of likely interest to you

- Provides instructions for joining any list

- Gives advice for taking part in lists and managing your list mail

- Highlights some of the best lists available to AOL members

MAILING LIST ABCS

Lists vary in a couple of ways. Some support active discussion, while others are one-way newsletters. Some are moderated, but most are not. And lists are administered by different kinds of list software that have different commands for doing basic things like subscribing and unsubscribing. These mechanical nuances are spelled out in the "Reference" section at the end of this chapter.

4

What You Really Need to Know About Mailing Lists

Behind the minor mechanical variations from list to list, you'll find the same vibrant, self-regulating microcommunities of interest and passion. Lists are probably the best way to meet other people on the Internet, to get current information about any topic of personal or professional interest, and to keep up with new Internet resources about any topic. Lists are where "community" happens on the Internet.

Here's another thing to remember about mailing lists: all you need in order to use them is e-mail; the fancy list software that does all the work is located on some Internet computer that you don't need to worry about. You communicate with people on the list and with the list software itself by e-mail.

Although the specifics vary from list to list, joining a list entails three basic steps:

1. *Find a list to join.* Whatever your interest, you'll learn to uncover good mailing lists in "Finding a Mailing List for You." A selection of lists is provided in "Good and Great: A List Sampler," which includes many easy-to-get electronic newsletters created especially for AOL members.

2. *Subscribe to the list.* "Subscribing" means sending a simple e-mail message to the list's administrative e-mail address, as explained in "Subscribing to a Mailing List." Subscribing to a list isn't like subscribing to a magazine—it doesn't cost anything, for one thing. To subscribe and *unsubscribe* (as it's called on mailing lists), you send a message to software (usually not a person, but a program), which handles these tasks. Once you're subscribed, there are usually all sorts of options at your disposal, such as receiving all the lists' messages in a single e-mail *digest*. The software handles these options too. For more details about the mechanics of joining and customizing lists, see the "Reference" section at the end of this chapter.

Tip *Whenever you learn about a list, make sure to get the information spelled out in the "What You Need to Subscribe" box later in this chapter.*

> **3.** *Take part in the list.* Taking part means actually sending messages to
> the *people* on the list. Tips for making your messages to others as
> effective as possible are provided in "Mailing List Netiquette." To
> avoid getting swamped by e-mail, have a look at the guidelines for
> "Managing Your Mail" later in this chapter.

Discussion Lists and Distribution Lists (Newsletters)

Some mailing lists let everyone on the list talk to everyone else. David belongs to a
great list called **our-kids**, for example, which is a small community consisting of
about 500 parents of kids with developmental disabilities. Parents share their
problems, offer suggestions, give support, and generally prove themselves to be
good listeners. This kind of *discussion* list is genuinely interactive. There are other
lists for parents with "spirited" kids, asthmatic kids, deaf kids, and kids of every
other variety. You'll find thousands of other discussion lists devoted to topics such
as body piercing, violin playing, Japanese animation, and Internet advertising.

The other type of mailing lists arrives in your mailbox, but does not let you send
mail to the list. These *distribution* lists are really electronic newsletters, like the one
shown in Figure 4-1. They can tie a community together by providing everyone with
the same information at the same time. The difference with electronic newsletters
is that you usually do not know who else subscribes and what they think of the topics
discussed in the newsletter. These electronic creations cost nothing to print, very
little to distribute, and don't add to the world's garbage.

AOL's channels and many individual AOL forums make active use of the
Internet's list software to distribute forum and channel newsletters. You can read
about some of them later in this chapter ("Good and Great: A List Sampler").

MODERATED LISTS AND UNMODERATED LISTS

For the most part, only people who are serious about a list's topic will take the trouble
to subscribe to it (although it's not much trouble once you get the hang of it). In
practice, some lists have an additional level of control to make sure the people on
the list are serious about a topic or stay *on topic*. This second level of control takes
the form of a person, the *list moderator* or *editor*.

A list moderator, if there is one, must personally approve every message sent
from one member to the whole list. This screening of messages can keep a list on

FIGURE 4-1   Excerpt from the Your Business newsletter, created by AOL's Your Business channel and available at keyword: Mail Center

topic, but it violates some people's sense of free speech. (It's also a lot of unpaid work for the moderator.)

However, moderated lists can be more informative and can prevent Internet rituals such as flaming from getting out of hand. A moderator can be especially welcome in large groups and groups devoted to contentious topics. But there are some moderators who define the list's topic more narrowly than some subscribers are comfortable with—and from such tensions new lists are born.

A list I belong to for computer book authors is moderated, and the moderator does step in from time to time to end "off-topic" threads or patently commercial messages. The effect is not chilling, but then again I have never been the one to overstep the list's bounds. Mostly, lists moderate themselves collectively, with subscribers sharing a purpose and gently (or sometimes not so gently) reinforcing it, especially among newcomers.

How do you tell whether a list is moderated? One way is to read about the list before joining it, using one of the resources described in the next section. Or, when you subscribe to a list, you should receive a message including details about the list, including whether it's moderated or not.

FINDING A MAILING LIST FOR YOU

If you're looking for a mailing list to join, here are two places to start. First, America Online's Internet Mailing List Directory (keyword: Mailing Lists) brings together descriptions of several thousand lists. A handy subject directory (Figure 4-2) makes it easy for you to find a list of interest to you, and you can find useful guidelines for taking part in lists and interacting with people on lists (also have a look at "Mailing List Netiquette," later in this chapter).

Note   *On the Net you'll often find half a dozen ways to do the same thing. Searching for mailing lists is no exception. Several other ways of tracking down mailing lists of likely interest to you are available at keyword: Nethelp (click General Internet Help, then select Mailing Lists).*

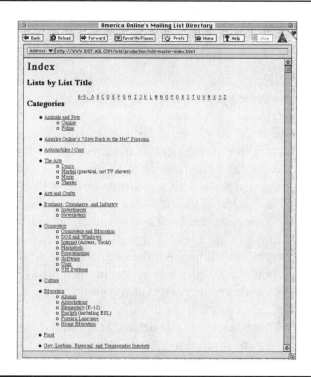

FIGURE 4-2   Browse AOL's Internet Mailing List Directory by subject to find a mailing list you're interested in

The AOL directory is small (relative to the number of lists on the Internet), but it does offer complete information for each list, including the purpose of the list, how to subscribe and unsubscribe, and where to find related information about the list's mission.

If AOL's directory doesn't have what you're seeking, try Liszt on the World Wide Web. Keyword: Liszt takes you there directly. This gigantic searchable database provides information about more than 60,000 mailing lists (Figure 4-3)! It doesn't offer the same level of detail for each list as AOL's mailing list directory, but it's fairly complete and, more important, it's searchable.

Like AOL's mailing list directory, Liszt gives you useful information about specific lists and an overview of other people's favorite lists. Chapter 9 introduces you to Liszt in detail.

"Good and Great: A List Sampler," later in this chapter, provides subscription information for some lists you might want to join.

FIGURE 4-3   Liszt has become the preeminent Internet tool for finding and joining Internet mailing lists

SUBSCRIBING TO A MAILING LIST

Lists vary in some fundamental ways, as described in the previous sections. Some are fully interactive discussion lists, while others are for distribution only (newsletters). Some are moderated, but most are pretty much self-regulating. These factors can shape your experience of belonging to a list.

There's another way in which lists differ: they are administered by different kinds of software, which you use to subscribe to (join) and unsubscribe from (leave) lists. The oldest and most widely used list software is *LISTSERV*, created by Eric Thomas in 1986. *LISTSERV* is the actual name of the software to which you send e-mail whenever you join or leave a LISTSERV-based list. LISTSERV is widely used because it can support very popular lists (such as C|net's Dispatch) and because it offers a ton of options. It's the software of choice at America Online, so it's a good idea to learn how it works (see "LISTSERV: Joining, Leaving, and Customizing").

 A product called Unix Listserv (only the L is capitalized) is used to run some lists. It is not the same as the LISTSERV product in use at AOL and other sites. This chapter capitalizes LISTSERV to make the distinction from the Unix product. Traditionally, you'll see LISTSERV lists and their associated commands in capital letters, but you can use lowercase.

But there are other mailing list programs. *Listproc* is another piece of software modeled after LISTSERV. Its commands are broadly similar to LISTSERV's. The third big name in mailing-list software is *Majordomo*, created by Brent Chapman. Majordomo isn't generally used to support large lists with many subscribers.

You'll also find lots of lists that are run from other programs such as Smartlist, Mailbase, Mailserv, and a host of improvised *reflectors,* which are simple distribution lists with primitive features that merely redistribute a message to several individuals when it was originally sent to a specific address.

 At the end of this chapter, in "Reference," you'll get the specifics of how you join and use these mailing lists.

What You Need to Subscribe

For every mailing list, you'll need three pieces of information to subscribe:

1. The list name (for example, there is **Roots-l**, the list name for the Genealogy Discussion List). Sending a message to the list causes your message to be sent to all the individuals who have subscribed to the list. Many list names end in hyphen *l* (*-l*), for *list*. Note: that's the letter *l*, not the number one (*1*).

2. The administrative address, that is, the e-mail address to which you send your subscription and unsubscription requests (in the example of the Genealogy Discussion List, it is **roots-l-request@ rootsweb.com**). Some administrative addresses indicate the type of list software (*listserv*, *majorodomo*, *listproc*), while others take the list name and tack on *-request*. Sometimes, the "-request" lists are maintained by a person who individually approves all new subscriptions rather than automated software.

3. The list address, that is, the e-mail address to which you send messages to the group when you want to take part. Generally, the list address consists of the list name, the @ sign, and the domain name. For example: **roots-l@rootsweb.com**. Note that the domain name (the bit after the @ sign) is usually the same for the administrative and the list address (e.g., **rootsweb.com**).

Common Mailing List Commands

The many types of list software vary in the commands they make available, but they all offer commands for joining and leaving (subscribing and unsubscribing), and many offer the important option of receiving a digest. The slight variations between names can be confusing, but Table 4-1 can help you keep the major commands straight.

	LISTSERV	**Listproc**	**Majordomo**
To subscribe	**subscribe** *listname [your full name]* or **sub** *listname [your full name]*	**subscribe** *listname your name* or **join** *listname your name*	**subscribe** *listname [your@address]* Note: *your@address* is the e-mail address at which you want to receive the list, if different from the address you're subscribing from—useful if you're using AOL's "bring your own access" service.
To get a digest	**set** *listname* **digest**	**set** *listname* **mail digest**	**subscribe** *listname-digest* Note: The list owner can choose not to set up a list as a digest. To get a digest (if there is one), you must first subscribe to the regular list. When requesting the digest, you should also send a message (it can be in the same e-mail message) simultaneously *unsubscribing* from the regular list (see below)
To unsubscribe	**unsubscribe** *listname* or **signoff** *listname*	**unsubscribe** *listname* or **signoff** *listname*	**unsubscribe** *listname [your@address]* Note: Use *your@address* if you receive the list at a different address from the one you used to send the unsubscribe message.

TABLE 4-1   Popular mailing list commands

Note   *In this chapter, whenever text is just bold, that's exactly what you type in the Compose Mail window:* **listserv.nodak.edu** *(for example). Whenever text is bold and italics—***domain.name** *(for example)—you must type something, but what you type will depend on the name of the list, its address, domain name, or your address. Any text in square brackets—[ ]— is optional.*

What do you do with these commands in Table 4-1? In the Compose Mail window, the administrative address goes in the To field, the Subject field is blank, and the actual command goes in the message box. Just click Send when everything's in order. See the example a little later in "Subscribing to a LISTSERV List."

Tip   *You can place several commands in one message, **help** and **subscribe** **listname**, for example. Just make sure they're on separate lines. Some commands are contingent on others, however, so you'll have to send separate messages. For example, you can't get a LISTSERV digest without first subscribing to the list. Finally, don't worry about case. Mailing list purists (like AOL's David O'Donnell) capitalize everything associated with LISTSERV, from list names to command names, but in fact, the software will accept lowercase.*

4

Every List Has Two Addresses

Never, ever send your administrative e-mail—messages about joining, leaving, or customizing—to the people on the list itself. They're not interested in your efforts to join the list or to leave it, and they may give you a hard time about it. Administrative e-mail goes to **listserv@***domain.name*… or **majordomo@-** *domain.name*… or *listname***-l@domain.name**. Real e-mail (to the other people who subscribe to the list) goes to *listname@domain.name*.

MAILING LIST NETIQUETTE

Chapter 3 modestly offered some general guidelines for communicating effectively by e-mail ("Putting Your Best Foot Forward"). All of those guidelines—quote aptly, stick to one subject, respect the other guy, signal your feelings, etc.—apply to mailing lists as well, because the communications problems are just the same. In addition, mailing lists have their own sets of guidelines that mostly have to do with the mechanics of lists. Sending a message to a list is a shade more anonymous than sending a message to an individual, and the netiquette requires that much more sensitivity since you'll be communicating with people you may not know personally. Here are some things to keep in mind:

- Don't send a message to the members of a list when it should be sent to the list-management software.

- Joining a list is not like visiting a Web site or browsing a newsgroup. Make sure the list's for you before joining it.

- Read the list for several weeks before posting. *Lurking* (just reading the messages) is the way to take the pulse of an e-mail microcommunity and decide whether it's for you.

- Keep your messages to lists on topic. Messages go into the mailboxes of all subscribers, and subscribers will not appreciate junk mail.

- Remember that list owners control their lists. America Online has no control over lists or list owners. Obscenities that might not faze one moderator might be cause for a TOS violation on AOL (see keyword: TOS).

- Save the Welcome message you automatically receive when you subscribe to a list. It contains useful information about how best to use the list, how to unsubscribe, and so on.

Tip *On some lists, you'll regularly (usually monthly) receive a FAQ—a list of frequently asked questions about the list. This FAQ will include an overview of the list's scope as well as instructions about customizing your subscription and leaving the list. Save the FAQ with the Welcome message. Sometimes the FAQ will include the same information as the Welcome message but will be more up to date.*

- If you are going to be away from your computer for some time, either leave any lists to which you subscribe or (if it's a LISTSERV list) use the LISTSERV NOMAIL feature (see Table 4-2) to temporarily suspend your subscription.

- Do not send a commercial solicitation to any mailing list. The only time it's okay to send a commercial solicitation is when buying or selling has been explicitly approved by the list's leader or in the list's charter or FAQ (Frequently Asked Questions) document.

- If you are going to delete a screen name that is subscribed to one or more lists, or if you will be closing your AOL account, please be kind to everyone and unsubscribe from any list(s) you are on. Steps for unsubscribing can be found in the list's Welcome message.

■   Respect people on the list. People from different cultures and persuasions might not understand or appreciate jokes and irony. When personal comments are appropriate, send them to an individual, not the list.

■   Take personal responsibility for what you write. A strong opinion will probably be taken more seriously if it's associated with a real name than if it's associated with an AOL screen name that doesn't reveal a real first or last name. However, while it is a good idea on Internet mailing lists to let people know your true identity, it's *not* a good idea to provide contact information such as address and phone number.

4

MANAGING YOUR MAIL

A single discussion list, if it's busy enough, can fill up your mailbox in a few days. If that happens, messages will start bouncing—getting returned to the list. In this case, list owners are within their rights to remove you from a list. Moreover, unless you have infinite time at your disposal and a list is of grave professional importance to you, you won't want to read every message that every subscriber sends. Even the best lists have their share of off-topic messages (usually known as *noise*) or messages that don't interest you.

Here are some tips for keeping up with the traffic and avoiding a full mailbox:

■   If a mailing list offers a digest version, get it. LISTSERV-type lists offer digests as a rule, as do some of the newer software packages. Majordomo offers digests too, but instead of first subscribing to a list and then *setting* it to digest mode, you subscribe to a separate list called (for example) **majordomo-users-digest**. Listproc is like LISTSERV in that you first subscribe to the list, then set it: **set anthro-lib mail digest**, for example. Note the addition of the word *mail* to the Listproc command. When in doubt, inquire with the list's owner, as described in "Finding Out Who Owns A List" at the end of this chapter.

■   If you subscribe to several mailing lists, consider creating a screen name for each list or group of related lists. For every AOL account, you can have five screen names, and each can keep up to 550 pieces of mail in the New and Old mailboxes combined. (To create additional screen names for use with your account, go to keyword: Names, and follow the simple onscreen instructions.) If you follow this advice, *do not delete screen names without first unsubscribing from any mailing lists to which the screen name belonged.*

- Use Automatic AOL to download unread e-mail and send outgoing e-mail. See "Taming E-Mail with Automatic AOL" for the how-to.

- If your mailing list is also carried as a Usenet newsgroup, you should consider quitting the mailing list and participating in the newsgroup. Information on how to do so will be given in AOL's Internet Mailing List Directory entry for that list (available at keyword: Mailing Lists under the Browse the Database button), on the list's Welcome message, or possibly in both places. The *bit.listserv.** newsgroups *mirror* more than 300 Internet mailing lists and are available at keyword: Newsgroups. Chapter 5 is all about newsgroups.

  The word mirror, *on the Internet, refers to a site or service that carries an exact copy of another site or service in order to improve service, relieve network pressure, or make a popular service more widely available. The best FTP and Web sites have FTP and Web mirrors, and AOL features a set of FTP mirrors for members' favorite sites.*

- The archives for some lists are available on the World Wide Web. They lack the interactive quality of mail-based lists but are a useful way of accessing old information. A very useful set of computer-related list archives can be found at **http://alt.venus.co.uk/hypermail/**. Inquire with a list's owner to find out whether the list has a Web archive. Otherwise, you may have to learn a list's *index* commands by sending the **help** command to any list's administrative address.

Taming E-Mail with Automatic AOL

Here's another feature that sets AOL apart. Using Automatic AOL, you can retrieve your new unread mail automatically, either at a specified time every day or on demand when you're online. With this feature, AOL automatically performs a series of tasks you request, and, if you want, signs off afterward. Messages downloaded via Automatic AOL are stored for you in your Personal Filing Cabinet, where you can read them offline, without incurring the cost of being online or the bother of tying up the phone line. Your outgoing mail (messages you send to mailing lists) can also be composed while you're offline then sent with Automatic AOL. Incoming and outgoing mail messages transferred with Automatic AOL are also available from the Mail menu on the main AOL menu bar: Read Offline Mail.

Automatic AOL is called FlashSessions by Windows-using AOL folk. Same thing, different name.

Setting up Automatic AOL requires two basic steps:

1. Indicate *what* you want to do during Automatic AOL: From the Mail menu, select Set up Automatic AOL. From the Auto AOL Preferences window shown in Figure 4-4, specify whether you want your automatic session to handle your incoming mail, your outgoing mail, the files attached to incoming messages, your file downloads, or your incoming and outgoing newsgroup messages. The AOL guide will walk you through the preferences. Click Activate Now to do it now, or Scheduler to schedule your automatic sessions.

2. Many people run Automatic AOL on demand. If you want to run Automatic AOL at a fixed time each day, use the Scheduler to indicate *when* or *how often* you want AOL to sign on automatically for you and carry out the activities you requested in Step 1. First, make sure there's a check mark in the Perform Scheduled Auto AOL Sessions check box; click in the box if there's not. Then, specify either a time or interval to run the session. Figure 4-5 shows a session scheduled for every day at around 6 A.M. Click OK when you're done.

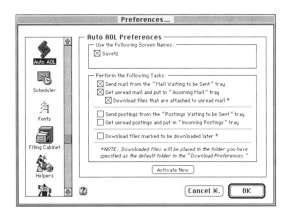

FIGURE 4-4   Automatic AOL lets you automatically send and retrieve batches of e-mail—a good way of taking part in high-volume lists

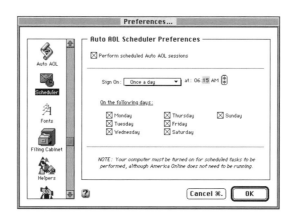

FIGURE 4-5 Setting up the times when you want the automatic sessions to occur

Note *If you are* offline *when you start Automatic AOL, there must be at least one name and password specified, and the session will run for those screen names. If you are online, you needn't specify any screen name, and it doesn't matter which ones you do specify; your Auto AOL session is only going to download messages for the screen name with which you signed on.*

Tip *The AOL software doesn't have to be running when it's time for a scheduled Auto AOL session. If you have it scheduled for Friday at 5 AM, but AOL isn't running, the software will automatically run and log in Friday morning to retrieve your mail and so on (if your computer is turned on, of course).*

GOOD AND GREAT: A LIST SAMPLER

Once you have a taste of how easy it is to subscribe to a mailing list, it's tempting to start subscribing right away. Where to start? If you are searching for a list devoted to a particular subject, start with the "Finding a Mailing List for You" section. If you'd just like to browse and try out some of the best mailing lists, have a look at the following lists. These are general interest electronic newsletters, not highly focused discussion lists. Distribution lists, by their nature, have a clear voice (they come from a single person) but aren't interactive. They can be a superb way to stay informed about a subject.

Tip In the Mail Center, available from the Mail menu, you can find a long list of online newsletters, created by AOL partners, forum leaders, and channels. The following AOL lists should all be available to you on that list. You can subscribe to most of them by clicking a button.

AOL's Mailing Lists

Mailing lists support thousands of communities on the Internet—but the mechanics of joining and customizing them can seem a bit unfriendly, with all those inflexible computer commands! America Online has recently begun to integrate LISTSERV-based mailing lists throughout its channels. Figure 4-6 shows the AOL Marketplace's newsletter. To join and leave an AOL-sponsored mailing list you will probably never have to send messages with arcane commands—just click a button to subscribe or unsubscribe. For the most part, AOL forums and channels use distribution lists (one-way electronic newsletters).

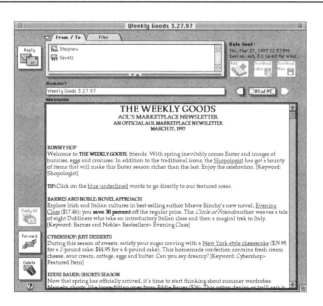

FIGURE 4-6   Attention shoppers! The AOL Marketplace newsletter, with deals of the week highlighted and linked to the AOL Store

Top Tips

At keyword: Top Tips, you can sign up for several newsletters that will deliver a tip a day, or every few days, to your mailbox. Tips for beginners (such as how to forward your e-mail) are at your fingertips, as are more advanced tips. For Internet tips, start with the AnswerMan Internet Extra.

AnswerMan Internet Extra

This weekly newsletter serves AOL members who enjoy the AnswerMan forum, the fun, interactive half of the Internet help forum on AOL (keyword: Nethelp). The newsletter is written by Kevin Savetz, forum leader and co-author of this book. Each newsletter contains Internet tips and resources and focuses on a specific topic each week, such as FTP or Music. You can subscribe at keyword: AnswerMan. From the main AnswerMan screen, click on the Internet Extra Newsletter button. You can also see the current issue and read past issues there.

> *Tip*   *Many of AOL's mailing lists use LISTSERV software, and all are run at* **listserv.aol.com**. *To unsubscribe to any of them, just send an e-mail message to* **listserv@listserv.aol.com** *with anything in the Subject line, and put the following in the body of the message:* ***signoff*** **listname,** *substituting* **AnswerMan,** **NetGirl, InBusiness,** *or whatever for* **listname***. Instructions for unsubscribing are provided at the end of every AOL newsletter.*

NetGirl Newsletter

The NetGirl forum, devoted to the world of online relationships, is one of AOL's most popular. The weekly newsletter brings romance-starved AOL members selected questions and answers about cyber-relationships, together with information about upcoming NetGirl events, new Web sites, questions and answers, and the like. You can subscribe to the newsletter at keyword: NetGirl; click Newsletter on the navigational bar at the bottom of the screen. You can also unsubscribe here, read the current edition online, and read earlier editions.

Most AOL mailing lists are weekly; they won't clutter up your mailbox. All include information for unsubscribing. On some you'll find AOL-only features such as text that's been enriched with color, formatting, and even hyperlinks (Figure 4-6).

4

Parental Controls on Mailing Lists and AOL's Policy

If you're a parent who has taught your children to be wary of strangers, you may be concerned about the strangers they can encounter on mailing lists or anywhere on the Internet. There's no better way to meet new people—strangers—on the Net than on mailing lists, so you might want to take a moment to read AOL's policy about allowing kids access to mailing lists:

"Internet mailing lists are not monitored, censored, or otherwise filtered by America Online, and America Online is not responsible for any content distributed via a mailing list. It is important for parents and guardians of minors to be aware of this fact and exercise discretion when evaluating how their children participate in mailing lists.

"The Internet is similar to real life in the sense that it is possible to electronically meet people and interact with them. Minors should be cautioned to never give out personal information, such as complete real name, telephone numbers, or addresses, to any strangers. If your child receives unsolicited or objectionable Internet e-mail, you should forward a complete copy of the e-mail to AOL screen name Postmaster and explain that it was unsolicited. You should send objectionable or unsolicited mail received from America Online members to AOL screen name *TOSEmail1* or *TOSEmail2*. In general, you should apply common-sense guidelines from the non-electronic world to your child's online sessions…. If you have specific questions about Internet mailing lists, you can send e-mail to AOL screen name ListMaster."

To provide even better protection, AOL offers Mail Controls, which enable parents to restrict the mail received by their kids. See Chapter 3 for more information.

Your Business Newsletter

This weekly newsletter for small businesses is created by Your Business (keyword: Your Business), AOL's small business resource center. A sample is shown earlier in this chapter, in Figure 4-1. In addition to schedules and promotions of the channel's chat sessions and other events, the newsletter contains guest columns and information from AOL partners such as *Business Week, Inc.* and *Home Office Computing.* Automatic subscription is available at keyword: Your Business.

BEYOND AOL: NET NEWSLETTERS

The following small sampling of what the Internet has to offer shows the kind of information you can have for free on the Internet. These newsletters can be a great way to stay informed about the things you're interested in. I'm leaving out of the picture the many excellent interactive mailings I've belonged to over the years, such as com-priv (devoted to issues surrounding the commercialization of the Internet), the Children with Special Health Care Needs list, and Community Memory (devoted to the history of cyberspace). Using Liszt and the AOL Internet Mailing List Directory, you can identify lists that address your specific personal and professional interests. For a profile of a classic Internet discussion list, BELIEFS-L, see "A Community of Believers."

A Community of Believers

BELIEF-L
Subscribe To: listserv@list
Subject line: *anything*
Body: subscribe belief-l *your name*

David O'Donnell, AOL's Postmaster, is the owner of this lively mailing list, hosted on AOL's mailing list computer. The list focuses on discussions of personal ideologies. Subscribers debate everything from religious, ethical, and moral issues to political upheaval in Bosnia, along with more whimsical subjects. Belief-L has developed quite a special community over the years, so it's important to carefully read the FAQ and Welcome message. You should also check out the Belief-L Web Site at **http://www.idot.aol.com/atropos/elf-bile/** before jumping into the fray. Beware: Belief-L is a *high* volume list, sometimes exceeding 150 messages a day, so be prepared to spend a lot of time trying to keep up.

Tour Bus

Subscribe To: listserv@listserv.aol.com
Subject line: *anything*
Body: subscribe tourbus

   Bob Rankin and Patrick Douglas Crispen write this very popular newsletter (hosted at AOL), which each week focuses on new or must-see Internet resources. These Internet old-timers have much experience helping newcomers make the most of the Net. Two things to note about this newsletter: because so many people subscribe, this newsletter accepts advertising (the more "eyeballs" a newsletter has, the keener sponsors' interest); don't be surprised or shocked to see ads in this and other newsletters. Also, this newsletter is available, as are more and more newsletters, on the Web (**http://www.worldvillage.com/tourbus.htm**).

Scout Report

Subscribe To: listserv@lists.internic.net
Subject line: *anything*
Body: subscribe scout-report

   This weekly newsletter containing serious new Internet resources is written by Susan Calcari and supported by InterNIC, an important Internet institution that keeps American universities informed about the Internet. With all the emphasis on "hot" and "cool" sites elsewhere, the Scout Report is committed to discovering and sharing useful and informative sites. The Scout Report is also available on the World Wide Web (**http://www.cs.wisc.edu/scout/report/**).

Yahoo!'s Picks of the Week

OK, you *are* interested in hot and cool sites. The folks at Yahoo have created a very big directory of Web sites, and they add to this list daily (Chapter 9 has more to say about Yahoo). Each week they post their favorite-site picks at their Web site. You can find out their favorites by e-mail, too, by simply visiting **http://www.yahoo.com/picks/** and (at the bottom of the page) typing in your e-mail address and clicking a button. You unsubscribe by sending a message to **yahoo-picks-request@yahoo.com**, with anything in the Subject line and **unsubscribe** *your.e-mail.address*.

REFERENCE: JOINING AND USING LISTSERV, LISTPROC, AND MAJORDOMO MAILING LISTS

Mailing lists are adminstered by different kinds of software. You communicate with this software by e-mail, sending messages and receiving replies. You'll find great lists of both kinds—discussion lists and distribution lists (newsletters)—on all the major types of mailing-list software. The slight variations in software commands and capabilities is a small price for the incredible community experience available on mailing lists. *Just remember that it's not important to understand exactly what ACK and Repro mean, as long as you know what they can do for you and how you can use them to make the most of your mailing list experience.*

LISTSERV: Joining, Leaving, and Customizing

LISTSERV bristles with features. The majority of these features are not used by most people, but they can add substantially to the power and usefulness of the program.

If you are interested in subscribing to a particular LISTSERV-type mailing list and know the administrative address, you can usually get information about the list (what it's about and who it's for) by sending a message to **listserv@*domain.name***, putting anything in the Subject line, and typing **info** *listname* in the body of the message. To get information about the famous Tourbus mailing list, for example, send a message to **listserv@listserv.aol.com**, put anything you please in the Subject line, and write **info tourbus** in the body. Then click Send.

Subscribing to a LISTSERV List

When you subscribe to a LISTSERV list, you're talking (by e-mail, that is) to a piece of software called *LISTSERV*—its e-mail name is **listserv**. All your *administrative* dealings with the list go to the administrative address (**listserv@*domain***), not the actual list address (*listname@domain*). LISTSERV administrative addresses look like this:

```
listserv@peach.ease.lsoft.com
listserv@listserv.aol.com
```

To subscribe to a LISTSERV list, follow these general steps. (Figure 4-7 shows a sample subscription message.)

1. Open the Compose Mail window (choose Compose Mail from the Mail menu). Type **listserv@***domain**.name* in the To field (for example, **listserv@peach.ease.lsoft.com**). LISTSERV ignores the Subject line, so you can leave it blank.

2. Put the following in the body of the message:

   ```
   subscribe listname [your real name]
   ```

   Whether you include your real name is optional. If the list supports a command that lets people view a listing of subscribers, your name will appear on the listing.

3. Click Send Now.

> *When you use AOL's Internet Mailing List Directory or one of the Net's directories, such as Liszt (keyword: Liszt), you'll find all the information you need to join, leave, and customize individual mailing lists. Always follow those instructions, because the exact subscription method is a little different for every mailing list.*

If the address seems generic, it is; one piece of LISTSERV software can be used to administer any number of mailing lists at a specific domain. There are dozens of mailing lists at **listserv.aol.com**, for example.

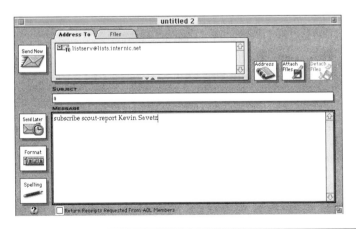

FIGURE 4-7   What a subscription message looks like

Remember that it's a piece of software that's reading your message, not a person. Any human message such as:

```
hi, please sign me up for the kennel management list. thanks,
wendell poodle
```

will be read as if it were a computer command, and returned to you via another e-mail message, because the words you've typed, beginning with the "hi," are not recognized commands.

Unless you've made a typo, you'll usually get a response by return mail saying that you have been added to the membership list. For larger LISTSERV lists, you may be asked to reply within 24 or 48 hours to the confirmation and say *ok* or something similar in your message (see Figure 4-8).

Once you are added, you usually receive a message welcoming you to the list (see Figure 4-9 for an example). Some Welcome messages provide an overview of the scope of the list's topic, and some lists provide a monthly FAQ to answer administrative and substantive questions. You may also receive a message called "Output of your job," which summarizes the computer time used to process your request. You can delete this message.

Tip *Save the Welcome message by selecting Save to Personal File Cabinet from your File menu. You can then retrieve the message at any time by selecting Personal File Cabinet from your File menu and looking in Incoming Mail.*

Customizing Your LISTSERV Experience

For many, the most useful way to customize a LISTSERV list is to get a *digest*. The automatic availability of a digest mode is a great advantage of LISTSERV. A digest is a single message you receive in which all the day's messages are compiled. The benefits? If you belong to more than one high-volume list, your mailbox will soon be overrun with messages, but a digest packages the day's traffic in one tidy little (or not so little) message. Having the day's messages in a single message makes it easy to skim the list and follow *threads*—discussions about the same topic. Usually, each digest is preceded by a numbered list of the day's topics, so you can jump to messages of likely interest, especially if the digest is so big that it arrives as an attached file that you must read in a word processor.

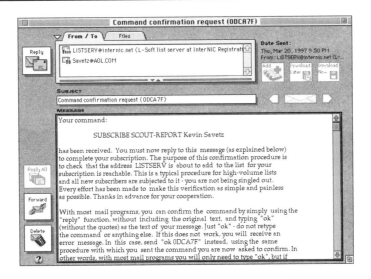

FIGURE 4-8   LISTSERV sometimes wants to verify your interest in the list before signing you up

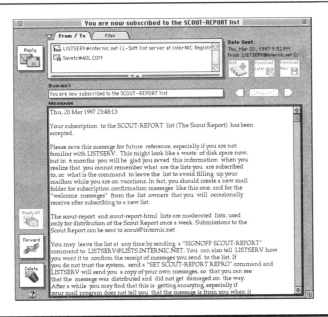

FIGURE 4-9   A typical Welcome message that you will receive when you join a list. Keep this message for future reference

To get a digest, you must first subscribe. Once you've requested the digest, the individual messages will stop coming to your mailbox.

The downside? Digests usually exceed the size limit AOL sets on messages, so they're automatically turned into attachments that you must download. Since every day's digest (attachment) will probably have the same file name, you'll have to rename each attached digest if you want to save it and not overwrite it with the next day's digest. Also, it's a bit more difficult to respond to messages if you're reading a message within a word processor!

To get the daily digest of a list to which you are subscribed, send a message to **listserv@*domain.name***, put anything in the Subject line, and put the following in the body of the message:

```
set listname digest
```

Other LISTSERV commands let you turn off digest mode, retrieve files (archived messages, usually), and get help. These options for customizing LISTSERV are outlined in Table 4-2.

Leaving a LISTSERV Mailing List

To leave any LISTSERV mailing list, send a message to **listserv@*domain.name***, with the following command in the message body:

```
signoff listname
```

That's it. You don't have to provide your name or any other information. Unless there's a typo, you will be unsubscribed and your unsubscription attempt will be confirmed.

 LISTSERV automatically makes a note of the e-mail address when you ask to subscribe to (join) a list. Make sure to leave the list using the same address! Using different accounts, different service providers, or different screen names can confuse LISTSERV.

To...	Send this message to listserv@*domain.name*
Get help	**help**
Subscribe to list	**subscribe** *listname [your name]*
Unsubscribe to list	**signoff** *listname*
Get a copy of messages you send to the list (as a record and to verify that the list is distributing messages appropriately)	**set** *listname* **repro**
Don't get a copy of your messages	**set** *listname* **norepro**
Temporarily "turn off" the list (when you go on a vacation, for example)	**set** *listname* **nomail**
Turn a list back on—after you get back from vacation	**set** *listname* **mail**
Get the list in digest form	**set** *listname* **digest**
Return to regular form (lots of mail)	**set** *listname* **nodigest**
Get a brief acknowledgement of messages you send the list	**set** *listname* **ack norepro**
Turn off acknowledgement	**set** *listname* **noack norepro**
Get a list of files associated with the list (usually archived messages)	**index** *listname*
Get a complete, long list of all the things you can do with LISTSERV	**info refcard**

TABLE 4-2   A few ways of customizing a LISTSERV-type mailing list

Basics of Listproc Lists

Listproc, a popular variant of LISTSERV, is another program used to administer many mailing lists. In other words, to join, customize, and leave a Listproc list, you must send messages to the Listproc software (not to the people on the list). The basic Listproc commands are summarized in Table 4-3. Sometimes the Listproc administrative address is *listserv* or *listserver*, which can be confusing, since the commands for LISTSERV and Listproc differ in slight ways.

To...	Send this message to listproc@*domain.name*
Join	**subscribe** *listname your real name* **join** *listname your real name*
Leave	**unsubscribe** *listname* **signoff** *listname*
Get digest	**set** *listname* **mail digest**
Get a list of people on the list	**review** *listname*
Get help	**help**

TABLE 4-3 The most important Listproc commands

Basics of Majordomo Lists

If you're familiar with other types of list software, Majordomo won't present any shocking departures from your experience. Majordomo is a popular type of list software for smaller lists. To join, customize, and leave a Majordomo list, you send messages to the Majordomo software. Table 4-4 summarizes the stuff you can do with Majordomo. As with Lisproc, Majordomo's options are limited relative to the myriad LISTSERV options. Note that the digest is a separate mailing list, not a version of the regular mailing list, so to request the digest you must first subscribe to the regular list, then request listname-digest, and then unsubscribe from the regular list.

Tip *Once you've taken part in (or at least subscribed to) a mailing list for a long time, it is quite easy to forget what kind of list it is (LISTSERV, Listproc, etc.), and it is also easy to forget to keep your Welcome messages. If you study the* **headers** *of your messages, you will find lots of useful information about the list's address, the owner's address, the type of list software being used, and even information about how to unsubscribe. If you receive a digest, the header will tell you the e-mail address of the original sender and of the list itself, so you can reply to an individual or to the group, as appropriate.*

To...	Send this message to majordomo@*domain.name*
Join	**subscribe** *listname* [*your e-mail address*]
Leave	**unsubscribe** *listname* [*your e-mail address*]
Get digest	**subscribe** *listname*-**digest** **unsubscribe** *listname*
Find out what files are available for the list	**index** *listname*
Get files related to the list	**get** *listname filename*
Find out who's on the list	**who** *listname*
Get the Welcome message again	**intro** *listname*
Get help	**help**

TABLE 4-4   The most important Majordomo commands

Finding Out Who "Owns" a List

Every mailing list has at least one "owner"—the person who sets up the software and makes sure that it's working, that messages don't bounce, and that patently inappropriate messages don't find their way onto the list. It's useful to know this person's e-mail address, just in case you have problems *using* the list—posting messages or accessing archives, for example. Such "administrative" problems should be shared with the list's owner and *not* with all the actual subscribers. Before asking the owner a question, it's wise to consult the help file available for every kind of major list software.

How do you find out who owns a list? When you first subscribe to a list, chances are good that you will receive a Welcome message. This message will often include the name of the list owner and his or her e-mail address. In general, it's always a good idea to read and save this message. AOL's LISTSERV software has the address **listserv@listserv.aol.com** (or just **listserv@list**), and you can write that address for "automated" help (put anything in the Subject line and the word "help" in the message body, then click Send Now).

Here is advice from AOL's Postmaster General, David O'Donnell, about finding out who owns a list if it's not obvious from the Welcome message:

"First, determine the type of software that's administering the list by sending the Help command to the software administering the list. For example, send a message to **listserv@listserv.aol.com** with **Help** as the body of the text, then press Send Now. In the reply, there may be a line in the headers that indicates what particular server software is being used—LISTSERV, Listproc, Majordomo, and so on."

- For a LISTSERV list, you can contact the list owner by writing to *listname*-**request**@*domain.name*. For example, the owner of **belief-l@listserv.aol**.com can be reached at **belief-l-request@ listserv.aol.com**.

- For a Majordomo list, you can typically contact the list owner by writing to *listname*-**approval**, although a number of sites are now adopting ***owner**-listname* or *listname*-***owner***. For example, to contact the list owner of **2020WORLD@seatimes.com**, you could write to **2020world-approval@seatimes.com** or perhaps **owner-202world@seatimes.com** if the former didn't work.

- As a last resort, you can attempt to write to the *Hostmaster* at the site where the list is hosted. The Hostmaster (if one exists) may choose to forward the message to the list owner, provide you with an address, or ignore the request. If there isn't a Hostmaster, you may attempt to contact the site's *Postmaster*, who may take any one of those steps. If you choose to write to either of these accounts, provide the details of how you've already tried to contact the list owner and a brief description of why you are doing so; it may just make the difference between being ignored and getting a response, especially at larger sites.

FROM HERE...

Without special software beyond your e-mail program, mailing lists let you join any of tens of thousands of communities and receive information about anything you're likely to be interested in. Mail on every subject, from like-minded people located anywhere in the U.S. and the world, comes reliably, securely, and in great volume to your mailbox. Join a mailing list today!

The next chapter introduces newsgroups, which are more public, less cozy places than mailing lists. While mailing lists can be private, newsgroups can be noisy and raucous. Mailing lists and newsgroups are at the heart of the traditional community experience on the Internet.

4

Chapter 5

Discovering
Newsgroups

If you wanted to tell your neighbors about your garage sale, you might put a notice in the local newspaper or attach a sign to the phone poles in your neighborhood. If you wanted to announce something to attendees at a large conference, maybe you would thumbtack a scrap of paper on a bulletin board designated for the purpose. And if you were selling something at work, you'd probably post a notice where everyone would see it—on the bathroom doors, the bulletin boards, the candy machines. On the Internet, you can reach a public audience by using newsgroups, collectively known as *Usenet News* or just *News*.

News is like a big bulletin board insofar as it's (1) public, (2) usually not controlled by anyone, and (3) a little wild at times. Instead of a single bulletin board serving a single public, however, News consists of thousands of *newsgroups*, organized by subject and serving thousands of small communities—groups of people with the same belief, passion, or interest. It's a big world with many passions, so whether you have a taste for Indonesian music, a particular TV show, or a certain Mexican fast-food chain, you're likely to find a newsgroup devoted to it. The newsgroup communities can become tightly knit social groups with their own cultures and traditions. The AOL feature that's most similar to newsgroups is the message board, where members can ask questions, provide help, and just mingle.

Newsgroups were invented in 1979 by several graduate students at the University of North Carolina as a way of sending and receiving messages between their university and Duke. Using the same technology, a network of discussion groups, or newsgroups, grew very rapidly in the 1980s. This collection of newsgroups came to be called *Usenet*. AOL's News servers receive some 20,000 newsgroups and send AOL members' postings around the world.

With so many newsgroups, it's hard to know where to start. America Online can make it easy. This chapter tells you all you need to know about the workings of newsgroups as a global system for sharing information among millions of people. Among other things, you'll discover ways of :

- Finding newsgroups of interest to you

- Keeping track of your favorite newsgroups

- Taking part in newsgroups

- Saving and printing postings

First, let's get a better idea of what newsgroups are by looking at how they're different from mailing lists and how they're organized.

HOW NEWSGROUPS AND MAILING LISTS ARE DIFFERENT

Mailing lists and newsgroups are often lumped together as "discussion groups." It is true that they both involve groups of people discussing topics of shared interest; sometimes, mailing lists even find their way onto Usenet and become available as newsgroups (see "Mailing Lists That Masquerade as Newsgroups"). And they're both great ways to meet people who share an interest. I have a friend who met her husband on a newsgroup.

Mailing lists and newsgroups are different animals, however, and it's good to keep the differences in mind, especially if you'll be using both. For one thing, mailing lists aren't really public; they're semiprivate. You must take the time to subscribe to them. Newsgroups, on the other hand, can be read by anyone. No subscription is necessary.

Note *AOL allows you to keep a list called Read My Newsgroups, which makes it easy for you to access the newsgroups you like best and to keep track of the articles you've read in those newsgroups. You do not formally "subscribe" to newsgroups the way you do with mailing lists.*

Because newsgroups are public and because they are rarely moderated, no one guarantees that they are kept civil or even that they remain on topic. Larger and more popular newsgroups can get wild, but smaller newsgroups on more focused topics can be every bit as informative and intimate as a mailing list.

The beauty of newsgroups is the absolutely uniform way you use them. While mailing lists require that you learn to subscribe and unsubscribe in a slightly different way for each type of mailing list, on Usenet you access **alt.gothic.fashion** in just the same way as you access **sci.chem.analytical**. America Online makes it easy to browse newsgroups too. There is no good way to browse mailing lists.

A final difference is that newsgroup articles can contain attached files. While mailing lists are used primarily to send text, newsgroups can contain both text and files, including software, sounds, and images. All these files are available to anyone with full access to newsgroups, and America Online's unique FileGrabber tool makes it painless to retrieve them.

Mailing Lists That Masquerade as Newsgroups

Several hundred mailing lists are also available as newsgroups, simplifying access and reducing the volume of incoming mail for those who take part. Unlike mailing list messages, newsgroup postings, or *articles*, have to be retrieved—but only when you want, on the specific subjects you want. The **bit** hierarchy (see the next section, "How Newsgroups Are Organized" for more information on hierarchies) contains hundreds of mailing lists in newsgroup form.

A list of mailing lists available over Usenet is also available via FTP at **ftp://rtfm.mit.edu/pub/usenet-by-hierarchy/news/groups/Mailing_Lists _Available_in_Usenet**. (Chapter 8 covers FTP, which you use to send long documents and other files over the Internet.) All lists available as newsgroups accept articles from both Usenet and mailing lists.

HOW NEWSGROUPS ARE ORGANIZED

There are more than 20,000 or so newsgroups available to you via AOL's News servers, which form a big link in the network of worldwide News servers that exchange postings with each other. Here are five newsgroups you might find some evening on America Online:

- **alt.animation.warner-brothers**
- **alt.fishing**
- **misc.taxes**
- **rec.autos.antique**
- **sci.diseases.med.cancer**

At first glance, these newsgroup names look like the addresses you see in e-mail articles (like **answerman@aol.com**) and on Web pages (like **http://www.aol.com**).

Actually, newsgroups are organized and named in a way that's unique to Usenet (see "Which Is It? Internet Address or Newsgroup Address?").

Which Is It: Internet Address or Newsgroup Address?

Unsure whether you're looking at an Internet address or a Usenet newsgroup address? Both kinds of addresses consist of elements separated by a period (pronounced "dot," when spoken). But here's how they differ:

- In an Internet address, or URL (uniform resources locator), the most general element (*com, edu, gov,* etc.) is the *last* part: http://www.aol.**com**, for example. See Chapter 3 on domain names and Chapter 6 on URLs.

- In a newsgroup address, the most general element (*sci, comp, news, alt,* etc.) is the *first* part: **biz**.jobs.offered, for example.

There's another difference: Internet addresses identify actual computers or banks of computers, together with the networks to which they belong. That's why URLs begin with *protocols,* such as *http://* and *ftp://* and *news:*, which govern how physical machines "talk" to each other. Newsgroup names, by contrast, are abstractions used to classify and keep track of people's postings.

Newsgroups are organized in big categories called *hierarchies*. There are two big types of hierarchies on Usenet: *standard* and *alternative*. Each contains subhierarchies, abbreviated in such a way as to indicate their subject matter. At the lowest level are thousands of individual newsgroups. In the standard hierarchies, for example, you'll find the **misc** subhierarchy, which has *miscellaneous* personal-finance and family-oriented newsgroups such as **misc.taxes**. The **misc.taxes.moderated** newsgroup is even more focused, thanks to the presence of a human moderator who keeps conversations on topic and who shares expertise.

Tip *Newsgroups are the best place to learn about newsgroups, and the most useful hierarchy for beginners is* **news** *(devoted to* newsgroups, *not the* evening news). *The* **news.newusers.questions** *and* **news.answers** *newsgroups, in particular, have a wealth of information if you're just starting out.*

A Matter for the Name Police

On the Internet, newsgroup messages—the documents written by individuals—are called *articles* or *postings*. On AOL they're usually called *messages*, even though e-mail messages and News messages are different.

On the Internet, people refer to clusters of articles devoted to the same topic as *threads*; on AOL, threads are called *subjects*.

And while Internet folks are used to speaking of *hierarchies* and *subhierarchies* of newsgroups, on AOL you'll usually see *categories* and *topics*.

The Standard Hierarchies

Newsgroups were originally organized into the standard—sometimes called the Big Seven or "traditional"—hierarchies listed in Table 5-1. Think of a hierarchy as a sort of bucket in which newsgroups about a certain large theme are stored. Newsgroups in the **sci** hierarchy all have to do with science, and serious, academic science at that. Newsgroups in the standard hierarchies have general circulation via News servers around the world. These newsgroups are created according to a strict protocol (see the "Creating a Newsgroup" box) and tend to be a bit more serious than the alternative hierarchies. The need for a new newsgroup must be established and

Standard Hierarchies	Subject Matter
comp	Computers, networks, hardware, operating systems, multimedia, and the Internet
misc	Taxes, family, kids, investing, education—family matters
news	Usenet news-related topics (*not* the evening news)
rec	Sports, movies, the arts, entertainment, and the like
sci	Serious science—archaeology, biology, chemistry, physics, etc.
soc	Social issues, foreign cultures
talk	Controversial issues—gun control, abortion, etc.

TABLE 5-1   The standard, or traditional, newsgroup hierarchies

accepted by other members of the community, then voted upon. On America Online, you can reliably expect to be able to find all of the standard newsgroups.

Creating a Newsgroup

If you want to create a standard newsgroup, check out "Guidelines for Usenet Group Creation," which is regularly posted to the **news.answers** newsgroup. If you want to create an alternative newsgroup, there's a document for you called "So You Want to Create an Alt Newsgroup," which is regularly posted to the same newsgroup. You can get a sense of the two cultures of the alternative and standard hierarchies by skimming these documents. "Guidelines…" has rigorous protocol that must be followed. In the instructions for creating alt newsgroups, you will read: "Votes? Did someone say vote? Let me repeat. There are _no votes_ in alt. Period." Voting or no voting, both types of hierarchy are deeply democratic in process—no individual or organization controls them.

The Alternative Hierarchies

Alternative hierarchies consist of newsgroups that are relatively easy to form. These hierarchies are growing faster and contain more newsgroups than the standard hierarchies. Sometimes alternative newsgroups pop up before a need for them has been established and then fade away before a community has been able to form.

Because of their low volume and the sometimes limited audience, not all alternative newsgroups are carried by the entire network of News computers. Some alternative newsgroups, however, are devoted to exactly the sort of topics you find in the standard hierarchy, nicely complementing the standard newsgroups. Many alternative newsgroups were, in fact, created to accommodate the volume of a popular standard newsgroup or to handle a fundamental disagreement or because they weren't approved by the Usenet community.

AOL makes an effort to carry a full "feed" of alternative newsgroups, that is, they try to carry all the newsgroups and all their postings. One result of this openness is that some newsgroups are available via AOL that have no articles in them; these newsgroups are "extinct." You can post to them, but it's unlikely anyone will respond. AOL can't do anything about extinct groups. Another result of the vast scope of the newsgroups carried by AOL is that some alternative newsgroups may be highly objectionable to some AOL members, especially parents.

NEWSGROUPS AND PARENTAL CONTROLS

 America Online does not censor what you see within a newsgroup. It blocks only those few newsgroups that plainly break U.S. law (because they're used as distribution sites for pirated software, for example). Some newsgroups are thus available on AOL that may contain offensive content.

AOL offers parents several sets of controls to make it more difficult for kids to use objectionable newsgroups. First, AOL makes it difficult to browse any newsgroup that's likely to be objectionable. For more about browsing, see the "Keeping Track of Newsgroups" section.

Parental Controls offer a more powerful second line of defense. For any screen name under a master account, parents can restrict or prevent access as follows:

1. From the Newsgroup window (keyword: Newsgroups), click Parental Controls.

2. Specify a screen name for which to set controls, and click OK. The Blocking Criteria screen comes up (Figure 5-1).

3. Set controls as appropriate, placing a check in one or more of the check boxes for the following options:

Block Expert Add	Prevents a child (if the child has her own screen name) from accessing a newsgroup available on AOL using Expert Add but not listed using the Add Newsgroup feature. Both features are discussed later in this chapter.
Block All Newsgroups	Prevents a child from using *all* newsgroups.
Block Binary Downloads	Prevents a child from downloading possibly objectionable pictures. A binary download may be an image file, included with a newsgroup article.
Use Full Newsgroup List	*Doesn't* restrict newsgroup access, unless you single out specific newsgroups for exclusion (see Step 4).

4. In the first big text fields at the bottom of the Blocking Criteria window, indicate which parts of newsgroup names, if any, you wish to block (*sex* or *binaries*, for example). In the second big text box, indicate which specific newsgroups you do not wish the screen name to use.

5. Click OK to confirm your choices.

The Regional Newsgroups

Regional newsgroups are a type of alternative newsgroup. They're easy to form, but instead of being focused on some subject, they're focused on a geographical area (a city, university, country, or region). For that area, newsgroups can be devoted to all subjects. Like other alternative newsgroups, the regional newsgroups are not universally carried by the globe's News computers. These alternative newsgroups reside primarily on News servers in the region to which they are devoted.

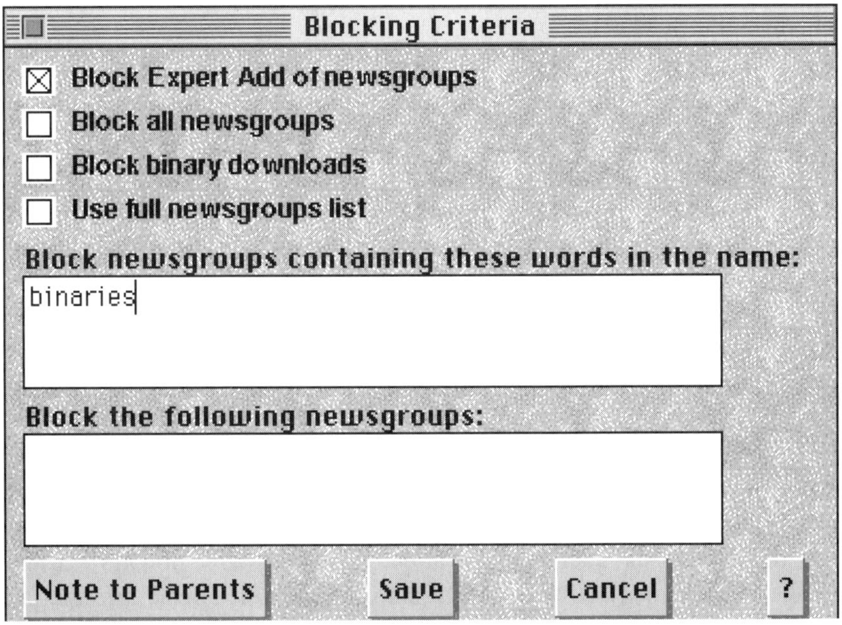

FIGURE 5-1   Parental Controls are used to restrict access to all newsgroups, certain newsgroups, and downloads

Because America Online is available throughout the U.S. and, increasingly, throughout the world, AOL's News feed includes regional hierarchies ranging from **bermuda.*** and **boulder.*** to **utah.*** and **utexas.***.

Note   *An asterisk (*), as in bermuda.*, refers to the entire family of newsgroups in a hierarchy, such as **bermuda.jobs.offered**, **bermuda.general**, **bermuda.politics**, and **bermuda.sports**.*

More Alternative Hierarchies

Many alternative newsgroups focus on topics of somewhat limited interest but are every bit as serious as the standard newsgroups. At keyword: Newsgroups, click Add Newsgroups to get a list of dozens of alternative hierarchies carried by America Online. Here are a few alternative hierarchies devoted to specific topics or professions.

bionet	For biologists
biz	The proper place to sell commercial products and services
hepnet	For physicists
k12	For teachers in grades kindergarten through twelfth grade

Note   *AOL does not carry the well-known hierarchy called **Clarinet**, whose newsgroups consist of edited newsfeeds from the commercial wire services. Instead (and better), AOL offers the newsfeeds available in the News channel; the cool news "ticker tape," also in the News channel; and the custom "clipping service," delivered right to your mailbox, available at keyword: News Profile. On the Web, you will find numerous news sources that now compete effectively with the Clarinet service. See the "Today's News" section of Chapter 11.*

FINDING NEWSGROUPS

Where do you start? How do you find newsgroups you'll want to read? The standard approach is to either search, if you know just what you're looking for, or browse, if you want to see what's available. If you already have the name of a newsgroup you want to read, you can use the Expert Add feature, as explained in the "Keeping Track of Newsgroups" section.

Searching for Specific Newsgroups

If you're looking for a newsgroup about a specific subject but don't know the exact newsgroup name yet, follow these steps:

1. Go to keyword: Newsgroups. This brings up the main Newsgroups window, shown in Figure 5-2.

2. Click Search All Newsgroups to go to the Search Newsgroup Titles window.

3. Type in a simple but specific search phrase such as *cooking*. Click Search.

4. If your search had results, they'll appear in the Search Results window. Select any newsgroup you want to read and click Add, to add it to Read My Newsgroups. To read the newsgroup, close the window, then click Read My Newsgroups on the main Newsgroups window.

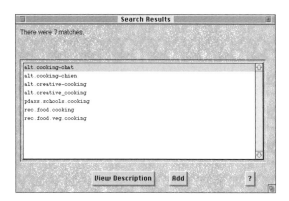

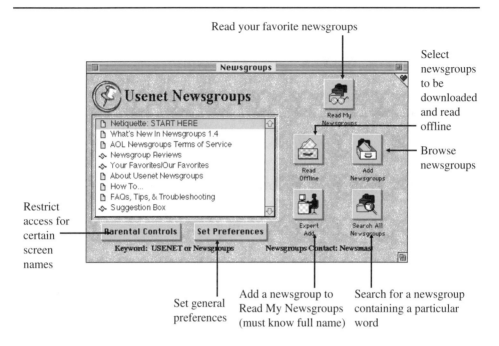

Read your favorite newsgroups

Select newsgroups to be downloaded and read offline

Browse newsgroups

Restrict access for certain screen names

Set general preferences

Add a newsgroup to Read My Newsgroups (must know full name)

Search for a newsgroup containing a particular word

FIGURE 5-2   The main Newsgroup window on AOL

Searching Newsgroups

You can "search newsgroups" in three ways.

First, you can *search for a specific newsgroup*. The easiest way to do this is by using the Search All Newsgroups feature, available from the main Newsgroups window (Figure 5-3). Second, with a newsgroup displayed, you can *search for an article about a specific subject*. (See the "Searching a Long List for Something Specific" box.) Finally, you can *search the body of articles for specific words*.

The first two types of search are easy with AOL. The last kind of search is covered in Chapter 9, which introduces easy-to-use search tools such as DejaNews, Excite, and Infoseek.

Browsing for Newsgroups

You can also *browse* for newsgroups that interest you.

1. From the main Newsgroup window shown in Figure 5-2, click Add Newsgroups.

2. A list of categories comes up—all the standard and alternative hierarchies plus all the local and alternative ones. Select a category by double-clicking. The Topics window comes up (Figure 5-3). For each topic, or subhierarchy, you'll see how many newsgroups are associated with it. Double-click to see the associated newsgroup(s). You'll know you're at the bottom of the hierarchy when the window's title bar (at the top) changes from *Topic* to *Newsgroup*.

3. In the Newsgroups window, shown in Figure 5-4, double-click the newsgroup name to go directly to it and start reading (but not posting).

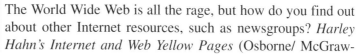 ### Newsgroup Scoop

The World Wide Web is all the rage, but how do you find out about other Internet resources, such as newsgroups? *Harley Hahn's Internet and Web Yellow Pages* (Osborne/ McGraw-Hill, 1997) is an excellent place to start if you're looking for groovy newsgroups.

You can find out about great newsgroups on AOL as well. Each week, in the Newsgroup Scoop (now a part of AOL NetFind and found at keyword: Scoop), you can read the reviews of newsgroups. Each newsgroup is rated for its Traffic, Insight, Technical Level, and Flaming. A full review gives you a good idea what you're in for if you decide to take part in the newsgroup. If a newsgroup name (such as rec.arts.anime) is unfamiliar to you, the introductions provide valuable context. Part reviews are conveniently organized into categories such as Sports, Practical Stuff, Computers & Tech, Fun & Interest, Mind & Body, and more.

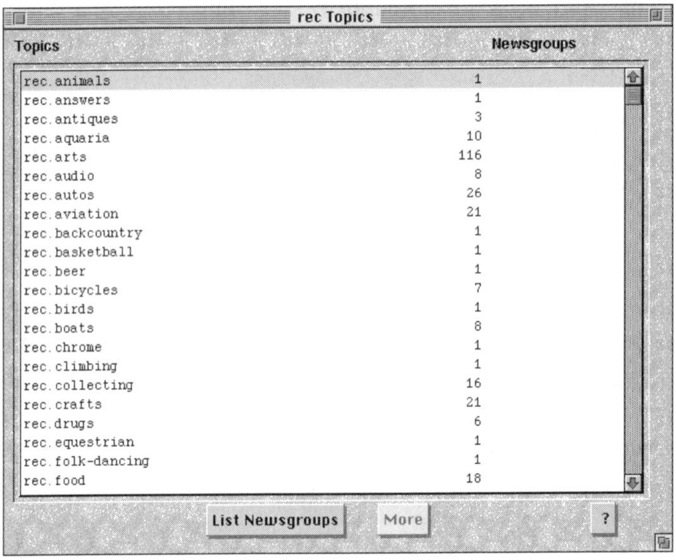

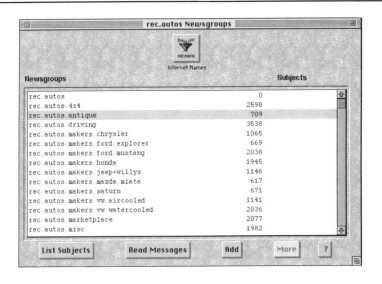

FIGURE 5-3   A list of recreational topics

FIGURE 5-4   Use the Add Newsgroups window to "drill down" to the
rec.autos.antique newsgroup; double-click to browse

KEEPING TRACK OF NEWSGROUPS

With so many newsgroups to read, how do you keep track of the ones you like? America Online lets you do just that in its Read My Newsgroups list. When you register as an AOL member, you will find several newsgroups included in this list. You can add and remove newsgroups to and from this list as you please, making it easy to return and read your favorites on a regular basis.

Adding newsgroups to Read My Newsgroups doesn't really "subscribe" you in any formal way; you can read newsgroups without subscribing, and there are times when you want to do just that (see "Just Passing Through: Browsing Newsgroups").

The Read My Newsgroups list has three benefits for you:

- It's a convenient way of quickly getting to the newsgroups you like.

- It's a way of keeping track of articles you have read *within* a newsgroup.

- You can read offline only those newsgroups included in Read My Newsgroups.

 There's another good way of keeping track of your favorite newsgroups—see the "Favorite Place It" text box.

Just Passing Through: Browsing Newsgroups

If you're just browsing, you may *not* want to keep track of all the newsgroups you stumble across. If you're looking for a newsgroup with a particular focus, you won't, for instance, want to keep track of every newsgroup you read on your path to the right one. An easy way to browse is by using Add Newsgroups, as described in "Finding Newsgroups." Or, use keywords. When you browse newsgroups, you read them but can't take part in them (Figure 5-5).

 ### Keywording to a Newsgroup

If you know a specific newsgroup's name—from the newspaper, a book, a friend, or a search of newsgroups, as explained in the previous section—you can go *directly* to the newsgroup using the Keyword window. This is a great, direct way to read newsgroups, but it doesn't give you the option of saving a newsgroup in Read My Newsgroups.

1. From the GoTo menu, select Keyword.

2. In the Keyword window, type in **news** and a colon (**:**) and the name of the newsgroup. For example:
   news:comp.internet.net-happenings.

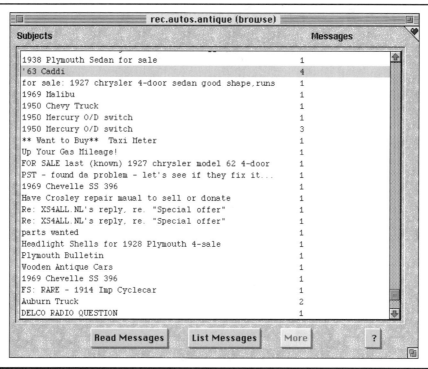

FIGURE 5-5 When you're browsing, you can only *read* newsgroup postings

Staying a While: Adding to "Read My Newsgroups"

The main reason for keeping track of newsgroups you like is pretty obvious—it makes it easier to return in the future, even when you're offline. If you *don't* know the exact newsgroup name you want to add, start by clicking Add Newsgroup. Burrow down through the hierarchy to the particular newsgroup, and click Add, as described above. If you *do* know the name, you use AOL's Expert Add feature:

1. Go to the main Newsgroup window, and click Expert Add to bring up the Expert Add window.

2. Type the newsgroup's name, and click the Add button. (The field is called "Internet" name, but in fact you're using the "Usenet" name.) Your choice will be confirmed; click Add.

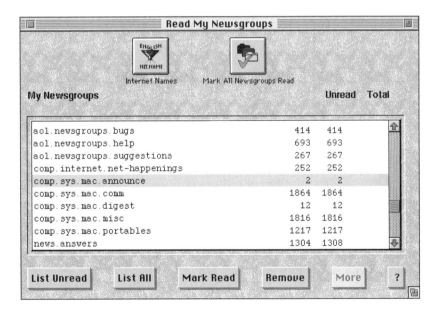

3. Close the Expert Add window.

4. To go to the newsgroup you've just added, click on Read My Newsgroups (Figure 5-6).

5. To open any newsgroup you've ever added, double-click its name to bring up the screen shown in Figure 5-7. To delete a newsgroup from Read My Newsgroups, click on it and click Remove.

FIGURE 5-6   Read My Newsgroups keeps track of newsgroups you want to revisit. AOL automatically includes several general-interest newsgroups in this list

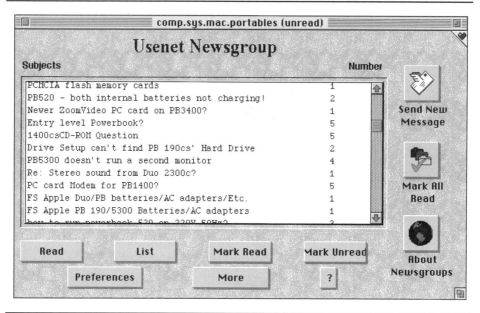

FIGURE 5-7 When you open a newgroup from Read My Newsgroups you can take part instead of just browsing

From time to time, you'll get an Invalid Group article when you attempt to read a particular newsgroup using Expert Add. You've either incorrectly entered the newsgroup's name, or the newsgroup is not carried by America Online. Double-check the name, and re-enter it. If you're having persistent problems and you feel the newsgroup should be carried, send e-mail to screen name **newsmaster***.*

Using the Browser to Go to a Newsgroup

Every newsgroup has a URL, or Internet address (see Chapter 6 on URLs). This means that a World Wide Web page can have a link pointing to a newsgroup; click on the link and you go directly to the newsgroup.

A newsgroup's URL is simple. It consists of **news:** *plus the newsgroup name, without any spaces and also without slashes (//). You are using URLs when you use the Keyword window to go directly to a newsgroup, as in* **news:comp.internet.net-happenings***.*

With AOL 3.0, clicking a Web link that points to a newsgroup takes you directly to the newsgroup. When you click a link to a newsgroup in this way, you bring up the AOL Newsgroups window.

Favorite Place It!

Using AOL 3.0 you can add a newsgroup to your Favorite Places folder (available from the AOL tool bar). With Favorite Places, you can store links to most kinds of content you like to use on AOL and the Internet—AOL forums, Web pages, and newsgroups. Here's how: With the main window of a newsgroup displayed (you'll see a list of Subjects and Number of articles per subject, as shown in Figure 5-2), there's a heart in the title bar. Just click the heart to add the newsgroup to Favorite Places.

To access the newsgroup, pick Favorite Places from your Go To menu and double-click the entry for the newsgroup.

With Favorite Places, you can create a folder for newsgroups, AOL, and Web content—all related to the same subject, for example.

What's the difference between Read My Newsgroups and Favorite Places? Read My Newsgroups consists only of newsgroups, while Favorite Places can be just about any kind of resource. Favorite Places are available offline as well: while offline, open Favorite Places, double-click a newsgroup, and you'll sign onto AOL and open that newsgroup.

Note   *AOL does not yet allow members to directly use third-party newsreaders such as Newswatcher, but you can use such programs if you take advantage of the "bring your own access" billing plan and access AOL over a TCP/IP connection, as described in Appendix A. If you use a third-party Newsreader over your other connection, you won't be using AOL's News servers, and you must make the appropriate settings for that reader (NNTP server, signature, organizational information, etc.).*

Tip   *Several Web sites allow Web access to newsgroups. One particular favorite of AOL members is Zippo, at **http://www.zippo.com/**. In Chapter 9, you can read about several search services on the Web (notably Excite and DejaNews) that give you access to specific newsgroups and posting through the* *browser. Zippo (an AOL Members Choice site) also provides lists of favorite newsgroups.*

SCANNING NEWSGROUP ARTICLES FOR THE GOOD ONES

Figure 5-7 shows a listing of articles in the **comp.sys.mac.portables** newsgroup. Whenever the More button is active (can be clicked), you know that not all articles are listed; keep clicking More until they're all there. On AOL you can control this listing in a couple of ways:

- Marking articles read or unread

- Ranking articles earliest to most recent or vice versa

Searching a Long List for Something Specific

With newsgroup articles displayed, you can search for articles of special interest by searching for a specific word in their subject lines.

1. From AOL's Edit menu, select Find in Top Window.

2. In the little window, type in the words of interest, and click Find.

You can use this trick to search your e-mail mailboxes and Personal Filing Cabinet as well.

Read, Unread—What's the Difference?

Figure 5-6 displays articles you have not yet read. This is similar to your New mailbox when you're using e-mail, which displays only new messages. However, unlike your New mailbox, you can't tell whether a newsgroup article has been read or not merely by looking at it.

When you read an article, it's automatically defined as *read*, and it won't display next time you open the newsgroup. You can also deliberately define ("mark") one or more articles as *read*. Why would you do this? Some newsgroups have a good deal of *noise*—off-topic, obnoxious, useless, argumentative, and offensive postings, for example. Marking such postings *read* can get them out of the way and help you focus on the articles you're really interested in. Or, if you've just returned from vacation and don't have the time to plow through thousands of articles, just mark them all *read* and close the window.

Why mark articles *unread*? So you can take the time to draft a well-thought-out response to the group (after reading subsequent articles on the same subject). Marking an article unread also lets you download it for offline reading (only unread articles can be downloaded).

With AOL, you can mark articles as *read* or *unread* one at a time, or a whole thread at a time. Clicking Mark Read or Mark Unread while looking at a single article will mark that single article. On the overview page for a newsgroup, it will mark or unmark all messages in that thread.

Listing Articles First to Last, or Last to First

AOL also gives you the choice of listing articles from most recent to least recent, or vice versa. Here's how:

■   From the main Newsgroup window, click Set Preferences, and click the appropriate button indicating whether you wish to see old or new articles first.

Following a newsgroup in chronological order (with the oldest articles posted first) gives you a sense of how discussions evolve and interrelate. Following in reverse order (from now to then) brings you up to date more quickly; most people are interested in the most recent articles, even though they may lack the context of the previous several weeks' articles. First-to-last (to see what's new) or last-to-first (to see how a thread evolves)—it's your choice.

ARTICLES AND THEIR PARTICLES

Newsgroup articles all contain *headers* and *bodies*. They can contain *files* and *signatures*. Figure 5-8 shows you what you see when you pull up a newsgroup on AOL.

Each line is either a single article or a *thread*. A thread, as the name implies, is a group of articles with the same subject line and, in principle, the same subject. It can consist of two articles or a hundred articles. When you're viewing one article in a thread, you can go to other adjacent articles in the thread by clicking the Previous and Next buttons. If you want to focus on a specific thread while reading a newsgroup, select it and click List to bring up a little window showing the individual postings in the thread, including their authors and the times they were posted.

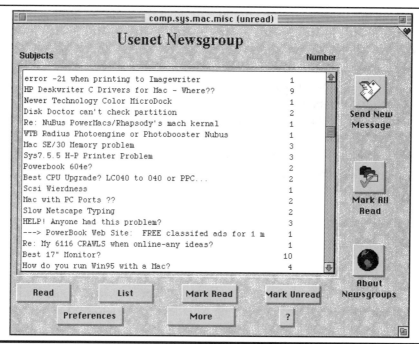

FIGURE 5-8   A list of articles and threads. If the Number on the right is greater than 1, there's a *thread* available—more than one article on the same subject

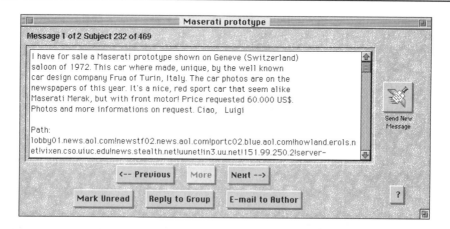

FIGURE 5-9   A newsgroup article, posted to **rec.autos.antique**. The head reads "message 1 of 2," so there's a reply to this article

Let's look at a single article (Figure 5-9). The *header* contains a little information about who sent the article (not shown here) and what the article is about (cars, in this case). Like an e-mail message, it can also provide a time and date. The subject line is uniquely important in newsgroups because it provides the "hook" used to catch the attention of people you don't know. When an article's Subject line is preceded by "re:" the article is a *reply* to another article, and the two form a part of a thread. Some newsgroup programs offers a range of other headers, including e-mail addresses to use for responding. Here's what a full header can look like:

```
Path:
newsbf05.news.aol.com!newstf01.news.aol.com!audrey01.news.aol.com!not-for-mail
From: lindad72@aol.com
Newsgroups: rec.autos.antique
Subject: Buick 340 V8 crank in 215 block?
Date: 28 Nov 1996 04:42:30 GMT
Organization: AOL http://www.aol.com
Lines: 6
Message-ID: <19961128044400.XAA13056@ladder01.news.aol.com>
NNTP-Posting-Host: ladder01.news.aol.com
X-Admin: news@aol.com
```

Tip   *With AOL you can choose whether to have headers appear at the beginning of articles or at the end or not at all. Placing them at the end makes it easier to get to the article but harder to see essential information such as the sender's name. To place headers at the end of messages, click Set Preferences from the Newsgroups window, click the Headers at Bottom button, and click OK.*

The *body* of the article is its content. If an article is part of a thread, content from earlier articles will probably be quoted, with each quoted line preceded by a particular character (often ">") or "spaced in" from the left (Figure 5-10).

Messages can contain *files*—anything from image and sound files to Macintosh utilities. Using other Internet providers, it can be a time-consuming and technical matter to download, convert, and use files. Using AOL's unique FileGrabber feature, however, you can extract a file with a point and a click of your mouse, as you'll see in "Getting Files from Newsgroups is a Breeze."

A final and optional element of an article is the *signature*. If you choose to use it, this bit of text that identifies you will be automatically added to the end of your postings. If you want to create a signature file, see the "Who You Are: Adding a Signature" section for instructions.

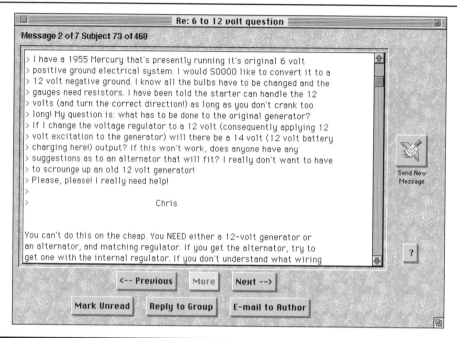

FIGURE 5-10 Part of the body of a reply to the article shown in Figure 5-9. An original article and a reply to the article form the start of a thread

RESPONDING TO AN ARTICLE

So, you've read an article. Now what? With an article open (as in Figure 5-9), there are a couple of things you can do:

- Read it and move on. The article will automatically be marked *read* and won't be displayed next time you visit the newsgroup. If you want the article to be displayed next time you visit the newsgroup, click the Mark Unread button. If the article you've just read is part of a thread, clicking the Previous and Next buttons takes you to the neighboring articles in the thread. If you're at the beginning or end of a thread, Previous and Next take you to the previous and next threads, respectively.

- Respond to the article by sending a reply to the newsgroup. AOL does not let you respond to other newsgroups at the same time (this is called cross-posting). You can respond only to the newsgroup you are reading.

Note   *With newsgroups, your postings go from News server to News server, so it can take a while for your posting to become available to all of the ten million-plus people in the world with News access. Because of the volume of postings worldwide, most News servers get rid of (expire) postings after a couple of days or weeks.*

- Respond only to the author, using e-mail, instead of responding to the entire newsgroup. Click E-mail to Author.

Tip   *Responding to the author is appropriate for personal, heated, and off-topic responses to an author's posting to the newsgroup. It's the right choice if what you have to say would not be of likely interest to the group at large.*

- Start an entirely new thread, or at least send an article to the newsgroup on a new topic, by clicking Send New Message (read "Threads of Your Own: Starting a New Subject").

Who You Are: Adding a Signature

If you plan on sending articles to a newsgroup, it's a good idea to add a signature. A *signature* is a bit of text that will be automatically added to every posting you make to any newsgroup. It's a way of tacking on information about yourself, contact information, or perhaps a favorite short joke or motto. You can also advertise a Web site or feature information that promotes your business. You can even add elaborate ASCII (text) drawings of dragons, cows, and other pictures, though some people on the Internet object to signatures longer than four lines as a waste of shared computer resources.

To add a signature:

1. From the main Newsgroups window, click Set Preferences (note that this is different from the Preferences button on the window you use to read an individual newsgroup).

2. In the Signature box at the bottom of the window, type in the text you want to use (see Figure 5-11). Click OK.

Tip   *Before you share your signature with the world, you might want to post a test article to one of the newsgroups devoted exclusively to this purpose, such as **alt.test** or **misc.test**. Do not post test messages to any newsgroup that isn't explicitly a "test" group!*

FIGURE 5-11 Supply a signature to *automatically* add a personalized message on every article you post to any newsgroup

Threads of Your Own: Starting a New Subject

If you don't want to respond to another person's posting but do have something to say, start your own thread! From the newsgroup window, click the Send New Message button to send an article.

The Post New Message window asks you for only two things: a Subject line and a Message, and lets you make the choice of whether to include a signature file as well (see the "Who You Are: Adding a Signature" section). When you've polished your article, click Send. Your article will join a global flow of information that reaches every continent and is accessible by millions of people. The window appears very similar if you are replying to an article, except the Subject line is filled in ("re: such and such"), and you have the choice of sending the post to the author of the original post, by e-mail.

READING AND POSTING OFFLINE

Automatic AOL is a feature that lets you take care of some Net chores even when you are not logged on. For communication such as e-mail and newsgroups, where people aren't communicating in *real time* (at the same time), working offline makes perfect sense.

With Automatic AOL, your computer signs on automatically at times you specify, performs a task such as reading newsgroup articles, then logs off again. You can download all your newsgroup postings at regular intervals, then browse them in leisure.

To read your newsgroups offline with Automatic AOL:

1. In the Newsgroups window, click Read Offline to bring up the Choose Newsgroups window (Figure 5-12).

2. The Subscribed Newsgroups list shows the newsgroups you've put in the Read My Newsgroup list—*these are the only newsgroups you can read offline.* The Newsgroups to Read Offline list shows the newsgroups you want to read offline. Highlight the newsgroup you want to read offline in the Subscribed Newsgroups list and click the Add > button. You can quickly select all newsgroups in your personal list by clicking the Add All >> button. Any newsgroups you select are moved to the Newsgroups to Read Offline list. To remove a newsgroup from offline status, select its name in the Newsgroups to Read Offline list and click the < Remove button. Click << Remove All if you don't want to read any newsgroups offline. *You must click OK to save any changes you have made.* If you don't want to save your changes, click the Cancel button.

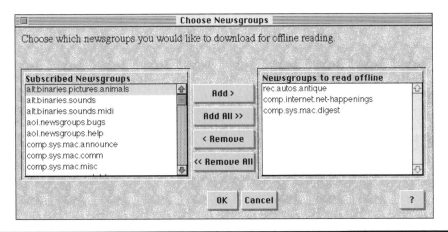

FIGURE 5-12   Add newsgroups from your Subscribed Newsgroups list for offline reading

Now, set up Automatic AOL:

1. From the Mail menu, select Set up Automatic AOL. The window shown in Figure 4-5 comes up. Look for checkboxes marked "Get Unread Postings" and "Send Postings."

2. Place checks in one box or both. Click OK.

> *Tip* *If you use "Copy author of original article by e-mail" when replying to an article and then do an offline session, you must also check the Send Mail box in order to send your e-mail response(s).*

3. To participate in a newsgroup while offline, you need to activate Automatic AOL. You have a choice. From the Mail menu, select Run Automatic AOL then click Begin. AOL immediately downloads or uploads articles for you. To schedule regular sessions, click Set up Automatic AOL and click on Scheduler. Then indicate your time preferences, and click OK. Your computer must be on during the times you have indicated.

4. Your selected newsgroups are downloaded into your Personal Filing Cabinet. To read them, click the Personal Filing Cabinet icon on the tool bar. Double-click on the Newsgroups folder. To read newsgroup articles, double-click on any article.

Because all of the items in the Personal Filing Cabinet are stored on your computer, it is a good idea to delete folders and articles that you've read and don't want to keep.

DON'T BE A JERK!

In your private e-mail, netiquette is important because it's easy to be misunderstood. E-mail is so ubiquitous that good netiquette can make a big difference in how you get along with others. On mailing lists, netiquette becomes more important because you're dealing with people you probably don't know—people who won't extend to you the benefit of the doubt. But in newsgroups, netiquette is even *more* important, because you are communicating with people you definitely don't know—unlike mailing lists, no one really knows who reads newsgroups. Your words can get you in trouble in countless ways. They can make the wrong impression or rub people the wrong way. Newsgroups themselves can be damaged by careless language, if quarrelsome behavior and flaming distract from their purpose.

What follows are some guidelines, distilled from Chuq Rosbach's classic "Primer on How to Work With the Usenet Community." If you're serious about newsgroups, read this document from beginning to end; it's regularly posted to the **news.answers** newsgroup.

- Lurk before you leap.

- Respect your reader.

- Respect people who *might* be your readers.

- Be brief.

- Write carefully.

- Use clear and descriptive subject lines.

- Post to the correct newsgroup.

- Avoid sarcasm and irony.

- When responding, summarize.

- Do not use a newsgroup as an advertising medium.

- Don't post the same message repeatedly.

GETTING FILES FROM NEWSGROUPS IS A BREEZE

Newsgroups are a source of more than text articles. They are also a source of files such as software, images, and sounds. You can use the Search All Newsgroups button on the main Newsgroups window to find such newsgroups.

In e-mail, you can get files *attached* to articles. With newsgroups, files are *inserted* inside articles. How? They are "encoded" using a technique called UUE (UNIX to UNIX Encoding). Encoding articles is a way of taking *binary* files (programs or the documents used by programs) and turning them into text files. To the eye, these files look like gibberish, but, rest assured, they're meant to be understood by computers, not people:

```
begin 644 Dannyboy.mid
M351H9`````8`0`("A-5)K````0@#_?PH@#_#PH@_?PLC`0`%`@L`/#'41A,FW
M($)O>0#__$`^`,`,@#_^^@$(_@^_L@_^_#'@^@@`_U@$^@@_)'#`'$`^$U4
M<FL``1^/#'#!#L@L='@^9L5=;F@^^##^`^^,&__&
M2`@F^L@@@&&!-$$#'B[5@#'$@#'$/^%!<=@##$''#%P.'FA
M`[IA'$H`$A`@$^$A@@#%`@$%%Mm
M`[pa'$o`$aa^@`$5a@@1$@
M46$@40`3V$3P`3&$3`3``2&$2``3&#3``2F&"'+$H`$M<`A`A
```

The great virtue of these files is that they can be transmitted the same way plain old text is transmitted. The resulting text files can be very long, so files encoded as text are often automatically broken up (by the encoding programs) into several files. In the olden days, decoding UUE files took work, luck, and time: you'd consolidate many files into one file, then run that one file through a special *de*coding utility. The result: the same file (an image, a sound, a program, whatever), but on someone else's computer.

AOL's FileGrabber tool makes it easy to extract and use files that have been UUEncoded. Here's an article in a newsgroup that contains a file, or part of a file (in this case a tuneful MIDI file with an electronic version of "Danny Boy"):

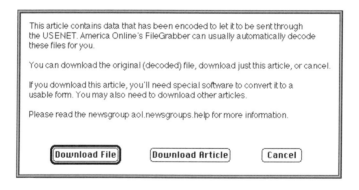

1. Click Download File.

2. Indicate where to put the file on your hard disk and click OK. Make sure to keep track of where on your Mac's hard drive you store the file. A progress bar tracks the download, letting you know approximately how long the download will take. If the file is spread out over a couple of articles, FileGrabber automatically finds all the articles and puts them together before downloading and decoding.

If you're downloading an image file (GIF, ART, JPG format), you will see the file as it's downloaded. If it's a sound file (WAV, MIDI format), AOL displays or plays the file automatically after it is completely downloaded. Chapter 8 goes into file types, with tips for handling types of downloaded files that aren't automatically played or displayed.

When Files Aren't Immediately Usable

FileGrabber is a neat feature when it works, and it usually does. If you've ever decoded a UUEncoded file, you will be instantly impressed by FileGrabber's power and ease of use. But sometimes, FileGrabber is unable to handle the files inserted into newsgroup articles for the following reasons:

- Some files you extract from newsgroups will be compressed for quicker downloading, or "zipped" up to make it possible to retrieve several files at the same time. You'll need special software for decompressing or unzipping these files. StuffIt Expander, from AOL's software libraries (keyword: FileSearch), can help you with most files. (See Chapter 8.)

- Some files won't be usable because they are spread out over several articles and at least one article is missing. There is nothing you can do about this except to send e-mail to the poster of the file and request a reposting.

- Some files are in an unusual format or are "MIME-encoded," and can't be handled by FileGrabber. You will have better luck decoding the file with a stand-alone MIME decoder utility program. Go to keyword: MIME for the software and more information.

Sending Files in Newsgroups

AOL makes it very easy to retrieve files from articles, but you'll need extra software to post files to newsgroups, because you'll need to convert a binary file into a text file—you may also need to split the text file into several smaller files. At keyword: FileSearch, you can search for programs that UUEncode. Follow the instructions of any of these programs for converting binary files. (I'm fond of a little shareware program called UULITE, which you can also get from *http://www. peanutsw.com/.*) Once a file has been converted, it's a simple matter to paste the article(s) into the Post New Message window and to post it to the appropriate newsgroup.

ESSENTIAL READING: FAQS

Many claims are made about the Internet as a source of information about everything under the sun. Much of this vaunted treasure, especially on the Web, is not systematic. In newsgroups, however, information has been systematically collected and, more important, *cooperatively* reviewed and refined, sometimes over many years. The result is a large collection of Frequently Asked Question documents, or FAQs. These FAQs address questions about either individual newsgroups or the topics to which the newsgroups are devoted. Sometimes they look at both.

What's special about FAQs is that they are written and commented on by many members of a newsgroup's community. Over time, they become widely accepted as authoritative within the community and genuinely useful beyond it. In theory, everybody can recommend changes to the FAQs' maintainer, who is as a rule prominently identified in the FAQ.

Note — *The assumption behind FAQs is that it's a waste of people's time and network bandwidth for old-timers to repeatedly answer beginners' routine questions. So, the idea that the Net has lots of people ready and eager to answer your questions is not always true. If you need human help, the best place to start is on AOL in a forum such as AnswerMan.*

Some FAQs make for good reads and serve as useful introductions to difficult topics. Some provide great sources for self-instruction if you want to learn more about anything Internet-related, for example, MIME, graphics formats such as JPG, access forms such as ISDN, and Usenet itself. Look for FAQs on non-technical subjects such as dogs, puzzles, specific disabilities, running, medicine, model rockets, and on and on.

FAQs are routinely published in the newsgroups they grow out of, as well as in the **news.answers** newsgroup. The FAQ archives of **news.answers** are available in a famous collection called **rtfm.mit.edu**, an FTP site. (Think of an FTP site as a big public hard disk on someone else's computer—a collection of files contained in folders contained in more folders. Chapter 8 goes into more detail about FTP.) Several Web sites carry this FAQ archive as well, including:

```
http://www.cis.ohio-state.edu/hypertext/faq/usenet/
http://ps.superb.net/FAQ
```

The good news for AOL members is that the FAQ archive is easily available on AOL as well. Here's how to access it:

1. Use keyword: FTP to go to AOL's FTP area. Once there, click the Go To FTP button.

2. From the listbox of FTP sites, double-click on **rtfm.mit.edu:/pub**. Information about the site comes up. Click OK.

3. Navigate the site by double-clicking the **usenet-by-hierarchy** folder, then the **news** folder, and finally the **news.answers** folder—the archives of the **news.answers** newsgroup.

4. Browse the list for topics of interest. Note that topics are alphabetically arranged, and that topics with capital letters precede topics with small letters.

SAVING AND PRINTING MESSAGES

Newsgroups, especially FAQs, are extraordinary repositories of information and knowledge. Saving and printing them is a way of extending their value by making them easily available when you're not online. As always on the Internet, do not incorporate any content from FAQs in your own writing without explicit mention of the source and without permission from the writer of the original material.

To save an article:

1. Display the article and then, from the File menu, select Save.

2. Give the file a name and move it into the appropriate folder, then click Save.

To print an article, display the article and click the Printer icon on the tool bar.

FROM HERE...

Community is what draws people to the global Internet. Traditionally, community on the Internet can be found in newsgroups and mailing lists, the 100,000 or so discussion groups in which you are likely to learn something new and meet other people with similar interests. On AOL, you have no effective limits on your access to these small but planet-circling communities.

The next chapters focus on *information* on the Internet. The World Wide Web, the driving force in today's Internet, is the focus of the next two chapters.

Chapter 6

Exploring the Web
with America Online

If it's human, it's on the World Wide Web. People use the Web to advertise products, market services, celebrate their ideas, amuse their friends, make friends, vent frustrations, campaign for President, publish magazines without cutting down trees or paying postage, and teach children how to discern stars and dissect frogs. The Web has been called a publishing revolution comparable to the invention of movable type. Maybe, maybe not, but it has produced approximately 100 million globally distributed pages of information, on every subject, in an amazingly short period of time. The entire experience of exploring the Web and creating Web pages is available to you through America Online.

What *is* the Web?

The Web is just another way of getting information and sharing information on the Internet—as are newsgroups, Telnet, and FTP. The physicists and computer scientists who launched the WWW Project in 1989 shared the vision of hypertext: linking related information located on networks anywhere in the world into a seamless and easy-to-navigate web of information. At first, the Web was just used as a way of getting to information available through the *other* Internet tools.

What happened next made the Web the white-hot center of the Internet. Thanks to the fundamental simplicity of the hypertext language, called HTML (Hypertext Markup Language), the Web quickly evolved into a way for people, and not only scientists, to both access and publish information, thereby creating even more sources of information.

Then came a major change in the software you use to navigate the Web—tools to help regular folks browse. The first browsers were meant for reading text. In 1993, the browser Mosaic, with a "graphical" interface, displayed images as well as text and allowed users to get around by the click of a mouse. In 1994, a new company called Netscape Communications improved on the Mosaic browser. In a brilliant marketing ploy, Netscape distributed free Macintosh, Windows, and Unix versions of their browser to almost anyone who wanted the software.

In 1995, software giant Microsoft got into the act with a competing browser, Internet Explorer, also free. With free software such as Netscape and Internet Explorer, and with an exploding universe of information people wanted to get, the Web went mainstream in 1995. The Microsoft browser is now integrated into the AOL software, and Macintosh users can use Netscape with AOL as well (Chapter 10).

Where Is the Web on AOL?

Eager to get started? You can get the hang of the Web yourself by just playing around. For all the fine points, you can use this chapter as a reference. The Web's always a click away when you're on AOL. There are several ways to get on the Web:

- From the main AOL window, click the Globe on the toolbar to go to AOL's Web site.

- In the Keyword window, type in the entire URL (Web address). Try it now if you want, using any of the hundreds of URLs provided in Chapter 11. Or, just go to keyword: Web or keyword: WWW, a quick way to get to the AOL Web site.

- Whenever you see one of the following icons in an AOL channel, double-click it to go directly to a Web site:

  Whenever you see underlined text in a different color, you can click on it to get to related information. For more information on finding specific places on the Web, see "Getting From A to B: How to Visit A Web Site Using AOL's Browser."

America Online gives you everything you need to enjoy the World Wide Web's multimedia feast of sounds, pictures, and animation. (For the technically minded:

AOL 3.0 for the Mac includes a customized version of Microsoft's Internet Explorer version 3.0.) This chapter provides everything you need to get started. You'll learn how to:

- Use the AOL browser

- Get from place to place on the Web

- Search for information on the Web

- Enjoy multimedia files

- Use the browser to access other Internet services—Gopher, FTP, e-mail, and newsgroups

- Get out of a jam

How It Works

A page is the unit of the Web. When you access the Web on America Online, you are requesting a single page of information. Your request goes to one of AOL's big computers, or servers, which opens up a connection over a very fast communications line to the computer (also called a server) where the page is located. AOL then requests a copy of the page. When it arrives, the page is transferred to your computer. When you browse the Web, you're really bringing the Web, or at least a page (with links to other pages), to yourself.

If the page you're requesting has built-in graphics—as AOL's home page does—the graphics files come to your computer, too, along with any links, which are bits of text or pictures you can click to get more information. Click a link and presto, another page comes to you, taking the place of the one you were just visiting. The browser does no more than request a page and present it to you—its formatting, pictures, and other elements ("A Page and Its Elements").

TERMS THAT CHANGED THE WORLD: URL AND HTML

A Web page is the basic unit of the World Wide Web. Every Web page has its own address, or URL (Uniform Resource Locator). The page itself is a simple text file, created in HTML (Hypertext Markup Language), which your browser displays as a more or less polished document. Let's look closer at these two fundamental aspects of every Web page.

Where Is That Page? URLs

A URL is simply an Internet address. Every piece of information on an Internet server has its own separate address.

A URL such as **http://www.aol.com/search** has three parts:

1. The first bit, *http*, specifies a *protocol*. A protocol is just a set of rules for exchanging information between two computers. That may sound complicated, but it just indicates which Internet service you want to use, such as the Web (http), e-mail (mailto), file transfer (ftp), or news groups (news).

 More information about non-hypertext protocols is available in the "Your All-Purpose Browser."

2. The next bit, *www.aol.com*, is the domain name, which tells you a little more about the site—whether it's a company and perhaps where it's located, for example. The domain name scheme used for Web domains is the same as that used for e-mail messages (see Chapter 3). Reading a domain name from left to right, you go from a specific computer to its domain. Many Web servers begin with *www* and end with *com*.

3. The final bit of the URL, */search*, is the specific page or directory path to the page you are requesting. A path is the directory or folder where the Web page resides. On an Internet computer, a path is a series of folders and subfolders, each level separated by a forward slash (/), such as */dpeal/myfamily/mykids/ella/circus.jpg*. You can tell an actual file because it usually ends in a file "extension" such as .HTML, .JPG, or .GIF.

URLs always take you to a specific file on the Web. If you type in a URL without a file name (like **http://www.aol.com/search/**), it's because a specific filename is assumed as the starting point in a directory, such as index.html or main.html.

How Is That Page Put Together? HTML

Web pages are ordinarily formatted in the Hypertext Markup Language (HTML). Figure 6-1 shows a page of marked-up text, and Figure 6-2 shows the corresponding page as the AOL browser displays it.

HTML is easy to learn, and AOL makes creating a Web page even easier using the Personal Publisher service (keyword: PP2). Personal Publisher writes the HTML code for you automatically. If you know even a little HTML, you can tweak and refine your Personal Publisher page into a thing of beauty. Chapter 7 gets you up and running with Personal Publisher.

```
<html>
<head>
<body bgcolor="#ffffff">
<TITLE>Welcome to the CHILE-HEADS home page </TITLE>
</head>
<center><h1> The Chile-Heads home page </h1></center>
<BR><IMG vspace=6 SRC="dot_clear.gif"><BR>
<IMG Align=left SRC="images/pepper3i.gif" alt="Chile Heads logo">
<h4>Illustration courtesy of <a href="shepherds.html">
Shepherd's Garden Seeds</a></h4>
<BR><IMG vspace=1 SRC="dot_clear.gif"><BR>
Welcome to the <b>Chile-Heads</b> home page.  Almost everything you might want
 to know about chile peppers is here!
Additions and updates are occurring constantly!

<BR><IMG vspace=10 SRC="dot_clear.gif"><BR>
<b>It doesn't matter who you are, or what you've done, or think you can
do.  There's a confrontation with destiny awaiting you.  Somewhere, there is
a chile you cannot eat."</b><br>
        <i>      -- Daniel Pinkwater, "A Hot Time in Nairobi"</i>

<BR clear=left><IMG vspace=10 SRC="dot_clear.gif"><BR>
<Center><ul>
<li><a href="misc.html">What's the hottest pepper?</a> and other Hot Topics!
<BR><IMG vspace=1 SRC="dot_clear.gif"><BR>
<li>Identify that unknown chile from the pictures in the
<a href="pre_gallery.html">Chile Gallery</a>
```

FIGURE 6-1   HTML never won a beauty contest

The Chile-Heads home page

FIGURE 6-2 Figure 6-1's Web page, with a title, some text, a graphic, and hyperlinks

How does HTML turn into something intelligible, even cool? The text you read is "tagged" to instruct browsers how to display it. The browser looks at the tags and displays text and pictures accordingly. If your browser sees a "bold" tag (), it displays text in bold until it's told to turn the tag "off" (). If it sees a "link" tag, it displays some blue (or some other color) underlined text that can be clicked to request another Web page from an Internet computer. If it sees a tag for a graphic, it fetches the graphic file and displays the image "inline." And so on.

> *Inline means part of the page, not displayed separately on a page of its own. Graphics are the most important inline elements of a Web page, but more and more you will see animated graphics, video, and other inline files as well.*

Different browsers will present the same Web page differently. What's graphical about the World Wide Web is a matter of how the browser on your computer presents a page. Netscape and Internet Explorer will take the same tag and render it slightly differently. Some tags or Web content can't be displayed by all browsers.

A PAGE AND ITS ELEMENTS

A Web page can consist of any or all HTML elements. These elements are the various parts of a Web page that you see (or hear or otherwise experience), which together convey some content or message:

- Text
- Graphics
- Links
- Forms
- Tables
- Frames
- Multimedia

If you'll be making Web pages, good design usually boils down to choosing the right elements in the most effective layout for a given message. If you'll be exploring the Web, it doesn't take long to become a Web connoisseur!

Text

Thanks to its academic origins, the Internet was built on words, and words make the Net a feast for the mind. HTML offers many ways to present text for maximum effect. Your AOL browser, like any good browser, can display many text effects, including:

- Headers, or titles, that vary in size
- Numbered and bulleted lists, as well as lists within lists
- Text of different sizes, colors, and fonts
- Emphasis such as bold and italics
- Alignment of text (and other elements) along the right margin or the left margin or centered between the margins
- Text links (or hyperlinks) to other pages

Even the modest bit of text in Figure 6-2 shows text with bold, italics, a centered headline, a smaller title, and hyperlinks!

Graphics

Pictures make the Web a feast for the eyes as well as the mind. You'll encounter several types of images on the Web:

- Backgrounds, or wallpapers, are the colors or repeating images that create a certain mood, usually to reinforce the content or message being conveyed. Backgrounds come in every imaginable color and pattern.

- Inline images are graphics files that are downloaded along with any HTML pages you fetch. Since it can take a while to download and display these images and they don't always provide a lot of information, you can choose to turn images off.

- Animated GIFs look like simple movies. Some inline graphics files contain several images, each different enough from the previous image to create the impression of simple movement. You'll see animated GIFs all over the Web; they're the easiest way to add action to a Web page. Chapter 7 shows how to add an animated GIF to your own page using AOL's Personal Publisher 2.

- Images can themselves be hyperlinked; click the image and you're linked to another page. Hyperlinked images can take the form of an image map—click a part of the image and you'll go to a specific page, click another part and you go to a different page.

Images of every kind are all over the Web. They can add pizzazz to a page but can also slow down the time it takes to download the page. AOL offers a patented

Turn Down the Picture!

Browsers, including AOL's, offer a standard option of allowing you to turn off images altogether, to speed up retrieval of Web pages. These days, with faster modems, better graphics, and image-compression technologies, turning off the images isn't necessarily a good idea; you can lose too much information. But if you have a 14.4K or slower modem, you still might want to do so: with the browser open, click Prefs, then make sure there's no check in the Show Images box. Click OK.

Before you turn off images altogether, try leaving Show Images on while making sure the Use Compressed Images button is also checked.

technology for compressing graphics files which speeds up their download times. And on AOL you always have the choice of turning off images altogether, though it can make the Web a less interesting place.

Links, Also Known as Hyperlinks

A link is something you click to move on to a Web page with related content. Links are often called hyperlinks, because they make hypertext possible—the transparent linking of related information, regardless of location. "Hypertext" uses clickable images as well as text links. You can spot linked text because it is underlined and generally in blue.

Tip   *To tell whether a word or a picture is hyperlinked, pass the cursor over the item. If it's a link, its URL will appear in the status bar at the bottom of your browser. Also, your cursor turns into a pointing finger, meaning you can click the link. That's the way things work on AOL, too: try passing your mouse slowly over any tool on the toolbar—the arrow turns into a pointing finger.*

Forms

A form makes a Web page into a mini-application, as in the Home Fair (Figure 6-3), a Washington, D.C.-area information service for people anywhere who are thinking of purchasing a home.

Forms give you many of the standard Mac features you know from other applications: radio buttons, check boxes, entry fields, drop-down listboxes, and buttons for processing or canceling your entries. You see forms in many places on the Web: when you register to use a site to buy something, when you customize a site, and when you answer a poll or enter a contest. Forms make the Web a more interactive, less static place because with forms you're giving data to a Web site, not just passively receiving data.

Tables

Tables allow for the formatting of text and images (and anything else) in rows and columns. They're a standard presentation technique. (Figure 6-4). The value of

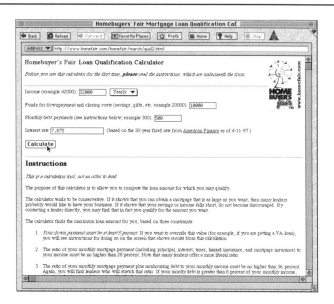

FIGURE 6-3   The Home Fair's mortgage calculator is a mini-application
that takes your data, runs it through formulas, and returns
useful information (see Figure 6-4)

tables is best appreciated when viewing a table through a browser that doesn't
support them—the text is often a mess.

Frames

Think of a frame as a way of dividing your browser into separate windows, each
capable of displaying a different page (Figure 6-5).

If frames are set up properly, each different page appears in a separate frame.
Click a link in one frame, and you're transported to a new page in that frame or
another frame.

Why do you need frames? Sites can be complex, and pages can be long—longer
at least than can fit vertically in a browser. Usually, a site's navigational bar—the
buttons you click to get to the various parts of a site—are at the bottom of the site,
though increasingly they're arranged along the side or positioned at the top of the
main page. With frames, the "table of contents" (the site's navigational bar) can be
made available at all times, so that it is easier to jump back and forth between
different parts of a site. It is possible to have several frames at a time.

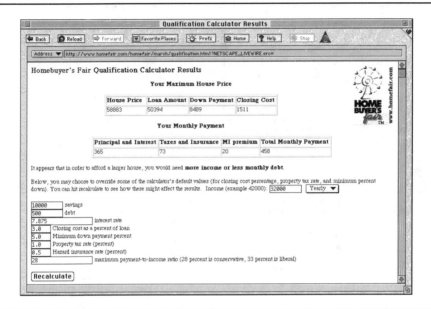

Homebuyer's Fair Qualification Calculator Results

Your Maximum House Price

House Price	Loan Amount	Down Payment	Closing Cost
58883	50394	8489	1511

Your Monthly Payment

Principal and Interest	Taxes and Insurance	MI premium	Total Monthly Payment
365	73	20	458

It appears that in order to afford a larger house, you would need **more income or less monthly debt**.

Below, you may choose to override some of the calculator's default values (for closing cost percentage, property tax rate, and minimum percent down). You can hit recalculate to see how these might affect the results. Income (example 42000): 32000 Yearly ▼

10000	savings
500	debt
7.875	interest rate
3.0	Closing cost as a percent of loan
5.0	Minimum down payment percent
1.0	Property tax rate (percent)
0.5	Hazard insurance rate (percent)
28	maximum payment-to-income ratio (28 percent is conservative, 33 percent is liberal)

Recalculate

FIGURE 6-4   The Home Fair presents information in the form of a table, for easy scanning and interpretation

Frames have other uses as well. They can present advertisements in such a way that the advertisement is always present in one frame even if you navigate somewhere else in another frame. It is even possible for ads to rotate within a banner every couple of minutes. Frames can also present the site's title as a constant feature, so you'll always know which site you're visiting.

The main problem with frames is that they can they take up a lot of space. Sometimes they leave too little space to read text; sometimes, as a result, you must resize them. To resize a frame, slowly pass your cursor over the frame border and, when the mouse cursor turns into a double arrow, click and drag the border to resize the two adjoining frames. But not all frames can be adjusted in this way: it depends if the person who created the page wants you moving the frames around.

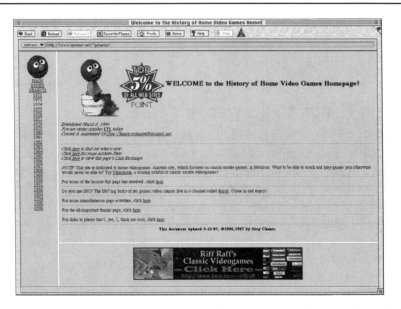

FIGURE 6-5 Frames used at the History of Home Video Games site. Note the ad (bottom frame), the index (left side frame), and the main information frame

Multimedia Gumdrops

A Web page can also be home to many multimedia elements as well, including sounds, videos, and animations. Some of these files play with the help of separate "helper applications" or "plug-ins" while others play right inside the browser. The "Sights, Sounds, Moving Pictures: Working with Multimedia Files" section provides a compact guide to using multimedia Web pages.

YOUR DASHBOARD: A CLOSER LOOK AT YOUR BROWSER

The Web's the same the world over—text, pictures, and any additional elements, packaged up as HTML pages. Browsers, however, behave differently, and they display Web pages differently. Let's take a moment to look closely at the AOL browser, which sports an AOL look but, inside, contains Microsoft's powerful Internet Explorer technology.

Buying Things on the Web: It's Safe!

It's a short step from being about to fill out a form that supplies a Web server with personal data to filling out an *order form* with your name, address, phone number, and credit card number. More and more companies sell products and services in this way. If the products are electronic (any publication or piece of software that can be digitized and sent over the phone lines), they can be delivered as well as purchased on the Web. All other products must use the postal or overnight services. The Internet Mall (**http://www.internet-mall.com**) collects links to thousands of merchants who sell items from jewelry to chocolates to books to CDs on the Web.

Is it safe to buy things on the Web?

The AOL browser supports an Internet security standard called Secure Sockets Layer (SSL). SSL protects your entire transaction, not just confidential data such as your credit card number. First, SSL *confirms the identity* of the company Web server from which you buy (this is called *authentication*). It also *encrypts the data* sent back and forth between you and the company Web server—scrambling the data packets so they are practically impossible to reconstruct. Finally, it *ensures the integrity of the data* transmitted between you and the server, so that tampered data will be considered invalid and rejected.

As a result of these measures, you can have confiidence that your transaction is safe on the Internet. *Completely* safe? No, but nothing is. Consider the following: (1) No one has yet lost money to "robbers" on the Internet, and very big companies such as Cisco are beginning to do a major share of their overall business on the Internet. (2) Your "real-life" transactions are subject to real-life risks through phone tampering, lost credit cards, and mislaid credit card slips. Virtual transactions are subject to fewer risks and are generally better protected.

There's another aspect to your security on the Web: the *confidentiality* of what you do and where you browse. See the "Cookies" box later in this chapter for more information.

Browsers are becoming mainstream applications, like word processors and spreadsheets, with the difference that the "documents" they view aren't located on your own computer and could be anywhere on the globe.

Opening Your Browser

The fastest way to get to the Web is to click the Globe icon of the main AOL toolbar, which spirits you directly to the AOL Web site, **http://www.aol.com**. You can also get to AOL's Web site by going to keyword: Web or keyword: WWW. The AOL Web site is automatically set as your home page, but in "Setting Your Preferences" you'll see how to start with any page you want (see "Changing Your Home Page"). Figure 6-6 shows the AOL Web site's opening page.

Naming of Parts

Notice that the integrated browser looks more or less like a standard AOL window and consists of standard Macintosh elements.

 You must be logged onto AOL to use the browser.

The *title bar* shows the name of the Web site (picked up from its "Title tag" in the underlying HTML code, in case you were wondering). Whenever you save a Web site in your Favorite Places folder, the site's name is based on what you see in the title bar. When you use Personal Publisher, you're prompted to provide a title.

The *buttons* do pretty much what their names say (Table 6-1). These buttons apply to what you're doing during the current Web session, which takes place from the time you opened the browser to the time you closed it.

You can open several browser windows at the same time, thus running a couple of sessions at once, and each browser window will have its own set of buttons.

Right below the browser's button bar is the *location box*, which displays the URL of the current Web page. Click the little downward-pointing arrow labeled Address to see a drop-down list, or menu, listing pages you've recently visited on the Web. You can jump directly to any one of those by simply selecting it and releasing the mouse button.

The title bar displays the Web page's title.

The buttons give you control over your browser.

The AOL logo spins as a page is being downloaded and stops when it arrives.

Click the arrow to see the pages you've visited this session.

The location box displays a page's URL.

Web page! →

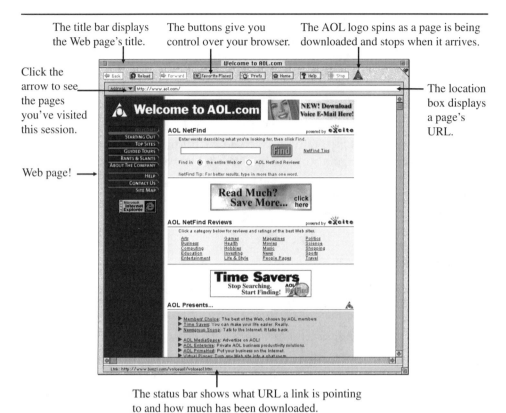

The status bar shows what URL a link is pointing to and how much has been downloaded.

FIGURE 6-6   AOL's Web site is a good place to start exploring the Web and to get an overview of AOL's broad range of Internet services

The *spinner*, the blue AOL icon to the right of the URL box, spins while a page is downloading. The spinner stops if a page is either successfully downloaded or the download got interrupted for some reason.

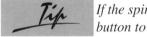   *If the spinner ever stops before a page has downloaded, click the Reload button to attempt to download it again, or try again later.*

The largest part of the browser is the *display window*, which is where you actually look at and respond to Web pages. If a Web page is either too long or too wide to fit

Button	What It Does
Back	If you've seen more than one site during the current session, Back takes you to the previous page you viewed.
Reload	If a page was partially displayed or if you've changed some preferences, Reload fetches a new copy of the same page.
Forward	If you've backtracked (using Back), Forward takes you to the site viewed after that site.
Favorite Places	Brings up your list of favorite Web sites and AOL forums.
Prefs	Lets you set preferences. The Preferences window differs in the two versions of AOL 3.0. See "Setting Your Preferences."
Home	Returns you to your home page, which you can set using the Prefs button.
Help	Brings up the Help area of the AOL Web site, with many pointers to help resources on the AOL service and on the Internet.
Stop	Stops a page from downloading if you change your mind or made a mistake, or if it's taking too long for all of the elements of the page to arrive.

TABLE 6-1   The AOL browser's button and what they do. If you linger with your mouse arrow over any button, a short description comes up

nicely in this window, horizontal or vertical scroll bars (or both) appear. Click the appropriate ends of the scroll bars to see content that doesn't fit.

Finally, there's the status bar at the bottom of the browser. Move your cursor over a link (word or image), and the URL of the page it's pointing to will appear in the status bar:

```
Link: http://www.apple.com
```

You can use the status bar to know where a link will take you before you commit to clicking on it. Click the link, and the status bar registers what's going on as the Web server is contacted, a connection is made, and the elements of a page are downloaded one at a time. You'll be notified in the status bar as each page element is downloaded, until all elements of the page have arrived and you can start clicking and browsing.

Fish and Fowl: AOL's Hybrid Browser

Across the AOL service you will encounter a customized version of the AOL browser called a "hybrid"—because it's part AOL forum and part Web browser. Hybrids are used to display Web sites specially chosen for a channel. In the Kids channel, all the Web sites appear in hybrids:

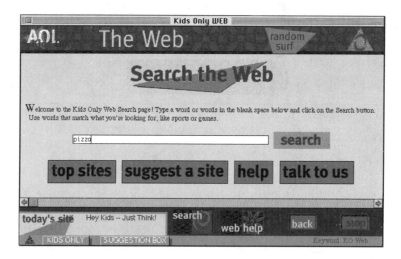

Hybrids ensure the best performance but sometimes lack one or another of the basic AOL browser features, such as the status bar, URL box, and the ability to make the window larger. But sometimes you'll get extra features, such as message boards and buttons pointing to related content.

Setting Your Preferences

The Web browser offers an array of ways to customize your preferences. To adjust the browser preferences, press the Prefs button on the browser window. (Another way to get there at any time is by picking Preferences from your Members menu, then picking Web from the list of preference types.)

You'll notice four areas on the Web preferences screen (Figure 6-7): Display, Warnings and Confirmations, Disk Cache, and Your Home Page.

Display

Four checkboxes give you some control of your browser's appearance:

- **Show address bar**   If checked (as it is by default,) the URL of the Web page is displayed near the top of the browser window. This is highly recommended.

6

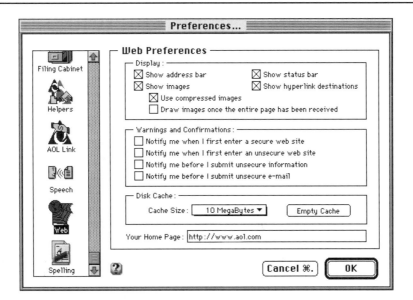

FIGURE 6-7   The AOL Web Preferences menu. Do not be alarmed

- **Show status bar**   Controls whether the informational status bar at the bottom of the browser window will be shown. It is recommended that you leave it turned on.

> *Tip*   *Removing either the location box or the status bar gives you a small bit of extra vertical space in which to display Web pages but at the cost of the vital information that URLs can provide.*

- **Show hyperlink destinations**   If the status bar is to be shown, this will let it tell you where a hyperlink goes when you pass the cursor over it. It's a useful feature—leave it activated, too.

- **Show images**   Controls whether images on Web pages will be shown. Turning off will speed up the transfer of Web pages, but you'll lose any graphics. Two more image options are below: Use compressed images (images will display more quickly but at a slight loss of picture quality) and Draw images once the entire page has been received. This option simply decides whether graphics will be shown as they download, or if the browser should wait for the whole enchilada to download before displaying it. Its up to you.

Warnings and Confirmations

These four controls decide whether the browser will warn you when you enter or leave a secure Web site (one that uses encryption to protect the information you send and receive) and when you submit information via a form. If you like to be reminded whether the information you are sharing is secure or not, turn these on. On the other hand, some people find these messages annoying distractions.

Disk Cache

The disk cache controls how much of your Mac's hard disk is devoted to storing information from the Web sites that you frequent.

You can set the size of this cache at anything from 1 to 100 megabytes. You can also turn caching off completely, but if you can spare the disk space, don't do that. Even a 1 Mb cache can speed up your Web access considerably. On the other hand, 100 Mb is overkill. If your Mac has the room, 5 or 10 Mb will do just fine.

To "purge" your cache, click the Empty Cache button. Why purge the cache? If the browser becomes inexplicably slow, or you start to get many "Network unavailable" errors, purging the cache may clear the problem right up.

Get Cache Fast

Going forward and backward can be a lot faster than downloading a page for the first time—if the pages you visit are being cached. A cache is a place where something is stored for fast retrieval. AOL uses caches at two points while you're browsing the Web, and both uses of caches can improve your experience of the Web.

First, sites that members most like to visit are stored on AOL's computers, so that members who subsequently want to visit the same sites can download directly from the cache, instead of going out to the Internet for a new copy of the page. These caches are frequently cleared to ensure that pages are as up to date as possible. Old pages are constantly reviewed, and pages that are no longer accessed are removed.

Second, there's a cache on your hard disk that keeps track of the pages you visit most frequently during a session. Loading the page or elements of the page from the cache can be quicker than getting the whole thing "off the Internet."

Your Home Page

Your home page is the page from which you choose to start your wanderings on the Web and to which you can usefully return again and again. Until you change it, AOL's Web site is your home page. But you can change it! If you frequently use a search engine, AOL's NetFind search page, **http://www.aol.com/netfind**, is a good place to call home. Or you can make any other site on the Net your home page.

In the Your Home Page field, type in the URL you wish to use as your home page. You can use anything under the sun: a Gopher menu or FTP directory, a search engine such as Excite, or your company's Web site.

Now, next time you click that Globe icon, or go to keyword: Web or keyword: WWW, you'll start with the home page of your preference.

Tip   *If you want to make a page with a long, hard-to-type URL your home page, try this: Go to the page. Highlight its URL in the location box and then choose Copy from the Edit menu. Finally, click the Prefs button, and paste the URL into the Your Home Page field.*

Your Home on the Web: AOL's Web Site

When you first install the AOL software, AOL's Web site is your *home page*, the hub of your travels on the Web, providing roadside assistance, roadmaps, and tips about what's worth seeing. It comes up when you click the Globe icon on the tool bar at the top of the screen, or go to keyword: WWW or keyword: Web. When you press the browser's Home button to "go home," you arrive back at the AOL Web site, one of the most visited sites on the Internet.

The AOL Web site (Figure 6-6) uses a set of long buttons to simplify access to the various parts of the site. These buttons are hyperlinks and are available in the upper left-hand part of every page. Click one, and you'll go to a different part of the AOL site.

Starting Out	An overview for beginners
Top Sites	New and notable Web sites
Guided Tours	The favorite Web sites of some of AOL's personalities
Rants & Slants	Opinions about the Internet
About the Company	All about AOL as a company

When you visit the "About the Company" portion of the site (where the company vision statement, corporate strategies, and press releases are located), you'll see lots of additional choices. (Figure 6-8).

GETTING FROM A TO B: HOW TO VISIT A WEB SITE USING AOL'S BROWSER

The comforts of home are fleeting on the Web, unable to compete with the pull of favorite haunts and the lure of new places to discover. America Online's browser gives you many ways to get to any site on the Web.

FIGURE 6-8   AOL, the company: vision, strategy, financials, opportunities, press releases

The easiest way to get from one Web site to another is to click a link. A nifty feature of the browser is that you can open a link in a new browser window while keeping open the page you're linking from. To do this, click on the link and hold your mouse button down for a second. A menu will appear—then select Open Link in New Window and release the mouse button. You can use AOL's Window menu to go back and forth between multiple browser windows. You can keep open as many browsers as you want. Bear in mind, though, that the more browsers that are open, the slower your computer will work.

Here are four ways to proceed directly to any page you please:

- *Hopping with keywords*   Gives you speedy access to the Web if you don't have a browser open yet.

- *Skipping to Favorite Places*   *Allows you to revisit sites you've already seen.*

- *Leaping to a Web site linked from an AOL forum*   Lets you go directly from an AOL forum to sites related to the forum's theme.

- *Jumping to new URLs* Gives you the most freedom after the browser screen is open. Just type a site's URL in the Location field and press RETURN.

Hop with the Keyword Window

Suppose you want to see what Disney is doing on the Internet. From the GoTo menu, select Keyword. Type in the URL, **http://www.disney.com**, and press RETURN. If you already have a page open (such as your home page, or anything else), keywording to a different page opens a new browser window.

AOL has assigned easy keywords to members' favorite Web sites, so that, for those sites, you don't have to know the URLs. In the Keyword window, you can type in **Pathfinder**, **Excite**, or **Disney.com** to go directly to those sites.

At keyword: Web keywords you will get a list of keywords that take you directly to Web sites, including all the major search sites (Altavista, Excite, Lycos, Liszt, Dejanews, Infoseek, Yahoo, Magellan, Switchboard, and Webcrawler), as well as popular sites such as MTV, NASA, and dozens of others. See Chapter 11 for a complete list of Web keywords.

Skip to a Favorite Place

Favorite Places give you quick access to your favorite things on AOL and the Internet. You can save any kind of content as long as it has a little heart in its title bar. After you've saved a number of places, you can organize your Favorite Places any way you want—in any order and with as many "levels" (folders within folders) as you want. To get to your Favorite Places folder, click the Favorite Places button in the tool bar:

Something like the window in Figure 6-9 comes up.

To jump to a Favorite Place, just open the folder and double-click a place.

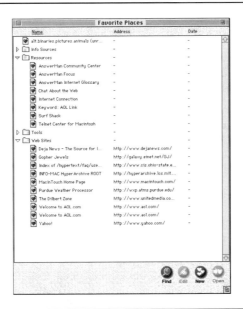

FIGURE 6-9 Favorite Places can quickly become an overgrown garden
(speaking of favorite places)

■ If it's a Web resource and the browser is already open, double-clicking the
Favorite Place opens up a new browser window.

 *Remember, you can add any Web site to your Favorite Places by clicking
on the heart in the browser's title bar.*

■ If you click the Favorite Place item and drag it from the Favorite Places
folder into an open browser, the Favorite Place replaces the Web site
displayed in the open browser.

Organizing your Favorite Places is a snap:

■ *To create a new folder for related Favorite Places*, just click New then click
the New Folder button. Give the folder a name and click Create. To move a
Favorite Place into the folder, just click and drag the item into the folder.

- *To change a folder's name*, click on its old name and wait a moment. The name will become highlighted so you can edit it. (Just like renaming a file with the Finder!)

- *To change the name of a favorite place,* (for instance, to shorten it or associate it in your mind more clearly with its content) you can click on its name and rename it just like changing a folder's name. Or, click on its icon and click the Edit button, type the new name in the Name field, and click OK.

Note *If you use AOL on several computers, each will have a separate Favorite Places folder. You can't currently copy Favorite Place folders from one machine to another.*

Leap to a Web Site Linked from an AOL Forum

All AOL channels integrate Web sites into other channel content. You'll find these sites arranged in listboxes, and "behind" buttons in your favorite channels. In the Health channel, for example, there's a large set of useful Web sites, such as:

⊕ Mayo Clinic

Keyword: Health Web takes you to the channel's best health-related Web sites. Chapter 11 provides a directory of the best of the Web sites for your favorite channels. To go to a Web site from the channel, just double-click (if the site's in a listbox) or single-click (if there's a button).

Jump to a New URL

With a browser open, you can use your mouse to select the current URL and type a new one over it. Press RETURN, and the site you've selected will appear in the browser window. Make sure you have the full and exact URL of the site you want to visit.

MANAGING YOUR WEB SESSION

Once you start visiting Web sites, you'll invariably start visiting *other* Web sites. That's the nature of the Web and of browsing. Clicking a hyperlink—underlined

Do You Know What Your Children Are Viewing?

"If it's human, it's on the Web." This means that there may be sites, pictures, and sounds that you, if you're a parent, might not want your child to experience. AOL does not censor the Web; it can't censor the Web. But it does give parents the tools to limit what members of their household do on the Web. To use these controls:

1. Go to Keyword: Parental.

2. Click Custom Controls.

3. Click Web, then Web Controls. You get four levels of control for every screen name on the master account: no access to the Web; access to kid-appropriate sites only; access to teen-appropriate sites only; and full access. Make a choice and click OK.

6

Cookies

A "cookie" is a little file on your hard disk that a Web site creates to track your visits to that site. It's a sort of message-to-itself that a Web site can create, then read back later that visit or the next time you visit. Cookies can help a site track which particular pages you have visited, for example. The marketing uses of such a file are obvious: sites get a clear idea of your browsing preferences (without knowing exactly who you are). A possible use of cookies is to present you with customized pages, based on your past browsing preferences. Some people, however, consider "cookies" a violation of their privacy.

The AOL browser allows sites to store cookies on your Mac. Unfortunately, if you don't like them, the AOL Web browser doesn't have an option that will disallow sites from tossing its cookies at you. But it is easy to delete cookies that sites have placed on your Mac after the fact. From the Finder, look in System Folder:Preferences:America Online:Browser Cache. If any sites have stored a cookie on your Mac, there will be a file called cookies.txt. Throw it in your Trash and they're gone. But next time you visit a site that wants to store a cookie, the file will reappear.

Unless you get tricky. To keep the cookies file from reappearing create a *new folder* named cookies.txt in the Browser Cache folder. Doing this will prevent the browser from saving any more cookies on your Mac.

text, or part of a clickable image, or image map—takes you to another page, or another site. With 100 million pages out there, linking never stops. Remember that you can tell if something's a link if a URL appears in the status bar when you pass your mouse cursor over it. The mouse pointer (arrow) turns into a pointing finger. At any point in any session, you can return home by clicking the browser's Home button.

Moving Around Within a Page

A Web page rarely fits within the browser window. To help you get around long or wide pages, vertical or horizontal scroll bars, or both, are available.

 The PAGE UP and PAGE DOWN keys are also available to help you navigate up and down a page.

AOL's integrated browser doesn't let you search for a specific word on a Web page, which can be a bother, for example, if you've used a search engine such as AOL's NetFind, and you're not sure what the page has to do with what you are searching.

Managing the Slow Page

Sometimes a page can take too long to download. This can happen because it's a badly built page, it's in great demand, network traffic is too heavy, or the page has lots of images. If you ever suspect a page has gotten "stuck" somewhere between the Internet and your Mac, click Stop. Sometimes the text (the part that downloads the fastest) will already have been downloaded, but the pictures haven't yet arrived. In this case, clicking Stop may cause the text to appear on your screen—and it may be what you were trying to get in the first place. Sometimes, nothing will have arrived, and your browser will be blank. If that's the case, you can click Reload to attempt again to retrieve the page.

Use the Reload button, too, if you've changed your settings while displaying a page. For example, you're viewing a site with very big, very slow images. You turn off the images by clicking Prefs and unchecking the Show Images box. The change won't take effect until you click Reload.

Going Back and Forth Between Pages

Using the Back and Forward buttons is straightforward. "Backward" and "Forward" are relative to the list of pages you've viewed in the current browser session. To see the list, click the downward-pointing arrow labeled Address to the left of the URL field at the top of the browser. You can jump to any of the pages on this list by picking its URL from the list and letting go of the mouse button.

6

Keeping Up with New Sites

The Web is growing so fast that you cannot possibly keep up with all the latest Web sites. How do you keep up with the ones of likely interest to you? Here are a few suggestions:

- The **NetGuide** forum on AOL (keyword: Netguide), *NetGuide* magazine, and the NetGuide Web site (**http://www.netguidemag.com/**) all provide a good selection of the best new sites, with clearly written annotations.

- **AOL's Top Site Picks** (**http://www.aol.com/top**). Includes a directory of Member's Choice sites and winners of the Member Home Page contest.

- Netscape's What's New (**http://home.netscape.com/escapes/ whats_new.html**). Uniformly high-quality Web sites.

- Three mailing lists described in Chapter 4 provide excellent updates on new Web resources: **Scout-Report, NetSurfer Digest,** and **Yahoo!'s Picks of the Week**.

- **Net-happenings**. Gleason Sackman's classic resource began as a mailing list, then migrated to a newsgroup (**comp.internet. net-happenings**).

- The **comp.infosystems.www.announce** newsgroup is used to publish notifications of new, noncommercial Web sites.

- **Yahoo! What's New**. At **http://www.yahoo.com** then click New or Cool or whatever it's called when you get there.

THE 15-SECOND WEB SEARCH

Suppose you want to find a fertilizer for your wild roses, look into beekeeping as a career, or plan a vacation to Wyoming. Where do you start? Much of your experience on the Web will probably begin with a search. The tools for searching have gotten dramatically better and easier to use in the past year, and changes are in store that will make for radically simpler custom-searching in the future. Chapter 9 helps you do really effective searches, regardless of where the information you need is located or how it's made available. For now, it's enough to introduce NetFind, AOL's exclusive search engine and perhaps the only search tool you need.

To use NetFind, simply go to keyword: NetFind or to **http://aol.com/netfind/** (shown in Figure 6-10). To search for information about roses, bees, or Wyoming, enter keywords in the box and click Find. *Wild roses* will do as an example. You can add more specific keywords, joined (if you wish) by words such as *and* and *or*. In

FIGURE 6-10   What aisle is it in? Start with the AOL Search page

general it's a good idea to conduct as specific a search as possible, to avoid being swamped by thousands of choices.

After NetFind has finished looking through its index of millions of URLs, it returns a list of pages that contain the word or words you've entered, along with a brief description of what's on that page. To visit one of the pages on the list, just click its link!

Choosing a Search Engine

Search engines vary in many ways, including:

- The number of URLs they track (how many tens of millions!).

- Their flexibility in allowing you to ask questions and then, from there, figuring out what you want.

- Their ability to return the URLs for which you're probably looking.

- Their additional bells and whistles, such as value-added reviews of sites, editorializing of one sort or another, and features such as Excite's City.Net and its directory of selected sites.

Chapter 9 goes into the endlessly interesting and rapidly changing world of searching for information on the Net. For now, try NetFind to get some sense of what searching the Net is all about.

SIGHTS, SOUNDS, MOVING PICTURES: WORKING WITH MULTIMEDIA FILES

FTP, the Net's File Transfer Protocol, was once the major way to transfer software, images, and other files across the Internet. Using FTP is like navigating someone else's hard disk, finding a file, then copying it over the Net to your computer. With FTP, however, you then have to find a word processor, or graphics viewer, or other program that can "play" the file. And all you get with FTP is files—no context, no discussion, no links to related files, nor any of the other essential content you get on the Web.

The Web has become an important alternative way of delivering files over the Internet, by means of links to sound, audio, or video files and as an interface to FTP (see "Your All-Purpose Browser").

 *No Web browser can play every type of multimedia file. The built-in Web browser can't handle Web pages with Java or JavaScript—it will show the page, but the interactive Java elements will be missing. If you must have Java access, you can use an external browser such as Netscape Navigator. More on this in Chapter 10.*

Using your browser, you see and hear files in two basic ways:

■ The most common image and sound files are displayed automatically by your browser.

■ Other files require special "players" that are more or less well-integrated into the Web browser, so the content of the files—the music, the video, whatever—is more or less smoothly integrated into the content of the Web page.

Playing Audio Files with the Browser—and Without

Some types of information can be automatically presented by AOL's browser—text, GIF and JPEG-format images, MIDI music, to name just a few.

Likewise, click a link to a common sound file (with the extension AU or WAV) and the file downloads and plays. AU and WAV files are digitized versions of actual music and recordings; thus, they can be large and slow to download. A 100K file might play only a few seconds. If you click on a link to a sound file, it will download to your Mac. When the download is complete, a tiny sound control window will appear. Click on the "play" arrow to hear the sound.

Procd_005742i

MIDI files are a different animal. Some Web pages have been "embedded" with MIDI files so the browser will play them automatically as a page downloads. AOL's Web browser can play embedded MIDI files, but won't play a MIDI file that is only accessible through a hyperlink. Here's a trick to get around the problem: Hold down the OPTION key while clicking on the link to the MIDI file. This forces the browser to download it to your Mac. Then you can play the file using MoviePlayer. If you don't have MoviePlayer on your Mac, you can download it from AOL: Go to keyword: Apple Computer, click Find, then enter **movieplayer**.

The beauty of MIDI is that files are small (and they download in a snap), while playing times are long. A 10K MIDI file of the Beatles' song "Eleanor Rigby" runs for more than a minute. Unfortunately, it sounds more like a music box than the Beatles rendition.

Working with Plug-ins and Helper Applications

More and more Web sites are delivering video and audio directly to your browser. The most important type of such files requires a plug-in program that runs automatically within your browser (or at least smoothly integrated with it) when you click a link to a certain kind of file

Where do you find the programs to run these newfangled files? The best place to start is at **http://multimedia.aol.com/addons/macaddons.htm**. This page offers several *plug-ins* that are designed especially to work with the AOL browser: RealAudio, ShockWave, and VDO. These plug-ins aren't built-in when you install AOL. If you want any (or all) of them, you'll have to download the plug-in installer, log out of AOL, then run the installer. Actually, the installation process couldn't be easier since these installers are built to work with AOL 3.0 for the Mac.

The other way to play files is with a helper application, a small program external to the browser. These programs, called "helper apps," load when you click a link to the file. The experience of helper apps can be similar to that of plug-ins, but helper apps are not integrated with the browser experience—a video clip will always play in a separate application, not in a little box on the Web page itself.

Three Major Plug-Ins

For (almost) instant gratification, your best bets to start with on your foray into Web multimedia are RealAudio, VDO, and Shockwave.

RealAudio

RealAudio is currently the most satisfying plug-in because of its ease of use, the number of sites taking advantage of it, and its relatively good sound quality. What's special about RealAudio is streaming sound: the sound starts playing while it's still downloading, no matter what modem speed you're using. The tiny RealAudio player (with forward, pause, and rewind buttons) runs automatically whenever you click a link to a RealAudio sound. Right-click on the RealAudio player, and you can pause, stop, and skip to a specific point in the sound clip. RealAudio offers the fidelity of AU but the good experience of MIDI.

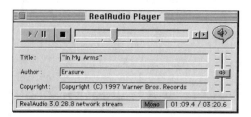

The potential for integrating sound into Web content is great. Interviews, news commentaries, sports reporting, music—all are being delivered via RealAudio. The following RealAudio resources are all a click away from the RealAudio site (**http://www.realaudio.com**). If you're interested in up-to-the-minute news, from the RealAudio site you can link to ABC, National Public Radio, and the Pacifica News Network. (For NPR's "All Things Considered" fans, the entire show is available via RealAudio, within a day or two of the original broadcast at **http://www.npr.org**.) WebActive (**http://www.webactive.com/**), for activists, brings an extensive collection of RealAudio content related to social causes. TimeCast (**http://www.timecast.com**) is a *TV Guide*-style directory of RealAudio sites. And for music, you'll find loads of RealAudio links at LiveConcerts (**http://www.liveconcerts.com**) and CDNow (**http://www.cdnow.com**).

VDO

What RealAudio does for sound, VDO does for video. Among the sample VDO files available when I visited the VDO site were tapes of a space walk that had occurred within the last 24 hours and a Bill Gates speech devoted to Internet technologies. VDO is only for PowerPC Macs—it won't work if you have a 68K Mac. Here's a sample of what it looks like. Just imagine that she's moving and talking.

Shockwave

Perhaps the coolest plug-in is Shockwave, the product of Macromedia, a San Francisco-based company that creates multimedia applications for use in graphic arts, education, training, and entertainment. When you click a Shockwave file, the Director program is launched automatically and plays interactive animations inside a new Web page. Shockwave also supports files that play CD-quality sound.

Links to lots of "shocked" pages are available in the Shockwave gallery at **http://www.macromedia.com/shockwave/epicenter/**. You'll find a Barney punching bag, NeuroGolf, an extreme snowboarding game, and other great stuff.

RealAudio, VDO, Shockwave—this stuff can be addictive. Over a modem, the experience is less than instantaneous, but the excitement of hearing music or watching a live broadcast must come close to the feeling of tuning into a scratchy radio broadcast in the early days of this century. The taste of the future and sense of connection with other people and places is more tangible, perhaps, than anything else on the Web.

Setting Up a Plug-In or Helper Application

When your browser can't play a file, you'll probably have to set up a helper application or plug-in. The procedure can seem technical, but it's not. Here's the background you need.

The Net's Multipurpose Internet Mail Extension (MIME) is the standard used by e-mail programs to identify attached files so they can be properly handled by the programs receiving them. When you download a file over the Web, it has a *MIME type*. AOL looks at the MIME type—based on a file's MIME type, the browser either plays the file itself or uses a helper app or plug-in to play it.

Tip   *All the helper apps you'll ever need can be downloaded from AOL's software libraries, as explained toward the end of Chapter 8. All the plug-ins you need are on the Web, free for you to download from the vendors' sites and from* **http://multimedia.aol.com/addons/macaddons.htm**. *A well-planned Web site directs users to the source of a plug-in if the site uses files requiring that plug-in.*

To set up your browser so that it can read a new type of file and launch the appropriate player (helper app), follow these steps:

1. With the browser open, click Prefs, and then click the Helpers button. Click the Create button.

2. In the "Open files with the following MIME type" field, enter the MIME type (the Web site where you found the plug-in will tell you what this is.)

3. In the "Or the following suffixes" field, enter the file suffixes, if any (again, the Web site where you found the plug-in will tell you what these are.)

4. Click the Select button and show it where the newly installed plug-in is on your Mac's hard drive. Then click OK.

YOUR ALL-PURPOSE BROWSER

URLs beginning *http://* (Web pages) aren't the only ones you can use with the AOL browser. In fact, the Web was originally designed to create a uniform way of viewing diverse information, not just Web pages. With your browser you can also access:

■ Gopher—the precursor of the Web

■ FTP—thousands of sites with millions of files for the downloading

■ Newsgroups—via AOL's Newsgroups window

■ The Compose Mail window—from which you can send an e-mail message

When you visit a Gopher or FTP site, everything takes place within the browser window; you use the browser's controls to get around. However, when you click a link to a newsgroup or an e-mail address, the browser calls up the appropriate built-in AOL tool (the Newsreader or Compose Mail window.) The trend in the next few years will be to integrate more and more in the browser, but for now it's good to get used to a mix: some protocols are directly supported by the browser, others launch a separate program.

Tip   *There's another type of URL that you may happen upon occasionally: telnet://. These are links to Telnet sites. Telnet is a text-only interface to computers on the Internet. You can access Telnet sites with AOL, but the browser can't automatically start the Telnet session for you. (If you try, the browser will report "This program does not support the protocol for accessing telnet.") However, you can run a Telnet client yourself to access the site. For more on this, see Chapter 10 and keyword: Telnet.*

Gopher's Swan Song

In 1991, after the Web was invented but before it became hugely popular, Mark McCahill and others at the University of Minnesota invented Gopher. This tool had a similar purpose as the Web—to provide easy access to different types of information located around the globe. However, while the Web uses hypertext as the model for how to find and link information, Gopher used simple menus to provide access (Figure 6-11).

A menu is just a list. Click a menu item and you either go to another menu or to actual content (such as a text file). While the Web integrates sounds and video into text information, Gopher was designed and is still used mostly as a way of accessing information one file at a time, particularly textual information such as statistics, government reports, books, magazines, current temperatures, earthquake reports, and the like.

FIGURE 6-11   Gopher—via the Web browser. Thousands of gopher servers still exist despite the popularity of the Web

When I first discovered Gopher in 1993, I was exhilarated by the easy access it provided to all kinds of information. As a researcher at heart I didn't mind the text-only nature of most of the information.

In 1994-95, textual information was still published via Gopher, especially on university campuses. But soon the Web absorbed almost all of the energy and resources that had gone into the creation and maintenance of Gopher sites. Today, even classic sites such as Rice University's Gopher subject directory and classic resources such as Gopher Jewels are no longer maintained. If you have serious information needs, however, it's important to know about Gopher.

Gopher It on the Web

Going to a Gopher site is easy using the AOL browser. Just enter the full URL, beginning *gopher://* in the keyword window or URL field. For instance, **gopher://spinaltap.micro.umn.edu** takes you to a collection of public domain books, reference works, and classics available at Gopher's birthplace, the University of Minnesota.

On AOL, at keyword: Gopher, you will find a list of "gopher treasures" that provide access to goodies ranging from the Congressional Record to 35 years of the speeches of Fidel Castro. Be forewarned, however, that many Gopher sites are no longer being maintained, and many have been converted to Web sites. You'll find increasingly that Gopher menus point you to Web pages, from which you browse the Web and leave Gopher behind.

File This: FTP on the Web

In contrast to Gopher, transferring files with FTP (the Net's File Transfer Protocol) remains a fundamental part of the Internet—it's the principal means by which files are stored on and transmitted across the Internet. When you use FTP, you log onto a distant computer in search of a file or group of files. You search for files in directories, going in and out of directories, subdirectories, and so on, until you find the files you're seeking.

With AOL's browser, you can visit any FTP site whose address you know by entering its full URL into the Keyword window or directly into the browser's URL box. An FTP site's URL consists of *ftp://* plus the domain name, for example,

ftp://ftp.aol.com. Using the browser to access FTP is an alternative to using AOL's FTP gateway at keyword: FTP. Chapter 8 makes a case for the browser being a better way to search FTP than actually downloading files from an FTP site.

E-Mail and Newsgroups Over the Web

Some Web sites hyperlink to newsgroups to take you to pertinent discussion groups. Clicking such a link brings up AOL's newsreader with the newsgroup displayed. You don't read newsgroups from the browser itself. (Chapter 5 is all about newsgroups).

The URL for a newsgroup is *news:* (without the usual forward slashes) and the name of the newsgroup. So, if you know a newsgroup name, such as **comp.internet.net-happenings**, you can type **news:comp.internet.net-happenings** directly into the Keyword window, click Go, and go directly to that newsgroup.

Some Web sites have hyperlinks that, when you click them, allow you to send an e-mail message to someone (the "Webmaster," the person who runs the site, for example). Clicking such a link on AOL calls up the Compose Mail window and inserts the e-mail address into the To window. Finish the message by supplying a Subject line and writing the message body, then clicking Send Now. You will return to the Web site so you can continue to browse.

SAVING WEB PAGES

Sometimes you'll come across information on the Web or gopher that you'll want to keep for reference. There are several ways that you can keep a copy of something:

- Saving a Link to the Page with Favorite Places
- Saving the text of a Web page to your Mac's hard disk
- Printing the Web page
- Saving the page's underlying HTML to your hard disk
- Saving a graphic from the Web page to your hard disk

Saving a Link to the Page with Favorite Places

As discussed earlier in this chapter, Favorite Places allows you to save links to the places you like. Instead of saving the actual Web page, you're saving the URL and title of the page, thus making it as easy as possible to return there in the future. You can add any Web site to your Favorite Places by clicking on the heart in the browser's title bar.

Saving the Text of a Web Page to Your Mac's Hard Disk

If it's the text of the Web page that you want to keep, you can save it to your Mac, automatically stripping the page of graphics, hotlinks, and other multimedia elements. Unfortunately, the browser will not let you pick Save from the File menu and be done with it—despite this, it isn't hard to save a Web page's text.

1. Click anywhere in the Web browser's window (well, not on a link, just in the window.)

2. Choose Select All from the Edit menu.

3. Choose Copy from the Edit menu.

4. Now choose New from the File menu to start a new memo, a blank page for text.

5. Paste the text of the Web page into the memo by choosing Paste from the Edit menu.

6. Finally, choose Save from the File menu. Save the file with a file type of Text Only to your Mac. You will be able to read this file with your word processor or SimpleText.

Tip *You can do all this in a jiffy by using keyword commands instead of the mouse: click in the browser window, then type COMMAND-A, COMMAND-C, COMMAND-N, COMMAND-V, COMMAND-S.*

Printing Out the Text of the Web Page

Printing's a snap with AOL's Web browser: you can print any page, graphics and all. With the Web page displayed, just click the Printer icon on the tool bar at the top of your screen, or choose Print from the File menu. Of course, you'll need a printer with paper, plugged in and properly set up.

Tip   *If you just want to print the text of a Web page without the graphics, you can use the trick in "Saving the text of a web page to your Mac's hard disk." After you've done step 5, click the Printer icon on the tool bar or choose Print from the File menu. (Or type COMMAND-A, COMMAND-C, COMMAND-N, COMMAND-V, COMMAND-P.)*

Saving the Page's Underlying HTML

You've seen what HTML is all about ("How Is That Page Put Together? HTML"). Why would you want to save the HTML file such as the one shown in Figure 6-1? For one thing, you can open the HTML file at any time, and the browser will display the page. It's a fast way of keeping a "local" copy of any page you like. If you're learning to make a Web page, this is a good way to see how your favorite pages were built.

To save a Web page:

1. Use the browser to display a page that links *to* the page that you want to save.

2. Drag that link from the browser window to your Mac's desktop. The page will download—but instead of being displayed, it will be saved to your Mac. If there are any inline graphics, they won't be saved, since they're not actually part of the HTML file.

To look at the page, drag the file's icon back from the Desktop to the browser's window. Or to view the HTML code itself, open the file with your word processor or SimpleText.

Saving a Graphic from a Web Page

More interested in the art from a Web site than the text or HTML tags? No problem. You can save any Web page graphic to your Mac with just a click. Click on the graphic and hold the mouse button down for a second. In the menu that appears, select Download Image to Disk. Give the file a name and a folder—that's it.

WHEN THINGS DON'T WORK

As Web sites get more complex, as more and more people pile in (like those phone booths in the 1950s), and as sites change owners and addresses, it is a miracle the Web works as well as it does. It's also a miracle how much better the Web experience gets from month to month. Still, things go wrong. Table 6-2 shows the details of the most common error messages you may see, and when possible it tells what you can do about them. In general, you can minimize problems by making sure the error isn't yours. Always type URLs carefully and exactly. Spelling, capitalization and punctuation count.

If all else fails, try contacting the Webmaster at the site. If the Web address is something like **http://www.xyz.com/** then the Webmaster's address would probably be **webmaster@xyz.com**.

 *AOL does not censor sites in any way. If you're ever unable to visit a site, it is never because AOL is blocking it.*

FROM HERE...

This chapter covers a lot of ground, but so does the Web! The best way to get comfortable with the Web is to start browsing. It's easy, fun, fairly intuitive, and you can't break anything. You can get tangled up in it, but it will never tear. The AOL Web site is a good place to start exploring.

The next chapter shows you how to create your own Web page using AOL's Personal Publisher.

Error Message	What It Means and What To Do
401 - Authorization Required 403 - Forbidden	You see one of these error messages when you attempt to access a Web page that has limited access. You may need a special password to access it. Double-check the source of your information.
404 - Not Found	The file is no longer available, is incorrectly linked, or has changed its URL. There's not much you can do except contact the person or organization responsible for the site or do a search for the new site.
500 - Server error	If the server has been incorrectly set up or is experiencing mechanical problems, you may see this message. Try again later!
Unable to Connect to Site	The browser cannot find the server specified in the URL. The URL you entered may be incorrect, the server on which the URL is located may be shut down or busy, or the URL may no longer exist. Try again, carefully. Or, click Reload if you're sure it's right.
Too much network traffic	%#$&%*%! The Web page to which you are attempting to connect has too many other people trying to access pages. Sometimes you'll get this message when there's a problem with your cache, the part of your hard disk that keeps track of the sites you visit. Use the Reload button to try to connect to the site again, or wait and try again later.
http couldn't be "parsed"	You made some mistake in typing the URL—adding a space, using backward instead of forward slashes, adding weird punctuation, using one forward slashes instead of two, etc. Try again but type your URL more carefully!

■ **TABLE 6-2**   Things that go bump on the Web and what to do about them

Chapter 7

Publishing on
the Web with
Personal Publisher

One reason the Web's growing so fast is that it's so easy to create new Web pages and make them available to the entire Internet. It probably doesn't get any easier than using America Online's Personal Publisher 2, which provides everything you need to create, publish, and refine a single Web page or an entire Web *site* (a collection of linked pages).

Why would you want to create a Web page? If you own a small business, you could probably benefit from your own Web "presence." The tens of thousands of American businesses with Web presence range from the smallest one-person outfits to giants like Microsoft and Cisco. Nothing can more effectively level the playing field in business than a Web presence. If you have a large (and wired) family and want to post the latest batch of pictures for everyone to see, a Web page may be the easiest way to stay in touch with loved ones. If you want to promote your organization or keep its members apprised of group gossip and events, a Web page may be, again, just the ticket. Finally, if you have a hobby or an abiding obsession, a Web page may be the best way to display your passion and discover who in the world, literally, shares your interest.

Tip   *For large, professional, and commercial sites, AOL also offers a Web-hosting service called PrimeHost, described later in this chapter ("In Business? Let PrimeHost Maintain Your Site").*

A Web page consists merely of a text file saved in a format called HTML, for Hypertext Markup Language (for a little background, see "How Is that Page Put Together? HTML" in Chapter 6). Figure 6-1 in the last chapter shows a page of HTML that consists of text (the words you see on a Web page) and "tags" (the formatting applied to the words you see when you browse the Web). Your browser's job is to turn tags—such as <b> for bold and <i> for italics—into an informative and attractive page, with links to other pages (Figure 6-2). In this chapter, you'll learn to create a Web page that anyone on the Internet can visit. Using AOL's Personal Publisher 2, the HTML is generated automatically for you.

This chapter starts out with a discussion of My Place—the free disk space AOL makes available to every member. It's helpful to know a little about My Place before you start storing and maintaining your Web pages there. Next, you'll learn the nuts and bolts of Personal Publisher 2, a simple way of making an attractive Web page. Then you'll learn to refine and perfect Personal Publisher 2 pages using some of the easy HTML effects possible with Personal Publisher itself or with an HTML editor such as AOLpress. Finally, and most fun, you'll see some of the cool pages created by other AOL members.

THREE WAYS TO MAKE A WEB PAGE

On America Online you basically have three ways to create a Web page:

- By hand, using a text editor such as SimpleText.

- Using an HTML visual editor such as AOLpress.

- Using Personal Publisher 2, which focuses strictly on the content you want to convey and not the HTML methods you use to convey it (they are automatically handled for you). Pages created with Personal Publisher can be refined using one or both of the other methods.

Making Web Pages by Hand

Many Web pages are created with nothing more than SimpleText, a program included with every Macintosh. You can create an HTML file with *any* text editor or word processor, for that matter, then upload it to a computer on the Internet to which other people have access (see "Publishing and Maintaining Your Web Pages in My Place"). However, to use a text editor or word processor requires that you hand-code the HTML.

Using an HTML Editor

A much easier way to make a Web page is to use an HTML editor, many of which are available on AOL in the software libraries. These graphical tools work in much the same way as your word processor. You simply type in the text, highlight it with your mouse, and apply HTML tags by clicking buttons on a tool bar or selecting items from a menu. The editing tool adds the HTML tags for you, makes sure they're correct, and usually lets you view the results as others will see them *before* you actually publish your pages. Such software makes it possible to generate a page using "visual" methods (menus, buttons, etc.), but you still need to know at least a little HTML to use the tools effectively.

 To download AOLpress, go to keyword: AOLpress and click on Download Free AOLpress. AOLpress is described later in this chapter.

Point and Click with Personal Publisher 2

The easiest way to make a Web page on America Online is with AOL's Personal Publisher 2 service. Once you've created a page, you can edit it either manually (using SimpleText or another text editor) or using an HTML editor, as described in "Using an HTML Editor to Edit Your Page (AOLpress)." An additional advantage of Personal Publisher 2 is that it provides a complete publishing solution—the ability to both create and edit pages and to make them available for people on the Internet to see. The next few sections look at My Place, the publishing area on AOL's computers that makes Personal Publisher possible.

PUBLISHING AND MAINTAINING YOUR WEB PAGES IN MY PLACE

ONLY ON AOL

My Place is the free Internet-accessible disk space available to every AOL member. Each AOL screen name automatically receives 2 Mb of storage space on an AOL computer called **members.aol.com**, in a directory called */screenname* (for example, **members.aol .com/answerman**). Since every account can have five screen names, that makes a total of 10 Mb per account. It's not yet possible to allocate space between screen names, but it's easy with Personal Publisher to link to pages in several locations. With up to 10 Mb of disk space to store your files, you can make an awesome Web site!

Tip   *The beauty of My Place is that you can use it to publish any Web page, whether you've made it with Personal Publisher, an HTML editor, or by hand. Many AOL members create and publish Web sites in My Place without even using Personal Publisher! The member pages highlighted at the end of this chapter were made with a variety of tools, including Personal Publisher and AOLpress.*

To get to your area of My Place, go to keyword: My Place. You will see the My Place window, the useful information hub shown in Figure 7-1, from which you get access to AOL's Web-publishing services, as well as to My Place.

Click Go To My Place to directly access the 2 Mb of disk space allocated to your screen name (Figure 7-2). If you'll be using this area actively, you should probably save it as a Favorite Place by clicking the heart in the title bar. Now My Place will be available in the Favorite Places folder on your tool bar.

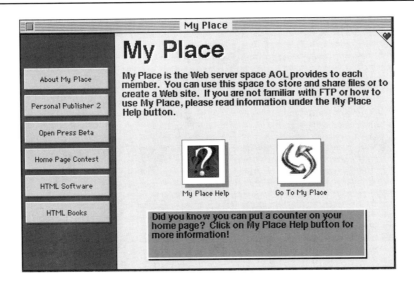

FIGURE 7-1   Start here to access your area in My Place

My Place is an FTP server (computer) that doubles as a Web (http) server. FTP is the Net's File Transfer Protocol—the chief way of storing and moving files around on the Internet (see Chapter 8 for the full story). While you ordinarily use FTP to *download* (retrieve) files from public FTP sites to your computer, My Place is chiefly used for *uploading* (copying) files from your computer to AOL's FTP server. From your area of My Place, *others* can download them as either Web pages or free-standing files (word-processed documents, sound files, programs, whatever). You can't use My Place to upload to any server other than **members.aol.com**.

Think of your area of My Place as a chunk of hard disk on someone else's computer where you can store files. Unlike the hard disk on your Mac, however, My Place can be made available to *other* people, once you publish your Web pages.

When you visit My Place (Figure 7-2), you'll find a handy FAQ (Frequently Asked Questions) document, which answers some basic questions about My Place. Double-click the file, then click View File Now. Read the FAQ and, if you want, print it. You'll also notice a **/private** directory, where you can store files that only you have access to.

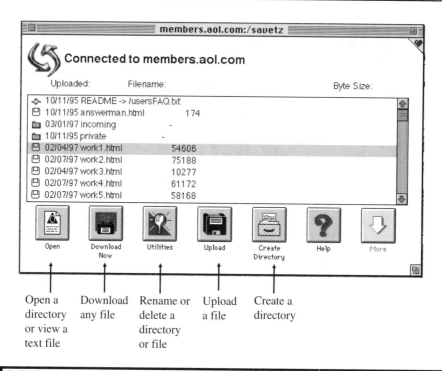

Open a directory or view a text file	Download any file	Rename or delete a directory or file	Upload a file	Create a directory

FIGURE 7-2 My Place is your storage space on an AOL computer; it's where you publish your Web pages

Uploading a File to My Place

When you use Personal Publisher to publish your page and any associated files (such as image and sound files), your work is automatically *uploaded* to My Place; that is, it's copied from your hard disk to My Place. You can also upload your files one at a time, when (for example) you change an image or add a sound file. And you can upload files that you want to make available to others simply as files and not as a part of a Web page.

Before you begin uploading your files, you must know the name and type of the file you want to upload and the location of the file on your hard drive.

1. Go to keyword: My Place, and click on GoTo My Place. Or, use Favorite Places if you've already saved My Place in your Favorite Places folder.

2. Open (double-click) the directory *into which you want to upload a file.* Click the Upload button. The following window comes up:

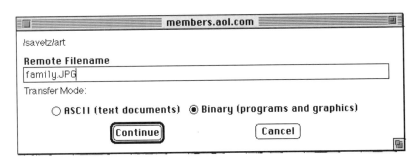

3. Type in the name that you want the file to have in My Place (yes, you first name the "target" name, then the "source" name). If the file is for your Web page, note that HTML files must have filenames that end in *.HTM* or *.HTML* and that graphics files must end in *.GIF* or *.JPG.* You must also select a Transfer Mode. Select ASCII for your HTML files and Binary for everything else.

Tip *Keep all of your filenames short and memorable. To avoid confusion and simplify management, use the same name in My Place that you use on your hard disk. If you upload a file with the same file as an existing My Place file, the existing file will be replaced by the new one.*

4. Click on Continue to bring up the Upload File window.

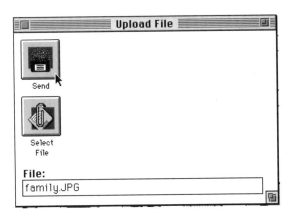

5. Click Select File, and browse your hard disk to select the file you want to upload. Click on Select.

6. Now click Send. The File Transfer window comes up and tracks the progress of the upload. When the transfer is complete, your directory window (Figure 7-2) is updated to display the file you just uploaded.

You can now view the file you've uploaded. Its URL is

```
http://members.aol.com/screenname/directoryname/filename
```

or, if you didn't put the file in a directory, the URL is

```
http://members.aol.com/screenname/filename
```

Managing My Place

Like your own hard disk, your space on My Place can easily get cluttered. If you're using large multimedia files, it can fill up. Just as you do with your hard disk files, you manage your Web files by creating directories, moving files around, and deleting files and directories as required to keep things orderly.

Creating a directory is useful if you either want to keep related information together (such as graphics files) or if you want to allow people to upload a file to you. To *accept* files, you'll need to create a directory called **incoming**. Bear in mind that an incoming directory can become clogged with files and eat up the 2 Mb of hard-disk space available to you.

Creating a Directory

Revisit the My Place shown in Figure 7-2 (yours will look different, of course, since you'll create it with *your* screen name):

1. Click Create Directory, to bring up the following little window:

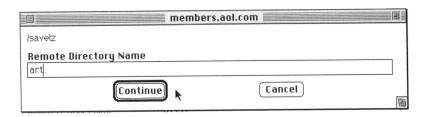

2. Type in a directory name (in this case, *art,* because it's for graphics files), and click Continue. A message confirms the creation of the directory. Click OK. Create more directories if you want, then close the little window.

 My Place (like FTP) is case sensitive, and uppercase letters precede lowercase letters (an Art *directory would come before an* art *directory).*

Deleting a Directory (or File)

Select the directory (or file) you want to delete, click Utilities, and click the Delete button. Be sure you want to delete it because there is no way to undelete! Once it's deleted, it's gone.

Renaming a Directory (or File)

What if you incorrectly entered the remote filename? Change it as follows: simply select the file, click Utilities, click Rename, and type in the correct name and click Continue.

USING PERSONAL PUBLISHER

Personal Publisher 2 makes it easy to create a Web page in a couple of minutes, adding images, sounds, backgrounds, and links to other Web sites. It's also easy to edit and refine your page, using either Personal Publisher 2 or an HTML editing tool such as AOLpress or SimpleText.

Let's get started and see how easy it can be. Keyword: PP2 takes you to the window shown in Figure 7-3.

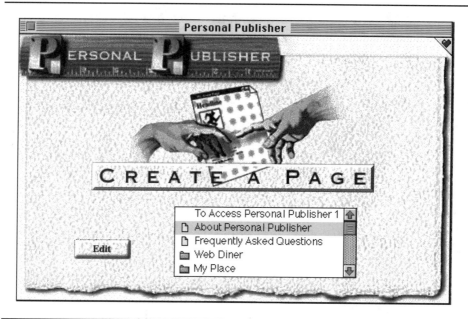

■ **FIGURE 7-3** Here's where you start creating a page or editing one you've already made

Click the big Create a Page button to bring up the window shown in Figure 7-4, where you choose one of three templates (Personal, Business, or Greeting) for your page. A *template* is a set of pre-defined *elements*, such as text, background, and images. All you do is "fill in the blanks" with the specific words and pictures you want to appear on your page. These elements include HTML tags, which are created for you behind the scenes. You never have to worry about the actual tags, because Personal Publisher creates them for you automatically. However, if you do want to create or edit your page either manually or with an HTML editor, you *may* need to work with the actual HTML tags.

When you choose either the Personal, Business, or Greeting template and make a page, you're guided through the process and prompted to add one element at a time. For the sequence of steps, see "Creating the One-Minute Web Page (Give or Take)." Even when you select No Template, you're really using the same elements that are in the templates. The only difference is that with No Template you're not

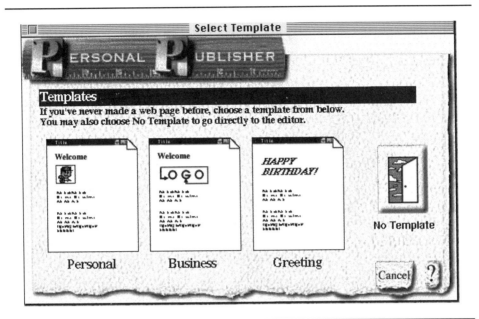

FIGURE 7-4 Choose a template and start publishing

7

guided through the process; you can choose any elements, any number of times, in any order, and you also get the choice of an additional element: HTML, which gives you the ability to add HTML code if you're comfortable with it.

No matter what template you use, you choose from the following elements in building your page. For a more complete overview of the page elements you'll *experience* when you browse the Web, see "A Page and Its Elements" in Chapter 6. You can't create every Web element with Personal Publisher, but it's a good place to start, and you can add fancier elements later, using AOLpress or another tool.

- *Title* and *heading*. A *title* is the phrase that appears in the title bar of the browser when someone looks at your Web page. A *heading* is the headline, the big bold letters on the Web page itself announcing its purpose or welcoming the reader (or whatever).

 In HTML-speak, a Personal Publisher heading is a level-one head (<H1>...</H1>).

- *Background.* Ever since the release of version 3.0 of the AOL software, AOL's browser has supported "backgrounds," a color or pattern, also called *wallpaper*, that covers the entire page and against which all text, links, and images appear. Personal Publisher lets you choose a colored background from a "color wheel," which you'll use in Step 2 below. With Personal Publisher 2 you can also choose a repeating image as a background. Or, you can choose not to use *any* background.

Tip *Nothing is more annoying than an overdesigned Web page whose loud background makes it impossible to read the text. Personal Publisher 2 gives you the ability to choose type color as well as background color/pattern. If you choose any colored background or any repeating image for your page, make sure to choose a text color that will display clearly. That may take some trial and error. Also, if you use a background on one page, you may want to use it on all pages—to give your site (collection of pages) a common overall look and feel.*

- *Image.* Personal Publisher 2 lets you choose a graphics file from either its own library of clip art or from your own hard disk. For more about using image files, see the "Images on the Web: What You Need to Know" box. "Image" is really shorthand for multimedia file: you would also use Personal Publisher's Add Image window to add a sound file or video clip to your page.

- *Personal information.* Short bits of unformatted personal or business information about you, your business, your hobbies, or anything else you please. Depending on the template you choose, you'll get one or two small text boxes for your personal information. You can change the names of the categories if you want, *hobbies* to *favorite sports*, for example, but you can't format this text (bold, italics, etc.) unless you play with the HTML directly or use an HTML editor.

- *Body text.* A personal statement, formatted in bold, italics, or other effects, with live links to your favorite AOL and Internet resources. If someone's viewing your page and clicks a link, he or she will go directly to the resource that you're pointing to. Of course, only members will be able to link directly to any AOL areas you link to (see Figure 7-5).

The three templates—Personal, Business, and Greeting—all use a mix of these elements, which differ slightly between templates. For instance, the images available in the Business template are a shade more serious than the images in the Personal

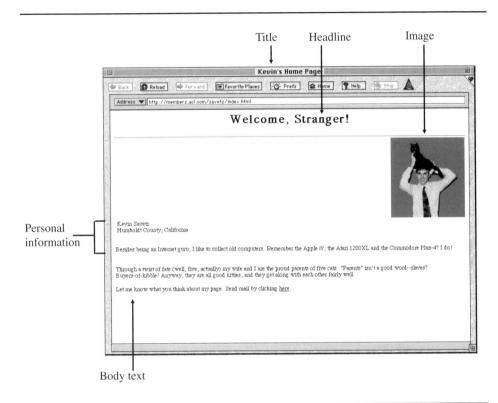

Title　　Headline　　Image

Welcome, Stranger!

Personal information

Body text

FIGURE 7-5 A personal page (my own) built with Personal Publisher and viewed with AOL's browser

template, and the Greeting template offers a box for a personal message as opposed to the more structured "personal information" (name, address, hobby…) in the Personal and Business templates. When you use No Template or when you edit *any* template, you get the option of adding "raw" HTML if you want to achieve a specific effect. The "Adding HTML" section provides the details.

Despite these differences from template to template, when you edit a page, you can change the wording, the images, and the links, and even change the order of elements so that you can get the same results no matter which template you choose!

The upshot: It really doesn't matter which template you use. Pages made with the Greeting template do offer some extra images, but the Personal and Business templates give you a choice of almost identical elements. A page made with any template is easily editable into a page that could have been made by the others.

Creating the One-Minute Web Page (Give or Take)

Let's see how easy it can be to make a personal page. Here's how I would make a personal page with Personal Publisher. I've kept the page self-contained and short; you can get as ambitious as you want!

1. Go to keyword: PP2, and click Create a Page. At the Select Template window, select Personal. The first window that comes up asks you for two pieces of information: your page's title and its heading.

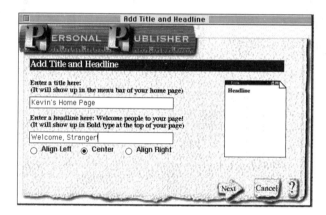

You don't *have* to supply either a title or a heading, but both provide important context to anyone viewing your page. Fill them in as appropriate. Click an alignment for your heading. (I chose Center.) Click Next.

2. Add a background, use a repeating image as a background, or choose no background.

If you want to use a repeating image, you can choose a "tile" from AOL's clip art collection or select an image of your own—a photo, say—that you have converted into a graphics file and saved on your hard disk. (See "Images on the Web: What You Need to Know.") Feeling earthy today, I'll use "Sand Tile" as my background by clicking the Image button and double-clicking on Sand Tile in the listbox. Click Next.

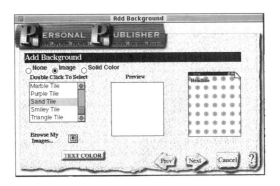

If you choose Solid Color for a background, you see a color wheel. Click on the small color wheel icon to bring up the standard Mac color wheel. With it, you can pick any imaginable color for your Web page's background. Slide the slider to change the intensity, then click on the wheel to choose a color. When you're ready, click OK.

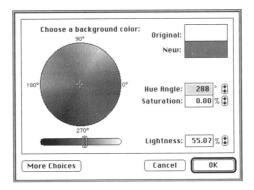

When you're happy with the color for your background, click Next.

Note   *If you ever want to revisit a previous screen in Personal Publisher, click Previous. If you want to do something else and quit the current page, click Cancel. Any elements you have created are automatically saved by Personal Publisher, even if you cancel.*

3. Now I'm going to add an image. Again, I can choose one of AOL's clip art files or browse my hard disk for an image of my own, which is what I'll do in this case. I click Browse, search for an old picture I happen to have handy on my hard disk (me with Arlo the cat on my head), and double-click.

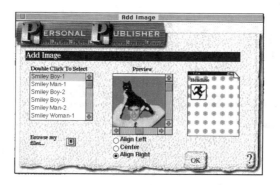

When using your own image, it must be in GIF, ART, or JPEG format. Trying to use other formats, including PICT, won't work. I click the Align Right button because I want the image to be on the right edge of the page. Click Next.

Images on the Web: What You Need to Know

Your Web pages can incorporate any graphics files of the common formats: GIF and JPG, as well as the less common ART format. In practice, you'll just be using GIFs and JPGs. How do you *get* such files?

■ For *clip art and generic art*, you could start at one of the AOL image archives such as the Mac Graphics Art Forum (keyword: MGR) or the "quick clips" that are downloadable from the AOL Web site at **http://www.aol.com/images/public/**.

■ More interested in using *your own images, especially photos*? But how do you turn those photos into files? Turning a photo that you can view into a file that a computer can use requires a scanner—a piece of hardware that works like a photocopier but that produces a file instead of a paper copy of an image. For more information about scanners and scanning, visit AOL's Digital Resource Center (keyword: Digital Imaging) and see the next item.

■ If you don't have access to a scanner, take a quick trip to your local service bureau and rent one for a few minutes.

■ *Make your own art.* If you're proficient using a tool such as Adobe PhotoShop, you can make your own graphics and backgrounds and save them as GIFs or JPGs suitable for uploading to My Place and using in your Web page.

■ *Get art on the Web.* Finally, don't overlook the Web itself as a source of free art, beginning with Web Diner host Laurie McCanna's Free Art Site at **http://www.mccannas.com/**. And Images from Planet Earth (**http://www.nosc.mil/planet_earth/images.html**) also includes files you can use in your Web page.

■ If you find graphics in some other format that you would like to use, you can convert them to GIF or JPEG easily with a fantastic shareware utility called GraphicConverter. You can download it from the Web at **http://members.aol.com/lemkesoft/**.

 Make sure not to use any image or other content that is copyrighted!

4. Now it's time to add Personal Information. For the Personal template, I get two boxes, one asking for my "name and location" and the other for my "hobbies and interests" (similar to the AOL Member Directory). I oblige:

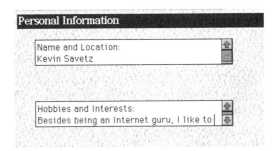

If you prefer not to provide this particular information, delete the text and use one or both boxes to say anything you want. Note that formatting (bold or italics, say) isn't possible here but is possible if you later refine the page using an HTML editor such as AOLpress. Click Next.

5. Now I'm asked to provide Body Text—up to 32K (a lot) of freeform text, formatted more or less as I please, with any *links* I want. I'm going to keep it simple, since I know that very few people like to read lots of text on the Web. Any text I enter can be formatted in the same way an e-mail message sent to someone on AOL can. Notice the small button above the Body Text box—click it to bring up the familiar Format tool bar. Just enter some text, highlight it, and click a button on the tool bar to apply bold, italics, or other effects. If it's unclear what the formatting buttons do, see "Adding Pizzazz to Your AOL Mail" in Chapter 3. The formatting "controls" are identical.

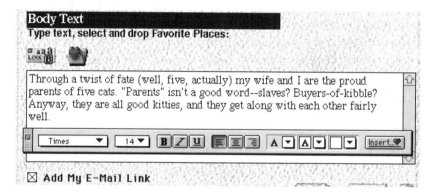

This window conveniently gives complete access to your Favorite Places folder, so you can easily create links from your personal page to one or many of your favorite places. First press the Favorite Places button to the right of the tool bar activation button. Now type and select your text, then drag a Favorite Place from the list onto your selected text. Or drag the Favorite Place anywhere in the Body Text window, and the title of your Favorite Place becomes the clickable text on your Web page.

I've placed a check box in the "Add My E-Mail Link" box, so readers can send me an e-mail message by clicking a "mailto" link (if their browser can automatically call up an e-mail program, as the AOL browser can).

6. To wrap things up, let's view the page by clicking the View button. A mini-browser comes up and displays the page just created as anyone on the Web would see it.

If you like what you see, click Publish. Your Web page and all associated image files are now uploaded to My Place, where your creation can be viewed by the entire world.

If you're not 100 percent satisfied with the results, click Edit Page and read on; the next sections are devoted to editing your Web pages.

Note   *With Personal Publisher 2, everyone with Web access, whether on AOL or the Net, can see your page. If you're serious about publishing for the world, you should get into the habit of viewing your page on different browsers (at least Microsoft Internet Explorer and Netscape), since there are many subtle differences in each that can cause the appearance of your page to vary. When you publish, Personal Publisher 2 names your main page **index.html**, so if you already have a page in PP2, it will be overwritten. PP2 notifies you if you're about to overwrite a page and lets you rename it.*

What's My URL?

When you create a page using Personal Publisher 2, this page and all associated files are kept in My Place, described earlier in "Publishing and Maintaining Your Web Pages in My Place." Anyone on the Internet can view this page by using your URL: **http://members.aol.com/*screenname*.** In place of *screenname*, your friend should type your actual screen name. It's not necessary to specify a file in the */screenname* directory, since browsers automatically attempt to open **index.html** if a page is not specified in a URL.

Sharing Your URL

On AOL, you can mail someone a hyperlink to your home page. The recipient must also be using AOL 3.0 or above to use the hyperlink. Start by going to your Web page—pick Keyword from the Go To menu and enter your URL—and adding it to your Favorite Places by clicking on the arrow in the title bar. Now to share your page:

1. From the Mail menu, select Compose Mail.

2. Fill in the To and Subject fields, then, in the message field, select the word or phrase that is related to your site and that you want to hyperlink.

3. From the Format tool bar, press the Insert ♥ button.

4. Drag the name of your Web page from the Favorite Places window onto the selected text in your message.

5. Finish composing your message, then click Send Now.

 You must edit your page using the same computer you used to create it.

The window contains two big sections: Add Contents and Edit Contents. Let's start with the Edit Contents section, on the right. This section lists the elements you created, in the order you created them. You can do two things here. You can double-click any element to tweak it—change the text, image, background, or whatever. Or you can rearrange the elements by clicking and dragging any element above or below any other element. This will change their order in the actual page after you publish it. You'll be able to see your changes immediately in the View window.

The buttons in the Add Contents section take you to one of the windows you saw in the previous section. Here you can *add* a headline, a background, an image, or whatever. Any element you add will go at the *end* of the elements listed on the right side of the window in the Edit Contents section. Feel free to move them around though.

If the list on the right is getting cluttered or you've inadvertently added elements that you don't want (which is easy to do), select the unwanted elements and click Delete. If you don't delete them, they will show up on your Web page.

Click View to see your page with the elements you've added or edited. Again, if you're not quite happy, click Edit Page; if you like what you see, return to the View page, then click Publish.

Editing a Page You Created a While Ago

You can edit anything you've ever done in Personal Publisher 2 by clicking the little Edit button on Personal Publisher's main window, shown in Figure 7-3. You'll see the following scrolling window, which gives you access to your life's work on Personal Publisher:

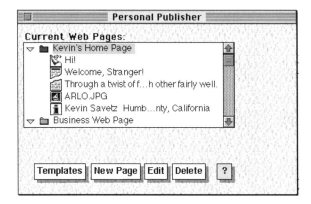

Select any element and click the little Edit button to bring up the mini-browser (pictured in Step 6 in the section "Creating the One-Minute Web Page"), in which you view and from which you can edit or publish a page. Click Edit Page to tweak it until it is perfect, view the page again, and either do some more editing or publish it.

Adding HTML

The HTML button of the Add Contents section of the editing window (Figure 7-6) gives you your first opportunity to add some raw HTML to your page. HTML is very simple in principle, but it can get as fancy as you want it to. It gives you the flexibility to add just about any effect you want to your page. Some of these effects are described in "Next Step: Refining Your Page."

Learning HTML on AOL

HTML is simple in concept but is getting more and more complex to master because of the many powerful features available to Web designers, such as tables, forms, precise font control, plug-ins, and JavaScript. This chapter won't teach HTML because there's not enough room, but here are some places to start if you want to learn HTML on AOL.

- For instruction in person, Web Diner (keyword: Web Diner) and Web University (keyword: Web University) offer HTML classes at regularly scheduled times in chat rooms.

- For a selection of books about HTML, go to keyword: My Place, where you can click a button to go directly to a selection of tutorials and reference guides, all for sale on AOL.

- On the Web itself many tutorials and references are available. A classic place to learn correct HTML is the *Beginners' Guide to HTML,* at the following address:

```
http://www.ncsa.uiuc.edu/General/Internet/WWW/HTMLPrimer.html
```

And Tim Berners-Lee, one of the inventors of the World Wide Web, has written a classic called the *Style Guide for Online Hypertext*, to help you write *good* HTML—tags that convey your content as effectively as possible:

```
http://www.w3.org/pub/WWW/Provider/Style/Overview.html
```

- At keyword: Answerman, click on the Answerman Focus button. There you'll find pointers to online HTML tutorials and links to free books on the Web, many of which are all about HTML.

NEXT STEP: REFINING YOUR PAGE

Now that you've created your Web page, you may want to know how to add Personal Publisher features to it that are not as obvious as the basics; or maybe you want to add features that you can't get by using PP2. For example, you may wish to add a visitor counter to your Web page. Or you may want to do something as simple as

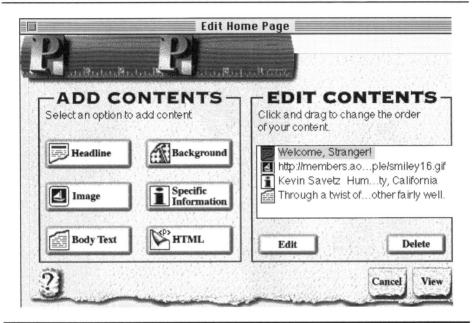

FIGURE 7-6 Add an element or double-click an element you've already created to edit it

bolding some of your text. The following sections barely begin to show how far you can go in building and refining a Web page. For more ideas, read the "Learning HTML on AOL" box or visit AOL's Web Diner (keyword: Web Diner), Web University (keyword: Web University), or Desktop and Web Publishers forum (keyword: DWP).

Adding a Visitor Counter

A counter is a neat gimmick many people use to keep track of the number of people who access their main Web page. Actually, it just keeps track of "hits," not unique individuals, so if someone visits your page twice, the counter will say *00000002*. To add a visitor counter to your Web page:

> **1.** From the PP2 main window, click Edit, select the page to which you want to add a counter, and click Edit. Your page now shows up in the view window. Click Edit Page to bring up the window shown in Figure 7-6.

2. Click the HTML button in the Add Contents section and type the following text in the big box, including the quotes and brackets:

```
<img src="/cgi-bin/counter?screenname">
```

Substitute your screen name for *screenname*, for example:

```
<img src="/cgi-bin/counter?ellamp">
```

3. Click OK to return to the Edit Home Page screen.

Note *HTML elements go at the end of the list of your Web page elements (see Figure 7-6). You can add more than one HTML element in a single box, but the elements will be adjacent on the actual page. Thus, it's a good idea to add HTML elements separately, so you can position them on the part of the page where they will be most effective.*

This little "script" won't really work until you've published the revised Web page to **members.aol.com**. Once it's published, you can open your Web browser and view your counter at the bottom of your Web page. You're visitor 00000001…of many more, I hope. By the way, don't forget to add some text before the counter, saying something like "Since June 1, 1997, you are visitor number…to my site. Thanks!"

Tip *To see other counters, visit one of the sites with counters at the end of this chapter. For more about counters, visit **http://members.aol.com/wwwadmin**, where you will find more useful tips for building interactive elements such as guestbooks, counters, and e-mail links.*

In Business? Let PrimeHost Maintain Your Site.

AOLpress can be used as a stand-alone application, but it also forms part of the more complete business service offered by AOL's PrimeHost (keyword: PrimeHost). *Hosting* allows a business to lease the technology required for an Internet presence on a monthly basis, so it can focus on business while the hosting provider focuses on the technology—running the server, installing the software, leasing fast connections to the Internet, and ensuring security.

> AOL's PrimeHost service offers companies fully supported publishing software (AOLpress), AOLserver software with a fully integrated database, and simple Web-based methods of gaining access to and information about your site. Customer service and technical support staff are always on hand to assist you with any questions you may have. PrimeHost also facilitates domain name registration if you want your own Internet address, such as **sunnyprospects.com**.
>
> For more information, visit keyword: PrimeHost.

Adding Animation

The simplest way to add animation to your Web Page is to use an animated GIF, a file that contains several images shown in sequence when someone views the page, creating the impression of animation. There are other more advanced types of animation you could use, plug-ins such as Shockwave, but they require more advanced software to create, and it's not a good idea to assume that users around the world will have the required gear (for more on plug-ins, see Chapter 6).

Tip *You can find animated GIFs at Web Diner (keyword: Web Diner). These GIFs are indistinguishable from regular GIFs since they have the same GIF extension. An excellent guide to animated GIFs has also been published by an AOL member: **http://members.aol.com/royalef/gifanim.htm**.*

As in the previous sections, you view and edit the page to which you want to add the animated GIF. In the Add Contents section (Figure 7-6), click Image. Click Browse and search for the GIF file on your hard disk, then double-click to select it. Back in the Add Image window, choose the proper alignment. Now, click View again and make sure that at least one frame of your animation appears on the page. Click Publish.

Now anyone viewing your Web Page with a browser that supports animated GIFs will be able to see your creation and is sure to be impressed by your technical prowess.

Using an HTML Editor to Edit Your Page (AOLpress)

Astonishing things are possible on the Web these days—animation (from animated GIFs to RealVideo, Shockwave, and beyond), CD-quality audio, Java-driven ticker tapes, and much more—but many of the coolest effects require that you get comfortable with HTML code, either manually (using a text editor like SimpleText) or graphically (using an HTML editor such as AOLpress).

Caution *Once you start editing an HTML page using tools other than Personal Publisher 2, you can no longer use Personal Publisher 2 with the file, so make sure you're comfortable with "going it alone" if you plan to use another tool!*

Let's take a quick look at an HTML editor you can get for free on AOL (see Figure 7-7). At keyword: AOLpress, you come to information about both PrimeHost (AOL's Web-hosting service for commercial Web sites) and AOLpress. To use AOLpress, you must download and install the program following the online instructions.

To use AOLpress, you can start with a blank slate to build a Web page—but you might find it easier to start with something that you're already familiar with. If you created a page with Personal Press, a copy of that page is on your hard disk in System Folder: Preferences: America Online: Personal Press 2: *Screen Name:* index.html.

To edit the file with AOLpress, choose Open from the File menu and navigate to the index.html file. The page will be displayed in the AOLpress window (Figure 7-7).

Here are some of AOLpress's features you might want to explore:

■ A graphical tool for making multicolumn, multirow structured tables, without the hassle of coding them in HTML. AOLpress doesn't yet provide simple tools for making forms, however.

■ Access to your HTML code just in case you want to tinker with it (Figure 7-7). A great way to learn HTML coding is to go back and forth between the graphical image of your page and the underlying HTML. You can edit in either mode—graphical or HTML.

■ A spell checker.

■ An easy way to link to other pages and anchors. Just highlight text, click the Links button, and type in or navigate to a URL. A *link* takes you to the top of a page, an *anchor* to some point you specify within a page. Although with Personal Publisher it's easy to link pages to your main page (**index.html**) using the Body Text element and dragging Favorite Places onto highlighted text, it's a bit more complex to create and link several levels of pages within your Personal Publisher site. You also can't create anchors with Personal Publisher 2. AOLpress makes it easy to create, link, and edit the links between pages in a complex site.

■   Really simple tools for making bulleted and numbered lists. Just select the text and click the appropriate button. Personal Publisher 2 doesn't let you create lists unless you know a little HTML.

■   Complete control of the appearance of text. For instance, the Personal Information can't be formatted in Personal Publisher 2, but you can format it in AOLpress.

Some of the most powerful capabilities of AOLpress can be used with PrimeHost but not with Personal Publisher 2. For instance, with AOLpress you can save files on a remote server and edit a large complex set of pages and links directly from your desktop computer! The related ability to view the remote files as a "mini-web" is a powerful tool for remote management of a more complex site. For the full scoop on these and other features, excellent online help, including a FAQ and a tutorial, is available from the AOLpress Help menu.

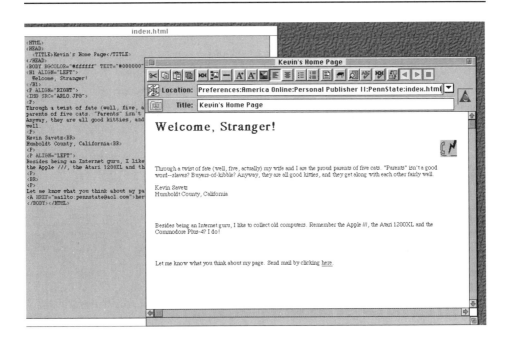

FIGURE 7-7   AOLpress lets you edit your page graphically or manually, by giving you direct access to the HTML script

Remember, after you create a page with AOLpress or any other editor, you'll need to upload it to My Place to publish it on the Web.

TELLING THE WORLD ABOUT YOUR SITE

So, you've built a page. What good does it do if no one knows it exists? There are search engines and directories that collect the URLs of Web sites around the world; for others to find your page, it has to be available on one of these search engines. Chapter 9 is devoted to the whole topic of searching. Some search engines automatically "crawl" the Web looking for sites, but most also accept URLs sent to them by Web builders eager for promotion.

The Submit-it service lets you provide information about your site to more than 300 search engines and directories at the same time, letting you reach both the general sites (like Excite) and the highly specific ones (like SBA's Guide to Computer Vendors). You can get more information at **http://www.submit-it.com**.

In Web Diner (keyword: Web Diner), check out the Web Developers Resource Center for a great deal of additional information about how and where to publicize your Web site.

Curious about who's actually linking to your page? Infoseek's Ultraseek (available at keyword: Infoseek) offers a "Link search" by which you can enter your URL and find out who's pointing to it! That in itself is a good way to seek out like-minded people on the Internet.

Adding a Guestbook

A guestbook gives you a way of collecting information about people who visit your site. You can find out what they think of the site, for example, or what they'd like to see you add. Making a guestbook requires the use of forms. AOL now supports the *CGI* (Common Gateway Interface) capability required for members to include guestbooks in their Personal Publisher sites. For complete instructions and sample scripts, see **http://members.aol.com/wwwadmin/guestbook/guestbook.htm**.

SHARING YOUR PAGE WITH OTHER AOL MEMBERS

The most important thing to do with your new Web page is to share it with others. Many individual areas throughout AOL offer collections of home pages created by AOL members who frequent the area and share interests. Here are a few AOL areas with big collections of member home pages, to which you can add yours:

- Digital City, Washington D.C.
  (**http://www.digitalcity.com/washington/Page1.html**)

- InBusiness (keyword: Inbusiness)

- Web Diner (keyword: Web Diner)

- Surf Shack (keyword: SurfShack)

The rest of this chapter is devoted to a handful of sites created by AOL members, and it shows what makes them stand out.

Learning Web Design on AOL

Mastery of HTML in itself doesn't make for good design. Here are some places on AOL where you can learn the fine points of the new art of Web design:

- Web Diner (keyword: Web Diner), led by Tim and Laurie McCanna, ostensibly focuses on designing business sites, but in fact offers abundant and free Web advice of very general interest, organized in areas with mysterious names such as "Byte of the Day" and "Blue Plate Specials." Visit Web Diner daily to figure out what the names mean—it's worth it. The tutorials are particularly useful for anyone taking the high road and writing their own HTML scripts. There's also a ton of graphics elements to download from Web Diner.

> - The Desktop and Web Publishers' forum (keyword: DWP) brings together design-minded desktop publishers and Web builders.
>
> - Jill Ellsworth's InBusiness forum (keyword: Inbusiness) is a great place to get pointers for making effective business pages—not *how* to make pages, but how to make them *work*.

NOTABLE AOL HOME PAGES

Here's a very small sampling of pages made by AOL members that were chosen because they exemplify one or another aspect of strong Web design. No offense to the countless excellent member pages not included here!

Out of Balance

http://members.aol.com/gerrym22

Winner of Member Home Page contest.

Creativity is the main theme of the site shown in Figure 7-8. Graphic artist and former Lockheed engineer Gerry Manacsa's home page combines rich graphic design and good readable content. The content is personal as well as creative. Manacsa, born in the Phillipines, displays his graphic art and photographs, and he shares his musings about surfing, life, and Fellini. The site has won more than 20 Website awards, including Point Communications' Top 5 percent award.

This site was published in My Place. It was created with Adobe PageMill, an HTML editor.

Ovarian Cancer Links

http://members.aol.com/mind2body/mind2body.html

Winner of Member Home Page contest.

This site, created with Personal Publisher, demonstrates the Web's powerful way of delivering essential information to a specific group of people, in this case women who have experienced, or who want to learn about, ovarian cancer. The one very

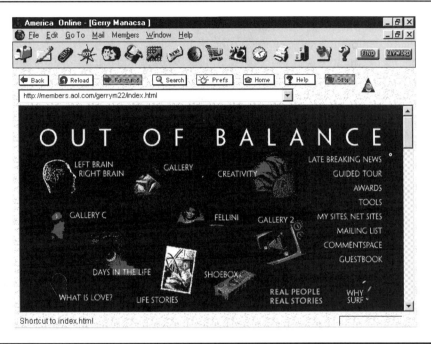

FIGURE 7-8   Gerry Manacsa's beautifully balanced—and very personal—page

long page consists only of links to information about ovarian cancer. They're carefully selected, attractively grouped, and effectively centered on the page. The categories include "your medical team," "support," "legal, finance & insurance," "general cancer links," and "general health links." This is a "must see" Internet resource for both women with this disease and their families.

Womanist is to Feminist...

http://members.aol.com/nshour

This site, recommended by the good people of the Web Diner, comes from Nancy Shour, who teaches American Studies and African-American literature at Union College in Schenectady, New York. It shows how someone can incorporate the Web into their actual work, in this case, into the literature classes Professor Shour teaches.

Shour uses her Web site as a resource for her students as well as a way of reaching a broader, "virtual" audience of anyone interested in the literature she clearly loves.

She uses both the Web and e-mail to make her class interactive and to publish students' work. She posts extra credit projects on her site, giving her students an incentive to explore the site and the larger Web.

A distinctive feature of the site is that it is self-contained—it has a clear purpose and just about all the content it needs to achieve that purpose—so readers aren't distracted by links that take them to other sites. Where there are links, as in the set of selected links to sites devoted to the writings of Alice Walker, they are fully annotated, so Shour adds value and probably unique content to the links themselves. Much of the site was hand-built with a text editor, then uploaded to My Place.

FROM HERE...

Browsing gives you somewhat passive access to Web sites. With Personal Publisher, My Place, and all the HTML tools and resources at your disposal on AOL, the Web comes alive. If you ever have a question about Web publishing, make sure to frequent Web Diner or another Web-related AOL forum.

FTP, the subject of the next chapter, is the final Internet service covered in this book. It's the other, more interesting side of My Place. While My Place lets you upload to a single site (**members.aol.com**), FTP lets you download millions of files from thousands of Internet sites.

Chapter 8

Downloading Software from AOL and the Internet

In human terms, the work you do at the computer consists of the letters you send people, the reports you prepare for work, and the images and videos you like to view. You might use your Mac to keep track of everything from recipes and resumes to jokes and addresses—perhaps you also play games and do your bills on it.

Files are the way your Mac stores and keeps track of all this information. They make activities such as playing games and paying bills possible. Everything you do on a computer requires files, that is, discrete pieces of data and software, each with a name and a location on a hard disk or other kind of "storage medium." Even the AOL software is just a huge set of program and data files.

On the Internet, the FTP (File Transfer Protocol) service gives you access to millions of publicly available files on every imaginable subject. America Online provides everything you need to search for files available by FTP and to help yourself to files you like—images, games, software of every type, even public domain literary classics, and much more. AOL's own software collection includes programs you can use to run the files you download via FTP.

Note *Copying a file from a distant Internet computer to your own computer is called* downloading. Uploading *means moving a file from one computer to another, usually from a home computer to a "larger" computer.*

America Online has a built-in FTP program, or client, that enables you to go quickly and easily to any publicly accessible FTP site. AOL's World Wide Web browser gives you an alternative way of going to FTP sites. Which do you use? Whichever you prefer. This chapter makes a case for the browser as a great tool for finding files to download, and the client as a great tool for actually retrieving them. This chapter begins with an introduction to filenames and types, and ends with an overview of the vast software libraries available on America Online itself.

UNDERSTANDING FILES AND FILE TYPES

Every file has a filename and a file type. Simply, a *filename* is the name that a person gives a file so that others know what it is for.

A file's *type* determines what it is for—a word processing document, an application, an image file, and so on. How do you tell a file's type? Click on the file's icon in the Finder and select Get Info from the File menu. This will tell you what application the file works with or if the file is an application itself.

   chapter 8

Kind : Microsoft Word document
Size : 62K on disk (5,918 bytes used)

   America Online
America Online v3.0

Kind : application program
Size : 2.1 MB on disk (2,259,730 bytes used)

You may also be able to tell what a file is for by looking at the extension of the filename. The extension is the part of the filename after the period. Not all Mac files have extensions, but many of the files that you'll get with FTP will.

Table 8-1 provides an overview of the most common file extensions of Mac and Windows files you'll encounter on FTP. The file extension can tell you a great deal, including:

- Which operating system you must have in order to use the file. Unix, Macintosh, and Windows are the primary operating systems for which files are available on the Net. Generally speaking, as a Macintosh user you won't have much use for non-Mac programs. Text files can be read on any platform. Many other types of files, such as graphics and sounds, can be used on different types of computers, if you have the software that can view or play them.

- Whether the file is *binary* or *text*. It used to be that when you downloaded a file using FTP, you had to specify whether it was binary or text. Now, AOL's FTP program takes care of that for you. Basically, everything is a binary file except "pure" text files (ASCII). If you know a file is text, you can count on being able to use it with any word processor. If it's binary, you must use a specific program. Table 8-1 provides some guidance, as does the "Using the Files You Download: Graphics, Sounds, and Beyond" section.

8

■ Whether the file is compressed. A *compressed* file has been run through a special program to reduce its size and thus decrease the download time. A compressed file may also be archived, which means that several related files are bundled together into one file. This makes downloading easier and assures that you'll get all the files that you need—such as a program and its documentation. When you download a compressed file, you must decompress it before you can utilize it.

Note   *Compressing a file is a good way to reduce the size of large individual single files. Thus, a compressed file can harbor a single file (such as a large graphics file) or be an archive of many files (such as several chapters of this book).*

■ What the file contains. Reading a file's name can tell you whether the file is a program; whether it's an image or a video file; whether it's compressed; whether it's a Word or Excel document; and more.

File Extension	Platform Compressed and Archived Files	Comments and Usage Notes
SIT	Macintosh	A compressed file produced by the StuffIt program.
SEA	Macintosh	Self-extracting archive file: run a SEA file, and all its parts are automatically uncompressed.
CPT	Macintosh	A file compressed with Compact Pro. May be decompressed with Compact Pro or StuffIt Expander.

TABLE 8-1   Standard Mac and Windows file types, platforms, and categories, with usage tips

File Extension	Platform	Comments and Usage Notes
HQX (BinHex)	Macintosh	A binary file that's been encoded and converted into a text file; requires another program (such as StuffIt Expander) to be decoded.
UUE	Unix, Windows, Macintosh	A binary file that's been converted to a text file for transmission, especially via newsgroups; requires another program (such as StuffIt Expander) to be decoded, but can be done automatically by AOL's FileGrabber (Newsgroups only, see Chapter 5)
ZIP	Windows	A zipped file. Zipped files are compressed, usually for Windows, but may be decompressed on a Mac.
EXE	Windows	Windows executable file; useless on a Mac.
Image		
GIF	Macintosh, Windows	Stands for Graphics Interchange Format, an Internet standard; requires no special software to view on AOL.
JPG, JPEG	Macintosh, Windows	Stands for Joint Photographic Experts Group; requires no special software to use on AOL.
ART	Macintosh, Windows	Compressed Johnson-Grace image file; requires no special software to view on AOL.
PICT	Macintosh	A Macintosh-standard graphics format. Can be viewed with SimpleText or a graphics utility.

TABLE 8-1   Standard Mac and Windows file types, platforms, and categories, with usage tips (*continued*)

File Extension	Platform	Comments and Usage Notes
PDF	Macintosh, Windows	Delivers highly formatted documents; requires Adobe Acrobat (freeware) to use (keyword: Adobe).
BMP	Windows	Bitmapped picture file in Windows format. With special software, may be viewed on a Mac.
PCX	Windows	Windows format graphic. Can be viewed on a Mac with special software.
Sound		
AU	Macintosh, Windows	Sound file; plays using AOL browser or a sound utility.
MID	Macintosh, Windows	MIDI (Musical Instrument Digital Interface) sound file, played with a Sound utility (such as Sound Machine).
WAV	Windows	Windows sound file; can be played with a sound utility.
Video		
MOV	Macintosh, Windows	QuickTime. Requires a player, available at keyword: Mac video (or keyword: MVD).
MPEG	Macintosh, Windows	MPEG movies require special software and a speedy computer to view.
Text		
TXT	All	Text file; open in any word processor, SimpleText, or AOL's text editor.

■ **TABLE 8-1**   Standard Mac and Windows file types, platforms, and categories, with usage tips (*continued*)

Why Use FTP?

FTP is perhaps most useful as a way of making available a specific file or set of files that many people want—a software product or group of sound files, for example. In

Where's It At? Files and Directories

On the Internet, a full filename consists of a name of the actual file and the path to that file. A path is the exact directory (a directory is another name for folder) where the file is located, including any directory to which it belongs, any directory to which that parent directory belongs, and so on up to the computer's root directory. A path starts at the top level of a site, or root, which is similar to the root of your hard disk—it's the folder that contains all other folders.

For example, the Anarchie program (a feature-laden FTP program you can run with AOL) is itself available by FTP and is located at dozens of FTP sites around the world. One of the myriad places the file is available is at an FTP server at Apple Computer. The directory path to the file is **mirror.apple.com/mirrors/Info-Mac.Archive/comm/inet/anarchie-201. hqx**. The Anarchie file is contained in the **inet** directory, which is contained in the **comm** directory...which is contained in the **mirrors** directory, which is on a computer named **mirror.apple.com**.

projects where people live in different places, FTP can be a superb means of allowing limited access to files and keeping files secure. In addition, FTP is the only practical way of uploading files to a place from which they can be referenced by a Web site you are building (see Chapter 7). Lastly, it's easier to "publish" a single file (a program, say) by uploading it than to design and maintain a Web page just to make the file available.

8

Ways of Retrieving Files over the Internet

FTP may be the most efficient way of transferring files, but it's only one of many. You can also get files in the following ways:

■ **Files via Newsgroups**. Using a technique called UUEncoding, many people insert binary files into newsgroup messages by converting them to encoded text files. As an AOL member, you can use FileGrabber to effortlessly download and decode these files. See Chapter 5.

- **Files via the World Wide Web**. The Web has become a popular way of making files available to a broad audience—not just as files to download onto your own computer, but in context. A NASA Web site, for example, lets you view images taken by the Hubble Space Telescope, together with information about the Hubble mission (**http://spacelink.msfc.nasa.gov/**). Web pages today are loaded with files—RealAudio, Shockwave, image, video, and more (Chapter 6). Many Web publishers prefer the Web as a way of distributing files, because its easy to include information describing the files, and possible to incorparate tools for searching the files.

- **Files via E-mail**. If you need to send a file to a single person or a small group of people, attaching it to an e-mail message can be easier than using FTP, because your recipients are more likely to have (and know how to use) an e-mail reader than an FTP client. Your messages' recipients do need "MIME-compliant" mail readers, however, as explained in Chapter 3.

FINDING FTP FILES

Unlike the Web or newsgroups, FTP is not meant for browsing. "Finding" a file usually means searching for a specific file. With FTP, browsing makes little sense, since you cannot usually tell what's in a file from its name. Moreover, almost all FTP sites limit the number of connections—the number of people who can use the file directories at that site at the same time.

Tip *Browsing an FTP site (going up and down the directories in search of interesting files) can be bad netiquette, because it ties up limited FTP server resources and can prevent access by people who know exactly what they are looking for.*

On AOL, you traditionally have two ways of discovering the FTP sites where a certain file resides:

- Using AOL's FTP search technique (the Search for FTP sites button at keyword: FTP)

- Using a Web-based file search tool.

Tip   *If you're ever in desperate need of a file, start with AOL's file libraries, which are available all over the service. The files can be searched at keyword: FileSearch (see "Downloading Files from America Online," later in this chapter).*

Anonymous and Non-anonymous FTP

When you use AOL or a Web-based file search tool to look for files, you're really searching only for publicly accessible files (after all, you don't have access to other peoples' private files.) These public files are available by a method called *anonymous FTP*. All this means is that the site is open to the public: you log on with the user name **anonymous** and your e-mail address as a password. You don't even have to do that yourself: logging on is handled automatically by the FTP client or browser.

USING NON-ANONYMOUS FTP   On AOL, when you use the FTP client, there's a little check box: "Ask for login name and password." (Go to keyword: FTP, click on Go To FTP, then on Other Site.) If you don't want to use anonymous FTP, put a check in the box, and, when you arrive at the FTP site, you will be prompted to supply a user name and password. This form of FTP is an excellent way of sharing confidential files with a small group of people.

8

AOL's Search FTP Service

At keyword: FTP, you can do a search of FTP sites by clicking the button labeled Search for FTP Sites. It seems easy, and it is. This search looks through a gigantic text document consisting of a list of FTP sites. This valuable list, maintained by Perry Rovers of the Netherlands, provides information on every known anonymous and non-anonymous FTP site in the world: its address, location, and date last modified.

Unfortunately, this document does not provide a list of the files actually available at these sites—only a characterization of the kind of files available and the names of some of the most popular directories. Here, for example, is a description of the files available at **brawls.mindlink.net**:

```
audio and textual information related to arcade one-on-one
fighting video games (Street Fighter II, etc.); pictures.
```

Thus, with AOL's FTP Search service, you can search by subject, but you also have to assume that the people who run FTP sites make the same assumptions you do about categorizing files. Sometimes you'll get good results, sometimes not: a search for "funny" turns up three sites, a search for "maps" reveals 73.

Here's how to go to an FTP site that you find using the FTP Search service:

1. Write down the FTP site name, then close the Search window.

2. From the main FTP window, click the Go To FTP button.

3. Click the Other Site button. Type in the FTP address in the Site Address box and click OK. An information window appears; read it and click OK. For help getting around an FTP site, see the "Navigating an FTP Site" section.

Using the Web to Search for Files

There are many Web sites that make it easy to search for a particular file, or just browse the treasure troves of goodies available for your Mac—applications, sound files, fonts, programs for kids, utilities—just name it and chances are excellent that you can find a program somewhere on the Internet that will help your Mac do it. These Web tools catalog and organize FTP sites so you can find whatever you're looking for.

FTP Site Names

FTP site names are a type of domain name (see Appendix B). They consist of little bits of text separated by periods, or dots. For instance, the FTP site **ftp.aol.com** is the site name of a set of FTP computers in the *aol.com* domain. Sometimes you'll find FTP sites beginning *ftp*, just as you'll find Web sites beginning *www*. Organizations with multiple types of services are likely to follow this convention, hence **www.aol.com** and **ftp.aol.com**. But, in general, you can't tell an FTP site from its address.

Info-Mac HyperArchive

The Info-Mac archive is an FTP site that contains a vast and well-organized collection of Macintosh software. It is truly one of the treasures of the Internet. The

Info-Mac HyperArchive Web site (Figure 8-1) makes a good thing even better. Visit the site at **http://hyperarchive.lcs.mit.edu/HyperArchive.html** and you'll see why. Just type in a few words describing what you're looking for and the HyperArchive will serve up a list of matches. You don't have to know the exact name of the file, because the HyperArchive quickly pores over small descriptions of each file—called *abstracts*—looking for words that match your search.

You can also just browse the archive by category: fonts, games, printing, and so on. When you've found what you want, just click on the filename and the browser will download the file to your Mac.

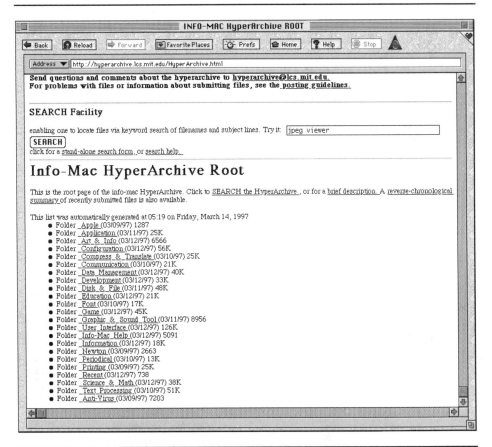

FIGURE 8-1   The Info-Mac HyperArchive Web site

Shareware.com

Shareware.com (at, you guessed it, **http://shareware.com**) is a much busier site—from a usage standpoint and a design standpoint. This site (Figure 8-2) has a lot going on, including a fast search interface, a free weekly newsletter, a "title of the day," and a way to see the most popular downloads.

This site is not devoted exclusively to the Mac, but it does make it easy to search for only Mac files. When you find the perfect file, one click will cause your browser to download it.

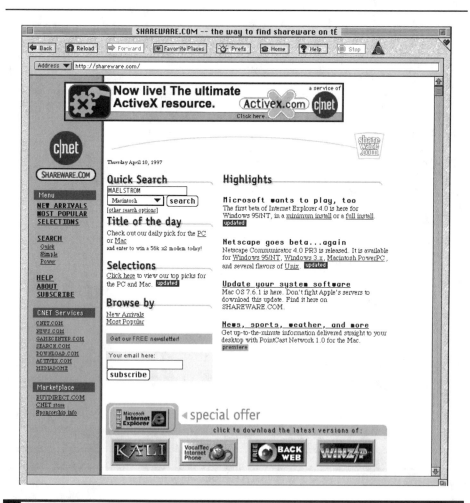

FIGURE 8-2   Shareware.com

Filez.com

At first glance, Filez.com (Figure 8-3) bears a resemblance to Shareware.com, featuring a flashy interface and an elegant search capability. But Filez.com is its own animal, with its own copious selection of links to FTP sites around the world. Filez.com claims to index some 45 million files. Not all of them are for the Mac, but the search tool lets you search through only the files that you're interested in.

You can also browse files by categories, such as movies and multimedia, system utilities, fonts and publishing, and hobbies. This resource is at **http:// www.filez.com**.

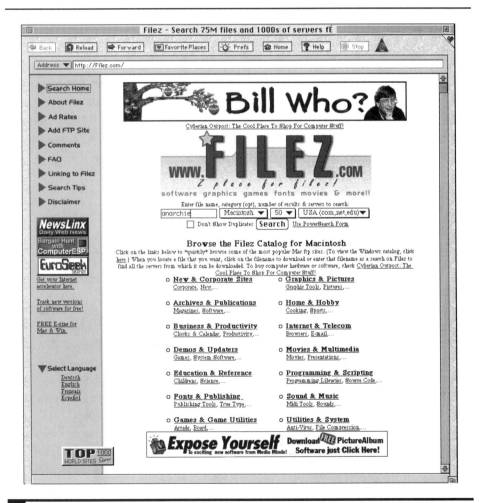

FIGURE 8-3   Filez.com

Archie

Archie is the original tool for searching for files on the Internet. Back before the Web was even around, Archie was the only tool that cataloged files available via FTP. Back in the "old days" of the Internet, you could only access Archie via Telnet or e-mail. Today there are a variety of Web interfaces that you can use to search Archie.

Archie searches a list of files and directories available at anonymous FTP sites around the world. Its gargantuan list is updated approximately weekly.

Using Archie's Web interface (Figure 8-4), all you do is type a keyword (part or all of a file's name) and click the Search button. The Web site contacts the Archie server, asks Archie to search its list of files, and presents the results back to you as hypertext. To go to an FTP site and get the specific file at that site, just click the link.

The fact that Archie is still around is testament to its lasting utility—but in many ways Archie hasn't kept up with the times. First, Archie searches are often unacceptably slow. Second, the only way to search is based on the filename—if you know what you want but not what the file is called, Archie won't be a big help. Finally, Archie doesn't offer a way to search for just Macintosh files.

Some Archie servers on the Web are at:

■ **http://hoohoo.ncsa.uiuc.edu/archie.html**

■ **http://www-ns.rutgers.edu/htbin/archie**

■ **http://cuiwww.unige.ch/archieplexform.html**

Here, Snoopie!

One tool I like these days is an Archie-like service that's available only on the Web at **http://www.snoopie.com**. It's quick and easy to use and it provides the following information for each site it returns: host (FTP site), directory, filename, size, and date of last modification. Snoopie is nice and fast, but there's no way to limit your search to Macintosh files, so a search for "Maelstrom" (a great game for the Mac) reveals many hits for a different program for the Linux operating system that happens to have a similar name.

According to John Matzen, Snoopie's Network Engineer, Snoopie currently indexes approximately four million files.

SNOOPIE
The Internet's Most Comprehensive File Search

Enter Query disinfectant

Maximum number of Results 50 ▼

[Submit]

Power Search

Submit comments to support@dtr.net

Archie Request Form

| ⬅ Back | 🔌 Reload | ➡ Forward | 💟 Favorite Places | 🔆 Prefs | 🏠 Home | ❓ Help | 🛑 Stop | ▲ |

Address ▼ | http://hoohoo.ncsa.uiuc.edu/archie.html

Archie Request Form

This is a form based Archie gateway for the WWW.
Please remember that Archie searches can take a long time...

You might just want to check out the Monster FTP Sites List instead.

Some people have requested the source to this script. Its available from http://hoohoo.ncsa.uiuc.edu/archie/AA.pl.

What would you like to search for? SPACE

There are several types of search: Case Insensitive Substring Match ▼

The results can be sorted ⦿ By Host or ◯ By Date

The impact on other users can be: Nice ▼

Several Archie Servers can be used: University of Nebraska ▼

You can restrict the number of results returned (default 10): 10

Press this button to submit the query: [Submit] .

To reset the form, press this button: [Reset] .

Guy Brooker
guy@w.estec.esa.nl
Martin Koster

What is archie ?

"Archie" is a database of anonymous ftp sites and their contents. The software for it was written by the "Archie Group" (Peter Deutsch, Alan Emtage, Bill Heelan, and Mike Parker) at McGill University in Montreal, Canada, and they maintain the database as well.

"Archie" keeps track of the entire contents of a very large number of anonymous ftp sites, and allows you to search for files on those sites using various different kinds of filename searches.

8

FIGURE 8-4 Archie

USING FTP THE AOL WAY

Searching for files and downloading using the Web browser is convenient. The browser can offer one-stop shopping for files: with most of the Web's file searching tools, once you've found the file that you want, you're literally one click away from downloading it.

There is another way to get files that are available via FTP: by using AOL's built-in FTP software. The browser is clearly better for searching for files, but AOL's built-in FTP (Figure 8-5) has some features that the browser doesn't do as well, or at all. So it pays to know how to use both.

Here are some reasons to use AOL's built-in FTP software (keyword: FTP) rather than the browser:

■ America Online maintains "mirrors" of many of the most popular FTP sites. (A mirror is an exact copy of a site.) Because the most popular FTP sites are usually very crowded with other users, it can be difficult to access them when you want to do so. Most FTP servers only allow so many users at once. If it's too crowded, you'll be turned away. When you want to download from one of these popular sites, the built-in FTP software will actually connect you to the private mirror site instead. This way, you have access to the exact same files, but you'll never see an annoying "Server is busy, try again later" message.

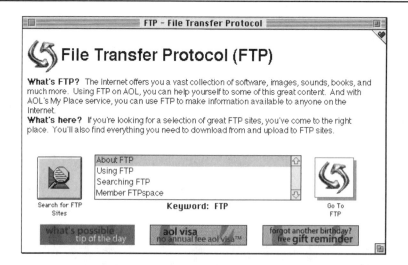

FIGURE 8-5   AOL's starting point for downloading files from the Internet (keyword: FTP)

■ The browser can be slower in connecting to and navigating FTP sites, and slower in downloading files.

■ The browser was created primarily to access the Web, not FTP sites. As a result, when you use the browser, you don't get all the options you get when you use keyword: FTP.

■ AOL's FTP client gives you the ability to explicitly request non-anonymous FTP (see the "Anonymous and Non-anonymous FTP" box). The browser does not gracefully handle non-anonymous FTP.

■ AOL's FTP client will estimate how long it will take to download a file (see "A Word About File Size").

■ The FTP client lets you finish an FTP download later. You can even queue up several FTP downloads—even files from different sites—for transfer late at night or when you're away from the Mac. The browser can't do that.

■ Using the Download Manager (from the File menu), you can keep track of files you've downloaded using FTP.

■ AOL's FTP client also lets you upload files—to My Place or to any other FTP site that allows uploads—something you can't do using any browser.

For these reasons, once you know where the files that you want are, you may want to close the browser window and use the built-in client to do your downloading.

Before using AOL's FTP client to download a file, make sure you have the file's exact directory path. Here's a useful exercise: retrieving StuffIt Expander, an essential program for uncompressing many of the files that you'll download from the Internet. Using one of the FTP search tools reveals that the file is available at **ftp.aladdinsys.com/pub/stuffit_exp_40_installer.bin**.

Follow these four broad steps below to retrieve any file:

1. **Connect to the site.**

   ■ Go to keyword FTP.

   ■ Click on the Go to FTP button. The Anonymous FTP screen comes up.

- Since the site that we want to visit isn't one of the most common ones available from the Favorite Sites list, click on the Other Site button.

- In the Site Address box, type **ftp.aladdinsys.com**, or whatever the FTP address is. Do not put a check mark in the "Ask for login name and password" box. Click Connect.

When you connect successfully with the FTP site, a message comes up from the FTP site itself. The welcoming message sometimes includes the name of someone at the site—the FTP administrator—to contact if there's a problem. This message can also provide the names of mirror sites—FTP sites with the same files as this one, if this one is busy. Read the message, then click OK.

2. **Navigate to the directory that holds the file you're seeking.**

   After getting past the welcome message, you'll find yourself looking at the top level of the FTP site—something like the main folder of your hard disk, the point at which you start looking for a file on your local computer. Where to start? In general, it's best to start in the *pub* directory—the publicly accessible directory of files available by anonymous FTP. As luck would have it, that's exactly where the file we're after is. Open the directory by double-clicking. A new window opens showing the contents of the pub directory.

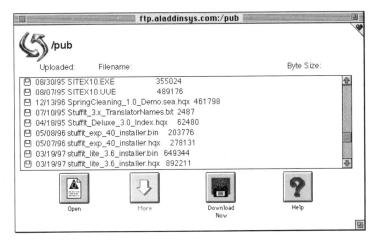

For other files, you are likely to have to open many directories as you burrow deeper in search of a particular file.

3. **Locate the file**

Identify the file you're seeking in the directory you've opened. You'll see three pieces of information for the file: the date it was uploaded, its filename, and its size in bytes. For more information about file size, see the text box called "A Word about File Size."

Note   *Throughout an FTP site, you'll notice the dates when a file or directory was last modified. Just because a folder was last modified on one date doesn't mean it won't contain files with more recent dates. So, don't be put off by old dates. Likewise, if a site's README file is really old, the individual files at the site may still be more recent; it's just that no one's updated the README file. Finally, the file least likely to be changed—the opening message—can make a site seem old, even if many individual files are up to date.*

To see how long it will take to download a file, select it and click the Open button (note that you're not actually opening the file, just getting some information about it).

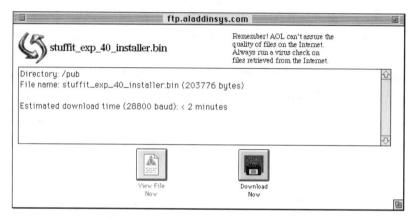

For text files, you'll be able to read the text without saving the file to your hard disk; just click View File Now.

Many FTP sites have README and INDEX files that can provide valuable information. A README file may provide advice about choosing and using files. An INDEX file usually provides a listing of files in a directory, sometimes with short descriptions. Using AOL's FTP client (keyword: FTP), you can read both types of file right on your screen without downloading the files to your hard disk. Just select the file and click View File Now.

A Word about File Size

A file's size matters because it determines, together with your modem speed, how long it takes to download a file. File size is also important because files take up space on your hard disk, and even a huge hard disk can become filled up if you do enough downloading.

Files are measured in *kilobytes* (about 1,000 bytes, the unit for measuring data). A thousand kilobytes is a *megabyte*.

On AOL, when you double-click a file at an FTP site to download the file, you first get a window that estimates how long it will take for the file to download. With a 28.8 modem, the estimated download for a 2 Mb file is *<18 minutes* or under 18 minutes, while for a 40K file it's under 1 minute.

In general, programs and binary files (such as sound, image, and video files) tend to be large (over 50K). Text documents are usually under that size, but you'll find Word documents weighing in at more than 100K and MIDI sound files of only 10K. Always bear in mind how much content you're getting for the time it takes to download a file. A 1 Mb WAV file might, for example, play for a minute, but so will a standard 15K MIDI file.

Using the Finder, you can learn the size of any file on your system (with the Get Info command); you can even arrange files by their size in order to find out which ones are taking up the most space (by picking By Size from the View menu.) That's the place to start if you're running out of hard disk space and need to make some room!

4. Download the file.

If you want a copy of the file, click Download Now. You'll be prompted to give the file a filename and folder on your hard disk. It's always a good idea not to alter the original filename and to download the file into a directory that won't be lost or accidentally deleted. The only time to change a filename is when there's already a file with the same name in the directory where you are downloading it. (You might want to create a special folder just for downloads.) After you've selected a directory on your computer and clicked Save, you'll see AOL's thermometer box telling you how much of the file has downloaded and how many minutes are left until it is complete:

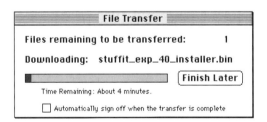

If you decide that you don't want to wait for the file to download right now, press the Finish Later button. The file will be added to your Download Manager for later retrieval. If you know that you want to download several files via FTP, you can use this trick to queue each file up one by one. Then, run an Automatic AOL session, click Signoff When Done, and go to dinner, to bed or to the opera. When you return, all the files will be waiting on your hard drive.

AOL's Download Manager

AOL treats downloading as pretty much the same kind of activity no matter how you initiate the download—whether it's from one of AOL's many software libraries, a newsgroup, an e-mail message, or with the built-in FTP software. Download Manager lets you adjust the way you use FTP in several important ways:

- Whether image files you download (GIF, JPG, and ART) are automatically displayed as they download.

- Whether compressed files that you download are automatically uncompressed when you log off.

- Whether the downloaded compressed file is kept on your hard disk after it's uncompressed.

To see your Download options, go to the Members menu, select Preferences, and click on Download.

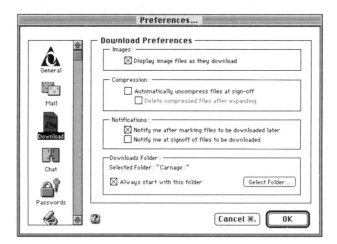

Need more help? A large set of answers to frequently asked questions is available at keyword: Download 101.

Navigating an FTP Site Using the AOL FTP Client

Navigating an FTP site means going "up" and "down" a directory path, from the top (or root) level to lower-level directories and any subdirectories. When you double-click a folder to open it, you open up a new window and go down a level. Close that window to go back up.

If you find yourself at an FTP site in search of a specific file, and the file does not appear to be where you expected, the best bet is to start with the pub directory and to browse downward through appropriate subdirectories. When you're using anonymous FTP, a pub directory is usually accessible from the root (top) directory.

NAVIGATING FTP WITH YOUR BROWSER

One reason for using the AOL browser to navigate FTP is that the only window that's ever open is the browser itself. Another reason is that the AOL browser itself can play many kinds of files (see Chapter 6). Or, maybe you just prefer the browser!

To use the browser, you need to know an FTP site's address, to which you tack on an *ftp://* at the beginning. For instance, typing **ftp://ftp.amug.org/** in the browser's location (URL) box and pressing RETURN takes you to a large FTP site at the Arizona Macintosh User's Group (Figure 8-6).

When a file or folder is clickable, the mouse cursor turns into a pointing finger. Open a folder and its contents appear on the screen. You can move back up a level by clicking the Back button. Or you can move back by clicking on any of the directory names in the "Path" line near the top of the browser window.

To download a file, just click it! You'll see the Mac's familiar Save As window. Give the file a name and select a folder on your hard disk, and click Save. The browser displays the progress of the download at the bottom of the browser window. When the entire file has arrived, the AOL logo stops spinning. You're done!

Note   *You can't use that browser window for anything else during a file transfer—doing so will cancel the download. (The browser will warn you before allowing you to do this by mistake.) But you can open another browser window—click the mouse button in the browser window and hold it down for a second. In the menu that appears, choose Clone Browser Window. Use the window that appears to further explore that FTP site or the Web while the other file downloads.*

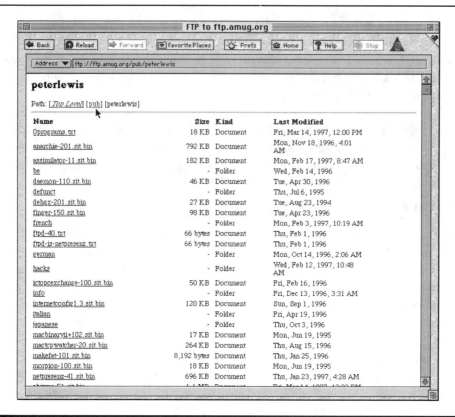

FIGURE 8-6   Viewing an FTP site from the browser. Notice the links on the Path line, which allow you to jump backward through a site with a single click

USING THE FILES YOU DOWNLOAD: GRAPHICS, SOUNDS, AND BEYOND

Many files that you download using the FTP client require an additional piece of software in order to use them. Sounds require a sound player so you can hear them, videos require a video player to watch them, and so on. There's one exception: images. When you download the most common types of image files using FTP, they'll display on your screen. Even so, you may want a more sophisticated program for viewing and editing your downloaded image files.

VIRUS ALERT

However you download a file—using the FTP client or the browser—you need to be careful about viruses! Every file you download from AOL has been checked for viruses—nasty little programs that can harm your programs and data. But files that you get from the Internet using FTP have not necessarily been checked for viruses. You need to check them yourself.

With one exception, viruses can only be spread by applications. One of the best (and cheapest—it's free!) programs for finding and eradicating viruses on the Mac is called Disinfectant. It is available from many FTP sites and in AOL's software libraries (keyword: FileSearch).

The exceptions to the rule are viruses that are spread in documents, by programs with complicated macro languages like Microsoft Word and Excel. Macro viruses, or "prank" viruses as they are often called, work by replacing the global template in applications like Word or Excel with a "new" global template. Any document you create or open that is normally dependent on the global template will be "infected." In addition, these macro viruses can be shared unwittingly simply by opening the document or spreadsheet. In AOL's software libraries, you can find macro virus removal programs to clean the affected files and replace the global templates.

AOL has excellent information in the Virus Information Center, at keyword: Virus, where you'll also find software for detecting and rooting out the little critters.

8

Note *Chapter 6 looks at how the AOL browser handles multimedia files displayed within Web pages. More and more, the browser itself plays multimedia files.*

Viewing Image Files

When you download an image file in one of the common formats, it displays automatically as it's being downloaded. (GIF and JPEG formats make up the overwhelming majority of the files available by FTP.) Actually, it's "progressively rendered," which means you gradually see more of the file until the whole thing is downloaded and the entire image is visible.

The first option of your Download Preferences gives you the choice of seeing images as they're downloading, whether you're using a newsgroup or FTP.

Downloading an image file automatically saves it. Once an image file has been saved, you can open it again by simply going to the File menu and selecting Open. Browse to the place where you saved the file and double-click it.

Where Do You Find Image Files on FTP?

AOL itself has great and easy-to-search image file libraries, some of which are listed in Table 8-2. If you get adventuresome, FTP has software treasures as well.

1. From the main FTP screen, click Search FTP sites and enter any keyword(s) you wish, such as **space and gifs**.

2. Double-click any FTP site that comes up for your search, and read the entry carefully. Write down the FTP address and as much file and directory information as you can glean from the site description.

3. Return to the Anonymous FTP window by closing the Search window. Click Go To FTP, then click Other Site to enter and connect to the site.

Where Do You Find Graphics Viewers on AOL?

If you want sophisticated display and editing capabilities, head for AOL's Multimedia Zone (see Table 8-2). At keyword: Viewers, too, you'll find a bushelful of recommended viewers. The viewers are screened, and like all AOL software, are guaranteed to be virus-free. For my money, the best Mac graphics viewers are JPEGView and GraphicConverter.

Using any stand-alone graphics utility or sound player, you can view images or play sounds when you're not online. Just open the program, go to its File menu, choose Open, and select the file you want to use.

Hearing Sound Files

Sound files are a bit more complex than image files. For one thing, you can't hear sounds automatically as they are downloaded from an FTP site. You must find a player—a separate program—if you want to hear a sound file.

Forum (Keyword)	Software Library & Other Features
Animation & Video (keyword: Software, click Animation & Video)	Video files and utilities for QuickTime and other formats; includes some animations and animated GIFs
Mac Graphic Arts & Animation (keyword: MGR)	Fractals, stereograms, clip art, utilities, and the like
Multimedia Zone (keyword: MMZone)	Staffed area, with message boards, and software libraries
Music and Sound Forum (keyword: Mac Music)	MIDI, MOD, WAV and other files, and much more, with sound-playing utilities and operating instructions
Mac Software Center (keyword: Software)	Browsable categories of files and utilities: Animation & Video; Business & Finance; Desktop Publishing, etc.
Mac Recommend Viewers (keyword: Viewers)	Recommended viewers for animation, image, sound, and other file types
AOL Link Center (keyword: AOL Link)	Collection of Internet applications (see Chapter 10)

TABLE 8-2   Software treasures on AOL. Many of the files you want are already there!

The solution is simple: a program called SoundMachine. This fantastic shareware application will play just about any type of sound file that you can find on the Net, including AU, WAV, and many others. SoundMachine is available in the AOL file library (keyword: FileSearch), or from the Web site **http://www.kagi.com/rod**.

 Huge libraries of sound clips as well as utilities for playing every kind of sound clip are available in the Music and Sound Forum (keyword: Mac Music).

MIDI files simulate musical instruments digitally, and they squeeze a great deal of content in some very small packages. A 15K file can run for a minute and delight any child within earshot. SoundMachine can't play MIDI files, but you can play MIDI files right from AOL by going to the File menu and selecting Open, then choosing the file. MIDI files can also be played with a little utility called MidPlay, available from keyword: FileSearch.

Watching Video Files

The first comment to make here is that video files don't quite stack up to the quality of the video on VCR. The images are jumpy, the box in which you see them is tiny (an inch or two square), and the experience is quickly over. What Hobbes said of life—that it's poor, nasty, brutish, and short—applies to video over the Internet as well. The "streaming" effect on the Web, which lets you experience multimedia as it's downloading, without special software, is a little better, but streaming video files (such as RealVideo) aren't widely available by FTP.

The common video file types available by FTP are QuickTime (MOV), MPEG, and AVI. Keyword: VIEWERS is the solution—there you can download viewer applications that can handle each of those formats. (Be sure to download Sparkle from there, a fantastic application that can handle QuickTime and MPEG files.)

Tip   *As always on the Internet, be wary of copyright violations. On a Hungarian site, I found short clips from Stephen Spielberg's movie, E.T. It may seem unlikely that the value of the movie was infringed in this way, but it's a short step from making low-quality clips available to pirating longer segments of higher quality. Were the clips illegal? Probably not. Using such files may not get you in trouble, but making them available to others is probably a bad idea.*

Grappling with Compressed Files

One common characteristic of multimedia files—sounds, images, videos—is that they're often big—500K, 1 Mb, and more. (See "A Word about File Size," earlier in this chapter.)

As a result of their size, they take up more and more space on servers, they can take a long time to download, and they can take up a lot of space on your computer. To deal with these problems, multimedia files are often physically shrunk, or compressed, before being made available via FTP. This reduces storage space at the FTP site and reduces download time. All that usefulness comes at a price, however, and you can't use compressed files until you've uncompressed them.

With Mac files, you can spot a file that's been compressed by its filename—which will end in .SIT, .CPT or possibly .SEA.

There are two ways to deal with compressed files.

UNCOMPRESS THEM AS SOON AS THEY HAVE BEEN DOWNLOADED.   To do so, you'll need a program such as StuffIt Expander. It is freely available on America Online (keyword: FileSearch) as well as on the Internet (see the earlier downloading exercise). You'll need to download the program, and run it from the Finder to install it.

After it is installed, you can use StuffIt Expander to uncompress other files that you download—just drag the compressed files on to the StuffIt Expander icon.

LET AOL UNCOMPRESS FILES AUTOMATICALLY WHEN YOU LOG OFF.   You can set your preferences to automatically uncompress files when you log off and even to delete the compressed file afterwards (thereby saving space on your hard disk.). The uncompressed files are placed in a folder within your downloads folder.

DOWNLOADING FILES FROM AMERICA ONLINE

On the face of it, America Online's collection of a hundred thousand or so files is modest in comparison to the Internet's millions of files available via anonymous FTP. But several factors make AOL's software libraries indispensable:

- FTP files are frequently available in many versions on multiple sites. The redundancy reduces the number of unique files available over FTP. Worse, the redundancy can be confusing, since it's not always possible to know which versions of a file are the best and most recent. Many of the best FTP files are available on AOL as well—and can be downloaded more quickly.

- All of AOL's files have been subject to virus checks. You can't be sure that the Net's files have been virus checked.

- Downloading files via FTP can sometimes be painfully slow if the FTP server's connection is very busy.

- Searching with many of the Web's file search tools requires that you know a filename, or at least part of its name. On AOL's software libraries, you don't need to know filenames. Instead, you can search by subject, author, date, file type, or several other criteria.

Great FTP Sites "Mirrored" on AOL

Curious about why the same files are available in so many places? Remember that the Net is a decentralized and "distributed" network. In part, there's redundancy because there's no central control, but there's also intentional redundancy in order to make sure important files will always be available in case one site is unavailable. For the latter reason, you'll find "mirror" sites of the most popular FTP resources.

AOL maintains such "mirrors" at keyword: FTP. Click on GoTo FTP. At the Anonymous FTP window, you'll see a list of Favorite Sites. The mirrors are the first ones listed: One such site is **rtfm.mit.edu/pub**, a mirror of MIT's famous archive of newsgroup FAQs (described at the end of Chapter 5). Another is **mac.archive.umich.edu**, a vast archive of Macintosh software. Between the sheer information locked in the newsgroup FAQs and the cool games, images, and utilities at the Info-Mac archive, you'll fill up your hard disk in no time.

WHERE TO FIND THE GREAT FILES ON AOL

Software, images, videos, all the utilities you need to run these files, and more, are available throughout the AOL service. Even great software such as Netscape Navigator is easily available on America Online.

Computers & Software Channel

The starting point in any search for files on AOL is the Computers & Software channel, available from the main Channel window. Here you have direct access to the Software Center and ZDNet, two large and well-categorized collections of files and utilities of every type. Also, from the Software Center, you can get help (keyword: Software Help) about every aspect of downloading files. Table 8-2 lists other AOL forums where you'll find files, utilities, and, in many cases, someone to turn to if you have questions.

Software Search

It's hard to avoid AOL's Software Search window (Figure 8-7), which lets you search an archive of more than 100,000 files. It's available in many ways:

- From the Software Center button in the Computer & Software channel click File Search.

- Use keyword: FileSearch from anywhere in the service.

- Click the File icon on the main AOL tool bar.

 Unless you explicitly request them by pressing the PC Search button, you won't see any DOS or Windows files when you search with File Search.

1. Choose one file release date: all dates, past month, or past week. Click the appropriate radio button. Searching for the last week's or month's files can filter out files that are outdated.

2. Choose a category (or several categories) of files to search for by clicking the check boxes—Games and Hypercard, for instance.

FIGURE 8-7   No need to use filenames to search for files using AOL's software library

3. If you want, you can narrow the search further by specifying a filename, author, or description of what you're looking for in the Search Definition field. Remember, you do not have to search by filename—you can type words describing what you're looking for, such as "JPEG viewer" or "Mille Bornes game."

4. Click Search to run the search. The results of this particular search appear in Figure 8-8, usefully organized by Category and Subject (short file description). Click any result to get information about the file. From the information window, you can choose to download the file now or download it later (using Download Manager).

The search service looks through the text descriptions available for each file, so files may be included because their descriptions contain a matching keyword, even if the filename does not. This can cause occasional unexpected—and unwanted—matches.

To search for a specific word in a long list of files, go to the Edit menu and choose Find in Top Window. Enter some text to search for and click Find.

Double-click any file you'd like more information about. You will get a short description of the file, information about the file's upload date and any requirements for using it.

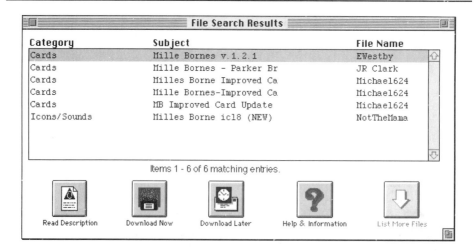

FIGURE 8-8   Files on AOL related to a classic card game

Shareware, Freeware, Commercial Software

It should be pretty obvious that the software available via FTP and on AOL differs in an important way from the software available in shrink-wrapped boxes that you buy at your computer store: it's distributed directly to you, and it doesn't cost anything (at least, there's no monetary outlay)! Otherwise, commercial software doesn't necessarily differ in quality from the variety available online. (I've gotten some wonderful programs from AOL and the Internet—and occasionally paid for commercial software that turned out to be rotten.)

Many software creators prefer to distribute software directly to users, since it reduces their distribution costs and creates the opportunity for valuable customer feedback. However, much of this software is shareware, meaning that the creator expects a nominal payment of $10 to $30 or even more. Sometimes the "free" software will lack some features until you pony up some cash. Sometimes it will expire 30 or 45 days after it's installed. Some of the best software on AOL is shareware, and many software creators both request and deserve your support (read: payment). A rule of thumb: if you use shareware, please respect the people whose hard work makes shareware possible.

Yes, some software is "freeware"—software that is completely free for you to use. If you download and use a freeware program, at least e-mail the author and thank them for their time and effort.

FROM HERE...

No other Internet service is as closely integrated into America Online as FTP. In many cases, AOL's features for working with files—Download Manager, FileGrabber, myriad software libraries, software forums—duplicate what's available on the Internet via FTP. The difference is that finding, downloading, and using files is easier on AOL than on the Net. The real value of AOL's file-related features is that they complement what you'll find on FTP; they make it easier to use the incredibly rich content available on the Internet. Since files affect everything you do on the Internet, the services you find on AOL—from the forums to the software libraries to the help resources—can enrich everything you do on the Internet.

This chapter wraps up the discussion of the Internet programs and services that are built into the AOL service. The next chapter takes a look at how to find information and people on the Internet. It moves away from how you use the tools to what you do with them, which is probably the reason for being on the Net in the first place.

Chapter **9**

Finding What *You* Want on the Internet

Browsing the globe is fun, but not everyone has unlimited time to read about things they're not that interested in. When you really need information—whether it's a recipe for pie crust, a guide to raising terriers, a phone number in Iowa City, a biography of Babe Ruth, or a local movie theater's schedule this week—how do you find it? There's yet another problem: some of the information on the Internet is not all that great. Unlike AOL, on the Internet there's an abundance of less-than-useful information; at any rate, it can be difficult to find information of direct use to you.

This chapter provides you with a guide to making *use* of the Internet, whether you need discrete facts or you're looking for people who have knowledge in their heads and information at their fingertips. You'll read about:

- A quick and easy search strategy ("Better Living Through Good Searching")

- Finding information on the World Wide Web

- Finding mailing lists and newsgroups, so you can get information from *people*

- Finding people's e-mail and street addresses

WHAT'S ON THE INTERNET AND WHAT'S NOT?

With so much information on the Net, many people assume everything is on the Net. It's not quite true. Here are some things you *won't* find on the Internet:

- **Books.** You *won't* find whole libraries or books that are still in print. Nor will you find free authoritative reference works (although you can pay for access to the Encyclopedia Britannica's innovative new service at **http://www.eb.com**). You *will* find a selection of public-domain books collected under the auspices of Project Gutenberg, including classics of English literature and Western civilization (**http://www.promo.net/pg/**). And you will find superb resources *about* current books and publishers (starting with BookWire at **http://www.bookwire.com**).

- **Really private information.** You *won't* find Social Security or credit card numbers, nor will you find tax records and employment information. Mega-reams of business information are online if you do company research, but if you need employee lists and meeting minutes—don't hold your breath. However, you *will* find street addresses and e-mail addresses for tens of millions of people and businesses.

- **Really important legal materials.** If you do legal research, you must still use a proprietary service such as Lexis-Nexis to get case law and court documentation. Although more and more of this information is going online, if you require reliable, comprehensive, up-to-date, and searchable legal records, a law library or proprietary service may be your best bet.

Better Living Through Good Searching

Sure it's easy to search the Net. But it's even easier *not* to find what you're looking for. Here are some tips for finding what you want as quickly and effectively as possible:

Step One: Ask Yourself: What do I Need? What do I Want to Know? How Will I Use the Information I Get?

- Does it have to be authoritative or hold up in court? The Web might not be the best place to start, but people on the Internet might have advice and useful information. Ask someone in a newsgroup or mailing list.

- Do you need software? Try FTP (see Chapter 8) or AOL's huge software library at keyword: FileSearch. Looking for image or sound files, or a *type* of file? Try Lycos or Hotbot, with their special file-searching features.

- Is the information discrete (the number of car washes in Houston)? Search the Web. Ask someone on an AOL message board!

- Are others likely to be interested in the question? Check out newsgroups and mailing lists, especially if your interest is long-term vs. a one-time need for a fact.

9

■ Just browsing? Then just browse! Use Excite's selective directory or a more comprehensive directory such as Yahoo.

Step Two: Choose the Best Tool.

Sometimes it's hard to know where to start, with so many Web search services. My advice? Get comfortable with a single tool, such as Excite, but understand the benefits of the other tools and use them when your standby doesn't return the results you need. Table 9-1 summarizes the relative strengths of the Web search indexes and directories.

Step Three: Turn your Question into a Query.

You have questions; computers understand only queries. How do you get from one to the other? The way you pose a query varies by search service. In general, use several highly specific words (from most to least specific). Use "Boolean" ANDs and ORs as necessary to expand or limit your search. Use filters to screen for specific results.

Step Four: Evaluate your Results.

If your query was specific, you can usually limit yourself to the top 10 or 20 sites returned by a query. If any of the sites returned are good, use a "More Like This" feature if it's available (as in Excite). If the results aren't useful, refine your query by adding more specific search terms or additional search terms. If *terriers* didn't work, try *short-haired terriers*!

Finding Information on the World Wide Web

The sheer size of the Web makes it a good place to start for many searches. Where exactly do you start your Web search? The first choice to make is between an *index* and a *directory*. The next choice is among indexes and among directories. Don't worry if this sounds complicated; it will become second nature in no time.

Engine/Directory (Keyword)	Strengths
AltaVista (Altavista)	Usenet searches; full-text searches of Web pages; powerful queries possible, but at the cost of complexity; speed.
Argus Clearinghouse (http://www.clearinghouse.net)	Contextual essays for serious subjects; access to all Internet resources, not just Web sites; ratings by experts and librarians; ratings of ratings.
Excite (http://www.excite.com)	Excellent directory of selected and reviewed sites; concept searching; Usenet searching; "query by example" with the More Like This feature, so you can zero in on the most relevant sites.
HotBot (http://www.hotbot.com)	Easy-to-use interface and full-text searches; simple, useful filters; Usenet searches; searches by media type (images, Java, particular extensions); speed.
Infoseek (Infoseek)	Searchable FAQs; excellent "essentials"—people finder, ZIP code directory, etc.; Usenet searching and browsing (but not posting) within the browser; natural language queries; speed.
Lycos (Lycos)	Directory; ratings (Top 5%); large database; people and places searches; multimedia file searches; latest news.
Magellan (Magellan)	Ratings, annotations; Green Lights (parental controls); clear editorial standards.
NetFind (NetFind)	Easy Web searching; links to other information search tools; kids only section; site reviews.
Virtual Library (http://www.w3.org/vl/)	High quality; serious content; international perspective.
WebCrawler (WebCrawler)	WebSelect, a directory; customized site reviews; backward searches; More Like This feature.
Yahoo (Yahoo)	Lots of goodies: packaging of sites by city and country; customization; kids' version; latest news by subject (politics, entertainment, etc.).

TABLE 9-1   Web search services: how they differ

9

Start Your Search on AOL

AOL NetFind, shown in Figure 6-10, was launched too late for coverage in this book. You'll find it at Net Highlights (off the Welcome screen) and behind the browser's Search button. It pulls together the best of the Net's search services: Excite (for searching the Web), DejaNews (for searching newsgroups), and Switchboard (for finding anyone's address). You also get tons of recommended sites, plus tips for making it fun and painless to search the Net.

Which Do I Use? Index or Directory?

Think of a book. Every nonfiction book usually has a table of contents and an index. The table of contents takes you to chapters—big clumps of related information about some subject (for example, "Plants of North America"). The index takes you to highly specific references (for example, "kudzu" or "azaleas").

Or, think of AOL: Channels take you to clusters of information about a big theme such as sports or entertainment. The Find button on your tool bar near the top of the main window takes you to a specific forum of the hundreds available.

On the Web you have a similar choice. *Directories* give you access to groupings of Web sites about some large subject, such as Business or, within Business, Marketing. Directories are meant to be *browsed*, which means you can poke around until you find something interesting or something you are looking for.

Indexes on the Web give you the same kind of targeted results you get with an index in a book. They are useful when you have a good idea what you are looking for—good enough to ask a specific question. The great indexes include AltaVista, Excite, HotBot, InfoSeek, and Lycos.

Using any index is pretty much the same experience: you enter a keyword in a field and click the Search button. Most indexes also ask you to indicate *what* you want to search: the Web, Usenet, or something else. But the technique's the same: type your keywords into a box, click a button, and scan a list of "results" that can run on for many pages.

Here's an important difference between the two ways of looking for information. Indexes such as Excite are created by *computers* and are useful if you know just what you are looking for. Directories are compiled by *people* and can be excellent starting places if you need general information or are just starting to learn about something. Indexes require that you know what you want; directories assume you're willing to let someone else do some of the choosing.

Search Terms and What They Mean

Here are some terms you are likely to see on the Web when you do searches.

Boolean operators: See the sidebar, "Boolean Operators Made Easy."

Browse: In a *directory*, you browse categories of sites such as Business or Recreation for whatever strikes your fancy, instead of doing a focused search for specific information.

Database: A structured list. Each row in the list has related information, for example a URL for a Web page and all the words appearing on that Web page. A database stores information and makes it available in the form of a searchable *index*.

Directory: A catalog of selected sites, often with ratings and short descriptions, arranged into topics for easy *browsing*. A good place to get an overview of a subject.

Engine: A geeky word that usually means searchable *index*. Excite is an engine, but Yahoo is a directory. A good place to start a search for specific information.

Hit: A single item returned by *query*.

Index: A listing of URLs and associated words. Indexes make it easy to quickly find a specific URL. Search for *wild roses*, and you bring up a URL for the Web page with one or both of those words on it.

Keyword: The word or words you type at a search site to indicate what you are looking for. When you're searching the Web, a keyword is what *you* are looking for. (When you use AOL, a *keyword* is the word assigned by AOL to a forum, which you type into the Keyword window in order to go directly to that forum.)

Phrase: Two or more words that together have a special meaning, such as "League of Nations" or "home run" or "Murphy's law."

Query: What you are searching for, put in terms the computer can work with. Queries can be simple *keywords*, optionally linked by *Boolean operators* (see the sidebar). A "natural language" query is one that is expressed in *your* terms, not the computer's.

9

> **Relevancy:** The computer's best guess about whether a Web page will meet your needs. Most search engines list the most relevant sites first. Relevancy takes into consideration such factors as how many times your keyword appears on a page, how many of the words you entered are found (if you entered several words), and where the words appear on a page.
>
> **Returns:** An *engine's* answer to your *query*: a list of clickable pages with a reasonable likelihood of containing the information you are searching. Returned sites are often ranked by *relevancy*. Also know as *hits*.
>
> **URLs:** The standard way of specifying the actual location of an Internet resource, such as a Web page or Gopher menu. See Chapter 6 and Appendix B.

SEARCH ARSENAL: THE BEST SEARCH TOOLS

On the next few pages you'll find short reviews of the best search indexes and directories. The reviews compare search indexes and directories primarily by how easy it is to use them—how easy it is to turn your question into a *query* that yields good results. When you compare search services, keep in mind how big they are, how fast they are, how easy they are for *you* to use, and how well they answer your questions.

AltaVista

Keyword: Altavista
http://www.altavista.digital.com/

This powerful search engine from Digital Equipment boasts a large index running on some very fast Digital computers (Figure 9-1). AltaVista does full-text searches of Web sites, and you're more likely to get good results if you follow the guidelines below. Because of its power, AltaVista is the site favored by the Yahoo directory as well as by Clnet's search.com service profiled at the end of this chapter.

Here are some tips for doing what AltaVista calls a "Simple" search; most of these tips apply to other search engines as well. For Advanced searches, help is available on the AltaVista site.

- Put phrases in double quotes, as in "guns or butter." Not putting phrases in quotes could get you in trouble in this case, since AltaVista would search for the pages with both the word *gun* and the word *butter*.

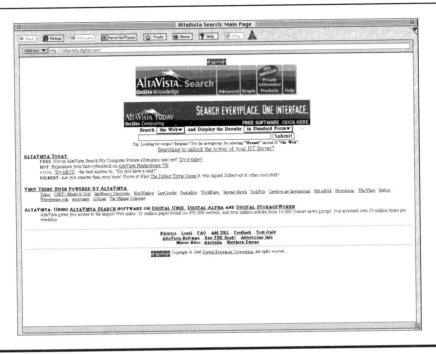

FIGURE 9-1   AltaVista, a powerful full-text searcher of either Web pages or Usenet newsgroups

■ Use several words in your query, beginning with the least common one.

■ Use capitalization and punctuation to limit a search. AltaVista interprets small letters as either lowercase or uppercase, but any word you *do* capitalize returns *only* pages containing the capitalized word. A search for "Babe Ruth's" birthday won't return the latest "hot babes" sites.

■ Precede words that must be included in the sites returned with a plus sign (+), as in *Babe Ruth +Yankees,* and words you definitely are not looking for with a minus sign (–), as in *"film noir"-pinot noir* (to use AltaVista's example).

Osborne/McGraw-Hill, publisher of the book you're reading, also publishes the official AltaVista book, The AltaVista Search Revolution *(1996). Ordering information is available at the AltaVista Web site (at the bottom of the opening page) as well as at Osborne's site (**http://www.osborne.com**).*

Since AltaVista searches the full text of Web pages, you can get good results with specific and complex queries. To use "Boolean operators" such as AND and OR, you must do one of AltaVista's Advanced Queries. See "Boolean Operators Made Easy" for some general background about words like AND and OR.

Boolean Operators Made Easy

Boolean operators were named after George Boole (1815-1864), an Irish professor of mathematics who contributed fundamental concepts to modern logic and algebra. Basically, in the Web context, "operators" are the terms AND, OR, and NOT, which, when placed between words in a search, change the way a search is conducted.

 In actual searches you don't have to capitalize them; it's OK to say "and" and "or."

These terms have two effects:

- *AND and NOT* **limit** *a search.* If you search for *bread AND wine,* you're searching for Web pages that contain both words. If you search for *bread NOT wine,* you're searching for only those pages with *bread* that don't include *wine.* You can use these operators to get fewer irrelevant sites.

- *OR* **expands** *a search.* If you search for *bread OR wine,* you're searching for pages that contain either word: pages that contain *bread* and pages that contain *wine,* a much broader search than using AND.

Not all uses of AND and OR are Boolean. Sometimes, you are actually searching for the words *and* and *or.* Suppose you're looking for pages with information about the book called *Bread and Wine,* by Ignazio Silone. You'd want to package up these three words and look only for that particular phrase. You do this by simply enclosing the phrase in quotation marks:"*Bread and Wine*".

Most search engines offer Boolean operators, and most let you search by phrase. Getting comfortable with these choices can dramatically improve the quality of your searches. *All engines differ slightly, however, so make sure to read the help text for your favorite engine.*

HotBot

http://www.hotbot.com/

HotBot is owned by the folks who bring you *Wired* magazine and the HotWired Web site. The underlying technology, called *Inktomi,* is the brainchild of a Berkeley professor who is trying to devise databases big enough to track the entire Web but fast enough to enable access by the entire Web community. By and large he has succeeded: HotBot is fast and easy to use. Of the search engines, it has, for now, one of the largest indexes.

Like AltaVista, HotBot does a full-text search, which in general means that if you search for very specific terms you are likely to have acceptable results. Using HotBot is a breeze. Figure 9-2 shows a sample search for information about a childhood syndrome called pervasive developmental delay. The search terms consists of a phrase (in quotes) and the acronym for the phrase, so I'll settle for pages containing either the phrase or the acronym. I'm searching the Web (not Usenet News) for a Boolean expression, *"pervasive developmental delay" or PDD.* I only want brief descriptions (as opposed to long descriptions or just URLs), and I apply a "filter"—I only want to see pages located on a North American server, because

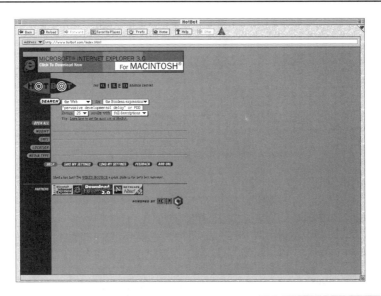

FIGURE 9-2   HotBot, from Wired Ventures, features filters and lets you search Usenet News as well as the Web

I'm especially interested in English-language resources and American organizations pertaining to the condition.

HotBot lets you use filters in conjunction with queries. With filters you specify some of the characteristics of the information you are seeking. If you're looking for information about *terriers*, you can use filters to search for information of a specific format or information more recent than a certain date.

> *Tip*   *HotBot is the only major search engine to allow you to limit your search to a specific domain or place (with places such as North America being defined as a cluster of domains).*

Currently HotBot offers the following filters:

Filter	Effect
Modify	Lets you build complex queries out of keywords, names, URLs, and phrases.
Date	Lets you specify how current you want the Web pages to be. A good way to filter out old or stale pages.
Location	Lets you specify a particular domain, such as **aol.com**, or a specific place, such as North America (all sites with top-level North American domains).
Media type	Requests only files of a certain format, such as Java, Shockwave, image, specific extension, etc.

> *Tip*   *Using the media type filter is an excellent way of tracking down Java, Shockwave, or other files that take advantage of plug-ins, as described in Chapter 6.*

Finally, HotBot lets you search newsgroup postings for specific words. If your query has results (and it probably will), you can bring up the full text of a newsgroup. However, you cannot read the rest of the newgroup for related postings, and you cannot respond to the posting with one of your own, at least not within HotBot. But clicking on the newsgroup name (which is hyperlinked in the newsgroup article) does bring up *AOL's* Newsgroups window, where you can browse and post as you wish. There's no "Back" to click to return to HotBot, so you'll have to use the Window menu to return to the Web browser.

Results in HotBot are ranked numerically (starting with 1) and by percentage, with the best results (in HotBot's estimation) at the top of the list.

InfoSeek's UltraSeek

Keyword: Infoseek

http://www.infoseek.com/

InfoSeek offers a simple interface and powerful underlying search technology. Let's focus on InfoSeek's especially strong UltraSeek engine (Figure 9-3), available at keyword: Infoseek.

When you use any index you want to know whether it's easy to ask your questions and whether the results are reliable. UltraSmart makes it particularly easy to ask a question by accepting "natural language" queries from you. In other words, you don't have to think up keywords (as in most other engines) but can simply ask your question in your own language; so, if you have a question, you already have a query! One strength of Infoseek Ultraseek is that it allows you to use common words (such as *a, to, an, the*) in phrases; some engines automatically ignore such words, even in phrases.

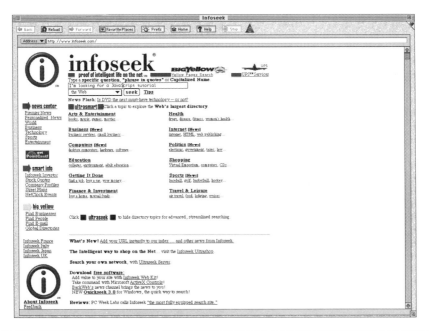

FIGURE 9-3   InfoSeek lets you ask "natural language" queries of a full-text index of more than 50 million Web sites

I compared two Web searches:

```
I'm looking for a javascript tutorial
javascript tutorial
```

and got good but different results from both and marginally better results for my own purposes from the second query. In Infoseek, capitalizing a name you are searching for automatically turns the name into a phrase (such as *Babe Ruth*, which won't return a bunch of sites about the movie *Babe* and the book of *Ruth*).

InfoSeek lets you search not just Web pages (more than 50 million of them), but also newsgroup postings, e-mail addresses, "timely news," company profiles, and Web FAQs. (Searching Usenet for *javascript tutorial* turned up an important Javascript mini-FAQ!) Unlike AltaVista, InfoSeek lets you read entire newsgroups containing the postings you are seeking. An icon shows you whether you're reading a thread or an article. Opening a thread lets you read all the articles in that thread, and you get "cross references" to other newsgroups with threads of likely relevance. Finally, when you do a Usenet search, you read newsgroups directly, as opposed to bringing up AOL's newsreader as in HotBot. You cannot post your own message to the newsgroup, though you can send e-mail to the author of a specific posting.

Like other great search indexes, InfoSeek is "growing" its own directory, with categories of selected, rated, and briefly described sites, in categories such as Politics, Sports, and Travel. InfoSeek is also putting together an excellent "information mall," complete with:

- A news center

- A people finder, with millions of e-mail addresses

- Big Yellow, the Internet version of the Yellow Pages, with 16 million entries (profiled later in this chapter)

- A ZIP code directory (you put in an address to get the ZIP code)

- A searchable *Webster's Dictionary* (the 1913 edition, alas)

- Street maps (enter *any* street address and get a local map)

- Currency exchange

- A searchable set of tens of thousands of company profiles, and more

All this good stuff is available from the main page (available with AOL at keyword: Infoseek).

Lycos

Keyword: Lycos

http://www.Lycos.com

Lycos has been around for a while, at least in "Web time." The search engine, developed at Carnegie-Mellon University, was the Net's favored Web engine for a period in 1994 (Figure 9-4). It was partly its success that paved the way for services such as Yahoo, HotBot, and InfoSeek. In the way it handles queries, Lycos hasn't kept up with the other engines, but it does still have some advantages in certain areas.

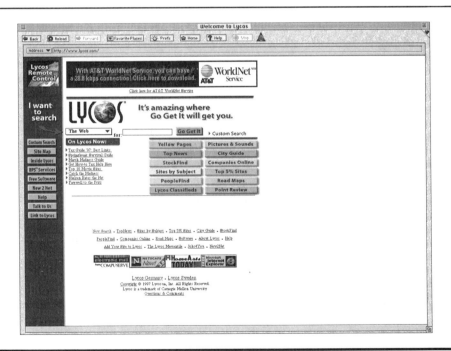

FIGURE 9-4   Lycos lets you search for sounds, pictures, and Gopher resources and browse directories of reviewed Web sites

One result of Lycos' maturity is its size. When this book was being written, Lycos was the biggest of the search indexes, with about 70 million pages indexed. Another advantage: instead of searching all the words on a page, Lycos does a statistical analysis of page contents. When it works, it's great. Keep in mind that in the opinion of some, Lycos doesn't offer the best customization choices to refine your query if it doesn't work on the first try.

Lycos accepts Boolean operators (AND, OR, NOT), but not filters (HotBot) or natural language queries (InfoSeek). One strong search feature it offers is "stemming." Adding a dollar sign ($) makes Lycos look for any words beginning (or ending) with a certain *stem*, or part of a word. For example, the search term *gard$* picks up both *gardens* and *gardenias*. (The *$* is a *wildcard;* Lycos searches for *anything* in place of it. Other engines don't yet do much with wildcards.) Add a period (.) to a keyword (*gardenia.*), and Lycos searches for exactly that stem; it won't pick up *gardenias.*

One downside to Lycos is that it strips out simple words such as *a* and *an*, even, it seems, in phrases. Sure, these words are everywhere—too common to be generally useful as keywords. But from time to time they *can* be essential to a query.

Lycos searches just the Web—not Usenet—but it does give you the option of searching for *images* and *sounds* on the Web. I used this feature to find some magnificent whale cries. To search for sounds, I used *whale* as the search term in the "Sounds and Pictures" area—not very tricky! (See "Searching for Sounds.") Also, Lycos includes FTP and Gopher sites in its indexes, unlike the other search engines.

In addition to a huge index, Lycos features a 16-subject *directory* of selected and rated sites called *a2Z*. It also offers a catalog of the "Top 5%," based on a catalog of rated sites that Lycos recently acquired (Figure 9-5). These top sites are rated for their design, content, and overall experience, and are assigned a number from 1 to 50. At the end of each description is a "Find Related Sites" link. Clicking the link causes Lycos to search its index for other sites with similar titles. (Results can be mixed. I did a search for sites related to the American Classical League and found, among other things, the *American Professional Soccer League* and *Composite Ratings for the American League*! Well, at least they're both *American* and *leagues* of some sort.)

Like the other great search sites, Lycos offers a bounty of essential information services:

■ CityGuide, Lycos's answer to Excite's City.Net. Though it is more narrowly focused on American cities, it does give quick access to about 10,000 Web sites.

- PeopleFinder, which lets you find street addresses if you just type in a name (see "Finding People One at a Time").

- Roadmaps for any address in the U.S.

- The latest headlines and news stories.

- Pictures and sounds of anything you want to see and hear (if it's on the Web).

- Club Lycos, membership in which (a sort of AAA for cyberspace) entitles you to discounts on travel arrangements and automatic entries in drawings for free books from Lycos Press.

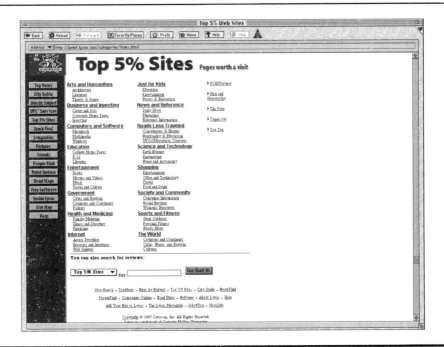

FIGURE 9-5 At Lycos you can browse some 16 categories or go right to the "Top 5%" of all sites

Searching for Sounds

Sometimes it's hard to know where to start a search. In the case of multimedia files, do you start on FTP or on the Web? More and more, the answer is the Web. If you don't find a file using Archie (see Chapter 8), you're likely to find it on the Web.

Lycos and HotBot let you do searches for files of a certain type, that is, with a certain file extension (such as MIDI or WAV). In Lycos, choose Pictures & Sounds from the main page, and follow the simple instructions for locating either picture files or sound files (you can search only one type at a time). Just click Sounds and type in **midi**, for example.

HotBot is also easy to use (**http://www.hotbot.com**). From the main window, click the Media button to bring up a set of media filters, which you search for files with specific multimedia formats. In the search window that comes up, check the box for the media types you want to retrieve, such as *Audio*. If you want, narrow the search further: in the Extensions box, enter the file extension of the audio file type you're seeking, such as **midi** or **wav**. Click Search.

Looking for good MIDI sites? Vikram's MIDI-Fest is a big collection of MIDI files located, unfortunately, on a slow FTP server, **ftp://sunsite.unc.edu/pub/multimedia/midi/midi.html**. Included are MIDI versions of most of the Beatles' music. The Classical MIDI Archive (**http://www.prs.net/midi.html#index**) contains thousands of classical MIDI clips from popular composers such as Bach and Mozart and hundreds of lesser-known composers. Smithsonian Folkways has collected hundreds of clips of folk, jazz, children's, blues, American Indian, Southern, and other American music, and made them easily available and searchable at **http://www.si.edu/organiza/offices/ folklife/folkways/genrlist.htm**.

Magellan Internet Guide

Keyword: Magellan
http://www.mckinley.com

Magellan and Yahoo are the most popular Web directories (see the description of Yahoo in a couple of pages). Yahoo came first and has always been among the most popular destinations on the entire Internet, but Magellan, from the McKinley Group, offers a more systematic editorial approach to selecting, describing, and rating sites. (Yahoo hand-picks and arranges sites, but doesn't describe or rate them.) In addition to a directory, Magellan offers a searchable database of URLs—its own index.

In 1995 Magellan assembled a large and talented editorial team, and set out to create a better directory. In mid-1996, Magellan was acquired by Excite Inc., but fortunately, the Magellan directory is still available.

Magellan can be browsed, which is the proper way to approach any directory. The two dozen or so main categories give you more starting points for browsing than the other directories. Magellan can also be searched for specific rated sites, and searches can be restricted to sites appropriate for the entire family ("Green Light" sites). Finally, you can also search Magellan's Rock Guide, created by *Rolling Stone* magazine.

Tip   *Looking for kid-appropriate sites? Magellan's Green Light sites are free of objectionable material, and AOL NetFind for Kids makes it easy for you to find children's sites that are fun as well as safe.*

NetFind

Keyword: NetFind
http://www.aol.com/netfind

NetFind is AOL's preferred search tool, and is one click away—just click the browser's Search button. The folks at NetFind urge you to use ordinary language for your keyword searches, and to do the following:

- Be as specific as possible in your query. Instead of *dogs* or *terriers*, search for *short-haired terriers*.

- Repeat those specific terms that are especially important. Instead of *terriers*, search for *terriers, terriers, terriers*.

- Precede required terms with a plus sign (+) and terms you don't want with a minus (-), as in AltaVista.

To search with NetFind:

1. In the "What are you looking for?" field, type your keyword or concept, such as **Babe Ruth's birthday**. As with other search engines, with

NetFind your query is not restricted to the length of the text box (keep typing and you'll "scroll" right).

2. *Below* the main text box, use the radio buttons to select *what* you want to search: the Web or NetFind's Reviews of Web sites.

3. Click Find.

NetFind is also notable in the way it returns Web addresses (URLs). It ranks them from best to worst (100% to 0%), in terms of how well the returned page matches what you are looking for. Extremely useful is the More Like This feature. Every site returned by your query has a More Like This link to the right of the main link. If any site answers your query especially well, you can click More Like This to see a refined search that combines words from your original search and the result you liked. You can keep clicking More Like This until you find exactly the information you are seeking.

NetFind doesn't stop at the Web. From the main screen, click on Newsgroup Finder for details on Newsgroup etiquette, and a link to the FAQ archive at Ohio State. The Newsgroup Scoop link offers insightful reviews of hundreds of newsgroups, with new ones added weekly.

Back at NetFind's main screen, the Find a Person and Find a Business links provide one-click access to the power of Switchboard for searching for people. And the Time Savers link will show you how you can use the Net to enhance your real life: by getting news, planning a trip, getting maps, and more.

NetFind is an index that has begun to grow its own *directory* and has hired a team of top-notch editors to select, annotate, and rate Web sites. The sites are organized in 20 categories, such as Business and Shopping, all available from NetFind's main screen. Choose a category, and you can "drill down." From the Science category, for example, you can click on General Science, then on History, and from there to a dozen carefully reviewed and rated Web sites.

  NetFind's thousands of reviews can be searched. Just choose AOL NetFind Reviews from the radio buttons at the main window.

Yahoo

Keyword: Yahoo
http://www.yahoo.com

Yahoo is the largest and most popular directory on the Net (Figure 9-6). Yahoo's categories range from "Arts and Humanities" to "Society and Culture." Sites are hand-picked, so in general you can count on the links working. However, they are neither annotated nor rated, although for some sites you'll find a short descriptive phrase.

Compiling a directory of Web sites is like building a sand castle during high tide. It seems futile because of the rate at which new sites are created. Yahoo confronts the problem by offering visitors easy access to a major search index, AltaVista. In addition, Yahoo adds many layers of value to its directory:

- The directory itself can be searched for specific sites, so you're not forced to navigate many levels of subcategories. Pages listing some of the subcategories can be quite long, so you'll appreciate searchability—especially if you know what you are looking for or if you want to find resources scattered across several categories.

- Two other aids to navigation: (1) For each subcategory, the number of sites is available in parentheses—a useful measure of the depth of Yahoo's contents for any area and of the length of time it will take for the page to download. (2) New sites have a special little picture by them ("New" in a starburst), as do especially cool sites (a pair of glasses).

- Yahooligans for Kids! is a large directory of kid-appropriate sites.

- Yahoo has created both national and metropolitan Yahoos—collections of Web sites about particular countries (Canada, France, Japan, etc.) and cities (San Francisco, D.C., Boston, etc.).

- Powerful customization features. From the top level of Yahoo, you can create something called "My Yahoo," which can serve as your private window into the world of Yahoo—with only the current news, sports, stock, and entertainment information (and more) that you want to see each day. (Expect to see such customization throughout the Web in the near future.)

- Yahoo offers current subject-appropriate news headlines for several categories of its main directory.

- Unlike the other search sites, Yahoo offers an e-mail newsletter to keep you informed of the week's top new sites. It's available by choosing Weekly Picks and looking for a subscription link. Online, you can get the same information, but getting it by e-mail is a major convenience if you use e-mail more often than you use the Web.

9

FIGURE 9-6 Yahoo, the Internet's leading directory

Yahoo alone is probably not the place to do a serious search for specific information (see "Essential Directories for the Serious Searcher" for that), but it does offer nicely packaged information on a large set of topics. If you're just browsing, it's the place to start.

Essential Directories for the Serious Searcher

The **Argus Clearinghouse** (formerly the Clearinghouse for Subject-Oriented Internet Resource Guides, available at **http://www.clearinghouse.net/**) consists of hundreds of hypertext essays, each reviewing the best resources on specific subjects. The essays were written by University of Michigan library-science students under the guidance of Lou Rosenfeld, a leading figure in the search world. Of the essays in the Health & Medicine category, for example, you will find essays dealing with AIDs, food safety, and holistic medicine Internet resources. Some of the essays are dated, but there is no rival resource as detailed and systematic.

The **Virtual Library** (**http://www.w3.org/vl/**) began at CERN in 1991 and moved to the World Wide Web Consortium in 1996. This serious directory of Internet resources is a labor of love, and it communicates the original impulse of the Web better than any of the commercial directories.

The Virtual Library consists of well over 100 categories of information. Many of the topics are of strictly academic interest (Mycology and Vision Science, for example), but dozens of others have broad appeal as well (Recipes, Men's Issues, Games, Gardening, and the like). Unlike the commercial services such as Yahoo, the Virtual Library categories are separately maintained by experts in the various areas, all with their own approach to selecting and organizing resources. The experts live throughout the world, not just in the U.S., so you will get an international perspective on many subjects—something that's surprisingly rare on the "global" Internet. You'll also find in-depth information *about* the rest of the world, and not merely travel tips. Special categories are devoted to Taiwan, Singapore, India, and many other non-Western places.

The Virtual Library will link you to *all* the pertinent information for a subject, not just Web sites. You can find out about Telnet sites, FTP sites, newsgroups, mailing lists, and more. It's not systematic or fancy, but it makes for a true information feast.

FINDING *PEOPLE* WITH INFORMATION: MAILING LISTS AND NEWSGROUPS

Mailing lists and newsgroups provide tens of thousands of microcommunities of interest. If you raise terriers for a living, a good first stop may well be the Internet discussion group that lives and breathes the subject (such as the mailing list for "friends of soft-coated wheaten terriers"). Getting to know the people who frequent a mailing list or newsgroup, you can often find better answers more quickly, and you can stay more current about any topic than if you just used a "passive" resource like the Web.

Tip *If you're just learning about a topic, make a point to read the FAQ first. The newsgroup or mailing list may have already gathered answers to the most common questions and posted them in that document.*

Liszt: Searching for Mailing Lists

Keyword: Liszt
http://www.liszt.com

Over the years, some great mailing list *directories* have been hand-maintained to provide guidance to people searching for lists. They were maintained by individuals such as Vivian Neou, Stephanie da Silva, and AOL's own David O'Donnell. The Liszt database is the first true searchable index of mailing lists—currently more than 60,000 of them. In other words, you enter a search keyword, and Liszt searches an index for mailing lists whose name or description matches the keyword. Note that Liszt just searches through the names and short descriptions of mailing lists; *it does not search through messages posted to lists.*

Note *A new service, Reference.com (**http://www.reference.com**), is trying to provide access to mailing list archives, but its success will depend on whether the owners and moderators of mailing lists make their archives available to the public. For now, it focuses on newsgroups.*

To use Liszt to find a mailing list about a specific topic, you enter a term as you do in any index, then click Search (see Figure 9-7).

You need to be explicit about what you want. If you want a phrase (*home run*), enclose it in quotes (*"home run"*). Otherwise, *home run* returns all mailing lists with either *home* or *run* in their title or in the short descriptions lists sometimes provide about themselves. Not only that, Liszt will return the names of mailing lists with the words *run*, *run*ning, and b*run*ch in them! Specificity can rescue any search, and not just on Liszt.

The result of your query is a list of hyperlinks of mailing lists whose names or descriptions contain the term you are seeking. Click one to bring up a description of the list.

You get two pieces of information for any mailing list. First, you get any information about the list that is archived at Liszt—the "information file," similar to the Welcome message you receive when you subscribe to the list. Such information is not always available, unfortunately. Second, you get the boilerplate How to Subscribe information shown in Figure 9-8 about the *kind* of software used to administer the list (LISTSERV, Majordomo, Listproc, etc.).

This text tells you how to get information about the list via e-mail and how to subscribe to it. Clicking the hyperlink in the How to Subscribe section brings up

FIGURE 9-7 Liszt delivers the news (er, mail)

AOL's Compose Mail window, with the list's *administrative* address plugged into the To field. Just complete the form as instructed, then click Send to subscribe!

 Chapter 4 is devoted to mailing lists, the Internet's best service for finding groups of people who share a serious interest.

Like WebCrawler and other *Web* engines, Liszt provides a directory-like feature with the best mailing lists by subject (such as Business and Social)—a useful feature, though it's not so clear how lists make it into this pantheon.

You can also do a Usenet search on Liszt. Currently this search looks only through the *names* of newsgroups, not the actual postings; AOL's newsreader does much the same thing and searches through a longer list of newsgroups. But this Liszt feature does allow you to do all your searching for good "discussion groups"—newsgroups and mailing lists—in one place. With Liszt, you can identify all the mailing lists and newsgroups whose members share an interest of yours.

FIGURE 9-8 Liszt provides point and click subscription to mailing lists

Search Newsgroups with DejaNews

Keyword: DejaNews

http://www.dejanews.com

Chapter 5 mentioned all the ways you can "search" newsgroups:

■ You can search for a *newsgroup* with a certain word in its title.

■ You can search for a specific *article* (posting) within a newsgroup, by searching subject lines.

■ You can search all the *text* you'll find in millions of postings by individuals.

DejaNews leads the pack of the Usenet search tools, giving you two out of three: You can search for specific newsgroups, and, more important, you can search actual content. A version of DejaNews is now available as Newsgroup Finder at AOL NetFind (just click the browser's Search button).

DejaNews boasts a database with close to 100 million articles from 15,000 newsgroups stretching back to March 1995! Despite its size, it's very fast.

From the opening DejaNews window you are presented with two text boxes (Figure 9-9). The first allows you to do a Quick Search for actual *postings* based on word or words used in them. The second lets you search for a *newsgroup* with a certain word or words in its title. To find relevant newsgroups, you enter a word in the second box ("Enter one of your interests below"), and click Find.

To search through actual articles, you enter a keyword (*banjo* or *puppies* or whatever) into the first box, click Find, and DejaNews does its magic, returning postings with your keyword. Your results are hyperlinked to actual postings. You automatically get hyperlinks to the e-mail addresses of the postings' authors as well, so you can send e-mail directly to those individuals. You can read the postings from within DejaNews, not in AOL's Newsgroups window.

Sending e-mail to the author of the posting is easy, but sending a posting of your own to the newsgroup requires registration, which is free.

FIGURE 9-9   DejaNews lets you find newsgroups and newsgroup postings about any topic. Register, and you can post to newsgroups from here

A final important feature of DejaNews is its ability to let you browse newsgroups as well as search them by title and content. This top-down approach is similar to what you do on AOL when you click Add Newsgroups and "drill down" through categories and subcategories to actual newsgroups. AOL seems to carry more newsgroups and offer faster performance, because it's not dependent on the Web or any intervening networks; it's all on AOL. But DejaNews does let you search postings and post-your-own in the same session.

SEARCHING NEWSGROUPS WITH OTHER SEARCH TOOLS

AltaVista, Excite, HotBot, and InfoSeek all do Usenet searches, searching the text of newsgroup postings for your keywords. None offers a database as old or big as DejaNews, however. Nor do they offer detailed profiles of posters or the ability to post your *own* articles in response to an article. What they *do* offer is the convenience of allowing you to combine Web and Usenet searches from the same site.

If you want to browse a newsgroup from which a posting comes or send a posting of your own, AltaVista, Excite and HotBot call up the AOL newsreader. From AOL you can browse and post to your heart's content. Only Infoseek allows newsgroup browsing *within* the browser, but it doesn't (yet) allow posting.

Of the Web engines that can search newsgroups, Excite is especially good: it allows you to do "concept" searches as well as simple keyword searches, and when you get your results you can click "More Like This" for any single result that's especially pertinent.

Yellow Pages on the Net: Finding Business Addresses

For any business, the Internet has drastically cut the costs and simplified the methods of doing competitive research. It's also easier for consumers to get contact information for both local stores and mail-order companies *anywhere*. When you're looking for business information you can use either a directory or an index; the best tools combine the two.

Big Yellow (keyword: BigYellow), from NYNEX, offers a searchable database of some 16 million businesses, plus a browsable directory of categories such as Automotive and Home Office. A strength of Big Yellow is its ability to search for all the listings for a specific type of business in a state, giving you the equivalent of a statewide yellow pages.

Switchboard (keyword: Switchboard, profiled a little later in this chapter), an AOL partner, also lets you search for a business by category (there are more than 2,000!) and by place. Unlike Big Yellow, with Switchboard you also get a huge White Pages listing of more than 100 million people. The combination of very big yellow and white page directories makes Switchboard a reliable one-stop site if you regularly need to look up a person or a business. (Big Yellow has a White Pages directory, too, but it's smaller.)

If you need more than an address for a company, **Hoover's Online** (**http://www.hoovers.com**) provides links to thousands of company Web sites as well as profiles of thousands of public and private companies. The profiles can be used by paying subscribers only, but you get free access to this information on AOL at keyword: Hoovers, with profiles nicely packaged to include links to company Web pages and stock charts for companies that are publicly traded.

FINDING PEOPLE ONE AT A TIME

A number of companies have put the real-world White Pages and similar print directories online and made them accessible via the Web.

The "people-finding" tools all work pretty much the same way. You:

1. Enter the name of a person or a business whose address (real or e-mail) you need. Provide as much address information as you can.

2. Click Find, or whatever the button is called.

3. Receive either an e-mail address or a real-world address for that person or business.

Caution *Searches for real addresses are likely to be a lot more successful than searches for e-mail addresses, because they're based on existing White Pages and other printed directories. E-mail addresses* cannot *be systematically collected or maintained, so the e-mail searches are less satisfying. All the "address finders" would love for you to add your e-mail address to their database!* **Yet another caveat:** *All the tools have a hard time with duplicate entries, since there is no sure way of determining whether the David Peal who lived in San Francisco is different from the one who lives where he currently lives. If the computers can't tell the difference, you probably won't be able to either! Why? If you haven't seen Harry Housebound in 20 years, there is no way to tell whether the Harry in Phoenix is different from the one in Piscataway.*

Despite these reservations, search tools have recently gotten light years better and easier to use, and they promise to continue perfecting themselves.

Switchboard

Keyword: Switchboard
http://www.switchboard.com

With more than 10 million business listings and more than 100 million residential listings, Switchboard (Figure 9-10) will almost certainly retrieve most people's street address; I even found my parents' address, neither of whom has ever used a computer. To find a person, all you need is a last name, though additional information (first name and city) will greatly improve your results. Then, just click Search.

Switchboard returns street addresses and phone numbers. If your search was a bit too broad, you can click Modify Search to add limiting information, such as state or city. For businesses, all you need is a business name, though, again, the more details the better. See the "Yellow Pages on the Net: Finding Business Addresses" sidebar for Switchboard's special Yellow Pages features.

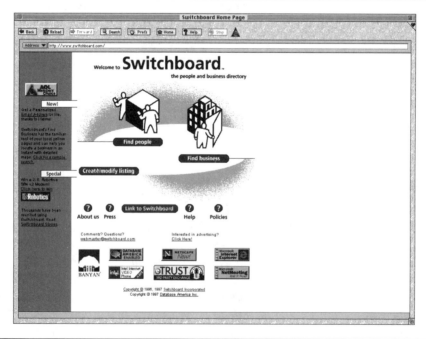

FIGURE 9-10 Switchboard is as close as you'll find to White Pages on the Internet

 *The power of Switchboard is now conveniently available in the new AOL NetFind area (just click the browser's Search button).*

Switchboard also has good *security features* that protect your privacy and keep junk e-mail out of your AOL mailbox. Your options include hiding your e-mail address from others and showing your e-mail as *knock knock*, so that someone who wants to send you e-mail can reach you only *via Switchboard*, not directly. Being unlisted in this way does *not* mean you've been deleted from the database.

Looking for Someone on AOL?

Use the AOL Members Directory. From the Members menu, select Member Directory. Click the Advanced Search tab to search for members with the same interests and professions, even members with the same interests who live in your community! I know of someone who found a handyman in her community using the AOL Member Directory.

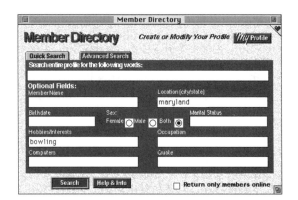

This particular search for Maryland bowlers returned more than 250 AOL members. Non-members don't have access to this directory. It's a privilege of membership!

You can find someone only if that person has filled in the Member Directory. So, it's your choice: if you don't want to be found, don't supply information about yourself. If you do want the AOL community to know about you, just click My Profile.

9

Four11

Keyword: Four11
http://www.four11.com/

Four11, one of the oldest Web-based directory services, claims "complete" and constantly updated Web access to U.S. White Pages as well as (at the time the book was written) ten million unique e-mail addresses. When you use Yahoo's People Finder service, you're using Four11's technology and listings. Special features include directories for the government and for celebrities.

Four11 searches for e-mail addresses as well as 100 million real-world addresses, though its real-world capabilities are stronger than its e-mail capabilities, simply because the white pages are reliable and there *aren't* white pages for the Internet. Again, I was able to find my parents' street address.

Like Switchboard, Four11 lets you register for free, then add or modify your personal information. Registering also gives you the privilege of keeping your e-mail address out of your listing and of using Four11 as an intermediary to intercept and forward mail to you. The only advantage of this particular service over Switchboard is its focus on creating a large database of e-mail addresses.

Bigfoot

http://www.bigfoot.com/

Bigfoot is notable for providing you with e-mail addresses, and it seems fairly aggressive in compiling them (with over eight million addresses when this book was written). Like other services, Bigfoot lets you edit your personal information when you move or change your preferred e-mail address. Bigfoot also lets you hide all your personal information, or parts of it such as your e-mail address, in order to protect your privacy online.

People Finders in Web Search Engines

Several of the best Web search indexes and directories have links to "people finders." Yahoo, for example, uses Four11's technology. Lycos uses a people finder from InfoSpace, which it nicely integrates with its Road Maps feature. For anyone whose street address you discover, Lycos will give you a local street map pinpointing that address. You can also link to community information and local buisnesses. Excite also offers the InfoSpace people finder.

SEARCHING THE MEGASITES: FINDING SPECIALIZED INFORMATION

More and more, you'll find search tools being adapted to narrower and narrower subjects. Instead of searching the Web universe from this or that speck of dust, they focus on a discrete subject and aim for comprehensiveness or at least depth within that subject. Or, they search no further than a megasite, a specific, content-rich site such as ESPN (**http://espnet.sportszone.com/**), which boasts 60,000 pages! These megasites seek to be meccas—the best sites for a specific field, whether it has to do with sports, parenting, travel, or something else. What follows are short descriptions of three specialized engines, of the thousands you can find on your own.

Medline: The World's Leading Medical Database

Keyword: Medline

A standard source for doctors and all healthcare professionals, Medline is now generally available on AOL and the Internet. This database of abstracts, gathered from more than 3,000 medical journals from all over the world, was created by the National Library of Medicine in Bethesda, Maryland. It grows by about 30,000 abstracts a month, and the database goes back to 1990. It's one of the most authoritative, focused resources on the Net. You can search for an article by author, author's affiliation, title, publication date, and journal; and you can search abstracts by keyword.

Tip   *Medline, as well as related medical databases (such as MEDLARS, the Visual Human Project, and various AIDS databases), is available at the National Library of Medicine Web site (***http://www.nlm.nih.gov/databases/ databases.html***), but many of these databases require accounts and fees, and some are available only by Telnet. On AOL Medline is always free.*

AOL adds value in many ways. You can share your Medline findings with others in the Disabilities Forum (keyword: Dis) or on the Better Health and Medical Network (keyword: Better Health). AOL has created online help for Medline, and AOL's Medline message boards allow members to share their Medline finds.

Note   *Medline offers abstracts; you must use a document retrieval service such as UnCover to get actual articles. AOL may be offering such a service in the future.*

City.Net: The World at Your Fingertips

Keyword: City.Net
http://www.city.net

Mecca is the right metaphor for City.Net, the brainchild of a former Intel engineer in Oregon named Kevin Altis. It began as an effort to provide a comprehensive directory of place-related Internet content for travelers, students, business people, and the curious. It became the Internet's single most comprehensive geographic resource for nonscientistis, and then was acquired by Excite Inc. Today, City.Net fits right in with the Excite interface (Figure 9-11).

With City.Net you can search for a specific location on any continent, and you'll get categorized sites. For example, I did a search for sites about Halifax, Nova Scotia and got sites usefully arranged in several categories, including travel and tourism, regional information, newspapers, parks and gardens, weather, and government. Maps were also available. Or, you can take a "top down" approach, and browse: just choose a continent and burrow down through countries, states, and provinces to local communities that interest you. Armchair travellers never had it so good.

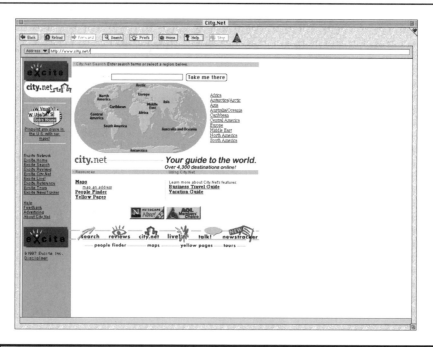

FIGURE 9-11 Leaving home on the Net

Searchable Megasites

Some Web sites are so big or so complex that special search engines are needed just to find information at them. Search.com (see the next section, "Pulling It All Together") makes dozens of such sites available in one place. Some Web sites can *only* be used with a search engine. Jeremy Hylton's Internet classic, the searchable Shakespeare database (shown in Chapter 1, Figure 1-5), was meant to be searched, and the nicely designed search form for doing so is available at **http://the-tech.mit.edu/Shakespeare/search.html**.

Clnet: The World of PCs

Keyword: cnet

http://www.cnet.com

Everyone on the Internet has access to a computer, so it's not surprising that some of the best resources on the Internet are computer-related. Publishers of computer magazines such as CMP (**http://techweb.cmp.com**) and Ziff-Davis (**http://www.zdnet.com**) have put together large sites based on the content of their print publications, with frequently changing and interactive material as well.

The current all-around leader in the category of computing megasites is Clnet, from the same-named company that creates programming for cable TV's Computer Network (Figure 9-12). The clnet megasite brings you computer-related news, feature articles, product reviews, regular editorials, site reviews, *plus* the ability to search this excellent content. Like every good Web site, there are rich interactive opportunities as well, so (unlike cable TV) you can speak your mind and meet other people who frequent the site. It's one of the best places to begin if you want to become well-informed about the Internet industry.

PULLING IT ALL TOGETHER

Search sites are getting more powerful and easier to use with each passing month. Currently you can find Internet search services that:

- Bring together links to the big search engines in one place, as AOL's Web site does (click the Search button with the browser open)

- Run queries against several search engines at the same time

- Collect hundreds of searchable megasites like Clnet and City.Net in one place

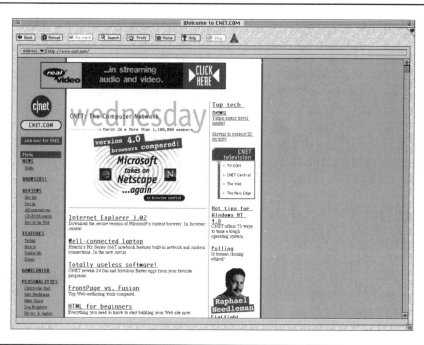

FIGURE 9-12 Clnet: a vibrant site devoted to the world's most dynamic industry

Note *Many sites are competing to provide comprehensive search capabilities. The following overview is just that—skim it, and perhaps try one or two, but don't feel like you have to master all these tools, since they overlap in many ways, and it's not clear which is going to emerge as the best.*

Sites That Link to Multiple Search Engines

An excellent resource of this type is InterNIC's **Internet Search Engines** page, which takes you to dozens of search engines by category—Web, mailing lists, FTP, "meta" search, and so on (**http://www.internic.net/tools**). Similarly, the **All in One Page** (**http://www.albany.net/allinone/**) lets you choose a search tool more by topic than by tool. Click "Desk Reference," for example, to get dictionaries, AT&T's

1-800 directory, and the like. Finally, Netscape's Web site, like AOL's, pulls together all the major search engines and offers a highly selective directory of the best sites, by topic.

Sites That Run Multiple Queries at the Same Time

Some services go a step further and run multiple searches using different engines *at the same time.* The innovative Inference search engine (**http://www.inference.com**) lets you search AltaVista, Yahoo, Lycos, InfoSeek, WebCrawler, and Excite all at once. What's unique about Inference is that it *clusters* similar items, drastically simplifying the work you have to do to scan returned sites. For example, an Inference search for *Bismarck* (the German chancellor and North Dakota capital) returns hundreds of sites, usefully grouped in categories such as Misc. European Sites, Misc. Commercial sites, Bismarck (ND), and the Bismarck Group (a Chicago-based Microsoft Solution Provider). Of course, the more specific the original query, the better the results, with Inference or any search engine. The query *Otto von Bismarck and Kaiser Wilhelm* returns sites about Imperial Germany, while the query *Bismarck North Dakota* returns sites about the American city.

Sites That Let You Search Any of Dozens of Megasites

Sites like **Internet Sleuth** (**http://www.isleuth.com/**) and **Search.com**, a part of the Clnet Web empire (**http://www.search.com**), let you do a broad range of focused searches for specific information in one place. Internet Sleuth currently lets you search any of *1,800* databases. A newer service, **WorldPages (http://www. worldpages.com**), pulls together people finders and business finders as well as searchable travel and business sites in the search for one-stop searching. A feature of WorldPages is the collection of White Pages and Yellow Pages for countries around the world.

Search.com is the current leader of this particular pack (Figure 9-13). Search.com looks like a directory, but it's actually a lot more. Pick a category such as Finance from the list of Search Subjects and you pull up 30 or so searchable sites such as CNN's Finance Network; SEC's EDGAR service; Hoover's online company profiles; Mutual Funds Online; and several currency converters. If you don't find what you're looking for, AltaVista is always available, as are searchable Yellow Pages (BigBook) and White Pages (Switchboard). You can also choose one of about

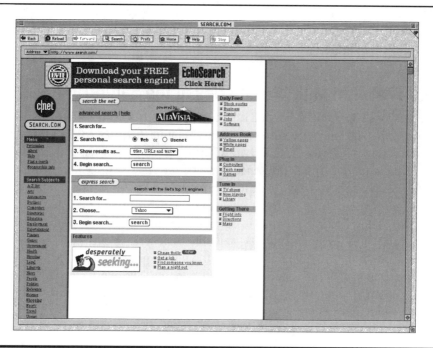

SEARCH.COM

FIGURE 9-13   Still can't find it? Visit Search.com

a dozen of the major search engines, including Excite. Flight information, maps, sports scores, stock quotes—it's all a click away as well. I searched for the kitchen sink, but it's the only thing I couldn't find at Search.com.

FROM HERE...

With these search tools and this chapter, you can start putting the Internet to *use* in your day-to-day life. Or, you can learn something new, do some armchair travelling, research your family's history, find out the capital of North Dakota, or search for the whereabouts of your favorite high-school teacher.

Everything up to this point in the book is possible with your basic AOL software. The next chapter looks beyond, to all the non-AOL software you can use with AOL, such as Netscape, Internet Relay Chat, and Telnet. It's not about software, though. In the next chapter you'll see how to extend the AOL *community* to the global Internet.

Chapter 10

Beyond AOL:
Exploring Internet
Applications

America Online provides first-rate software for browsing the Web, downloading files with FTP, reading newsgroups, and managing your e-mail, but AOL's Internet access doesn't stop there. A little file called AOL Link, which is automatically set up for you when you install the AOL software, opens an even broader world of possibilities on AOL.

This chapter takes a brief look at AOL Link itself, and then it looks at powerful AOL Link-enabled Internet applications you can use on AOL at no additional charge:

- Netscape—if you have a yen to use the world's most popular Web browser

- Internet Relay Chat—chat rooms on the global Internet

- Telnet—collaborative work and play, and a thousand electronic library catalogs

These few Internet applications are among the hundreds available to you. See "Where Do I Find Applications to Use with AOL Link?" for a list of places on AOL and the Internet where you can find truckloads of Internet software.

ALL YOU NEED TO KNOW ABOUT AOL LINK

The little AOL Link file makes it possible for "third party Internet applications"—programs that aren't built into AOL—to work with America Online. Most of these programs are available free or as shareware. The AOL Link file was automatically put in your Extensions folder when you installed AOL 3.0.

Where Do I Find Applications to Use with AOL Link?

Hundreds of Internet applications are available to download from AOL and the Internet, including browsers, games, FTP clients, Telnet, and Internet Relay Chat programs.

You can get Internet applications for the Mac from the following places on AOL and the Net:

- **Keyword: AOL Link.** AOL Link Central, featuring more information about AOL Link and related software.

- **Keyword: Net Software.** Part of the Mac Communications and Networking forum (at keyword: MCM), this area offers copious links to Internet software.

- The Mac Orchard at **http://www.spectra.net/~dsaur/orchard.html**, which features essential links and software for Mac users.

How Do I Use an AOL Link Application?

Using a program with AOL Link is like using any program—you must install it, run it, and learn what it does and how to get around. The only hitch is that since AOL Link programs require Internet access, you must be signed on to AOL to use them.

Assuming you have enough memory in your Mac, you can use more than one AOL Link application at the same time. You could, if you wanted, run an IRC program (such as IRCle), the Netscape browser, and a Telnet client all at the same time. You could even browse the World Wide Web using more than one browser at the same time (AOL's and Netscape's, for example.)

If you exit from AOL or your AOL connection is broken for any reason, all your AOL Link applications lose their connection to the Internet as well. When you're ready to log out, it's best to quit your AOL Link programs before logging out of America Online.

NETSCAPE NAVIGATOR

America Online members can use Netscape Navigator, the world's most popular Web browser. Navigator is fast and easy to use, a browser that supports and extends open Web standards.

With such a strong, integrated browser from Microsoft, why would AOL offer Netscape as well? In a word: choice. If you use Netscape at school or work, you may want to use Netscape on AOL as well. Also, Netscape offers a few features lacking in the built-in browser (such as Java and JavaScript). Finally, some plug-ins and a few Web sites will only work with Netscape.

Downloading and Installing Netscape

Here are the steps for downloading and installing Netscape Navigator:

1. Go to Netscape's Web page at keyword: http://www.netscape.com.

2. On Netscape's Web page, find and click the Download Netscape link.

3. Read the information on the screen that appears: fill out the form to tell the server what kind of Mac you have and pick the closest server to download the file from.

4. When the transfer of the file is complete, quit the America Online application. You will need to compress the file with StuffIt Expander.

5. Now run the installer application, and follow the prompts.

Using Netscape Navigator on AOL

Once you've finished downloading and installing AOL's Netscape Navigator, follow these steps to access the Web:

1. Sign on to AOL as usual.

2. Switch to the Finder and run Netscape. You'll find it in a folder called Netscape Navigator Folder on your hard disk.

 If you click on a Web link from America Online, the integrated browser launches. To access the Web with Netscape, you must manually run Navigator each time you want to go to the Web. You cannot make Netscape your default browser.

How to Get Parental Controls to Work with Netscape

At keyword: Parental Controls, parents have the ability to restrict children to Web sites approved by the Kids Only channel. Restricting children in this way limits the Web sites they can visit to the sites available in that channel. See "Do You Know What Your Children Are Viewing?" in Chapter 6.

The Kids Only setting will work, however, only when you use a modem to connect to AOL, not if you're connecting to AOL via the Internet.

If you want to limit your children to Kids Only sites, follow these steps:

1. Make sure your kids' screen names are locked in to approved sites, at keyword: Parental Controls.

2. While signed onto AOL, open the Netscape browser.

3. From the Options menu, select Network Preferences.

4. Click the Proxies tab.

5. Select Manual Proxy Configuration, then click the View button.

6. In the HTTP Proxy field, type **ie3.proxy.aol.com**.

7. To the right of the HTTP Proxy field, in the Port box, type **80**.

8. Click OK. You do not need to restart your computer for the change to take effect.

Netscape and AOL's Browser: How They Differ

Whole books have been written on Netscape Navigator, but browsing the Web with Navigator really doesn't take much explanation. If you're familiar with the basics of clicking, going backward, and jumping to a new Web page, then you'll pick it up in a few minutes. Figure 10-1 gives you a quick tour of the Netscape screen.

If you are not familiar with Navigator but are familiar with the Microsoft browser integrated into AOL, here are some of the more important ways in which they differ.

Netscape Gives You Many Keyboard Equivalents for Core Tasks

For example, to go forward and backward, you can either click the Forward and Backward buttons on the tool bar, or press COMMAND-LEFT ARROW or COMMAND-RIGHT ARROW. You can scroll down a page at a time by pressing the spacebar. For other keyboard equivalents, look at Navigator's menus; the equivalents, when available, appear to the right of command names.

Netscape Includes a Find Command for Doing a Search Within a Page

Search engines are often undiscriminating, so you will appreciate the ability to look for a word on a page returned by a search. Choose Find from the Edit menu to search

Location box   Easy searching   Netscape plug-ins   Tool bar   Directory buttons

and other software

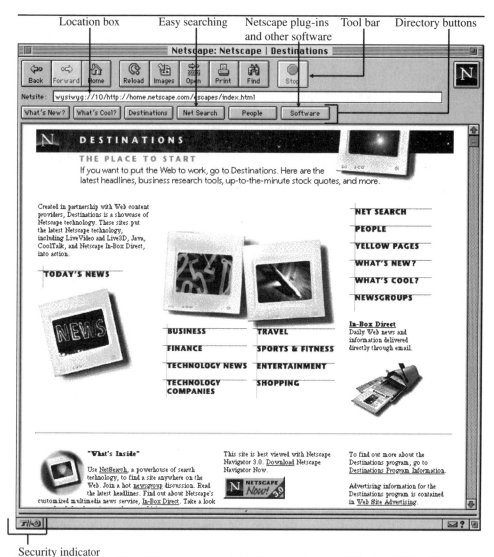

Security indicator

FIGURE 10-1   Netscape's Destinations area, with access to the best sites

for a specific word on that page! This feature is a lifesaver if, say, you use Excite to do a search for a keyword and get a long page that doesn't seem to include the keyword.

Grand Central Netscape

The default home page for Navigator is Netscape's Web site rather that AOL's home page.

Click the Destinations button in Navigator toolbar for instant access to one of the best starting points for exploring the Web. You'll find links to several hundred choice Web sites, in categories such as business, finance, and travel. Click Net Search in the tool bar for direct access to some of the best Web search tools—Excite, Yahoo, Magellan, Infoseek, and Lycos.

AOL Uses Favorite Places; Netscape Uses Bookmarks

Bookmarks, like Favorite Places, hold your favorite Web sites, but on Navigator you can keep track only of Internet sites—not AOL content. If you discover a great site while using Navigator, go to the Bookmark menu and select Add Bookmark (or just press COMMAND-D).

Preferences Are Available from the Options Menu, Not the Toolbar

Click General Preferences. As with the AOL 3.0 browser, you have a healthy choice of preferences, arranged in a "tabbed" interface. Click a tab, such as Appearance and Fonts, to get a set of preferences relating to that topic. Here are two key preferences you should know about: To change your home page, click the Appearance tab. Type your preferred home page in the "Browser Starts With" box, and click O.K. To adjust your cache (in order to devote more hard disk to your Netscape cache or to clear your cache), select Network Preferences from the Options menu and use the Cache tab. Note that AOL and Netscape maintain different caches.

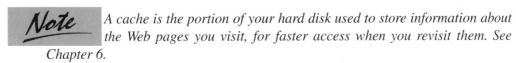 *A cache is the portion of your hard disk used to store information about the Web pages you visit, for faster access when you revisit them. See Chapter 6.*

You Can Open Several Browsers at the Same Time

On AOL, you open a another browser window by entering a new URL in the Keyword window or double-clicking a Favorite Place. With your mouse over a link, you can also hold down the button and select Open Link in New Window. In Navigator, holding down the mouse button does similar magic. In addition, you can go to the File menu and select New Web Browser.

Navigator Is Secure

Like the AOL browser, the Netscape browser is secure, which means you can transmit confidential information such as credit card numbers. On Navigator, however, you'll be more aware of security. The lower-left corner of the browser displays a key on a blue background to indicate a secure document and a broken key on a gray background to indicate an insecure document. Most documents—pages—are not secure, which only means they don't reside on specially secured servers. For security information about a specific page, display the page and select Document Information from the View menu. Netscape does a good job of explaining its multiple security features. From the Help menu, select On Security.

Telnet Support

Some Web sites have links to Telnet resources. Later in this chapter you'll encounter two superb sites of this type, Hytelnet and the MudConnector. The AOL browser can't launch the Telnet application when needed. Navigator, however, can work with a Telnet client to swiftly connect you to Telnet sites.

Java and JavaScript

Netscape Navigator gives you full access to sites that employ Java and JavaScript to enhance their pages. Java and JavaScript put all sorts of tricks up Web sites' sleeves. With Java, sites can create interactive programs, such as chat boards and games, that work within a Web page. Sites use JavaScript for useful additions like scrolling banners, and onscreen clocks that tick away automatically.

CHATTING ON THE INTERNET WITH IRC

Chatting on the Internet is pretty much like chatting on AOL, which is like chatting in the airport, at the checkout counter, or anywhere else. It's informal, lively, sociable, and usually has no purpose beyond itself. You'll also find rooms for serious discussion, fact finding, and emotional and moral support.

The Internet version of chat—Internet Relay Chat (IRC)—differs from chat on AOL primarily in its global reach. IRC also differs from AOL's chat in that it requires special software, and the software is more complex than AOL's. A few IRC programs are available for the Mac, and one of the best of them, IRCle, is conveniently available, with installation instructions, at keyword: AOL Link (Figure 10-2), or the official IRCle home page at **http://www.xs4all.nl/~IRCle/**. IRCle is shareware, so if you use it regularly, you are expected to pay for it ($15). To use IRCle, you must first download the program then uncompress it.

Note   *This section focuses on IRCle as an example of setting up and using an IRC client. But if IRCle doesn't suit you, several other IRC clients are available at keyword: Net Software.*

AOL Rules (and AOL's Rules on the Net)

AOL's Rules of the Road (keyword: TOS), Part II, reads: "Although AOL Inc. does not control the Internet, your conduct on the Internet when using your AOL account is subject to the AOL Rules of the Road. Because AOL Inc. wants to be a good Internet citizen, it prohibits Members from engaging in certain conduct…" Inappropriate conduct includes posting the following: chain letters, commercial communications in noncommercial places, and copyrighted material.

Don't forget that the "real world" also has laws against sending chain letters and violating copyrights.

Setting Up IRCle

The first time you start IRCle, you have to provide enough information for it to connect to an IRC server at AOL.

1. After the welcome screen, select Preferences | Startup from IRCle's File menu.

2. In the Server drop-down menu, choose Other Server, then type **irc02.irc.aol.com** in the server field. You'll see a long list of IRC servers, but most IRC servers do not work with AOL; you have to use one of the few that do.

3. Now enter your nickname (be creative—you've got to have a name that no one else on IRC is using), and your real name in the provided fields. Leave the name "ircle" in the Username field and click OK.

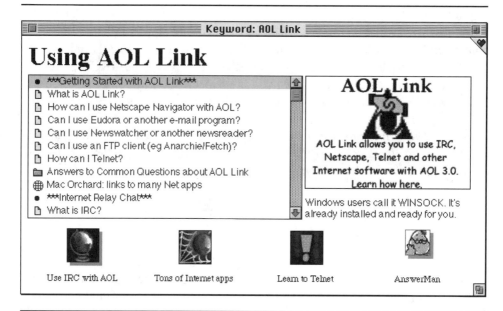

FIGURE 10-2 AOL Link is home to a plethora of information on using IRC and other Internet applications through AOL

4. Finally, choose Open Connection from the File menu and you'll be connected to the IRC server. From now on, when you start IRCle, all you have to do is choose Open Connection.

Choosing a Channel to Join

An IRC channel may remind you of an AOL chat room. Unlike an AOL chat room, however, an IRC channel can grow to be very busy—there's no 23-person limit. On average, however, IRC channels are pretty small—a lot smaller than the packed chat rooms you'll find on AOL! On IRC, you will find thousands of one- and two-person chat rooms—people waiting for the party to start. Sometimes the party never does start!

Now you need to pick a channel to join. Select List from the Commands menu, then press RETURN. Now select Channel List from the Windows menu to reveal the special window where the channel listing appears. You can join a channel by selecting "Join" from the Commands menu and typing its name. On IRC, all channel names start with the # sign.

Chatting

IRCle has many features and windows. The three most important for chatting are:

- A list of participants in the channel.

- The chat window, where chat text is displayed.

- The entry field, ("InputLine") where you enter either chat messages (text) or commands (preceded by a forward slash, /).

As in an AOL chat room, in an IRC channel you can either communicate with the group or chat privately with one individual in the group. To communicate with the group, type a message in the InputLine field and press RETURN. Your message appears in the main chat window.

To send a private message to someone, type:

```
/msg nickname your message
```

Something called DCC (Direct Client to Client) communication is also available with IRCle, for directly chatting and exchanging files with someone. Choose DCC from the Windows menu.

Leaving a Channel and Quitting IRC

The easiest way to leave a channel is to close its window. A channel remains in existence after the original operators have left, and the last person who leaves the channel automatically "turns off the light."

Leaving IRCle is like quitting any program: Selecting Quit from the File menu does the trick.

Finding Out More

To help get the hang of IRC, join a channel such as #new2irc (Figure 10-3) or #newbies. There you can try new things and ask questions you might have about the basics of IRC.

Here are some resources for getting more information about IRC.

■ The Official IRCle Web site at **http://www.xs4all.nl/~ircle/**

■ An informative FAQ on IRC is available at
http://www.cis.ohio-state.edu/hypertext/faq/usenet/irc-faq/faq.html

Chat windows   Participants

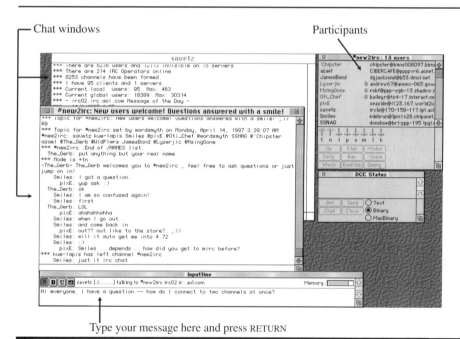

Type your message here and press RETURN

FIGURE 10-3 Using IRCle to chat on the Net

TELNET

What is Telnet? When you access a Telnet site on an Internet computer, your Mac becomes the terminal—a mere keyboard and display—for a distant computer (the word remote is sometimes used for distant; they both mean "out there" on the Internet). You type in commands and responses, and all the processing takes place at the distant computer, where you can do searches, make requests, and perhaps communicate with others who are also telneting to the computer. The goings-on are displayed on your monitor as old-fashioned and not very attractive text (Figure 10-4).

It may not be very sexy, but Telnet is useful and versatile precisely because of its low-end interface.

Telnet gives access to two essential Internet resources, which we'll look at here, plus dozens of others you can explore on your own. First of all, Telnet lets you search hundreds of library card catalogs, saving time and money if you are doing any kind of research. Every kind of Internet-accessible library catalog can be searched: law, medical, public, community, university, and K-12. See "Hytelnet: Gateway to a Thousand Libraries."

Telnet also provides a haven for people who love collaborative games and simulated environments. A whole genre of simulation, fantasy, adventure, and learning games has grown up over the past decade on Telnet, collectively known as MUDs—multi-user dungeons, or dimensions. See "Garden of MUD."

FIGURE 10-4   NYPL without the lions. The New York Public Library's CATNYP system allows you to do author, title, and journal searches of millions of titles in a fraction of a second

There's no Telnet client built into AOL, but like IRC, it's easy to download one and use it to connect to the Internet. A program called NCSA Telnet is the de facto standard for the Mac. It has just about every feature you could need, and it's absolutely free.

Downloading and Using NCSA Telnet

To start, you'll need to download NCSA Telnet and install it on your Macintosh.:

1. Go to keyword: Telnet (Figure 10-5). Download the NCSA Telnet program.

2. Uncompress the file.

To use Telnet, log onto AOL as usual, then double-click the Telnet application from the Finder to run it. You will see its title screen for a moment, then you'll be ready to Telnet. Pick "Open Connection..." from the File menu, then enter the address of the computer that you wish to connect to.

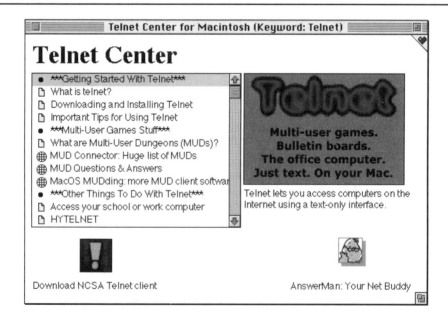

FIGURE 10-5 AOL's Telnet Center for the Mac, available at keyword: Telnet (where else?)

You should also read the NCSA Telnet Guide. You can read it on the Web at **http://www.ncsa.uiuc.edu/SDG/Software/MacTelnet/Docs/MacTelnet.Home. html**. If you want a copy for offline reference, it is also available in Microsoft Word and Adobe Acrobat formats.

Tip   *If you use Netscape Navigator, you can define a Telnet "helper" application. From Netscape's Options menu, select General Preferences, and click on the Applications tab. By the Telnet Application box, click the Browse button and navigate to the place where you've installed NCSA Telnet.*

Hytelnet: Gateway to a Thousand Libraries

Have you noticed that card catalogs have disappeared from your public library? Throughout the world, those inefficient and difficult-to-maintain space-wasters have given way to the electronic catalog, which can be easily searched by anyone, anywhere, using a "terminal emulation" program such as Telnet. Electronic searches allow you to search for books by title, author, year of publication, and other standard criteria.

Telnet makes it possible to do such searches from a distance and to do several such searches at a time. The books themselves are not available by Telnet. For that, you'll need to get in the car or on the phone. (Well, if you refuse to get up from the computer, you can go to an online bookstore like Barnes and Nobel—keyword: Barnes— to buy the book. But you'll have to get up when the book is delivered in a few days.)

Hytelnet is a piece of software written by Peter Scott, one of those Net heroes who have contributed an essential service to the larger Internet community. Hytelnet is available by Telnet, of course, but also by Gopher and, most important, by the Web.

10

Other Cool Telnet Resources

Hytelnet provides more than access to library catalogs. Click the boringly named Other category at Hytelnet's top level to get direct access via Telnet to all kinds of goodies: Archie servers (see Chapter 8); dozens of community free-nets (computer "online services" for communities from Canada to Finland); a large set of NASA databases of interest to students and teachers; stores such as CDNow; and all of the world's publicly accessible Gopher servers!

Hytelnet on the Web is available at many sites, including **http://www.einet.net/hytelnet/HYTELNET.html** and **http://moondog.usask.ca/hytelnet/**. With Hytelnet, you can take a top-down approach to finding a particular library, beginning with region (Americas, Europe, Asia) and "drilling down." (More than a thousand libraries are available for the U.S., which is more than for the rest of the world combined.) You can also do a search for a specific library.

Telnet 101

Logging onto a distant computer often requires that you know a password and log-in name. Hytelnet usefully provides you such information for libraries, but other kinds of Telnet sites may require that you first contact an administrator.

A key setting you may need to adjust in your software—or set at the site—is your "terminal emulation" type, which makes your keyboard behave in a way that makes sense to the distant computer. The most common terminal emulation type is VT-100, which NCSA Telnet handles with style.

Once you're signed on, you'll find that navigation differs from site to site. As a rule of thumb, you use the arrow keys on your keyboard to get around, and the mouse is useless at a Telnet site. When in doubt, try to get help at the distant computer by typing **H**, **?**, or **Help**. To end a Telnet session, you can simply close the Telnet window or (more gracefully) use the remote system's logout or quit command.

Garden of MUD

Community has come a long way on the Internet. Up-to-date, graphically spiffy programs are easy to use and a pleasure to watch but are still maturing. Dig a little, and you come to IRC, a graphically simple but fully mature environment for chatting with people around the world. MUDs have no graphics and are nothing but text (Figure 10-6), but they offer the most creative environment for meeting and interacting with others on the Internet. MUDs require an active imagination—and good typing skills. Like radio in the early decades of the twentieth century, subsequent innovations have not replaced MUDs; they've emulated and supplemented them. MUDs are alive and well.

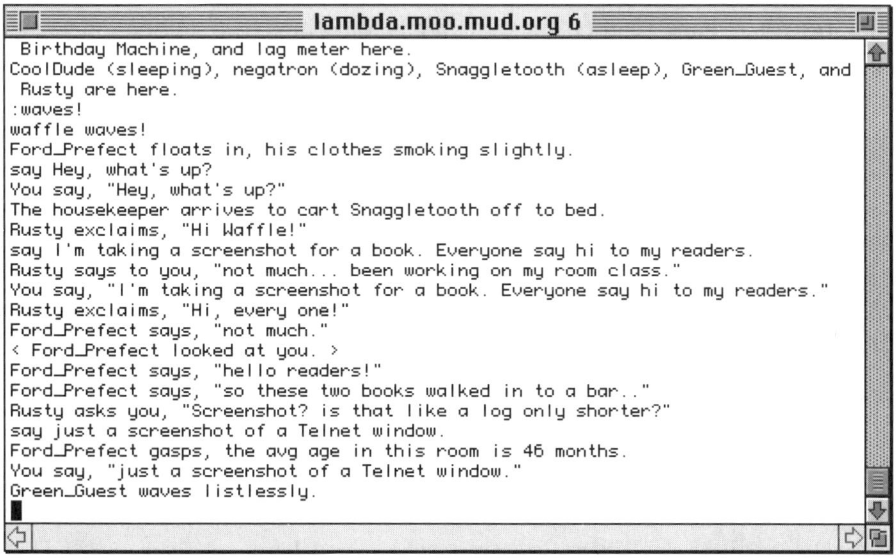

```
 ▣▤▤▤▤▤▤▤▤▤▤▤ lambda.moo.mud.org 6 ▤▤▤▤▤▤▤▤▤▤ ▣
  Birthday Machine, and lag meter here.                                    ▲
  CoolDude (sleeping), negatron (dozing), Snaggletooth (asleep), Green_Guest, and
  Rusty are here.
  :waves!
  waffle waves!
  Ford_Prefect floats in, his clothes smoking slightly.
  say Hey, what's up?
  You say, "Hey, what's up?"
  The housekeeper arrives to cart Snaggletooth off to bed.
  Rusty exclaims, "Hi Waffle!"
  say I'm taking a screenshot for a book. Everyone say hi to my readers.
  Rusty says to you, "not much... been working on my room class."
  You say, "I'm taking a screenshot for a book. Everyone say hi to my readers."
  Rusty exclaims, "Hi, every one!"
  Ford_Prefect says, "not much."
  < Ford_Prefect looked at you. >
  Ford_Prefect says, "hello readers!"
  Ford_Prefect says, "so these two books walked in to a bar.."
  Rusty asks you, "Screenshot? is that like a log only shorter?"
  say just a screenshot of a Telnet window.
  Ford_Prefect gasps, the avg age in this room is 46 months.
  You say, "just a screenshot of a Telnet window."
  Green_Guest waves listlessly.                                           ▼
 ▣◄                                                                    ►▣
```

FIGURE 10-6   Chatting on a MUD via Telnet. It's not pretty, but it is pretty fun

> *If you're serious about MUDding, then use a client program that's just made for accessing MUDs, like MUDDweller. It offers a much easier-to-use interface than relatively bland Telnet, makes it very easy to join any MUD, and gives you a level of control over your display that programs like NCSA Telnet don't provide. MUDDweller and other MUD clients are available from the MacOS MUDding Resource WWW page at* **http://www.eden.com/~hsoi/mud/,** *as well as keyword: Net Software.*

MUD stands for multi-user *dungeon* (after the Dungeons and Dragons games) or *dimension*. Unlike an IRC channel, a MUD is a structured environment in which people assume and develop online identities other than their "real" identities. Author and MIT professor Sherry Turkle considers MUDs a profound tool for exploring the parts of one's self that aren't fully expressed in day-to-day life. There are enough MUDs—hundreds of them—for you to find a comfortable place to try on a new persona. MUDs have been used in the workplace as a powerful collaborative tool and in the classroom to create virtual learning and role-playing opportunities. But they're mostly used for creative and interactive (not arcade-style) games.

MUDs tend to fall into two big classes. Traditional MUDs are devoted to adventure. You assume an often elaborate identity, defined by a set of traits you can choose. You name your character and join a specific clan or guild. You're now ready to interact with other personas, developing the characters and story in the process, in pursuit of giants, the Grail, evil, whatever. With practice comes recognition, advanced levels of play, and prestige. Characters engage in activities such as whispering, walking, fighting, and flying, and action unfolds in elaborate imaginary places, with rooms and neighborhoods. Bored with what's going on in one room? Try another.

The "social" MUDs—with names like Mush, Muck, and TinyMUD—have more in common with an AOL chat room than with Dungeons and Dragons. They're simply for socializing, although, with their objects, role-playing, and invented spaces, they have more structure than a chat room.

Learning about MUDs

All MUDs are different. Where do you start? Harley Hahn's chapter on MUDs in the *Internet Complete Reference, Second Edition* (Osborne/McGraw-Hill, 1996) is an excellent place to start. What Hytelnet does for library resources, the MudConnector (**http://www.mudconnect.com**), created and maintained by Andrew Cowan, does for the world of simulated environments. The searchable, annotated list of MUDs includes every variety of MUD, from aggressive galaxies to peaceable kingdoms, from the Age of Dragons to New Age. It's the place to find crisp descriptions of more than 600 MUDs, as well as usage statistics and links to MUD home pages on the Web. Most important, Telnet links take you directly to any MUD you want to explore.

Newsgroups on MUDs abound, including **alt.mud**, **rec.games.mud.announce** and **rec.games.mud.misc**, as well as newsgroups devoted to discussion of particular types of MUDs, on **rec.games.mud.diku**, **rec.games.mud.lp**, and **rec.games. mud.tiny**.

Dozens of MUD-related Web sites, plus the home pages for hundreds of individual MUDs, are available from MudConnector. Finally, an informative MUD FAQ is available at **http://www.math.okstate.edu/~jds/mudfaq-p1.html**.

The best way to learn about MUDs—like anything on the Net—is to jump right in. You can't break anything, and you will never be alone. Welcome to the Internet community!

Chapter 11

The AOL 300 Directory

The AOL 300 was designed to bring together in one place, *by channel*, the best Internet resources you'll find on AOL. For each of 19 channels, you'll find 15 Web sites and newsgroups closely related to the channel's theme. Most of the sites you'll find in the AOL 300 are integrated into channel listboxes. Some were added here to complement the integrated sites. The AOL 300 opens with some sites that AOL members like the best—AOL Members' Choice (which you can get to with the Hot button on the tool bar). It's a pretty remarkable list. Welcome to the feast!

HOW CHANNELS USE INTERNET RESOURCES

Web sites are everywhere on AOL, tucked into hundreds of listboxes. You'll see Web sites indicated in listboxes in different ways, as shown here.

W African Newspapers

⊕ Excite

Clicking any listbox item with one of these icons or the WEB label will usually take you directly to a Web site. Sometimes you'll first go to an AOL screen describing the site.

Some of the Web sites in the AOL 300 are siblings to AOL forums. What's the difference between a Web site and an AOL forum? The Web sites tend to be splashier, but as a rule the AOL forums will download *much* faster and offer more ways and more consistent ways to interact with others. The spectacular Rolling Stone Web site (MusicSpace), for example, takes forever to download for mortals using a normal-to-fast modem (28.8K) compared to the corresponding AOL forum. AOL forums have the additional advantage of linking you directly to the *most useful* parts of the Web sites, as you'll discover in the Personal Finance forums run by Charles Schwab, Dreyfus, and Fidelity.

From section to section you'll notice some overlap in content. In fact, AOL's channels overlap in lots of ways. Sometimes it's fun to watch the border skirmishes. For you, it means more choice but also a little less clarity. That's just the way it is.

The most popular sites have their own keywords, to simplify access. So, instead of typing **http://www.pathfinder.com**, you just type **pathfinder** in the Keyword window. Following is a list of "keywordable" Web sites. The most up-to-date list of such keywords is always available at keyword: Web keywords.

adobe.com
AltaVista
American Photo
Angelfire
Apple.com
Atlantic Financial
Big Yellow
BigBook
BingoZone
Boston Globe
CBS
CDnow
Census
City.Net
CNN.com
CNNfn
Compass.com
DejaNews
Digits
Discovery.com
Edmunds
Electronic News
Elle.com
Epicurious
ESPN
Excite
Family Tree
Firefly
FoodTV
Four11
GA Tech
Gameplayers

Gamespot
Garden.com
Gateway2000.com
Go Florida
HBO
Home PC.com
HomeArts
Homes
HotWired
HP.com
IBM.com
IDSoftware
iGuide
Indiana University
Infoseek
Intel.com
Intellicast
Internet Movie
    Database
Ivanhoe
Jumbo
LA Times.com
Link Exchange
Liszt
Look up
Macromedia.com
Magellan
Mapquest
McDonnell Douglas
Microsoft.com
Monster
MSU

MTV.com
Nando.net
Nasa.gov
Nascar.com
Navy.mil
NBA
NBC.com
NetGuide Live
NetGuide.com
Nintendo.com
Novell.com
NY Times.com
ON.com
Pathfinder
Purdue
Quantum Group
RealAudio
Riddler
RIT
Rockwell
    Automation
Salon
Sci Fi.com
Search.com
Sierra.com
Slate
Sony
Sportsline
Stanford University
Switchboard
TechWeb

The Weather
    Channel
Total NY.com
Travelocity
Treasury
Tribune.com
Tripod
U Iowa
U Mich
U Penn
U Texas
UIUC
UMD
United Media
Universal
Urban Desires
USAToday.com
Vacations.com
Warner Bros.com
Washington Post
Washingon
    University
Webcrawler
Webtivities
White House.gov
WinMag.com
Wisc
WSJ
Yahoo
ZD Net
Zippo

11

In the future you'll see more and more channels and forums creating their own Web sites, to reach a broader audience and tap some of the power of the Web. Digital City is already beginning to "aggregate" sites for major metropolitan areas such as Washington and Chicago, for example, and the Travel section of the AOL 300 includes a site created by the channel itself.

WHAT'S MISSING?

Missing from this guide are the Web sites integrated into the "subchannels" you'll find within AOL's channels: the Your Business subchannel within Personal Finance, for example.

Tip   *The Internet is an unparalleled source of information about business as well as a place to do business. If the subject interests you, visit the InBusiness forum, led by Jill Ellsworth. Dr. Ellsworth provides a sampling of the best business resources on the Net (keyword: InBusiness).*

Also missing are two AOL channels that as yet have no parallel on the Web. First, the People Connection channel is primarily a place—hundreds of places, actually—to *chat*. Second, the Marketplace channel is a unique AOL offering. Marketplace is a hundred-story mall, a marvelous maze of stores to browse, with opportunities to purchase books, steaks, flowers, and notebook computers, among a myriad of other things. The Net's still pretty much a flea market, though electronic commerce on the Internet is coming on very strong and will likely reshape consumer habits in the next 3-5 years. For now, it's nowhere as convenient or as safe to purchase *anything* as on AOL.

The sites in the AOL 300 are missing something even more important. They're missing the context AOL provides to make a coherent whole out of diverse content. Channels add descriptive text, attitude, a point of view, chat rooms, message boards, leading personalities such as NetGirl and the Motley Fools, and *much* faster download times. Members take all this content and turn channels into communities, creating a mix more compelling than anything the Internet yet has to offer.

In a channel with *many* communities, such as Life, Styles & Interests, the best idea is to find your niche (whether it's writing or birdwatching) and explore *all* the AOL and Internet resources for that niche. It's a good way to meet people on America Online.

HOW DO I USE THE AOL 300?

As a starting place.

These 300 sites are a very small sampling of what the Internet has to offer. New sites are cropping up daily, some, no doubt, as good as what you'll find here. Begin with sites of personal or professional interest, and see where they lead you.

■ If you're looking for something that's not here, Chapter 9 provides plenty of guidance in finding exactly what you're seeking.

■ If you're looking for a way to stay up to date with new sites devoted to your interests, subscribe to the appropriate mailing lists, as discussed in Chapter 4.

One final thing, to repeat a point made in Chapter 1: the Web's not the Net. The AOL 300 brings you primarily Web sites because they're fun and easy to use. In the search for good, cool, and even practical information don't forget the other core Internet services: FTP, Telnet, e-mail, newsgroups, and mailing lists.

Tip   *Osborne/McGraw-Hill publishes two resource directories for your reading and Web-browsing pleasure:* Harley's Hahn's Internet and Web Yellow Pages, 1997 edition, *and Jean Polly's* Internet Kids and Family Yellow Pages, Second Edition *(1997).*

FEEDBACK

If you ever encounter problems with a site—because its address changes, or the site disappears, or anything else—please send a message to **inetbook97**. Please use the same address to recommend sites for inclusion in the next edition of this book. Thank you!

AOL MEMBERS' CHOICE

City.Net

http://www.city.net/

This site is a must-visit for travelers. Here you can find extensive information on any major city in the United States and the world, and you can search for other cities, too.

If you are planning a trip soon, check out Concierge, a listing of resources on arts and entertainment, food and drink, travel and sights, and the weather for any particular city or region. In addition, **City.Net** offers a free interactive, customizable mapping service.

DC Comics

http://www.dccomics.com/

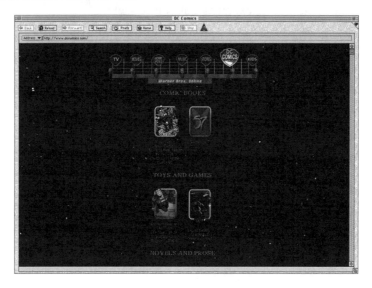

DC Comics fans frequent this site to find high-quality graphics, stories, and games. WeirdWeb, for instance, offers original and colorful online comic strips. If you enjoy interactive multimedia, explore the Toys and Games section to listen to the Superman radio serial and check out the digital trading cards. In addition, you can find original DC Comics fiction, complete with beautiful painted images, for adults, teenagers, and children.

EXTRA

http://www.extratv.com/

If you are an entertainment news addict, check out EXTRA, an insider's guide to Hollywood, fashion, business, and pop culture. Here you can read celebrity interviews, find exclusives on television shows and movies, and chat live with the stars. Movie buffs will appreciate the EXTRA film release schedule. If you are a fan of a particular celebrity, check out the Superstar Library to find specific information, images, and multimedia files.

Firefly

http://www.ffly.com

When the WWW first started to gain popularity, one of the biggest complaints was that it was "static." Surfers would access a page, look at it, and move on. There was no real interactivity. That's changing fast these days, and Firefly is one of the sites that is making the change. At its heart, Firefly is another database of movies and popular music, but the interface makes all the difference. Here you can rate music, and Firefly makes suggestions based on your ratings. You also have a special Firefly mailbox, where you can send and receive notes to other Firefly browsers. You can spend hours here.

HomeArts

http://www.homearts.com/

Welcome to the premiere Web magazine devoted to home life. This compilation of resources brings together the best content of popular magazines such as *Country Living, Good Housekeeping, Popular Mechanics,* and *Redbook.* Here you can find news and features on home improvement and decorating, crafts, family life, health, romance and relationships, and food. Some of the best features here include the extensive Recipe Finder database, the weekly horoscope, and the Botanica gardening newsletter.

iGuide

http://www.iguide.com/

A rich source of information—news, listings, and searchable databases—on television, movies, soap operas, music, and sports. If you enjoy interactive media, check out the TV show- or movie-specific games, quizzes, bulletin boards, and live chat auditorium. The features and databases are updated all the time, so keep visiting iGuide to stay abreast of the entertainment industry.

Jumbo

http://www.jumbo.com/

This is a huge—yet carefully organized—repository of free downloadable software available on the Net. Here you can find up-to-date software for various purposes, such as business (databases and finance), desktop (backgrounds and icons), education (tutorials and vocabulary-builders), and games (3D and adventure). The software runs on various platforms, and there's an archive of programs based on ActiveX and Java. Jumbo also offers value-added services, including What's New, to help you stay abreast of new software additions; the Resource Center to access a directory for Web sites; and Starter Kits for newbies.

Magellan Internet Guide

http://www.mckinley.com/

This Internet directory includes FTP, Gopher, and Telnet, as well as Web sites. Unlike many other directories, Magellan's resources are described and rated; a Green Light rating means a site's OK for kids. The directories, plus the Internet as a whole, are searchable. Magellan's People Finder helps you find long-lost friends. Surfers who want to sneak a peek at others' search entries will enjoy watching the automatically updating Search Voyeur.

MapQuest

http://www.mapquest.com/

Why spend money on a new road atlas when you can access MapQuest for free? This service allows to you customize your own interactive atlas and create a personalized home page. After entering address or city information, you can view detailed road maps of the area, zoom in and out, and identify points of interest for travel and business services. If you are planning a road trip, check out TripQuest, an easy-to-use, door-to-door mapping service.

MTV Online

http://www.mtv.com/

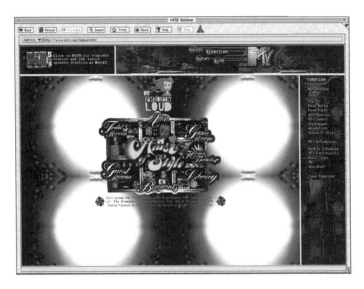

If you're an MTV fan, you'll love this site. MTV Online offers the latest in music news as well as information on shows such as *Real World, Road Rules,* and *Beavis and Butt-Head.* You can also find data, graphics, and audio clips of your favorite bands and vocal artists. The Java-enriched version offers live news and hot graphics. If you have a slower connection or prefer a more straightforward approach to surfing, you'll appreciate the Decaf version.

Riddler

http://www.riddler.com/

If you enjoy games and puzzles, check out Riddler, one of the most popular game sites on the Web. Riddler offers word searches, a solitaire game, and a trivia sampler to members and non-members alike. Membership registration is free, and once you are registered you may play the Daily Riddle, crossword puzzles, and a variety of trivia games. You may even win a prize!

11

Salon

http://www.salon1999.com/

This popular Web e-zine is one of the best reads on the Net. Salon offers a rich mix of feature articles, including some by famous writers and celebrities. Here you can also find updated comic strips by Tom Tomorrow, Carol Lay, and others. The most popular feature of this site may be Table Talk, Salon's interactive bulletin board, in which you can participate in discussions about books, television, movies, digital culture, music, politics, and more.

Switchboard

http://www.switchboard.com

A groovy people and business directory. This is a way to search for companies, addresses, and telephone numbers that's faster than your hardcopy telephone directory book. Your search is not limited by your own geographic region; Switchboard lets you search people and businesses in any city and state. Within its database, Switchboard contains additional contact information, such as e-mail addresses, affiliations, and personal comments. You may add and modify your own listings free of charge. If you wish, Switchboard will not make your actual e-mail addresses publicly known, but will forward any messages to you.

Tripod: Tools for Life

http://www.tripod.com/

Some Web sites focus on a particular subject; this one takes "life" as its subject. This appropriately named, practical Web publication is akin to an all-purpose guide to how to improve your life in a variety of areas: money, politics, community, living, and travel. The information is delivered in the form of how-to guides, bulletin boards, and interactive tools such as the Resume Builder and Retirement Planner. If you are a surfer and just want to relax and have fun, check out the Tripod Toybox for multimedia games, animations, and other goodies.

Warner Brothers Online

http://www.warnerbros.com/

The central information hub for WB media and services, including television, movies, music, videos, stores, and DC Comics. (Warner Brothers is also available on AOL at keyword: WB.) The site is chock-full of colorful graphics, cartoons, and animations. Kids will especially enjoy viewing WB Animation, which includes Looney Tune animations, downloadable media files, games, puzzles, and other goodies. The Warner Brothers Kids Page features Looney Tunes Karaoke.

11

COMPUTERS & SOFTWARE

CINet's Product Reviews

http://www.cnet.com/Content/Reviews/

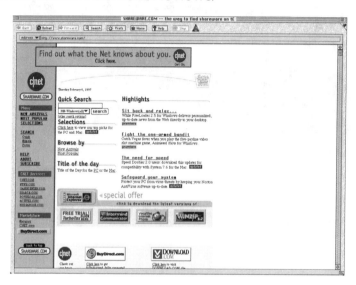

Nearly everyone knows about Clnet's Web site. It's one of the absolute best sites about computing and the Internet. The folks at AOL's Computing and Software channel have singled out the Product Review page though, and rightly so. Here you can read informed opinions on hardware and software. The page is updated often, so you'll want to check back regularly. The design is the typical confusing jumble that Clnet uses everywhere on their site, but what the heck—you're here for the information, and there's plenty of that!

comp.sys.mac.announce (newsgroup)

comp.sys.mac.announce is very low-volume newsgroup—there aren't many postings, but when there is one, you can be sure that it contains vital information for Macintosh owners. Here you can find information about software upgrades, news from Apple itself, and announcements of Mac-related Web sites. Add this one to Read My Newsgroups in order to keep tabs on it—you'll be glad you did.

Computer Virus Help Desk

http://www.indyweb.net/~cvhd

The Macintosh Utilities (MUT) forum on AOL is one of the best resources for Mac users around. One of the things they do very well is disseminate information about computer viruses. Their link to the Computer Virus Help Desk is one of their nicest features. The site provides visitors with guidance in preventing, detecting, and eradicating computer viruses. One thing to note about this site is that it is heavily Java-dependent. If you aren't using a Java-enabled browser, such as the one that comes with the Macintosh version of AOL 3.0, you may not have access to all the features of the site.

Design & Publishers Center

http://www.graphic-design.com/

This online center for visual communications includes information and links for anyone involved with graphics, writing, typography, printing, publishing, advertising, signs, displays—in short, for anyone in the design and publishing fields. The site includes Web chat, interviews, and links to online versions of several desktop publishing magazines. It also actively solicits submissions: "Guess what? Talent scouts cruise our Gallery all the time! They're looking for your masterpieces!"

FamilyPC on the Web

http://www.zdnet.com/familypc

This electronic counterpart to the Ziff-Davis print publication is devoted to family computing and features reviews of hardware and software and recommendations of family-friendly places to visit on the Internet. For kids, there are stories, projects, and contests.

11

Guide to Computer Vendors

http://guide.sbanetweb.com/

From SBA * Consulting, this simple guide provides a searchable and browsable directory to all the major and many of the minor vendors of software and hardware. Plus, there are links to dozens of computer magazines.

Macintosh Emulators

http://www.emulation.net/

Who says your Mac can only be a Mac? This unique site is devoted to emulators for the Macintosh—programs that let the Mac operate like other computers. If you need to run Windows 95, use an obscure program for the Amiga computer, or just have a hankering to play the old arcade version of Space Invaders, this site will show you how to do it on your Mac. Well-organized and filled with interesting news about Mac emulators.

MacinTouch

http://www.macintouch.com/

Mac news—official, unofficial and sometimes just rumors—abounds at MacinTouch. This site features news of interest to Mac users, from announcements of new system software to pointers to sites for Macophiles, like the Unofficial Apple Color LaserWriter Site. MacinTouch also announces updates to important applications and provides inside news from Apple Computer. Updated nearly every day, this will truly be a Favorite Place for people who love their Macs.

MIDI City

http://www.berkshire.net/~malancar/midicity.htm

A favorite of the PC Music & Sound Forum. MIDI is the Musical Instrument Digital Interface, a cool technology for simulating instruments, and putting a lot of music into very small files. Chapter 8 has more to say about MIDI. Dedicated to MIDI music by songwriters and developers, MIDI City provides original artists' MIDI songs which you can hear on your Mac. It includes links to a dozen or so sites where you can find bluegrass, big band, and light jazz tunes sequenced for MIDI. Best of all, it will play selections for you while you browse. The site comes in three flavors: frames, no frames, and free-flying frames. The last choice works properly only with Netscape Navigator 3.

Modems, Modems, Modems

http://www.rosenet.net/~costmo

The Costmo Modem page was created to be a hub where you can find links to just about any modem information that might be available on the Web. It succeeds. Here you can find links to more than 50 modem manufacturers, links to other sites about modems, initialization strings for all occasions, and the site-creator's personal experiences with a variety of different modems. The page design is very simple. Virtually all the links are on the same page, so you can either use the handy alphabetic buttons or simply scroll down until you find the modem manufacturer you want.

The Pixel Foundry

http://the-tech.mit.edu/KPT/KPT.html

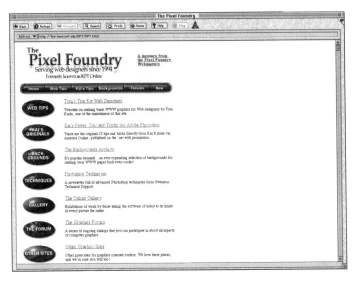

Formerly known as KPT Online, The Pixel Foundry has a wealth of information for users of Adobe Photoshop. It includes an interactive message forum and tips from Kai Krause, Tom Karlo, and Swanson Technical Support. There are also dozens of background tiles you can use for your Web pages or desktop. The design is clean and uncluttered, allowing you to move from page to page and get the information you want without delay. If you're a Photoshop or Kai's Power Tools user, this page should be one of your Favorite Places.

Print Magazine Online—1995 Regional Design Annual

http://www.printmag.com/

Print is America's leading graphic design magazine, and its online version shows you why. It includes every page of the printed design annual. Winning images are indexed and can be searched by category, designer's name, design firm, art director, client, and region. You can also click through the pages as though you are looking through the paper version of the book, or you can take a guided tour. It's a good thing they're so organized, because there are 2,000 images on this site! This may be one of the best-looking sites on the Web.

RealAudio

http://www.realaudio.com/

If video is the Web's future, then RealAudio is the present. Anyone who has tried to look at a video clip on the Web over a 28.8 kbps connection knows that we have a way to go before the technology is really useful. Sound is another matter. RealAudio has created a quiet revolution. You can get high-quality sound (near CD-quality over a fast connection) from a Web page without having to wait for the file to download. This is the Progressive Networks' home page, and you can either download your free RealAudio player here or purchase an enhanced player or server (the software that allows you to put RealAudio sound clips on your page). The best thing about this Web site is that it contains links to dozens of pages with interesting sounds. You can listen to live music at the House of Blues, hear the latest news being reported by ABC, or check National Public Radio's "All Things Considered."

Shareware.com

http://www.shareware.com

Shareware.com is a tremendously popular site for downloading software on the World Wide Web. By dividing the software up into easy-to-use categories (games, Internet, multimedia, etc.) and then writing short, breezy, and informative reviews of each offering, the C|net folks make it easy for you to find what you want and then decide if you really want it. Like the rest of the C|net site, the design here is busy, busy, busy. It is filled with advertisements, button bars, tables of contents, and search windows. Still, it loads quickly and is very easy to use. If you haven't seen any of the pages on C|net's Web site, this is a great place to start. It is also updated regularly, so you will probably want to bookmark it.

DIGITAL CITY

Alaska Internet Travel Guide

http://www.alaska-online.com/travel/alaska.htm

If you're planning to travel to Alaska, you'll want to explore this travel guide first. Here you can find statewide information on accommodations, adventures, hunting and fishing, cruises, parks, travel agents, and more. Say you're planning to visit Kodiak or the Kenai Peninsula. No problem—just click the particular region on the imagemap of Alaska to get more detailed information. Look over Alaska Lingo to learn fun terms like "bush pilot" (a pilot of small aircraft providing transportation

11

to isolated Alaskan areas), *cheechako* (a newcomer to Alaska), and "outside" (anywhere outside of Alaska).

Atlanta Traveler

http://www.georgia-traveler.com/

An excellent service for both Atlanta residents and travelers, this Web site offers a broad range of pointers to Atlanta information, including entertainment, professional sports teams, city sites, cultural events, and community services. The transportation section is especially useful and features continually updated maps of real-time traffic and a map of the Atlanta area freeway system, as well as information on public transit, MARTA parking, and route planning. Also, check the Atlanta project section to read about why Atlantans are the first to use the Intelligent Transportation Systems to ease the stressed metropolitan transportation system.

Boston Online

http://obi.std.com/NE/boston.html

An impressive and well-organized directory of Boston area community services, organizations, education, entertainment, culture, health care, environment, sports, and much more. While you're browsing the directory, you can learn something about Boston as the capital of Massachusetts, why Boston is called the "Athens of America" and the "Hub of the Universe," a bit about cod, and Roger Williams' recipe for Boston baked beans. Boston lovers won't want to miss Adam Gaffin's Good Guide to Boston English, where you can learn Boston pronunciation, place names, and neighborhood variations, as well as peruse an extensive glossary of vocabulary.

California Highway Conditions

http://www.dot.ca.gov/hq/roadinfo/

Everyone in California is affected by highway conditions; this Web site offers a reliable way of previewing road conditions before you start the car. Here you can get immediate information on all the interstate, state, and U.S. routes (listed by route number), an hourly compilation of all current reports, winter driving conditions, and alternate routes for damaged highways. If you'll be traveling through Nevada, check the data provided by the Nevada Department of Transportation at the bottom of the main page.

Chicago

http://chicago.digitalcity.com/

A visually attractive combination of a Web directory and metropolitan magazine for Chicagoland. Here you can find interesting articles on things like spas, Brenda Starr comics, and ballroom dancing. The Go Guide to recreational sports is jam-packed with helpful information on finding a local pickup game of basketball, billiards, or bridge. Similarly, the entertainment section provides calendars, club information, and tons of ideas for going out on the town. If you live in or are planning to visit a suburb of Chicago, check out Digital City's guide to Arlington Heights, Crystal Lake, Evanston, Hoffman Estates, Naperville, and Schaumburg.

Colorado, Arts to Zoo

http://www.artstozoo.org/

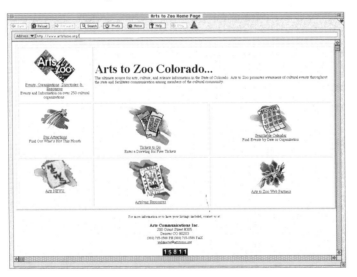

"The ultimate source for arts, culture, and science information" in Colorado, from A to Z. The Events, Organizations, Directories, and Resources sections contain a huge listing of arts, dance, music, theater, and other cultural and educational information. If you're interested in staying abreast of the Colorado arts scene, check the news section to read press releases that are posted several times a week. Also, you can jump to Star Attractions to find a listing of events during the current month.

Destination: Washington, D.C.

http://www.washingtonpost.com/wp-srv/local/longterm/tours/guide2.htm

Here's a unique tourist guide to Washington, D.C. provided by the Washington Post. Some interesting virtual tours you can take include the Scandal Tour ("a glimpse of Washington's seamy underbelly"), Black History and Latino Culture Tours (museums, schools, and historical houses), The Smithsonian and the National Mall, the Theater Guide, and the Restaurant Guide. Other fun stuff you can find here includes the Washington Trivia Quiz, a public golf course guide, an outdoor recreational guide, and a music calendar.

Experience New Orleans

http://www.neosoft.com/~bigeasy/acquaint.html

A virtual tour of the city famous for jazz, Mardi Gras, the Orpheus Parade, cemeteries, swamps, the Saints, and Cajun cuisine. You can learn about these and other facets of New Orleans culture and history at this Web site; it also provides a live Netcast from Mardi Gras (as well as a gallery of photographs after the event), authentic Creole and Cajun recipes, a useful shopping guide, and information on New Orleans celebrities such as Harry Connick, Jr. and Anne Rice.

Honolulu's Internet Café

http://www.aloha-cafe.com/

The aesthetically appealing Web site of "the World's First 24-Hour Cybercafé," located in Honolulu. This Web site is kindly offered in light (text), medium (text and graphics), and heavy (Java, Quicktime, and audio) versions. Here you can read news about both the café and about the Internet. If you're a serious news addict, click Brief to find a thorough index to famous columns and newspapers around the United States. Art lovers will want to visit the Gallery to view images of works by Hawaiian artists.

Houston Entertainment Network

http://www.steppingout.com/culture/maincu.htm

An interesting and useful collection of cultural, entertainment, and community information for the Houston area. In the attractions section, you can find information on such sites as the American Funeral Service Museum, Six Flags Waterworld, the

Houston Space Center, and the Beer Can House—and everything in between. Ballet lovers will want to peruse the Houston Ballet page to read about productions like *Swan Lake*, *The Nutcracker*, *Dracula*, and *Don Quixote*.

Las Vegas Leisure Guide

http://www.pcap.com/lasvegas.htm

A complete guide to Las Vegas, one of the world's most popular vacation destinations. In addition to everything you need to plan your vacation—tours, hotels, shows, restaurants, recreation, night life, shopping, transportation, attractions, and maps—you can also find an extensive guide to conventions and business services in the area. The main page offers news about casinos and hotels, which makes it easy to stay abreast of new attractions.

Meet Minneapolis

http://www.minneapolis.org/

Well-organized guide to the "City of Lakes." The Discover Minneapolis section is chock-full of fun and useful information, including "Minne-facts" about business and the economy, medicine, the quality of life, and trivia; original cartoons by Paul Davies in Minnesota Sights; and a message from the Mayor. If you need more information, you can fill out the Tourism Information Request Form to have pamphlets and guides sent to you via the postal service.

Pittsburgh Net

http://www.pittsburgh.net/

The official site of the city of Pittsburgh. Here you can find a variety of useful materials, such as the online Yellow Pages, visitors information, and residential and business relocation information. In addition, this site offers some fun stuff, like a special welcome message from Mayor Tom Murphy and a Quicktime video of Pittsburgh. Visitors will especially appreciate the special events calendar and the Top Ten Reasons for Visiting Pittsburgh.

Seattle P-I Plus

http://www.seattle-pi.com/

The official Web supplement to the printed *Seattle Post-Intelligencer* newspaper. Here you'll find four main sections: Getaways, Neighbors, Golf NW, and Classified. Although there isn't much news at this Web site, these four sections offer some worthwhile local information. In Getaways, for instance, you can find a multitude of materials on outdoors recreation, travel, and the natural environment. In addition, the Neighbors section profiles a different neighborhood or Seattle region once a week.

TotalNY

http://www.totalny.com/

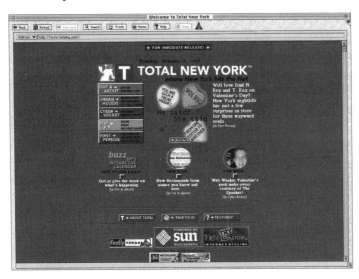

The motto "Where New York hits the Net" is a fairly accurate description of this site. Here you'll find five main sections—Out & About, Urban Access, Cyber Socket, Pop Fix, and First Person—all of which are chock-full of detailed information, reviews, and guides. In Out & About, for example, you can peruse Buzz, the event calendar; NY Essentials, a guide to eating, clubbing, and Web surfing; and NY Solutions, a quick-and-dirty collection of advice for real estate, fashion, and holiday problems and issues.

ENTERTAINMENT

alt.days (newsgroup)

http://www.io.com/~jlc/alt_days/

An alternative version of NBC's *Days of Our Lives,* **alt.days** has been in production since 1993 as a Usenet newsgroup and has been on the Web since 1995. While many of the same characters who appear on the television show also show up here, the plot is independent of the broadcast show. You can keep up with the episodes each week in the newsgroup, or you can check this Web site (where episodes are uploaded

11

biweekly) and read the complete series in the archives. The Web site has additional features such as cast lists and a readers poll.

Café Utne

http://www.utne.com/cafe

The magazine *Utne Reader* is a progressive version of *Reader's Digest*. The Utne Café has taken the concerns and interests of *Utne* readers and created a Web site with more than 40 conferences with hundreds of topics. As they say of their site, it is "a place in cyberspace where ideas and community intersect." Although it is free, you must register to use this service, and, because of Utne's concern about the male/female ratio of contributors to their site, men may find themselves waiting a few days.

Celebrities On-Line

http://www.mgal.com/links/celeb.html

Subtitled "Cool Links to Celebrity Sites," Celebrities On-Line delivers the goods. It has more than 70 links to specific celebrity sites as well as links to *People* magazine online, the Official Interactive Guide to the Academy Awards, information on autographs, and a TV index offering information on what celebrities are doing on the tube this month. There is one oddity here: among the links to pages for Christian Slater, Sharon Stone, and Madonna is a link to a Web page for jailed Native American activist Leonard Peltier. Here you'll find not just the "manufactured" stars but the people you want to know about.

Centre for the Easily Amused

http://www.amused.com

Your best bet for trivia and time-wasting tips, this site is an exercise in uncomplicated frivolity. The Centre's Short Attention Span Site of the week (SASS) offers truly useless Internet resources ranging from **RubberChicken.com** to the Home Lobotomy Kit to really awful sites. They'd also like to sell you stuff: T-shirts, caps ("not just for bad hair days"), and a CEA mousepad.

Dilbert Zone

http://www.unitedmedia.com/comics/dilbert/

The engineer-as-hero and management-as-obstacle-to-progress. That's *Dilbert* in a nutshell, one of the most popular comic strips in the country, especially among nerds. Read Dilbert at this site daily, but be aware that the strip is delayed a week before making it to the Web. Still, it's worth it, since you can read months of the cartoons at a time. You can read the original Dilbert strips submitted to syndication and see some of Scott Adams' pre-Dilbert attempts here as well. There are also contests, games, and a Dilbert store. On AOL, check out keyword: Dilbert.

The Doonesbury Electronic Town Hall

http://www.doonesbury.com/

News, opinions, real-time chat, and message boards—all with the flip but critical Doonesbury point of view. Curious about how the characters have aged? Check out a Doonesbury strip from 16 years ago. Want your own Zonker T-shirt? You can get that here, too. You'll also get some astute political commentary, a very amusing biweekly poll, and lists of activist organizations.

Graceland

http://www.elvis-presley.com/

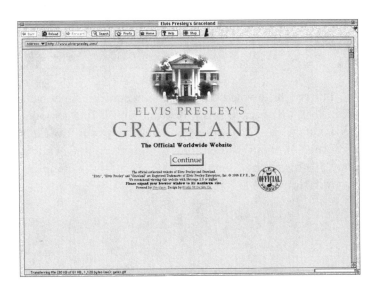

If you're planning a pilgrimage to the estate of the late Elvis Aron Presley, plan your trip here, the official Web page for Graceland that includes ample information on tours and hotels. You will also find a discography and filmography of the King here. Even if you aren't planning to visit Memphis any time soon, there's still a good reason to see this site. It's the home of the Graceland Shopping Mall, which claims

11

to have "the finest selection of Elvis Presley merchandise" anywhere. Finally, a source for the much-sought-after Elvis doll!

Hollywood Online

http://www.hollywood.com/

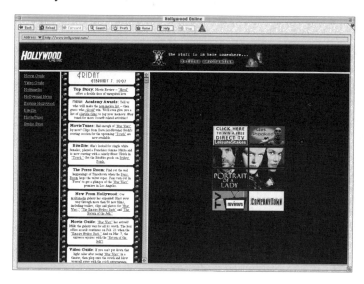

The, um, blockbuster site devoted to the quintessentially American industry of making movies. They don't leave much out, and you'll find reviews, box office statistics, video catalogs, gossip, multimedia clips from your favorite flicks, and a big source of information about (and samples of) soundtracks. Of course, you'll also find stuff to buy. It's owned by Time Mirror and beautifully complements AOL's version at keyword: Hollywood.

Internet Movie Database

http://www.imdb.com

One thing the Internet is good at is making available simple databases, enabling you to get the specific information you need. Take this site: it's got information about more than 80,000 movies and an even larger number of actors and actresses. Type in, say, *Fearless Vampire Killers*, and you get the plot summary, director, complete cast, some trivia questions, and a chance to rate the movie. For many actors and actresses, you'll get a biography and hyperlinks. You can search by keyword as well as movie name, making this site a superb research resource if you have serious film interests. Other goodies: local cinema schedules (they aim to cover the world, so it's not quite complete yet), info about movie-related mailing lists, a trivia quiz, and "This Day in the Movies." Bring some popcorn.

Mr. Showbiz

http://www.mrshowbiz.com/

Are you a Hollywood junkie? If so, this online magazine, brought to you by Starwave (the same people who produce the popular ESPNet), is for you. Updated daily, Mr. Showbiz brings you entertainment news, film reviews, interviews, biographies, fun polls, contests, a real-time chat area, and more. For a real hoot, try playing in the Plastic Surgery lab, where you can mix and match famous features to create bizarre new celebrities.

Personalized Shakespearean Insults Page

http://kite.preferred.com/insults/

Plug in a name and out comes an insult: "Thou art a knotty-pated beslubbering pignut, Jon!" "Thou art a bat-fowling currish pumpion, Vick!" The erudite way to insult a boss or in-law, more dignified than "I told you so."

11

rec.arts.tv.soaps.misc (newsgroup)

If you just can't get enough conversation about soap operas, there's a place for you in the Usenet newsgroups. In the **rec.arts.tv.soaps.misc** newsgroup, you can discuss the relationship between Josie and Gary on *Another World* or the machinations of Sami and Kate on *Days of Our Lives*. You'll even find the occasional posting from writers and others close to the shows who give hints about future developments and the background stories of characters. If this isn't enough, you might also want to check **rec.arts.tv.soaps.abc** and **rec.arts.tv.soaps.cbs**.

Scrolling Mystery Theater

http://www.fiction.com/

The Advanced Fiction Workshop explores the literary, creative facets of network-centric computing. Its first project is the launch of the Scrolling Mystery Theater, which brings groundbreaking detective fiction and thrillers to the World Wide Web. SMT's first production, "The Moving Face," written by the site's Webmaster Robert Richardson, premiered on February 20, 1996, and can be read here in its entirety.

The Squat

http://www.thesquat.com

The Squat is one of the world's first online comedy shows. It began as a satire of The Spot (a Web site that created a fictional situation similar to MTV's *Real World*) but has taken on a life of its own. Instead of a young, attractive, upwardly mobile group living together in a beach house, you have homely, incredibly stupid people living together in a trailer. Its clever animations and art are worth the price of admission (free, by the way), but it is the continuing comedic adventure that will keep you coming back. So pick up some Whup A** beer and join Earl, Woody, Val, Cleitus, and Elvis in their trailer park home.

Worldwide Internet Live Music Archive (WILMA)

http://wilma.com/

WILMA includes a database of concert schedules for more than 3,000 musical performers. You can search for concerts by artist, city, or venue. There are also sound clips, music reviews, and articles about bands, singers, and songwriters. You can join in the conversation in their musical chat room, or join the Intergalactic Freak Club to win free prizes. WILMA also has a mailing list that can be joined from here.

GAMES

Avalon

http://www.avalon-rpg.com

A beautifully designed role-playing game with a faraway, mythological feel. At this Web site you actually engage in and play the game, but the site also contains everything you need to get started and maintain the game's logical structure. The Introduction is a step-by-step tutorial that teaches you about creating a character, getting help, the geography of Avalon, cityports and guilds, and communicating with other players.

The Big List of Puzzle and Riddle Pages

http://huizen.dds.nl/~mahulsma/biglist.htm

A huge and well-organized compilation of puzzle and riddle pages on the Web. If you're a regular here, you can simply check the front cover page of this site to find new listings. Many of the listings are rated, and they all have reviews. For more lists, check Archives to find an index of **rec.puzzles** archives in North America, Europe, and Asia. If you like Escher, you'll find a handy list of optical-illusion sites.

Bridge on the Web

http://www.cs.vu.nl/~sater/bridge/bridge-on-the-web.html

Mecca for bridge aficionados. This is a simple, straightforward site where you can find just about anything pertaining to the popular card game. For fans, there's information about recent and upcoming tournaments all over the world, and, for players, there are laws and rules. For enthusiasts, there are bridge-related companies, periodicals, and even arguments for making bridge a new Olympic sport. There are several sections devoted to electronic bridge resources, such as bridge software, live bridge games online, FTP sites, Usenet newsgroups, and indexes of other bridge Web pages.

Chess Space

http://www.redweb.com/chess/

An award-winning resource for chess enthusiasts. Chess Space offers tons of links to chess sites on the Internet—and these links are impeccably organized, so you can easily find what you're looking for. Categories include Internet Archives, Audio Sites, Commercial Sites, Databases, E-mail Chess Games, and anything else you might want. Or you could skip all that and go directly to BEST, where you can find the most valuable and well-designed chess sites.

Computer Gaming World

http://www.zdnet.com/gaming/

If you enjoy playing games on your computer—any type of game—you've come to the right place. This is an excellent resource for not just staying abreast of the computer gaming industry, but for getting insider information on good gaming computers, peripherals, and networking connectivity. Here you can find news and features; reviews; sneak previews; strategies, tips, and cheats; worthy opponents; and interactive discussions on action, adventure, role-playing, simulation, space, sports, strategy, war, and online games, as well as discussions on classics and puzzles.

CyberLink Web Games

http://www.cyber-link.net/games.htm

Simple, straightforward index of interactive, multimedia Web-based games. Here you can find everything from puzzles and board games to casino gambling and horror-genre games. If you are drawn to the bizarre, check out Find-the-Spam and Piercing Mildred. Otherwise, the "normal" games are well represented: Tetris-style motion puzzles, racing games, crosswords, trivia and matching games, virtual construction sets, Yahtzee, Mastermind, Spirograph, scavenger hunts, and even the Sony PlayStation Web Game.

Dream League

http://www.dreamleague.com/

The Dream League is the original promoter of fantasy sports in the United Kingdom and Europe, as well as throughout the world. This is one of the best sources for easy Dream Team selection. Here you can find information on Gaelic Football, Cycling, Cricket, Golf, Tennis, and Motor Racing Dream Leagues, as well as daily updates during live events. The Football (*soccer*, in the U.S.) League is available on World Soccernet. Check out the competition results for the European Champions League and the U.K. Snooker Championships.

duJour

http://www.dujour.com/

New games, puzzles, and contests every day. Here you can play MondoTrivia, The Labyrinth (a maddening multidimensional maze), Jacques du Jour (casino card games), WordAngst (lexicon games), BigByte (brain twisters), and the Online Sphinx in Riddle du Jour. If you win a game, your name will be prominently displayed on the front page of duJour, and you may win some cool prizes. Just for the heck of it, check out Ce Jour to learn what is so special about today's date in history, including birthdays, death anniversaries, significant events, and holidays from around the world.

Games Domain

http://www.gamesdomain.com/

An internationally mirrored meta-index of gaming resources on the Net where you can download scores of free games for all personal computer platforms and check out hundreds of demos and previews. You can also run a sophisticated search for specific game information which covers a wide range of resources, such as commercial sites, game hints and cheats, and online gaming help. Families will be pleased with the Kids Area, where there's kid-appropriate software, contests, desktop decorations, and FAQs.

GameSpot

http://www.gamespot.com/

Home to a mountain of computer games of every stripe—action, adventure, role-playing, sports, simulation, and strategy. Each page provides in-depth review and test results according to game play, graphics, sound, learning curve, and difficulty. Shopping for a 14-year-old or closet gamer? Check out the Game Spot Top 10—or jump directly to GameSpot's Product Index to find an extensive alphabetized list of computer games.

House of Cards

http://www.sky.net/~rrasa/hoc.html

A central hub of card game information, with a focus on the different types of solitaire card games. Here you can find downloads and support for shareware solitaire games, including Solitaire Suite, Simple Pleasures, Four Seasons, FoxFire 13, Pyramid Deluxe, Poker Squares, and Chinese Solitaire. If you enjoy playing cards with others, this site is also a good resource for a variety of multiplayer card games. If you need more information, check the index of links to information on online rulebooks, books, newsgroups, e-mail lists, archives, and other shareware card games.

11

The Internet Role Playing Society

http://feeds.engr.ucf.edu/irps/

Official Web site of the Internet Role Playing Society (IRPS), a club "dedicated to the advancement of role-playing over the Internet." Here you can register to become a club member; it's free. Once you are a member, you may access a large database of other players and subscribe to a monthly newsletter. In addition, you can conduct club business, read about the IRPS, engage in Internet-based role-playing games, learn about upcoming conventions and tournaments, and find other resources such as e-mail lists and organizations.

The MUD Resource Collection

http://www.clock.org/muds/

Extensive index of Multi-User Dungeon (MUD)-related informational and gaming links. Both MUD users and researchers who study the communications and sociology of MUDs will find many useful resources here. For general information, jump right to the FAQs page to find a huge list of FAQs and Usenet newsgroups. Students and teachers may want to explore Research-Oriented Links first. Other resources you can find here include MUDlists and MudWHO, Web interfaces to games, FTP Archives, and lists of Multi-User Shared Hallucinations (MUSHes).

POKERwwwORLD

http://pokerwwworld.com/

There are many poker information and gaming resources here, although the Web page interface is a bit off-putting with its avant-garde design. Once you start roaming the site, though, you'll find an impressive compilation of links to poker-related newsgroups, rulebooks, IRC, and Web sites. Serious poker enthusiasts won't want to skip Razzo's Poker Archive, where they can uncover images and biographies of famous players, reference materials, and descriptions of poker events. And they'll appreciate the rule books provided for the varieties of poker.

Video Game Yellow Pages:
Your Guide to Computer and Video Games

http://www.gamepen.com/yellowpages/

Like the name says, this is a comprehensive reference to computer and video gaming sites on the Internet. It's your guide to electronic gaming mailing lists, online archives, publications, and documentation. There are specific sections for action, adventure, flight simulation, strategy, role-playing, and sports games. In addition, you can ponder indexes for cheats and hints, demos and downloads, multiplayer online and network games, fan sites, patches and fixes, commercial sites, and much more.

HEALTH & FITNESS

Achoo Online Healthcare Services

http://www.achoo.com

It's hard to dislike or overlook a site named Achoo, especially since *Consumer Reports* (keyword: Consumer) recently singled it out as one of the most useful Internet resources for people who need reliable medical information. Achoo aims to be the comprehensive directory of health-related resources. Included are links to 8,000 Web sites and hundreds of newsgroups, all helpfully arranged for both browsing and searching. The site is a service to the Internet from a company that (among other things) designs Web sites for companies and organizations in the healthcare sector.

American Cancer Society

http://www.cancer.org/

An award-winning Web site with information and support for medical professionals, cancer patients, and their families. You'll find information about ACS programs, events, offices, and meetings, and you'll find a large set of links to the growing number of Net cancer resources. You can also access news on cancer research and cancer prevention. This is a great place to learn how you can donate money or time to this cause and to find out exactly how your contribution helps.

American Diabetes Association

http://www.diabetes.org/

Start here for information on both diabetes and the American Diabetes Association itself. It's also a good source of health-conscious recipes, with a new offering each day and a review of the past week's recipes. A self-test for diabetes is offered as a way of learning more about the disease. A state-by-state listing helps you find the nearest ADA office, or you can search for specific medical information.

11

America's Housecall Network

http://www.housecall.com/

Some sites bury their treasure. On the Housecall Network, the treasure is the invaluable drug reference from U.S. Pharmacopeia, based on USP's consumer pamphlets, which contains reliable information about prescription drugs: warnings, usage advice, and the like. (In the Health Information section, click Medications.) The American Academy of Family Physicians also makes its pamphlets available, with information on dozens of common ailments such as nosebleeds and ulcers. (The link is in the Dictionary section of Health Information.) Two dozen bulletin boards let you ask questions and perhaps get answers via the Web.

Blindness Resource Center

http://www.nyise.org/access.htm

A Web site dedicated to making the Net accessible for the sight-impaired, it's available, naturally, in a large-print format. Tools and information for helping low-vision users to access the Web are readily available, along with discussions of considerate design. Learn about "talking" programs for the visually impaired and how blind people use computers. Other fascinating links offer information about organizations serving the visually impaired and an archive of the mailing list Blind-L, which discusses computer use by and for the blind.

CNN Interactive Health

http://www.cnn.com/HEALTH/

Cable News Network offers top health-related stories in a format that allows you to either scan headlines or plunge in for more depth. Prominent parts of the site promote CNN shows such as *Parenting Today* and *Your Health*. This is a great way to check the programming schedule for future shows that might be of interest to you and to check out transcripts of shows you may have missed or in which you have a particular interest. Direct access to the rest of CNN Interactive makes for a great way to get your minimum daily information requirement.

HospitalWeb

http://neuro-www.mgh.harvard.edu/hospitalWeb.nclk

Created and maintained by the department of Neurology at Massachusetts General Hospital, HospitalWeb is a small but growing list of hospitals on the Web, working towards offering a way for patients, medical researchers, and physicians to get information on any hospital in the world. Geographically arranged information makes finding your hospital's Web site easier. HospitalWeb offers an "Interesting Medical Site" of the week, medical school listings, and links to the sites of healthcare businesses.

Interactive Food Finder

http://www.olen.com/food/

Based on the book *Fast Food Facts* by the Minnesota Attorney General's Office, the Interactive Food Finder aims to break you of the fast-food habit. In a special form, you select a fast-food restaurant, type in your favorite dinner, and click Fire Up the Deep Fryer. You'll find out, if you can bear the truth, the number of calories and amount of fat, sodium, and cholesterol in your favorite fast foods. Not for the timid or those who won't pass up the fries.

KidsHealth

http://kidshealth.org/

The medical experts at the Nemour's Children's Clinic at the duPont Hospital for Children bring you KidsHealth.Org. This site is devoted to the health of children and teens and features information on growth, food and fitness, childhood infections, immunizations, and more. The interests of parents and professionals are nicely served. The Nemours Foundation also includes some fun for kids, with games, Shockwave animations, and cool activities. One area even covers kids' health questions, such as, "What makes you sneeze?" Big fun!

MedicineNet

http://www.medicinenet.com/

A free medical resource, presenting news and information on medical and health issues for the consumer. Included in the useful content in this site is a medical dictionary, pharmacy information, an alphabetical list of diseases and treatments, and *a state-by-state listing of 24-hour poison control centers*—a particularly valuable resource for families with small children. Here's a tip: print out a hard copy of your state's centers and keep it by your phone.

Medscape

http://www.medscape.com/

This site, one of the few health-related sites recommended by *Consumer Reports*, features full-text articles from leading medical journals, plus free searchable access to both Medline and the National Library of Medicine's AIDSLINE. Medscape caters to the needs of patients as well as physicians, even offering Continuing Medical Education credit. Click to subscribe to Medscape's mailing list, MedPulse. The simple, low-graphic interface makes it easy to get around.

Mental Health Net

http://www.cmhc.com/

Mental Health Net's award-winning site offers links to more than 4,200 individual resources covering information on disorders such as depression, anxiety, panic attacks, chronic fatigue syndrome, and substance abuse. Linger in the "Reading Room," browse resources for professionals and administrators, and spend some time with the self-help resources. These areas offer links to magazines, discussion forums, polls, news, a managed care glossary, and a Clinician's Yellow Pages.

Oncolink

http://cancer.med.upenn.edu/

Oncolink is the University of Pennsylvania's award-winning Cancer Center resource Web site. There is a search facility available, but many topics of immediate interest are available at a glance. Information on cancer can be found via the site's Disease Oriented Menus and FAQs. Issues of concern to patients and their families, such as psychosocial support and financing, are conveniently available. Links such as their Conferences and Meetings, Clinical Trials, and Journals will attract the medical professional.

Special Education Resources on the Internet

http://www.hood.edu/seri/serihome.htm

This is a massive directory whose resources cover more than special education. The topics are of interest to any parent or professional concerned about children whose educational needs aren't met by the existing system. The topics covered include learning disabilities, attention deficit disorder, autism, assistive technologies, and legal resources.

Women's Health Resources

http://sunsite.unc.edu/cheryb/women/resource/health-int.html

A clearinghouse of information about women's health concerns relating to breast cancer, pregnancy, and HIV. Also available are facts on homeopathy, caffeine, and computer-related repetitive strain injuries and their effects on women. More general guides to women's health resources can be found here, as well as a link to a women's health Gopher and several Web publications addressing these concerns.

THE HUB

AFU and Urban Legends Archive

http://www.urbanlegends.com/

Fun site to learn about a wide variety of urban legends as well as what an "urban legend" is. Here you can read the **alt.folklore.urban** FAQ and a few defining features of an urban legend: It "appears mysteriously and spreads spontaneously in varying forms," "contains elements of humor or horror," "makes good storytelling," and "does not have to be false." Among the list of categories, you'll find urban legends about animals, celebrities, drugs, food, language, politics, and religion; each legend page contains a lot of source material.

11

AIDS Research Information Center

http://www.critpath.org/aric/

Based in Baltimore, the AIDS Research Information Center (ARIC) aims to help people with AIDS (and those close to them) sort out the dizzying array of medical terms and data into understandable, medically accurate information. ARIC's Web site provides a comprehensive glossary of AIDS-specific terms, such as "antiretroviral," "prophylaxis," "maintenance therapy," "thrush," and "viral load." In addition, here you can read "The DIRT [Direct Information on Research and Treatment] (on AIDS)," a quarterly newsletter.

Amnesty International On-line

http://www.amnesty.org/

The official site for Amnesty International (AI), a renowned organization devoted to promoting awareness of human rights violations around the globe and taking action to stop them. To read news alerts and country political profiles, go directly to Stop Press. The AI Library is an excellent compilation of materials, including annual and campaign reports, an index of publications (by country and region), and 1994-1997 country reports (by year and continent). If you want to learn more about the organization and mission of AI, click About AI to read a FAQ on AI's stance on the death penalty, 15 Steps to Protect Women's Human Rights, and the 12-Point Program for the Prevention of Torture.

Archive X, Paranormal Phenomena

http://www.crown.net/X/

Compelling site in which you can explore the real X Files—that is, personal and news stories of paranormal phenomena. Here you'll find a wide range of fascinating tales of ghostly encounters and hauntings, angels, channeling, near-death experiences, and UFO sightings. There are over two hundred ghost stories alone. If you find yourself addicted to reading these stories, you can submit your e-mail address to the convenient service that automatically notifies you of Web site updates.

Center for Democracy and Technology

http://www.cdt.org/

In the aftermath of the telecommunications and Internet explosion, it's important that civil liberties are protected online as well as offline. The Center for Democracy and Technology is an organization committed to this cause. Under Headlines (at the top of the main Web page), you can read a number of continually updated news alerts on House and Senate hearings, FCC actions, FBI surveillance, and Supreme Court decisions. You can also browse Issues to jump to more in-depth reading material on Net censorship, cryptography policies, electronic privacy, Congress' impact on the Net, international cyberspace relations, and public digital access.

David Bowie: The Official Web Site

http://www.davidbowie.com/

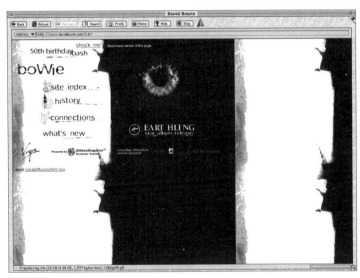

A visually enticing, multimedia-rich guide to this world-renowned and unique artist. Here you can find a gallery of Bowie's 50th Birthday Bash, including photographs, video from the Madison Square Garden concert, and a transcript of his America Online chat session. Another cool feature is the "EARTHLING" section, which includes RealAudio track samples and an interview. If you're a serious David Bowie fan, you'll appreciate the History section, complete with a biography, a discography, the Best of Bowie page, "OUTSIDE" album data, and song lyrics.

The GIG

http://www.thegig.com/

The Global Internet Gathering (GIG) is where the worlds of music and Internet technology meet. For a solid week, musicians, technicians, photographers, and journalists met online and in real life to form "the world's largest music festival." At this Web site, you can review the event and get information on the ongoing GIG. Check out Going GIGging, for instance, to access schedules, sponsors, and press releases. Musicians can submit audio samples to the Interactive Gallery. Other sections you won't want to miss include Digital Club Network (an index of GIG venues everywhere), The Bands (data on more than 600 bands), and Show Reviews & Photo Pass (editorial features and high-quality graphics).

MoJo Wire: Mother Jones Interactive

http://motherjones.com/

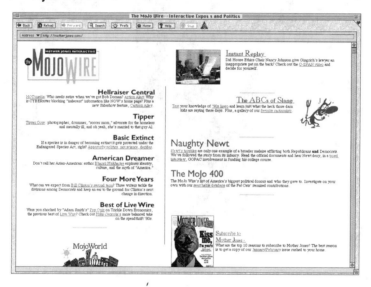

Here's a content-rich and exciting complement to the print edition of *Mother Jones* magazine where you can find a bunch of articles, tools, and goodies for those on the left side of the political fence. For example, check out MoJo 400, a searchable database of America's biggest political donors and their recipients. In addition, Hellraiser offers a variety of interesting features: HOT!media (reviews and profiles of good and bad films, television, books, music, and Web resources), Sideshow (illuminating and sometimes amusing analyses of pop culture, politicians, and big corporations), and Cartoon Alley (original comics by Mr. Fish and Callahan).

News of the Weird Archives

http://www.nine.org/notw/archive.html

As you might guess from the title, here you can find a large collection of extraordinary, amusing, and downright bizarre news stories. These stories—about news headliners, business, schemes and scams, politics, and even undignified deaths—are gleaned from a collection of Chuck Shepherd's News of the Weird articles. The index page lists the archives by month, and you can peruse over a year's worth of stories, all of which are displayed in a straightforward text format.

Poet's Corner

http://www.lexmark.com/data/poem/poem.html

A huge, organized collection of more than 1,700 poems written by more than 300 poets. Here you can search the poetry database, browse the alphabetical index of poets, or view the sampler of outstanding poetry. If you are looking for other poetry resources, try the Elsewhere section to find a list of links to events, magazines and journals, contests, collections, and other types of resources—or jump to the bibliography page to view a neatly compiled list of hardcopy poetry books and anthologies.

Safer Sex Page

http://www.safersex.org/

A very important page that explains a range of information along the safer-to-riskier sexual activity spectrum. Some materials you can find here include Safer Sex, AIDS Proofing Your Kids, Sex Myths, and How to Talk with a Partner About Smart Sex—all of which are written in a straightforward, down-to-earth, and sex-positive way. In addition, you can find information on women and safer sex, condoms, birth control, and

11

HIV and AIDS. If you need more information, check out the Multimedia Gallery, the archive of Safer Sex newsletters, and research data and resources for counselors.

Sierra On-line

http://www.sierra.com/

Sierra Entertainment produces hot software, including many game and multimedia titles. Here you can get information on Sierra software products, technical support, and hardware devices (like the 3D video card). Sierra fans will appreciate the Free Stuff section, where you can download demos, Internet games, sheet music, game utilities, hints, recipes, audio files, computer wallpaper, and more.

Surflink.com

http://www.surflink.com/

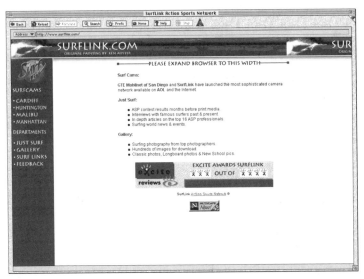

Surfing this Web site is possibly the second best thing to surfing the ocean waves. Here you can find a number of Surf Cams—for near-real-time pictures of the California Pacific waves at Cardiff, Huntington Pier, Malibu, and Manhattan Beach. Each Surf Cam page displays data on surf height, air and water temperatures, high and low tide times, and wind. In addition, you can explore Just Surf to find articles and interviews, and the Gallery to view photographs of Kelly Slater, Shane Beschen, Long Boarding, and other surfers.

Swank-O-Rama Cocktail Revolution Page

http://www.cyborganic.com/People/jpmckay/

If you're too tired to go out to a hip cocktail lounge at night, stop by this page for the cyberspace equivalent of the experience. You can start by enjoying a virtual mixed drink in the cocktails section; here you'll find recipes and reviews of various drinks and serving manners. Similarly, the Fabulous Lounge Sound section offers interesting reading material on such famous lounge musicians as Frank Sinatra, Sergio Mendes & Brasil 66, and Tony Bennett. Lounge lizards will also appreciate the style and dance sections.

11

Zipper: Gain a Voice in Washington

http://www.voxpop.org/zipper/

A handy tool to keep on your permanent Web page bookmarks list. You simply type your five-digit ZIP code into a form, and you can view all the contact information for your Representatives and Senators, including their e-mail addresses. If you're really in the mood to take some political action, check out Netgrams, another easy-to-use system for sending a message to your Representative, Senators, the President, and members of a variety of Congressional committees.

INTERNATIONAL

Afghan Cultural Info Center

http://www.gl.umbc.edu/~hqurba1/Afghanistan.html

Excellent resource on Afghanistan—its culture, religion, and history. Some unique features of this site include an index of Islamic resources for Afghans and information on other Muslim countries; downloadable movies of an animated Afghan flag, civil war in Tajikistan, and Tajikistan Muslims at prayer; and audio files of contemporary popular Afghan music. In addition, here you can find the *Jantari* (Afghan calendar), traditional recipes, and a variety of articles.

Africa Online

http://www.africaonline.com/

A visually appealing and content-rich guide to Africa. Here you can read continually updated news from Kenya, Uganda, and Tanzania. One particularly interesting feature here is Griots Talk. A *griot* is a storyteller in traditional West African culture; Griots Talk continues this tradition by providing information on African films, writing, and other media through cyberspace. Young Web surfers will enjoy exploring the Kids Only section, where you can read *Rainbow Magazine,* a Kenyan magazine for children; play interactive games and decode messages; learn about the various languages in Africa (over one thousand!); and meet African students.

Argentina!

http://www.middlebury.edu/~leparc/htm/argent2.htm

A collection of interesting and useful information about Argentina, all of which is written in English. Here you can find a compilation of encyclopedic articles on Argentine government, economy, transportation, communications, and other categories of country facts. Check out the Culture section to learn about *Yerba Mate,* a South American tea-like beverage; *Los Gauchos,* Argentine people of mixed ethnic backgrounds; *Lunfardo,* Argentine slang; *Tango,* the most well-known Argentine

11

dance; cuisine; and sports. You also won't want to miss the Geography page, which includes a map, photographs, and data on cities and regions, as well as the People section, which has information on Jorge Luis Borges, Evita Peron, and the Argentine Soccer Team, among others.

The Bahamas

http://microstate.com/bahamas

Straightforward, easy-to-use index to an information database on The Bahamas, "the country of islands." If you are traveling to The Bahamas soon, this is an excellent resource to use for quick facts about the country, pictures, cultural information, maps and travel information, and important telephone numbers. Other data you can find here includes the local time, a historical timeline, educational information, Bahamian folklore and myths, facts about the government, business and industry information, a list of holidays, and a bibliography.

The Brasil Page

http://charlotte.acns.nwu.edu/rio/brasil.html

Central hub of Brasilian information on the Internet. The Web Index is an organized list of pointers to sites pertaining to Brasilian business, culture, education, government, media, sports, and tourism. Each pointer has a one-line description and is marked with a "Portuguese-only site" or "exceptional site" symbol when appropriate. The coolest feature of this site is the Great Brasil Web Tour, which takes you on an automatically running, multimedia virtual tour of a variety of Brasilian culture, music, cuisine, and much more.

Discover Turkey

http://www.turkishnews.com/DiscoverTurkey/

One of the best Web resources for Turkey. Read the introduction on the front page to get a brief history of this globally significant region. In addition to standard reference material (society and culture, business and economics, tourism and travel, geography, sports, etc.), here you can find entire sections devoted to Turkish poetry, carpets, and Turkish/Cyprus unrest. Or you can peruse the Anatolia page to read about ancient Anatolia, the Hittites, the Byzantine Empire, the Seljuks, the Ottoman Empire, and finally, Turkey.

J-Links Meta-Index (Japan)

http://www.islandtel.com/j-links.html

A true meta-index of pointers to information on Japan and Japanese culture. For your convenience, each resource is accompanied by a symbol denoting text in English, Japanese, or both. A sampling of what you'll find here includes the Nihongo Yellow Pages, Internet Service Providers in Japan, Colleges of Technology in Japan, Anime (Japanese animation) and cartoons, ramen links, Furyu's Web Guide to Budo Sites, sumo links, The Anti-Japanophile Japan Page, and The Unofficial Shizuoka Home Page.

Madagasikara (Madagascar)

http://www.cable.com/madagas/madagas.htm

Central Web site of Madagascar information for the Malagasy community. Besides typical reference material, such as government, politics, and travel data, here you can find an interesting section on academic studies conducted in and about Madagascar as well as a page of Malagasy music. A very fun resource here is the section devoted entirely to lemurs, the most talked-about animal from Madagascar; from here you can explore galleries of photographs and lemur data.

New Zealand

http://nz.com/NZ/

Interactive tour guide to New Zealand. Here you can peruse the Aotearoa Guidebook to find recent New Zealand news stories, an automatic virtual tour, an illustrated gallery, travel and tourist information, and relocation information (immigration, job, and housing data). Or you can go directly to WebNZ: New Zealand Business on the Net to jump to commerce information on gold, platinum, and real estate. To meet other New Zealand travelers or residents, check out the Akiko Meeting Room, KiwiChat (a threaded discussion BBS), and real-time chat forum.

Peru

http://www.latinworld.com/countries/peru/

Latin World's guide to Peru. Some information is provided in English, some is in Spanish, and some in both languages; each pointer in the guide is denoted with the

11

language of the text. In this guide, you can find general information (in Spanish), business data (companies, exporters, organizations, products, and services), cultural information (art, magazines, music, and traditions), economy, education, politics, news, sports, and travel. The front page displays a beautiful photograph of Machu Picchu.

Portugal Home Page

http://s700.uminho.pt/homepage-pt.html

Everything you want to know about Portugal can be found through this Web site. Most of the information is provided in both English and Portuguese; check out the running marquee exclusively in Portuguese at the top of the front page. Immediately underneath the marquee is a large clickable imagemap of Portugal, from which you can learn more about specific cities and regions, including Braga, Porto, Aveiro, Coimbra, Lisboa, and Faro. If you need more information, peruse the indexes to general and cultural information about Portugal.

The Tonga Page

http://user.cs.tu-berlin.de/~minibbjd/tonga/

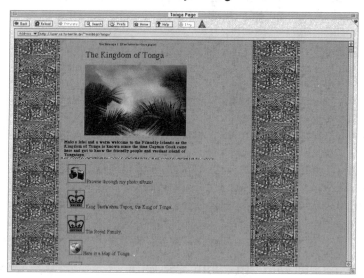

A compilation of materials on the Kingdom of Tonga, a group of islands in the South Pacific. Some unique features here include texts on King Taufa'ahau Tupou (the King of Tonga), the Royal Family, human rights in Tonga, an article about Pacific Islands Independence, and Tonga in the newspapers. In addition, you can find other such useful data as maps of Tonga and Polynesia, an excerpt from the 1994 *CIA World Factbook* about Tonga, a bibliography, and a list of Internet resources.

Ukraine FAQ Plus

http://www.std.com/sabre/UKRAINE.html

Excellent reference to educational, financial, political, and other types of information about Ukraine. Here you can find everything you've always wanted to know about this region, including business and commerce, culture, economics, history, language, law, and more. Some of the most useful and interesting features here include maps, entries from the Encyclopedia of Ukraine, information on the Ukrainian Diaspora, the Directory of Business Contacts, the Country Marketing Plan for Ukraine, and an exclusive preview from *The Ukrainian Weekly*.

Virtual Tour of Israel

http://dapsas.weizmann.ac.il/bcd/bcd_parent/tour/tour.html

Just as the title describes, this site is a virtual tour of this unique Middle Eastern country. Here you can follow the guide through Galilee (Western, Upper, and the Sea), Mount Carmel, the Negev desert, Golan, Tel Aviv, the Sharon Valley, Jerusalem, the Coastal Plain, and the Dead Sea. Each section offers color photographs, data, and often a sensitive map. You can also learn a lot of general and historical information about Israel just by reading the introduction page.

Welcome to Mexico!

http://mexico-travel.com/mex_eng.html

Make this your first stop on the Internet before traveling to Mexico. Here you can find a searchable compendium of resources and information geared towards the tourist looking for a high-quality vacation. If you need travel ideas, you can explore the Showcase to find content-rich brochures on beach destinations, archaeological zones, copper canyons, and colonial treasures, all provided by the Ministry of Tourism of Mexico. Other information you can find here includes travel tips, fiestas and events, Mexico states, and much more.

INTERNET CONNECTION

Beginner's Guide to HTML

http://www.ncsa.uiuc.edu/General/Internet/WWW/HTMLPrimer.html

This is the premiere source for learning HTML. Although the presentation is simple and straightforward, this guide is chock-full of material—in fact, it contains everything you need to get started making your own Web pages. Here you can learn what HTML is; what the differences are between head, title, and body tags; when it's appropriate to use headings and preformatted text; how to link and arrange graphics; how to create a table, and much more. Consult this site while you're making *your* site; you may not need a book!

Electronic Frontier Foundation

http://www.eff.org/

This is the home page of the Electronic Frontier Foundation (EFF), an organization famous for championing Internet-related civil rights and advocating a global cyber-community. In the EFF library, you can find a huge collection of online civil liberties material. In addition, you can stay abreast of new civil rights issues by checking the EFF Alerts regularly.

Gamelan

http://www.gamelan.com/

The Web's premiere Java directory, this site sports a nicely organized collection of thousands of useful and fun Java applets for entertainment, business, and development purposes. There is even a category for related technologies, such as ActiveX, JavaScript, VRML, and Castanet Channels. Java enthusiasts will appreciate EarthWeb Direct, a supply of professional development tools, class libraries, and applets, as well as EarthWeb Chat, a live forum for meeting other developers and users. Be sure to check out Special Features to find Our Favorite Games, Java Jolt with BackWeb, Gamelan Staff Picks, and other goodies.

HotWired

http://www.hotwired.com/

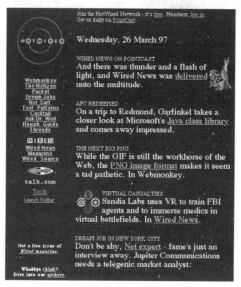

One of the most famous e-zines, HotWired is exemplary of the best digital publishing on the Internet. This site is the center of the HotWired Network. If you want to browse the contents, you must register for free membership to the HotWired Community. Once you are a member, you can explore the gamut of HotWired content, including Dream Jobs (opportunities, especially in multimedia), Netizen (Internet-related politics), Cocktail (cultural events and information), Ask Dr. Weil (health alerts), and The Rough Guide (virtual travel guide), as well as subscribe to a number of e-mail news services and participate in live forums.

HTML Bad Style Guide

http://www.earth.com/bad-style/

There are plenty of HTML how-to guides available on the Web. In contrast, this is a guide to what you should *avoid* when designing your Web pages. Here you can learn to avoid sloppy and ambiguous HTML coding, keep your page design consistent, and create Web sites that are readable and look good on any platform and in any browser. The author of this guide may seem to be a bit obsessive about proper HTML code, but if you follow the instructions, you're guaranteed to produce clean, inoffensive Web pages.

Info-Mac HyperArchive

http://hyperarchive.lcs.mit.edu/HyperArchive.html

Fantastic Mac freeware and shareware collection. This site brings thousands of programs for your Mac under one roof. This Web site is a mirror of the FTP-based Info-Mac archive, but the Web interface makes it very easy to browse the software by category and search for specific programs. Its priceless "abstracts" feature lets you read descriptions of programs before you download them, helping to assure that you'll get what you want.

Internet Index

http://www.openmarket.com/intindex/

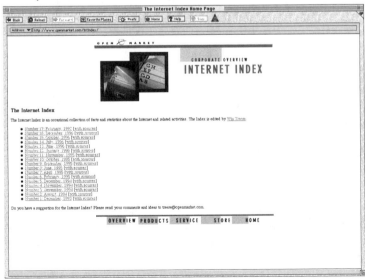

How many Brazilian orphans were available for adoption over the Internet in October 1996? How many copies of Mosaic were downloaded per day from NCSA in 1994? You can find answers to all kinds of obscure questions here. Published several times a year since 1993, the Internet Index provides a "collection of facts and statistics about the Internet and related activities." Win Treese, the editor, painstakingly organizes these factoids into bite-size statements. These trivia questions and answers convey something of the Internet's astonishing scope and growth.

"The List" of Internet Service Providers

http://thelist.iworld.com/

Now that AOL offers the "bring your own access" plan, you can access the service via the plain-vanilla access offered by an Internet Service Provider (ISP). This service from Meckler provides a directory of several thousand ISPs. Here you can search for an ISP by commercial name or domain name, and you can browse the list by country, state, or area code. International users can check the World Wide Listing and browse by country or country code.

Internet Society

http://www.isoc.org/

The official Web site of the Internet Society, an organization that works to ensure the viability and scalability (growth) of global networking and to promote networking in developing countries. Go directly to Information Services to find Internet-related conferences and forums, *The ISOC Forum* (the Internet Society's newsletter) archives, press releases, a global connectivity map and table, articles on the history of the Internet, and international Internet news. In the Papers and Presentations section you can find a statement on cryptographic technology, Vinton Cerf's "Truth and the Internet," and the Internet Code of Conduct.

Internet Tools

http://www.december.com/net/tools/

A must-visit (and must-frequent) site for Internet developers. Here you can find abundant information about tools for network information retrieval (NIR), computer-mediated interaction (CMI), and computer-mediated communication (CMC). Learn the nitty-gritty of "ping"; tools such as Archie, FTP, and Telnet; interfaces such as Netscape; and much more. This material can be displayed in three views, each providing different amounts of detail.

JavaScript Authoring Guide

http://home.netscape.com/eng/mozilla/Gold/handbook/javascript/

What is JavaScript, how does it differ from Java, and how might you use it? The answers begin here, at the official Netscape guide to creating your own JavaScript code. If you are ready to begin scripting, just follow the guide. Start with JavaScript Basics to learn Netscape Navigator scripting, objects, and using windows and frames. Then, explore Language Concepts to learn about values, expressions, operators, objects, and functions. For additional help, the Reference section provides information on methods, properties, event handlers, statements, reserved words, color values, and more.

Net-happenings

http://www.mid.net/NET/

(also available as a newsgroup at **comp.internet.net-happenings**)

Every day's a feast on the Internet, and here's your menu. Moderated by Gleason Sackman, this is an announcement service in which you can read recent postings about new Internet resources. It's one of the best ways to stay informed about new Web and Net resources. For your convenience, each message is categorized to indicate the type of resource being announced: CONF (conferences and event calendars), EMAG (electronic magazine, or e-zine), K12 (educational), LISTS (mailing lists), MISC (miscellaneous), NETLINK (list of Web pointers to similar resources), NEWSLTR (online periodicals), RESOURC (useful resources on the Net), and SOFT (software). Together with NetScout (a mailing list mentioned in Chapter 4), this resource will keep you apprised of the best serious new content on the Internet.

Unofficial Netscape FAQ

http://www.sousystems.com/faq/

The Unofficial Netscape FAQ, nicknamed "The UFAQ," offers a wealth of useful, often witty information on browsing the Web and developing pages with Netscape Navigator. Here you can learn ways of dealing with font problems, get tips on using Netscape applications (the newsreader, mailer, etc.), figure out how to connect to the Internet from specific platforms, and implement workarounds for Netscape product bugs. Further assistance you can find here includes a descriptive list of pointers to official Netscape sites and newsgroups as well as other useful FAQs.

11

Web Developer's Virtual Library

http://www.stars.com/

If you're involved in any way in creating Web content, bookmark this site, a one-stop compendium of information and tools for Web developers. Here you can find a massive set of links to technical information about site development, including entire pages of resource links on meta tags, Web page style, VRML, HTML, graphics, CGI programming, Perl scripting, Java, and browser plug-ins. You can also jump to other Internet information, such as legal issues, news, and glossaries. Check the Top 100 to find out what are the most widely used—and often the most important—sites for developers.

Web Diner

http://www.webdiner.com/

The Web sibling to AOL's popular Web Diner forum (keyword: Web Diner), Web Diner aims to teach "people how to use the Web to enrich their lives and their businesses." Jump directly to Web Utensils to find useful templates for Web pages, a collection of classes and tutorials, graphics tips, galleries of free graphics, and Web Diner links. The bibliography points you to high-quality books on business, HTML, graphic design, and the Web.

KIDS ONLY

Bill Nye the Science Guy

http://nyelabs.kcts.org/goodies/goodies.html

Can't pry the kids from the TV set when Bill Nye the Science Guy is on? Just show them this site, which offers videos in the Screening Room, still graphics in the Photo Album, and sounds in the Sounds of Science. If you've ever seen Mr. Nye's popular children's science show, you know that it manages to impart as much information as Mr. Wizard used to but with all the kinetic energy of an MTV video. It's not surprising, then, to find that the Web page is goofy and fun but also simple to use. The videos and sound files themselves come from the television show.

Blue Dog Can Count!

http://kao.ini.cmu.edu:5550/bdf.html

Who is Blue Dog? If you haven't seen or heard of her yet, you probably will soon. Thanks to this Web page, the dog that appears in the surreal paintings of the Cajun artist George Rodrigue has taken on a life of her own on the Internet. Click on the painting of Blue Dog, and she will bark at you. Fill in numbers in the arithmetic form on this page and she will bark out the answer. Typing **2+2=4** elicits a bark. This

11

page is a top choice for pre-schoolers and kindergartners, but with over 1,000 hits a day, it looks suspiciously like moms and dads are getting help with their addition and subtraction, too!

Boy Scouts of America

http://www.bsa.scouting.org/index.htm

The BSA home page offers information about scouting for boys ages 7 to 20 and scout-leading for adults. A link to BSA activities lists links to their High Adventure bases, Jamboree pages, and Learning for Life program for schools. Check out official BSA gear such as the Pinewood Derby kits and order an official catalog. Family Fun offers ideas for engaging and educational activities for the scout and his family. The Index takes you to scouting and other related sites for more in-depth information, and the Local Councils link will help you to find active scouting groups near your home.

CollegeNET

http://www.collegenet.com/

So it's time to go to college and you can't figure out where to start? Well, there's always the guidance counselor, but if you want to search for yourself, CollegeNET is a good place to start. You can get information on colleges and universities based on geography, tuition levels, and the size of the student body. There is information on financial aid and graduate programs, too. You can search through the MACH25 Scholarship Search Engine and can even try for a $5,000 CollegeNET scholarship by sending in your application electronically!

Cyberspace Middle School

http://www.scri.fsu.edu/~dennisl/CMS.html

The Cyberspace Middle School is designed for students in the sixth, seventh, eighth, and ninth grades who are using the World Wide Web for educational assistance with their science fair projects. It includes lists of possible science fair projects, links to libraries, and personal help from the Web author. There is also an excellent list of educational Web sites on any number of science-oriented subjects.

Empowered Young Females

http://www.eyf.com/

Here is the electronic edition of *XX Empowered*, a magazine dedicated to helping teenage girls grow up into well-adjusted women. With articles on subjects such as "No, I Am Not Anorexic" and "The Inner Beauty Contest" and topics like judo, it's pretty clear where they're coming from. This is a magazine with an attitude, and that attitude is expressed with clear writing and good graphics. EYF includes surveys, archives of earlier issues, e-mail, and regular features on games, television, and films.

ExploraNet

http://www.exploratorium.edu/

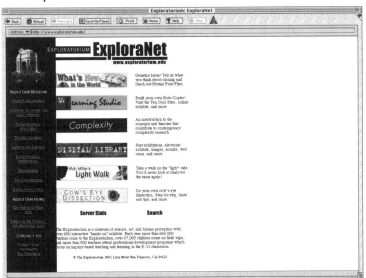

This Exploratorium is as good as science museums get. In the coolness and hands-on department, it rates a solid ten. The museum's Web site brings some true magic to the Net. The Exploratorium teaches about the senses by playing tricks on your sight and hearing. At this site you can hear the Doppler effect and view the Golden Gate Bridge live from a Web cam on the museum's roof. You can dissect a cow's eye and imagine a nuclear bomb. Each month the Exploratorium presents ten cool Web sites, some of which are as good as the Exploratorium itself. The Learning Studio features links to the current project there, as well as favorite recent projects. One visit offered a look at planets outside our solar system, satellite images of the earth, information on auroras, the ozone, and electronic versions of popular exhibits from the Exploratorium itself. The Exploratorium's Science Snackbook Series offers ideas and plans for fun and educational science projects that can be built and enjoyed in the classroom or home.

FishNet

http://www.jayi.com/jayi/

How many sites on the Web are called "FishNet"? There are probably quite a few, but this site is especially designed for teens. It includes a college guide, message boards, a quarterly e-zine, daily "weird facts," and a discussion of street language. It also has a random link and a list of age-appropriate links so kids can browse safely. FishNet is the free portion of a subscription service called Students Online, which gives kids the opportunity to set up their own Web pages, run forums and surveys, and much more.

Girl Scouts of the U.S.A.

http://www.gsusa.org/

Girl Scouting is open to girls between the ages of 5 and 17, and scout leading is open to men and women over the age of 18. The GS USA home page offers information on membership, history, publications, council sites, and, of course, cookie sales. This page should be particularly helpful for families looking to get involved in Girl Scouting as well as for those with girls already involved, with information on volunteer opportunities, current news, forthcoming events, and a product catalog. For those with questions about Girl Scouts, a click of a button will send e-mail directly to the Girl Scouts' U.S. administrative offices.

Homework Tools

http://www.zen.org/~brendan/kids-homework.html

The Kids on the Web: Homework Tools is just the place to go when you've put off that assignment until the library has closed and your bike has a flat tire. Links on the page will take you to electronic versions of *Webster's Dictionary*, *Roget's Thesaurus*, the *Encyclopedia Britannica*, *The Elements of Style*, and *Bartlett's*

Familiar Quotations, but the electrons weigh a lot less than all those books! Other assorted links such as Researchpaper.com can give you a jump-start on your project, with ideas and assistance on school-related research projects.

The National Zoo

http://www.si.edu/natzoo/

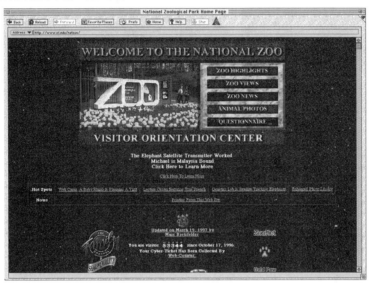

Washington, D.C.'s National Zoo has a state of the art Web site (as if a real, free, world-class zoo weren't enough). It has all the bells and whistles including a lecture center with streaming audio and Web cameras set around the zoo so you can see what's going on while you're visiting the site. It also includes a flashy marquee that moves randomly, changes color, shrinks, and grows. Pictures of animals are the mainstay, but there is much more. Just like the National Zoo itself, there's no way to see everything here in just one visit.

11

Seussville

http://www.randomhouse.com/seussville/

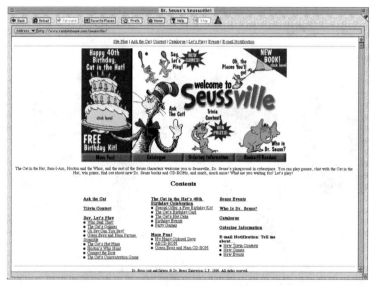

For Dr. Seuss fans of all ages, this bright page opens spattered with color and Seussian critters. Information about Theodore Geisel can be found on a link right out front, but kids will want to go right for the "Say, Let's Play" area. You will need to have the Shockwave plug-in to play Grab the Grinch, but other games need nothing more than agile speaking for the tongue twisters. Humorous pictures, contests, events, and special holiday sections round out this site full of fun for kids.

Teen Movie Critic

http://www.dreamagic.com/roger/teencritic.html

When someone is talking about a movie critic named Roger these days, they probably mean Roger Ebert. At some point in the future, though, they may well mean Roger Davidson. Roger's a teenager who loves films and shows it by reviewing a movie a day on this Web site. His reviews aren't just for kids either. From classics like *It's a Wonderful Life* to the latest releases, he always has something interesting to say, and he's often insightful.

Theodore Tugboat

http://www.cochran.com/tt.html

Web sites for small children must be hard to build. How else can we explain why there are so few good ones? Cochran Communications' Theodore Tugboat comes to the rescue with a site that is loads of fun for little kids. It includes an interactive story, postcards to be sent, and coloring book pages to be printed. Theodore Tugboat is the star of his own children's television show (which appears to be in rather limited distribution at the moment), but even if your kids have never seen it, they will enjoy this Web site.

Yahooligans

http://www.yahooligans.com/

Yahooligans is the Web directory just for kids from the folks at Yahoo. This bright and cheerful site features a special content-filtered search that was designed with the young user in mind. Kids can choose special search topics such as "Around the World" for culture, politics, and history; "School Bell" for educational programs and some homework help; and "The Scoop" for comics, daily news, and the weather. A link to "Stay Street Smart on the Internet" brings up the Yahooligan's rules for online safety, a document every young surfer should read and discuss with his or her parents. Resources for parents concerned about their children's safety on the Internet are also provided.

LEARNING & CULTURE

American Memory

http://rs6.loc.gov/amhome.html

The key contributions by the Library of Congress to the National Digital Library are available at the American Memory Web site. Here you will find photographs, documents, movies, and sound recordings from various times in American history. The format of this site is a little confusing (you sometimes have to work your way through four or five intermediate pages to get from the main screen to the actual text of a document), but all the pages on the site load very quickly, and the information is wonderful.

11

Ansel Adams

http://www.adamsgallery.com/

The photography of Ansel Adams is immediately recognizable by most Americans. Once seen, the magnificent black and white shots of Yosemite cannot be easily forgotten. It's readily apparent that a lot of people with Web sites haven't forgotten Adams' art—there are dozens of pages devoted to him and his photographs. This one is operated by the Ansel Adams Gallery in Yosemite. You can see examples of the artist's work here and can even buy prints for yourself.

Art on the Net

http://www.art.net/

Art on the Net is a virtual space where artists join together in sharing their art with others on the Internet. One hundred artists from around the world—poets, musicians, painters, sculptors, digital artists, performance artists, animators, and others—create and maintain studios and rooms in this virtual gallery. Because this site is graphics-intensive, some pages may be a bit slow to load, but it can be well worth the wait. Each area of the gallery contains thumbnails or descriptions of the art, allowing you to view larger representations simply by clicking. Beautiful.

ArtSource

http://www.uky.edu/Artsource/artsourcehome.html

If you are interested in art or architecture, this award-winning Web site is a great place to start looking for things. Although, as the Web owner points out, "For help in locating specific art-related information, the *BEST* source of information is your local art librarian," this isn't bad either! The site, regularly updated, features links to museums, image collections, online exhibitions, art journals, and vendors.

BookWire

http://www.bookwire.com/

A true mecca for anyone with *any* kind of interest in books, whether you write, work for a print or electronic publisher, or just like to read. You'll find reviews of the books you like to read, including poetry books, high-brow books, novels, and computer books. Get a schedule of author tours. Link to hundreds of publishers, big and little bookstores, and all manner of libraries. Follow the *Publishers' Weekly* bestseller lists. Learn about new book-related sites. Or, just have a look at the cartoon of the day.

Carnegie Library, Pittsburgh

http://www.clpgh.org/

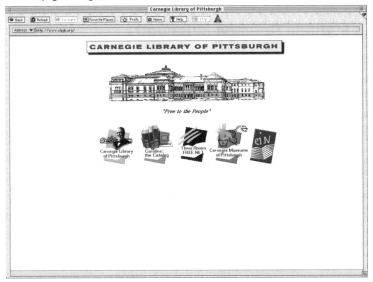

With Andrew Carnegie's help, Pittsburgh was the center of industrial America in the early 20th century. The Carnegie libraries and museums he left behind remain the cultural center of Pittsburgh today. Carnegie, who dreamed of using his millions to make cultural treasures "free to the people," would be pleased with this Web site. From here you can search all public (Carnegie) libraries of the Pittsburgh area. Or, you can link to any of Pittsburgh's great Carnegie museums: the Carnegie Museum of Natural History (where they keep the dinosaurs), the Carnegie Museum of Art (with a superb contemporary collection), and the Andy Warhol Museum. You'll also find much of the current edition of *Carnegie Magazine*.

11

Fine Arts Museums of San Francisco, ImageBase

http://www.thinker.org/imagebase/index.html

Maybe it was the earthquake of 1989 that gave Bay Area curators an inkling of mortality or at least a sense of the immense value of the fragile cultural treasures stored by the DeYoung Museum and Palace of the Legion of Honor. At any rate, they are currently digitizing their entire collection, including all the paintings, sculpture, jewelry, and furniture *not* on public display. Search for your favorites, including great works by Cassatt, Durer, Blake, and Homer. In respect to the artists represented and the museums who are supporting this endeavor, no images seen here should be reproduced without permission.

Franklin Institute Science Museum

http://sln.fi.edu/

The Franklin Institute in Philadelphia is one of America's best science museums. Here at the official Web site you can tour virtual versions of some of the exhibits currently on display at the museum and get brief exhibit summaries of the rest. There is also a publications library and the information you need to plan a visit.

Guide to Museums and Cultural Resources

http://www.lam.mus.ca.us/Webmuseums/

Every self-respecting museum has a Web site these days, and many museums exist *only* on the Web. Start here for a nearly comprehensive directory of such real and virtual museums. Each museum in the directory gets a brief review, and, for most, an e-mail contact person is also provided (useful if you need permissions and further information). The guide, created as a service to students, scholars, and the public by the Natural History Museum of Los Angeles County, can be indispensable for anyone planning a trip, even to less-traveled places like Tunisia and New Zealand. In your own area, you can use the site as a handy source of hours and directions.

The Hopi Way—Cloud Dancing

http://www.timesoft.com/hopi/

The songs, speeches, prayers, and stories of the Hopi Nation make moving reading. You can learn the history of the Hopi at this site and savor excerpts from their rich culture. This is not just a tourist site, although anyone visiting here will come away entertained and enlightened. It's also for the Hopi themselves, and included here is a mailing list and points of contact for various outreach programs for members of the Hopi community who need them.

The Nine Planets

http://seds.lpl.arizona.edu/nineplanets/

Did you know that the moons of Uranus were named after Shakespearean characters? That tidbit and countless more are available to you here on the Nine Planets Web site. This site has the modest goal of providing an "overview of the history, mythology, and current scientific knowledge" of our solar system which includes not only the nine planets, but also our moon, the moons of the other planets, and other celestial bodies such as comets and asteroids.

Online Reference Book for Medieval Studies

http://orb.rhodes.edu/

The Online Reference Book for Medieval Studies was put together by scholars to create a source on the Internet for papers and articles about Europe in the Middle Ages. It includes original essays, teaching resources, links to other related sites, and graphics. One area of particular interest is called Media. It discusses how the Middle Ages are represented in film, on television, and in literature.

The Smithsonian Institute

http://www.si.edu/newstart.htm

When most people think of the Smithsonian, they think of "the castle," the strange red-brick building on the Mall in Washington, D.C. that housed the original Smithsonian collections 150 years ago. The Web site conveys the sheer scope of the organization, which encompasses more than two dozen museums and research centers, including the Museum of Natural History, the National Museum of American Art, the Air and Space Museum, and the Museum of Native America. All of the museums, plus *Smithsonian Magazine*, can be accessed from this site. Plan to spend hours here, and don't worry about the parking!

11

Sundance Film Festival

http://www.sundancefilm.com/festival/

Actor-director Robert Redford created the Sundance Festival in 1981 to "develop new talent and preserve the voice of independent film." The festival itself is interesting because the search for exceptional independent movies has led to a few films—most notably *Sex, Lies and Videotape*—that have made quite a bit of money at the box office. You can cruise through the festival on this Web site, checking out past festivals, studying this year's entries, and reading a note from Mr. Redford.

Victoria and Albert Museum

http://www.artnet.co.uk/30VandA.html

Founded in 1852, at the height of Victoria's reign, the Victoria and Albert Museum is today the largest museum of the decorative arts in the world. The beautiful Victorian and Edwardian buildings house 145 galleries containing some of the world's greatest collections of sculpture, furniture, fashion and textiles, paintings, silver, glass, ceramics, jewelry, books, prints, and photographs. At this site you will also find masterpieces from their watercolor collection, including works from William Blake and Dante Rossetti.

LIFE, STYLES & INTERESTS

The AARP WebPlace

http://www.aarp.org/

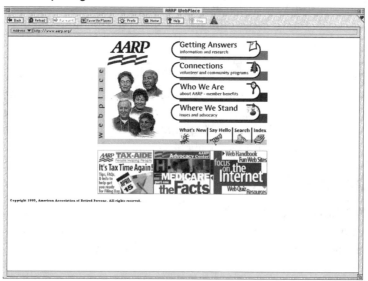

The American Association for Retired Persons (AARP) Web site is a place for "wired" seniors to hook into one of the most important resources for retired people.

Folks who are new to the AARP can learn more about this organization and find chapters and resources close to home with abundant information provided in their "Connections" section. Issues of importance to seniors are presented and discussed in "Where We Stand," featuring news releases and advocacy for members. "Who We Are" details the benefits of AARP membership, while the "Getting Answers" section helps members to more deeply understand the concerns of family, health, money, and other issues central to senior Americans. If you like the site, make sure to visit SeniorNet on AOL.

Backpacker Magazine

http://www.bpbasecamp.com/

Here's the view from base camp. There are articles here on cooking, grizzly bears, and just about anything else that would be of interest to a person walking alone through the woods. This electronic edition of the popular Rodale Press magazine has most of the features of its print sibling, plus the encyclopedia (a database of useful information on the wilderness), gearfinder (a guide to equipment retailers), an online store, and an archive of past issues. There are also message boards available in the Trail Talk forums for backpacking enthusiasts to discuss matters with one another.

Black Information Network

http://www.bin.com/

From its directory of African-American businesses and employment opportunities to its lists of available real estate and information on missing children, the Black Information Network is a Web site that packs in a ton of information. As if the information offered isn't enough, nearly every page of this site includes the enjoinder to "Add Yours!" This sense of being a cooperative project, along with its striking layout, makes the Black Information Network an engaging place to visit.

BoatNet

http://www.boatnet.com/

There's just something about being out on the water that—if you can get past the motion sickness—speaks to something deep within many of us. If you've been bitten by the boating bug, sail on over to BoatNet. It contains information on new and used boats for sale, charter yachts, marine supplies and services, maritime art galleries, and boating magazines. You'll also find information on weather, tides, and navigation, as well as online yacht clubs and links to related Web sites.

Cat Fanciers

http://www.fanciers.com/

The cat fanciers' Web site offers general information about cats and descriptions of virtually all cat breeds. You will find a wide selection of cat shows, clubs and registries, the latest news on veterinary medicine, and much more. This is a great place if you're thinking about buying a purebred cat. The breeders registry lists hundreds of Internet-connected breeders of pedigreed cats. This site is run by the same people who moderate the excellent Cat Fanciers Mailing List.

Comparative Religion

http://Weber.u.washington.edu/~madin/

Mike Madin's page on Comparative Religion is a directory of Internet resources for the academic study of religion. Links to directories and pages on world scriptures, religious tolerance, and studying religion in the electronic age can be found here, as well as information on less well-known religions such as Baha'i. Other religions are presented with directories, reference tools, and links to online publications. The Academic Departments of Religion in universities from many countries are accessible through links found here. This simply presented page can be a great starting place for personal research into the religions of the world.

Fly Fishing Broadcast Network

http://www.fbn-flyfish.com/index.htm

You might expect a Web site on fishing to be of limited interest to anyone who isn't an angler, but the Fly Fishing Broadcast Network (or FBN as they like to call themselves) works hard to change that expectation. Not only are there intriguing articles such as "The Wonders of Fly-fishing in Ireland," there are also great pictures of beautiful scenery and some games to play. Of course, if you are the sort of person who thinks the characters in *A River Runs Through It* were too casual about their fishing, there's a lot of great information for you, too! Fishing reports, a yellow pages directory, and a real-time chat room are just the beginning of the wealth of information you can find here.

foodwine.com

http://www.foodwine.com/

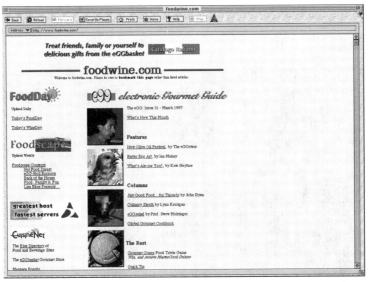

Foodwine.com is the Electronic Gourmet Guide's home on the Internet. eGG is one of AOL's premiere food resources (keyword: eGG), and this Web version handles the subject with the same cheerful and colorful flourish. The daily FoodDay and weekly Foodscape columns ensure that this site is one that you will want to visit often. You'll find recipes, of course, but there are also plenty of tips and tricks guaranteed to make you a better (or at least more interesting) cook. Drop in and take the trivia quiz or shop at the eGGbasket gourmet store.

Genealogy Home Page

http://www.genhomepage.com/

Here is a resource for people who are beginning to research their family history. The Genealogy Home Page includes help files, guides, libraries, maps, deeds and photographs, lists of associated newsgroups and mailing lists, and links to

11

other online genealogical information, home pages, and resources. You will find commercial services, software, and lists of genealogical societies here as well. This is a great place to visit after dropping by AOL's own Genealogy Forum (keyword: Genealogy)!

HouseNet

http://www.housenet.com/

This Web version of Gene and Katie Hamilton's popular HouseNet AOL forum (keyword: Housenet) might fool you at first glance. It has the same pleasant graphics as the AOL forum, but there is plenty of additional great information. The daily tips are a treasure trove for people who are interested in home repair and home remodeling, and the message board and Do It Together projects allow homeowners to discuss their work with each other. The genuinely useful Paint Calculator lets you enter the dimensions of the walls you want to paint, then figures out how much paint you'll need. If that isn't enough, there is also the Handy Homeowner contest where you can win Craftsman tools.

NetNoir

http://www.netnoir.com/

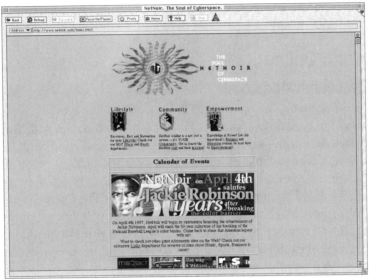

NetNoir is a popular America Online forum dedicated to and run by African-Americans (keyword: Netnoir). This Web site expands many of the popular NetNoir forum features, such as Club NetNoir and interview archives, to reach people who are not yet AOL members. It also has plenty of material that is different from AOL's offerings. The information here is "presented in such a way that anyone, from any walk of life, that has any interest in Afrocentric culture, can participate..." The site's clean, fast-loading design is appealing and makes browsing a breeze.

rec.antiques.marketplace (newsgroup)

Are you looking for a place to sell grandma's old griddle? Or maybe you're trying to find the piece of Depression-era glass that will complete your collection. If you're interested in buying, selling, or just pricing antiques and collectibles, the Usenet newsgroup **rec.antiques.marketplace** can be an invaluable resource. This is a fairly

11

high-volume newsgroup, but the signal to noise ratio is also fairly high, which means you're almost certain to find useful postings, whatever your collecting pleasure. This is a friendly and informative newsgroup, but as with any electronic forum where money changes hands, you should make sure you know who you are dealing with before parting with money or a precious heirloom.

ScubaWorld Online

http://www.scubaworld.com/

Sport Diver Magazine's Scuba World Online opens with a bright watery scene offering links of interest on every facet of this sport. A fascination with scuba diving can be explored here with magazines, club information, bulletin boards, and more. Photos and videos are available, as well as links to online catalogs produced by dive retailers. An area on science and the environment addresses issues of importance to divers and presents information on organizations such as The Cousteau Society and The JASON Project. A click on the sidebar of links will bring information on training, travel, and weather, or you can choose to take a virtual expedition to follow the work of teams of explorers on location. Data and findings are posted as they are available to make it possible to share them with enthusiasts everywhere and also to involve other experts out on the Net.

Softworld's Sewing Resource Guide

http://www.softworld.com/sewing/sewdir.htm

Sewing enthusiasts on the lookout for patterns, instructions, and ideas need look no further than this wonderful site. There are dozens of links to resources here. You can find information on equipment and, in many cases, follow links directly to the manufacturers. There is advice for beginners as well as challenging projects for more accomplished sewers.

World Wide Quilting Page

http://ttsw.com/MainQuiltingPage.html

This isn't just information on quilts, although there is plenty of that. There are intriguing features, such as the "worst quilts in the world" contest and overviews of changes in quilting styles here as well. This site is chock-full of photos of quilts. Whether you are an experienced quilter or are just thinking of trying your hand at this traditional craft, this site will get you thinking about piecing together your next masterpiece.

MUSICSPACE

Addicted to Noise

http://www.addict.com/

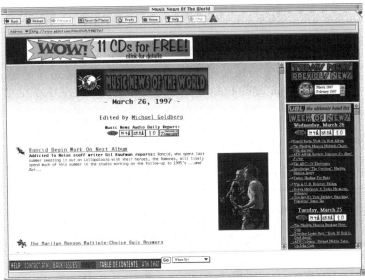

This is a hip and professionally designed electronic magazine covering the world of new rock and alternative music. This excellent resource will help you discover reviews of new albums, musician interviews, columns, features, and hype. If you're an audiophile, skip the text and go directly to Radio ATN, where you can listen to song samples by a variety of musicians, interviews with bands or individual artists, and exclusive programs. Film addicts may want to jump right to Cinemachine—Addicted to Noise's movie review search engine—to access thousands of film reviews.

All Music Guide

http://allmovie.com/amg/music_root.html

"A complete online database of recorded music." After you search for music information by artist, album title, or musical style and sub-style, you'll find a multitude of data, tidbits, and charts, including artist biographies, detailed discographies, chronology, ratings, and reviews. New Releases contains a long listing of new music and ratings, and Reissues provides the same information for rereleased music. Check out Monthly Columns to find features chock-full of links to artists and albums. Got a question about music itself? Browse the Music Glossary.

American Music Center

http://www.amc.net/amc/

The official Web site of the American Music Center (AMC), an informational and promotional resource for American contemporary music and jazz. Find out about the AMC itself as well as its information services (general as well as specifically for jazz, AMC publications, scores, grants, and more). Musicians may be able to network with each other and find new opportunities every month in Opportunity Update. If you want to know more about what AMC has to offer, be sure to read the FAQ.

Antidote

http://www.spiv.com/antidote/

If you're tired of the Top 40, check out Antidote. This is a visually appealing resource for underground and independent music. Rant, Gig, and Pulse contain in-depth reviews and features on a variety of bands and independent recordings. Ranarium is where you can find weekly music and culture information from specific cities, including Louisville, Chapel Hill, Portland, Seattle, Chicago, and New York City. You can also select from an extensive list of music samples in the Gramophone online listening center.

Classical Chat

http://members.aol.com/hostbri/classicalchat/index.html

This is the official Web site of AOL's Classical Chat (keyword: Classical). In addition to finding information about the forum (chat schedules, rules, an archive of chats and interviews), you can find a number of other important classical music resources here. In Composer Biographies, for instance, you can research birth and death dates, teachers, compositional media, and items of interest about the great composers. In Recommended Recordings and Music Website Links, you'll discover related resources.

Guitar World

http://www.guitarworld.com/

Impressive Web magazine where you can find guitar information, product guides and resources, and news and gossip about famous guitarists—all complete with high-quality photographic images. Here you can find features on a variety of guitarists and bands, from recent artists like Smashing Pumpkins to classic groups like The Who. If you are a guitar player, you won't want to miss the Lessons section, where you can read advice, tips, and techniques on soloing, playing rhythm guitar, improving your riffs, making the most of power chords, and using alternative string tuning.

History of Rock 'n' Roll

http://www.hollywood.com/rocknroll/

The Web companion to the television rockumentary series *The History of Rock 'n' Roll*. If you're interested in the television program, click Show Buzz to find an episode guide, performers, behind the scenes, and a local station listing. The rest of the site is a multimedia gallery of such rock legends as Bono of U2, Bruce Springsteen, Quincy Jones, Green Day, Pete Townshend, Alice Cooper, Van Halen, Aerosmith, and many others. You can read entertaining nuggets in Quotables, listen to interviews in Sound Bites, view photographs in Sights, and watch mini-movies in Video Vault.

The Internet Beatles Album

http://www.primenet.com/~dhaber/beatles.html

When you visit the front cover of this site, you'll see a simple image of a Beatles LP vinyl record. Click any of the songs or names listed on the record, however, and you'll access a huge compilation of Beatles facts, trivia, history, and much more.

Here you can also find a complete portfolio on each of the Fab Four. Other gems you won't want to miss include the photo gallery, trivia game, Today in Beatles History, and the entire section devoted to the "Paul is dead" mystery.

Music Previews Network

http://www.mpmusic.com/

Preview new recordings in just about any style of music, including rock, alternative, jazz and blues, classical, spiritual, rap and hip-hop, country, R&B, and more. Each music sample is provided in several sound formats and is displayed with a record cover image and a brief review and description of the album. You can search the entire database for something specific or check out the weekly list of picks.

National Anthems

http://world.std.com/~clm/anthem.html

Whatever national anthem you're looking for, you'll find a link to it here. The types of resources vary, but you can check the key to find out which links offer English or French translations of lyrics, historical notes, original lyrics, musical sound files, sheet music, and other national songs. Check the top of this home page to find links to the National Anthem of the Month, synthesized national anthems, and national flags.

Peeps Republic

http://www.peeps.com/

This is an entertaining source of R&B and similar contemporary music. Check out the Celebrity Guest Book to get an insider's perspective of vocal artists in a recording studio. The Book offers such fun tidbits as samples of musical free-styling, recordings of casual conversations, and autographed pictures. Peeps News is where you can read the latest about Grammies and other awards, movie soundtracks, a variety of vocalists and other musicians, and new albums. If you live near or are attending a university, visit Peeps Posse to find information on local music and cultural events.

resrocket

http://www.resrocket.com/

You'll feel as if you're in outer space when you're exploring this site, although this is really a gathering area for musicians. Players and artists of all levels meet in this online world to exchange ideas, chat, and—best of all—jam. Once you register, you'll get an avatar (little picture representing yourself) and a locker (personal space to store your tools and data). Then you can meet hundreds of other creative souls from all over the world to engage in this unique forum.

Rock and Roll Hall of Fame and Museum

http://www.rockhall.com/

Jerry Leiber, John Lennon, Bob Marley, Led Zeppelin, Frank Zappa—they're all here, in Cleveland's extravagant museum of rock, design by I.M. Pei. Each year, half a dozen or so new inductees are enshrined in the museum, chosen by a panel of rock historians. Every inductee is represented at this site by a biography with pictures and audio clips (in Real Audio, AU, and WAV formats). Every Web museum of any worth has a museum shop, and at this one you can purchase T-shirts, caps, and rock and roll ball-point pens. Well worth a visit, and the best way to plan a visit to the real museum.

Rollingstone.com

http://www.rollingstone.com/

An interactive, multimedia companion to *Rolling Stone,* the print magazine that pioneered rock music journalism. Here you can find new music reviews, opinions and regular columns, news from the university campus music scene, music award charts, critics' picks, contests, and an impressive photo gallery. Media addicts will

11

appreciate the up-to-the minute music and pop culture news in Random Notes Daily and the audio interviews with musicians and writers in Raw Tape.

TAXI

http://www.taxi.com/

Online service in which unsigned musicians and songwriters can network with major record label companies, publishers, and television, and film music supervisors. Here you can learn all about the TAXI service, including how to become a member, who the A&R staff is and what their credentials are, and what new recording companies are looking for in a variety of musical styles. Visit The A&R Insider to find monthly articles on A&R staff perspectives, industry advice, interviews with artists, and vocal techniques.

NEWSSTAND

Amazon.com

http://www.amazon.com/

Megasource of books; bigger than any physical bookstore— you can find a selection of over one million books. Don't be overwhelmed by the volume, though; it's easy to search the entire database by author, title, subject, and keyword. You can also browse the "shelves," which are logical categories of book types. If you're looking for a suggestion, peruse Editors' Favorites and Customer Reviews. An automatic search agent, Eyes, will send you e-mail notifying you of a requested title.

The Atlantic Monthly

http://www.theatlantic.com/

The Web companion to *The Atlantic Monthly,* a magazine devoted to politics, society, the arts, and culture. Here you can find excerpts from the print publication, and you can also read Atlantic Unbound, the Web-only edition. Atlantic Unbound contains features about Internet and digital culture, arts and entertainment, food, and books. To engage in The Atlantic Monthly community, go to Post & Riposte to join interesting discussions on a number of topics.

Better Homes and Gardens

http://www.bhglive.com/

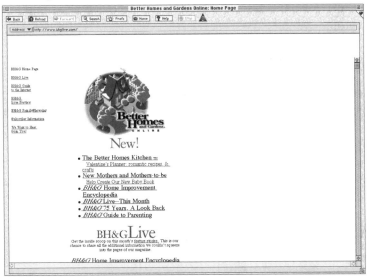

Online companion to the *Better Homes and Gardens* print magazine. The best resource here is the Home Improvement Encyclopedia, where you can find advice and instructions for home improvement basics including plumbing, landscaping, house structure, electrical and telephone, decks, and yard structure. The encyclopedia also contains a handy tool dictionary and home improvement glossary. If you need help with the holidays, check out the Holiday Entertaining Guide, which contains interactive guides to cooking and planning, as well as recipes and holiday decorating tips.

Car and Driver

http://www.caranddriver.com/hfm/

Companion to *Car and Driver* print magazine. The most valuable feature here is the Buyers Guide for this year and last, where you can get information on more than 400 cars

11

and trucks. Simply search the database by manufacturer, vehicle type, or price range; then check the list of winners. You can also read excerpts from the print publication, such as road tests, previews, and favorite articles from the past. Check the Daily Auto Insider to find continually updated news and information about the automotive industry.

Dell Magazines Daily Crossword Puzzle

http://www.bdd.com/puzzl/bddpuzzl.cgi/puzzl

A must-visit for crossword puzzle addicts. Dell Magazines offers a different original crossword puzzle every day. If you're stumped on yesterday's puzzle, sneak a peak at the solution. The crosswords are presented in Adobe Acrobat format, which makes the puzzles look clean and professionally published. From the puzzle page, you can explore other areas of the Dell Magazines Web site, including the catalog, new releases, author of the week, young readers section, daily horoscope, and forums.

Electronic Newsstand's Monster Magazine List

http://www.enews.com/monster/body.html

Jumpstation to a huge list of magazines on the Web. The types of magazines are divided into many categories, some of which include the arts, business and economics, computers and Internet, education and academia, entertainment and pop culture, health and medicine, hobby and craft, kids and family, news and politics, science and nature, sports and leisure, recreation, and travel and destinations. Check out the Enews Top 20 to find the most popular periodicals. You can conveniently search for a specific magazine or article.

Elle

http://www.ellemag.com/hfm/index.html

High fashion Webzine. What you can find here that you can't get in the print version of *Elle* is the Online Exclusive, a special fashion features section produced only for this Web site. If you want to see beautiful pictures of supermodels, check out the model gallery to find the likes of Claudia, Naomi, Cindy, Linda, Christy, and Elle. There is always new information on fashion trends in TrendReports as well as next season's fashion predictions. If you're a fashion buff, try your hand at Woody Hochswender's fashion quiz.

Forbes Magazine

http://www.forbes.com/

Extensive online companion to the print magazine. Business readers will appreciate the company databases, including the 500 Largest Private Companies, the 200 Best Small Companies in America, and the Forbes Four Hundred, which allows you to create a customized list. Other useful tools include the stock fund calculator, which helps you manage money between tax-sheltered and taxable accounts, and the investment primer, a collection of advice for investors from past issues.

Inc. Online

http://www.inc.com/

"The Web site for growing companies." Here you can read exclusive articles and interviews from *Inc. Real Time, Zinc, Online Entrepreneur,* and *Between the Pages.* Also, check out Virtual Consultant, a collection of interactive worksheets, searchable databases, and other online business references. Registered Inc. users can create, publish, and announce a Web site free of charge. If you're a regular Inc. visitor, you can create and modify a customized view. Don't miss the daily highlights and interesting questions posed in the weekly chat forum.

Life Magazine

http://pathfinder.com/Life/lifehome.html

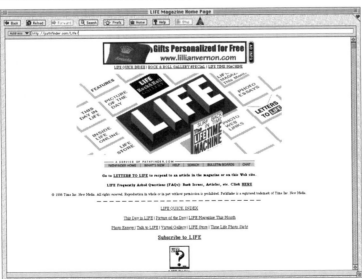

11

Beautifully designed Web companion to *Life Magazine*. Here you can read *Life* features, a FAQ, and This Day in Life, as well as view the Picture of the Day and photo essays. A fun feature is the Time Machine, which allows you to search for a specific *Life* cover by date, photographer, or subject and view it in a high-quality graphic image. You can also participate in an interactive forum or check out articles on subjects like alternative medicine, the 50 most influential baby boomers, and the band called Phish.

National Journal

http://www.politicsnow.com/news/NJournal/

Journal of political news and analysis. This site offers a ton of feature articles conveniently indexed on one page. Check back each week to find a new collection of articles. There is a year's worth of material stored here, and you can peruse the article titles, which are sorted by month. By reading this Webzine, you can stay abreast of a vast assortment of political information, including news and opinions about the President, government agencies, laws and regulations, legislative branches of the government, and more.

Osborne/McGraw-Hill

http://www.osborne.com/

Timely source of Internet development news and information. Here you can find press releases on new telecommunications products, software releases, programming language and protocol developments, security tools, and Internet business and culture. The Busy People Series includes timesaving tips and information on Microsoft business applications, America Online, the Internet and Web publishing, PCs, Intuit Quicken, and operating systems. There are also previews of Internet development and computing books with ordering information.

Scientific American

http://www.sciam.com/content.html

One of the premier journals of scientific research and discoveries. Here you can read current and past articles; news and analyses; reviews; commentaries; the "50, 100, and 150 Years Ago" editorial column; the "amateur scientist" column; and letters to the editors. One of the most valuable sections is Weekly Web Features, where you can find large collections of explorations and exhibits on genetic and subatomic research, questions on quantum mechanics, famous scientists like Carl Sagan and Mary Leakey, and more.

Swoon

http://www.swoon.com/

Fun publication all about "dating, mating, relating." Here you can read stories and advice on cohabitation, coping with loss, friendships, pets, and of course, sex. Some of the original columns include "Jan's Makeout Music," "Jane Err," "Cheap Date," and the "Who's Doin' Who?" gossip column. There are other fun areas, such as the Meet and Greet community area, personal ads, and horoscopes. Don't forget to add your two cents to the Daily Scoreboard.

Time

http://pathfinder.com/time/

The Web wouldn't be complete without *Time* magazine online, and here it is. Readers visit this site to find excerpts from the print magazine and special reports found exclusively online. Time Daily provides news highlights and photographs every day. In the Community area, you can participate in a discussion with others; the most popular forum is All Politics. You can also read transcripts of online discussions with celebrities and leaders. Don't miss the special multimedia section, which presents cool features in a variety of multimedia formats.

11

PERSONAL FINANCE

Best Rates from the Bank Rate Monitor

http://www.bankrate.com/

If you're shopping around for a new bank or consumer financial institution, you can't afford to miss this site. Here you'll get easy access to up-to-date rates on mortgages, credit cards, home equity loans, auto loans, personal loans, bank fees, and more. Other services offered here include the automatic e-mail interest rate alert for mortgage, deposits, and federal discount rates, as well as the handy monitor for personal stock, bond, and mutual fund portfolios.

Career Magazine

http://www.careermag.com/

This is an excellent resource for anyone looking for a new job or profession, graduating from college or graduate school, or climbing the corporate ladder. Here you can find articles on networking with colleagues, improving social skills in the office, and legal issues in the workplace. If you need specific job-seeking services, check out the Job Openings Database, Resume Bank, Employer Profiles, and Career Forum. You can keep abreast of *Career Magazine* by subscribing to the e-mail announcement list.

CNNfn Stock Quotes

http://cnnfn.com/markets/quotes.html

Stockholders frequent the Cable News Network, Inc.'s Financial Network (CNNfn) to find a reliable source of updated stock quotes provided by Standard & Poor's ComStock. Simply enter a stock's ticker symbol into the form or look it up in CNNfn's directory of company Web sites and symbols. In addition, you can keep abreast of the financial world by reading Breaking News and This Hour's Top Business Stories.

401(k) Retirement Calculator

http://www.awa.com/softlock/tturner/401k/

Have you calculated the estimated return on investment of your 401(k) retirement plan lately? If you haven't, or if you find the prospect daunting, check out this online retirement planning tool. After inputting some simple data such as your age, current salary, 401(k) balance, and planned retirement age, the calculator does all the work for you and allows you to experiment with different figures. You can also download a Macintosh version of the calculator, which includes more features.

Home Buyer's Fair

http://www.homefair.com/home/

If you are planning to buy a home or you are interested in noncommercial real estate, stop by this Web site. Here you can find Popular Exhibits—interactive tools for calculating your salary required for relocation, moving expenses, mortgage qualifications, and more. Be sure to check out the Main Booths, which offer extensive guides and resources for first-time homebuyers, mortgage finance resources, relocation information, and free services available to homebuyers.

Insurance News Network

http://www.insure.com/

If you have questions about Auto, Home, or Life insurance, you can find answers here. This insurance news resource provides reliable news about natural disasters' effect on insurance, automobile safety tests, and pending litigation against insurance companies, as well as guidance on how to best protect yourself. The comprehensive Insurance Glossary can help you make sense out of the confusing array of insurance terms. For further assistance, be sure to check out the InfoSources section to find insurance-related informational groups and trade associations.

IRS's Digital Daily

http://www.irs.ustreas.gov/prod/cover.html

This is a free publication brought to you by the IRS. When you visit this page, you'll see that tax information doesn't need to be dry and boring; this publication is colorful, easy to read, and even fun. Here you can find tax information for both individuals and businesses, as well as tax forms, educational publications, and electronic services. If you're interested in how taxes work on a national scale, check out the proposed tax regulations and statistics.

misc.invest.stocks (newsgroup)

This immensely popular newsgroup is a gathering area for stock investors. Here you can meet other stock holders and potential investors to exchange market tips and advice; discuss brokers and investment firms; find online stock tickers, investment Web sites, and software; and debate about what is currently hot on the market—and what is not. This is also a good forum for discussing mutual funds, precious metals, and currency trading.

misc.taxes (newsgroup)

If you need tax help or advice, this free resource is available to you. Here you can meet with others to discuss a variety of tax strategies, including vesting, gifts to children, tax shelters, and IRAs. You can also find questions and answers about avoiding and dealing with audits, determining the appropriate tax forms to use, and using tax software. Other discussion threads focus on tax codes and regulations and how they may affect you.

Money Online

http://quote.pathfinder.com/money/

This is the online version of *Money Magazine.* Like the print publication, Money Online is an excellent resource for news, features, and tools to help you manage your money and increase your wealth. This Webzine, however, offers some useful services which are impossible to get from the print magazine, such as the Financial Tool Kit, which helps you calculate your debt, investment portfolio return, mortgage, retirement savings, and net worth, as well as a stock lookup service and online portfolio tracker.

Motley Fool

http://fool.web.aol.com/

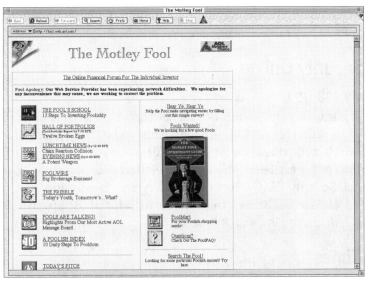

Welcome to one of the most popular America Online forums. This is an online resource devoted entirely to stocks; you won't find information about any other type of investments here. Appropriately named, Motley Fool is entertaining when it serves up its timely stock investment information. Check out The Fool's School, FoolWire, Lunchtime News, Evening News, and The Fribble for news and advice. If you enjoy playing games, try your hand with Today's Pitch and Foolball.

Networth's Insider: Mutual Funds

http://networth.galt.com/www/home/insider/fund.htm

If you invest in mutual funds, check out this site. The Insider provides an extensive index of Web-based information on mutual fund in the United States, Canada, Great Britain, and other countries. You can explore the NETworth Mutual Fund Market Manager to find the Fund Atlas (a directory of mutual funds), Net Asset Values (recent and historical fund prices), Morningstar Profiles, and Top Performers, as well as feature articles and a mutual fund search tool.

Retirement Zone

http://www.bookpage.com/kiplinger/

You have a good chance of finding answers to your retirement questions here. In the Zone, Kiplinger Retirement Services offers several free publications and tools, including an easy-to-use worksheet for calculating your retirement needs, a table to help calculate and build your nest egg, retirement guidance for members of the baby-boom generation, and a countdown-to-retirement to-do list. While you're here, check out the other publications by Kiplinger for money management, education, and career guidance.

Social Security Online

http://www.ssa.gov/

This is the official Web source of Social Security information. One unique application you'll find here is a Personal Earnings and Benefit Estimate Statements computer, which incorporates the annual cost-of-living adjustment. You'll also find a compendium of government publications including everything you need to know about Social Security, FAQs for various services, tax information, Medicare information, and forms. Some publications are offered in Spanish. To access information quickly, use the search tool.

Taxing Times

http://www.scubed.com/tax/tax.html

This is a convenient index of tax information available on the Web. Here you can find all the forms you need, including federal tax forms and instructions, state tax forms and instructions (with specific information for the California Franchise Tax Board), and Revenue Canada Taxation forms. In addition, you can find links to the entire tax code, The Tax Digest, tax newsgroups, IRS Code & Subject Telephone Directory, and other sources of tax help.

REFERENCE

Acronym Dictionary

http://www.ucc.ie/info/net/acronyms/acro.html

Database of definitions of acronyms—abbreviations made from the first letters of each word of a phrase. Simply enter an acronym into the form; the results are displayed with links to more information about your entry. Two options for searching are available: either search for an acronym and see its expansion, or search for a word in the expansions and view the related acronyms. You can also use e-mail to access the Acronym Dictionary; check the Mailserver page for information on the acronym and dictionary/thesaurus automatic e-mail services.

Biography

http://www.biography.com/

Provided by A&E Television Networks, this beautifully designed site features biographical information on over 15,000 people. You can read reviews of biographies, view a calendar of biographical television programs, and participate in a discussion forum with other biography fans. If you're a serious biography addict, try your hand at the Biography Quiz and Biography Anagrams, both found in the Play area. For quick access, go directly to the Find section to search for a name or to check the alphabetical listing.

CIA 1995 World Factbook

http://www.odci.gov/cia/publications/95fact/index.html

Complete reference of country facts and information published by the Central Intelligence Agency. Every country in the world is listed here, from Argentina to Zimbabwe, and each entry contains a map and information about geography, climate, terrain, land use, and more. Another huge resource here is the Notes, Definitions, and Abbreviations list, which defines terms and explains how each fact is acquired. For further information, check the appendices and reference maps.

Familiar Quotations

http://www.cc.columbia.edu/acis/bartleby/bartlett/

Online edition of Bartlett's Familiar Quotations. Here you can browse indexes of authors listed both alphabetically and chronologically. Within the huge list of literary works, you can find selected quotations from the complete works of Shakespeare and the Bible. Each author or written work in the list is linked to a page of quotations in straightforward text. Also provided here is information taken directly from the book, including the bibliographic record, front matter, and preface.

FAQ Finder

http://ps.superb.net/FAQ/

Searchable database containing a comprehensive list of approximately 1,800 links to FAQs on a wide variety of subjects. You can also read the FAQs by specific topic, including animals, art, audio, comedy, computers, countries, education, food, games, health, hobbies, Internet, lifestyles, literature, movies, music, people, personal finance, politics and law, programming, religion, science, social science, software, sports, technology, television, and video. Whether you are looking for a FAQ on birds, books, or toys, you'll find a link to one here.

FedWorld Information Network

http://www.fedworld.gov/

Central source of federal government information and documentation. Some examples of the many available resources here include Federal Aviation Administration service, training, and regulatory information; the federal job announcement search service, IRS tax forms and instructions, Bureau of Indian Affairs law enforcement services information, the EPA Clean Air Act database, United States Treasury information, and U.S. Customs Service information. From this Web site, you can access the Telnet service and FTP site.

Internet Public Library Reference Center

http://ipl.sils.umich.edu/ref/

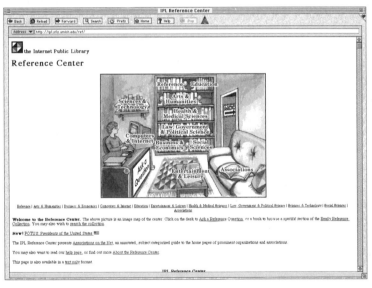

11

University of Michigan's virtual public library reference desk. You have the option of clicking the straightforward text links or using the cool imagemap of a library reference area. The selection of main topics includes arts and humanities, business and economics, computers and Internet, education, entertainment and leisure, and health and medical sciences. Then choose from a list of subcategories to find a descriptive list of resources. Be sure to stop by the Multi-User Object Oriented (MOO) environment for some live interaction.

iTools Research-it

http://www.itools.com/research-it/research-it.html

Instant research tool for many purposes. You can input strings of text into forms to look up language translations, biographical information, religion-related information, maps, facts, telephone numbers, financial information, postal and shipping addresses, and e-mail discussion groups. The snazzy table interface is cool and easy to use; simply type in an entry and click the Action button, and you'll get instant results. Each reference is listed with a link to the original Internet resource, so you'll know exactly which tool you're using.

My Virtual Reference Desk

http://www.refdesk.com/outline.html

A convenient and well-organized jumpstation of a variety of useful Web resources. The most valuable features are First Things First, which is a list of recommended sites to visit first thing in the morning; My Favorite Applications and Utilities; My Search Engines, which is an organized compilation of more than 150 search engines; My Virtual Encyclopedia; and My Virtual Newspaper. Here you can also find a huge list of computer and Internet links. Be sure to check out the current time, United States national debt, U.S. population clock, world population clock, and online calculator.

Periodic Table of the Elements

http://mwanal.lanl.gov/CST/imagemap/periodic/periodic.html

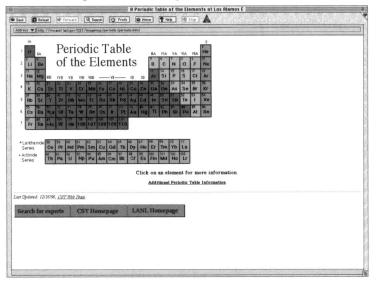

Graphic periodic table. Not only is this chemistry reference colorful and beautiful to look at, it's fully interactive. Because it's one big imagemap, you can click any element to find out its atomic number, symbol, and weight, as well as its electron configuration. You can also read an extensive history of how each element was discovered and used. Each page contains a link to other useful chemistry reference sites.

Roget's Thesaurus

http://humanities.uchicago.edu/forms_unrest/ROGET.html

Simple interface to this useful reference. Unlike the hardcopy edition of *Roget's Thesaurus,* however, you can use programming techniques to search for a word with

11

multiple endings. For example, if you look up the word "drive," you'll find synonyms for this word; however, if you add an asterisk to the end of the word ("drive*"), you'll get a list of synonyms for "drive," "driving," and "driver."

U.S. Census Bureau

http://www.census.gov/

Official online source of social, demographic, and economic data. Here you can check out Census news to find press releases and tip sheets, recent economic indicators, radio broadcasts, statistical briefs, this year's economic census, Census 2000, Web clips, and upcoming events. The Data Access Tools page is a handy index of applications for generating maps, viewing profiles, and extracting data. Another important feature of this site is the Subjects A-Z index, an extensive encyclopedia and jumpstation.

WWW Bible Gateway

http://www.gospelcom.net/bible

Complete Bible lookup service. You can use the simple form here to find any passage in the Bible. You can also select from a list of common Bible versions. A cool feature is the "What The Bible Says About" search, where you can find passages relating to more than 22,000 topics. This reference is offered in German, Swedish, Latin, French, Spanish, and Tagalog.

WWWebster Dictionary

http://www.m-w.com/netdict.htm

Web edition of *Merriam-Webster's Collegiate Dictionary*. Use the simple interface to look up the definition and synonyms of any word. If you want to conduct a more powerful word search, read the Help page. Here you can learn about wildcard searches, search results, cross-references, spelling, inflected forms, and illustrations and tables, as well as pronunciation guides, symbols, and keys. To expand your vocabulary, click Word of the Day to read a new word's definition and interesting fact.

Zipcode lookup

http://www.usps.gov/ncsc/

Official U.S. Postal Service (U.S.P.S.) ZIP code lookup and address information. Even more convenient than your trusty hardcopy ZIP code directory, this resource offers everything you need to complete the most important part of an address. Here you can use the ZIP+4 Code Lookup tool, which provides the entire 9-digit ZIP code for any address; city, state, and ZIP code associations; the Address Management Systems Office Locator, which finds the office that can correct local address and ZIP code errors in the U.S.P.S. database; and the list of official abbreviations, which are U.S.P.S. preferences of abbreviated address components.

SPORTS

Balance: Health and Fitness on the Net

http://hyperlink.com/balance

This high-quality online magazine about sports, health, and physical fitness is an excellent source of a wide variety of materials, including articles on sports injuries, the effects of exercising upon diseases, and sports equipment and clothing. You can also learn how to tailor a physical fitness program to fit your needs, from beginning a simple morning aerobic routine to training for a marathon. Special sections include Fe-mail (devoted to women's health), articles in Spanish and German, and The International Directory of Personal Trainers.

ESPNET SportsZone

http://espnet.sportszone.com/

A rich complement to the ESPN television channel, the SportsZone boasts more than 60,000 pages within its Web site. In addition to professional sports information and front page news headlines, you can read columns by Peter Gammons and Dick Vitale and check out the Extreme Sports section to find out about the Winter X and ESPN X games. You'll also be entertained by such fun stuff as "The Science of Sports," a monthly series by Bill Nye the Science Guy; the ESPN Multimedia Gallery; and goodies such as Sports Trivia, Players Directories, and LineTracker.

GolfWeb

http://www.golfweb.com/

The premiere golf resource on the Web. Here you can get the latest on such golf pros as Tiger Woods, Karrie Webb, John Daly, Annika Sörenstam, Kelli Kuehne, and Nick Faldo, as well as the LPGA and PGA tours. If you need some golf instruction, you can take the Lesson Tee. Avid golf players will appreciate OnCourse, an impressive database of courses. You can throw in your two cents in Tiger Talk, Architecture/Golf Courses, Women in Golf, and other discussion forums.

11

Major League Baseball

http://www.majorleaguebaseball.com/

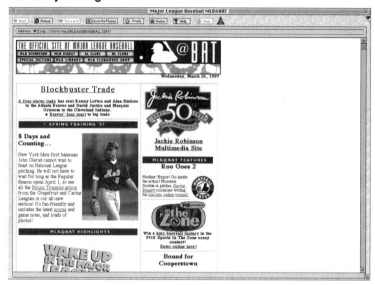

Official site of Major League Baseball (MLB). The Kids section is particularly fun; here you can create your own Dream Team, get tips from the pros (such as Barry Larkin and Bret Boone), and explore the World of Card Collecting. To view vintage pictures of World Series games and famous players, check out the MLB Library. Other important features of this site include The Arizona Fall League, Major League International, and The Business of Baseball.

NandoNet's Sports Server

http://www.nando.net/SportServer/

Authoritative news source for professional sports, including football, basketball, baseball, and hockey. At this site you can read daily news and view high-quality photographs in the Photo Galleries. If you're interested in other professional sports, check out Racing Circuit (auto racing), Corner Kicks (soccer), Aces (tennis), Fairways (golf), In The Ring (boxing), and the Olympics. In addition, there are tidbits of news on horse racing, cycling, Nordic and alpine skiing, yachting, track and field, swimming, cricket, rugby, biathlons, and more.

NASCAR Online

http://www.nascar.com/

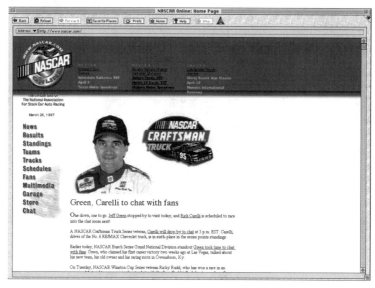

The official site of the National Association for Stock Car Racing (NASCAR). You can get the lowdown on the Winston Cup and Craftsman Truck Series, including information on the teams, tracks, schedules, and standings. You can also keep up with your favorite driver by reading Inside NASCAR. If you want to stay abreast of NASCAR news, you can subscribe to the weekly e-mail newsletter which includes information on every race weekend and announcements of NASCAR Online's new features.

National Basketball Association

http://www.nba.com/

The official site of the National Basketball Association (NBA). Here you can get continually updated news about games, teams, and players. If you're a serious basketball fan, you can try your hand at Trivia Today and send your fan e-mail to basketball stars. Be sure to check out the Top 10 Teams in NBA History to find in-depth bios of the best teams. The NBA at 50 section contains articles on the original NBA teams (Celtics, Knicks, and Warriors) and the Top 10 Coaches in NBA History.

National Football League

http://www.nfl.com/

Official home of the National Football League (NFL) on the Web. Every day, you can get NFL.com highlights, including divisional players of the week, player acquisitions, and Kevin Hardy's Rookie Journal. You can also find in-depth information on your favorite team, the complete season schedule, post-season recaps and previews, and the injury report. If you can't keep your opinions to yourself, you can add your predictions to the weekly Gatorade Dunk of the Week poll and chat with other NFL fans.

National Hockey League Players Association

http://www.nhlpa.com/

The official site of the National Hockey League Players' Association (NHL). Here you can check out Player Stats to find complete playoff and final regular season stats indexed by player name. If you're curious about how much money these guys earn, sneak a peak in Player Compensation to view salaries indexed by defencemen, forwards, and goalies, as well as by team. Other fun stuff includes trivia, World Cup information, NHL Picks, and a handy *Be a Player: The Hockey Show* schedule.

The Olympic Movement

http://www.olympic.org/

The Web home of the International Olympic Committee, provided in both English and French, at this site you can get Olympic news highlights, read the Olympic Charter, check the official IOC Medical Commission's medical code, and explore the Olympic Museum in Lausanne, Switzerland. If you're a devoted Olympics fan, you'll appreciate the International Olympic Federations section, where you can find a new page for each International Olympic Summer and Winter Federation. This site also hosts the official countdown clock for Salt Lake 2002.

11

Professional Rodeo Cowboys Association

http://www.prorodeo.com/

Rodeo die-hards will not want to miss the world champions section, PRCA record book, hall of fame, and circuit information. Here you can also find a weekly news release and Today's Rodeo Fact. If your heart is on the animals' side, you might find solace in the Humane Facts section, where the PRCA Animal-Welfare Guidelines are located. This section also includes a FAQ on rodeo equipment.

SnowLink

http://www.snowlink.com/

Popular information source for "on-snow" sports, mainly skiing and snowboarding. If you jump directly to the Hot News/Cool Tips section, you'll find the New Products report, articles featuring on-snow trends, and seasonal snowsports news. Avid snowsporters will appreciate the listing of current snow conditions throughout the United States, Canada, and Europe. In addition, you can view informational calendars on lessons and demos as well as descriptions and contact information for clubs, teams, and organizations.

The Tennis Server Home Page

http://www.tennisserver.com/

Information resource for tennis players. A prominently displayed tidbit on this page is the huge listing of countries from which Web surfers visit—an interesting statement on the global appeal of tennis and the global reach of that other Net, the Internet. There's tons of tennis information available here, for both fans of professional tennis and tennis players. You can subscribe to the free Tennis Server INTERACTIVE e-mail newsletter and read exclusive columns by David Higdon, John F. Murray, Ron Waite, Emma Peetz, and tennis pro John Mills.

U.S. Soccer

http://www.cs.cmu.edu/~mdwheel/us-soccer

A Web site "for soccer fans by soccer fans." Here you can find U.S. soccer news, information on media resources for soccer fans, and numerous links to the sites of professional leagues, including Major League Soccer, the American Professional

Soccer League, the United Systems of Independent Soccer Leagues, and the National Professional Soccer League. If you're interested in how it all began, peruse the Soccer History page to read about the National Soccer Hall of Fame, Society of American Soccer History, and U.S. Open Cup.

VeloNews Interactive

http://www.velonews.com/

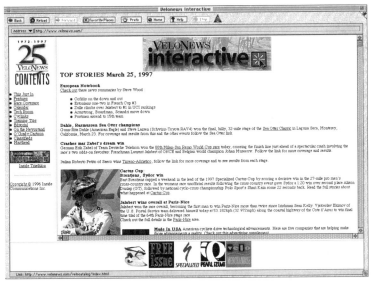

A Web magazine for people who love cycling, here you can read news, features, and race coverage highlights. The Tech Room features a series on metallurgy for cyclists, including data on steel, aluminum, titanium, carbon fiber, and exotic materials. If you're an avid cyclist, you'll want to explore the training area to find some useful articles by Joe Friel, a professional cycling coach. In addition, you'll be amused by Patrick O'Grady's cartoon, a colorful funny about bicycling and triathlons.

11

STYLE

Beauty Net

http://www.beautynet.com/

A hip compilation of fashion articles, services, and virtual community forums. If you need a head-to-toe makeover (or any part in between), you can jump to such columns as "Hair Studio," "Skin Care Suite," "Makeup Counter," "Nail Bed," "Style Showroom" and more from the Table of Contents. Are you ready to hit the beauty parlor? Search the Salon Finder for the best place for your location, your budget, and the services you require. Don't miss the Chat Room message board and Tip of the Week.

The Body Electric

http://www.surgery.com/

Nervous surgery recipients can go under the virtual knife before going under the real one. This Web service offers in-depth information for those who are serious about undergoing liposuction, facelifts, hair transplants, breast reconstruction, or other beauty-enhancing surgical procedures. Each procedure's page offers "before" and "after" pictures, typical costs, and a FAQ about the operation. You can find a plastic surgeon in Europe and throughout the United States by running a search through the Physician Locator.

Cosmetics Cop

http://www.cosmeticscop.com/

Everyone who uses cosmetics—which leaves few people out—should read this page. The author, Paula Begoun, a.k.a. the "Ralph Nader of Rouge," has done years of research on many aspects of the cosmetics industry, so she'll give you the low-down on what goes into popular products and which products make false claims. This Web site provides some excerpts from Ms. Begoun's books, as well as the *Cosmetics Counter* newsletter, the "Dear Paula" column, and Paula's Choice Skin Care System.

Diet and Weight Loss/Fitness Page

http://www1.mhv.net/~donn/diet.html

Inspiring and content-rich resource for anyone who wants to lose weight and get into better shape. Here you can read "The $1,000 Challenge," "A Powerful But Spooky Technique," "The Three Day Habit Breaker," and other articles written by a nonprofessional, self-taught expert from personal diet and fitness experience. Then move on to the huge collection of useful links, divided into categories of general information, diet and food, exercising and fitness, newsgroups, and health and fitness indexes.

11

Fashion Internet

http://www.finy.com/

Second best thing to attending a runway fashion show. The site has a New York focus, looking at the show rooms, design trends, and influential personalities in the fashion district. It's not parochial, though; start here to identify the ethnic and international influences on the best American designs. With Fashion Internet you'll stay a season ahead and find out what Isaac's up to.

Fashion Net

http://www.fashion.net/

Central search tool and directory of fashion-related Internet sites and services. Here you can find professionally compiled lists of message boards (fashion, beauty, modeling, and health and fitness) and top sites (magazines, shopping, fashion houses, beauty, modeling, and shows). You can also browse the industry-specific annotated guides for message boards, yellow pages, directories, trade publications, and shows and exhibits. There's hardly any fashion content per se within this site, but it is a comprehensive jumpstation to anything that may interest you.

Fashion Page

http://www.charm.net/~jakec/

Fashion maven Lynda Stretton produces this award-winning page, bringing fashion sense, style, and predictions to the Web world. For quick access, go directly to the table of contents to find new articles on current and past seasons as well as reviews of fashion television programs, magazines, books, and movies. If you're in the fashion industry, you'll appreciate the index of modeling agencies and fashion bibliography.

The Fragrance Foundation

http://www.fragrance.org/

The official Web site for The Fragrance Foundation. Here you can read about the history and mission of this organization and get perfume tips, fragrance trends, and information about the Olfactory Research Fund. The Features section offers articles that explore the importance of aromas and fragrances, such as using scent as a memory device and giving gifts of perfume. After touring The Fragrance Foundation, you'll wish that scents could be transferred over the Internet.

HairNet

http://www.hairnet.com/

Popular opinion asserts that hair is never unimportant. HairNet is dedicated to that proposition. Here you can find advice and services that help you make the most of your hair. Some of the features offered include *Beauty Online,* a Webzine devoted to beauty; *American Salon,* a leading beauty industry magazine; Salons Online, a database of beauty salons throughout the United States; HairNet Hotline, a community forum; and Beauty Schools Online, a database of beauty schools in a number of states.

11

The Lipstick Page

http://www.users.wineasy.se/bjornt/lip.html

Imagine an entire Web site devoted to lipstick: it would probably be full of color, advice, beauty tips, and pretty pictures. You're right—it is. Welcome to the Lipstick Page, where you can find everything you need to know about lipstick. The Lipstick Library provides a detailed catalog of colors, from "coral, peach, and apricot" to "reddish browns, brick, and terracotta." Learn who wears what lip paint in Lipstick of the Stars. Other useful sections include Cosmetics around the World, Tips and Consumer Issues, and the *FashionStance* mini-magazine.

Look Online

http://www.lookonline.com/

Insider perspective of the fashion industry. If you're interested in real fashion news—not just PR campaigns and ambiguous advice from waffling fashion critics—start here. Read about recent fashion shows (who showed up, who sat next to whom, and who was wearing what) and fashion politics (AIDS benefits and anti-fur and anti-exploitation demonstrations). Here you can also find interviews with designers, runway photos, and an updated list of Who's Who in New York Fashion Public Relations.

Lumiere

http://www.lumiere.com/

High-quality fashion Webzine; from funky and floral to shiny and sheer, you can read about it here. Every month, you'll find a variety of features on new seasonal fashions, trends, designers, models, photographers, fragrances, makeup, hair, and fashion in the entertainment industry. The site is chock-full of beautiful photographs, so you can see exactly what the authors are talking about. If you'd like to share your opinions with other fashion addicts or read about upcoming industry events, check out the message board.

Maximum Exposure

http://www.maxxp.com/

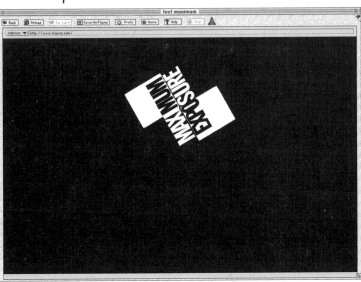

Webcast of Maximum Exposure, a live fashion industry event. This event is a charity benefit for Design Industries Foundation Fighting AIDS (DIFFA) and Photographers + Friends United Against AIDS. When Maximum Exposure is Webcasted, you'll be able to access live interviews with many celebrity models, photographers, performers, and actors. Some of the co-chairs of this event include Giorgio Armani, Fabien Baron, Kelly Klein, Peter MacGill, Isaac Mizrahi, Todd Oldham, and Anna Sui.

Redbook's Best Beauty Buys

http://homearts.com/rb/beauty/11bestf1.htm

Straightforward and down-to-earth guide to buying beauty products that are easy on your face and on your wallet. The pages on this site are divided into short advice blurbs on why some prices are so high, what to look for and what to avoid, which products can be substituted for more expensive brand products, and where to find the best deals on common products. Each blurb is presented with a photograph of the product and listed retail price.

Work Style

http://www.workstyle.com/

Where professional men and women come to get useful fashion advice for the working hours. Some fun features include Tip of the Day, Question of the Week, What They're Wearing in the [Music, Publishing, Computer, Legal, etc.] Industry, the Ask Kim advice column, the What to Wear column, and the Guess My Job? multiple-choice quiz. You can also read about a makeover and view "before" and "after" pictures of someone just like you!

TODAY'S NEWS

Campus Newspapers on the Internet

http://beacon-www.asa.utk.edu/resources/papers.html

A huge index of college and university newspapers, hosted by the University of Tennessee, Knoxville. You can browse the site listings by categories of how often the newspapers are published (daily, almost daily, or weekly, biweekly, and monthly). You can also find prototypes, demonstrations, and experimental newspapers which are still being developed. If you work on a student-run newspaper, you'll want to check the college journalism resources to find valuable Internet sites for editors and advisors.

Capitol Steps

http://www.capsteps.com/

An irreverent look at Washington. This site is produced by a group of current and former Congressional staffers who monitor events and personalities on Capitol Hill, in the Oval Office, and in other typically serious places of political action. Audiophiles will love the satirical collection of songs about former Speakers of the House. You also won't want to miss the New Year's Radio Special about Ross Perot.

The Chicago Tribune

http://www.chicago.tribune.com/

Web edition of Chicago's renowned newspaper. You can start your morning by reading the main page, which contains daily headlines and top stories. In addition to the typical sections found in a print newspaper—national and local news, weather, business, sports, culture, special features, and editorials—the online Chicago Tribune offers some unique features, such as sports career profiles and archives; a search tool for finding homes for sale or rent; a real estate transactions database; and a database of Chicago-based community profiles, statistics, directories, and school information.

The Christian Science e-Monitor

http://www.csmonitor.com/

A distinguished source of international and U.S. news, cultural reviews and features, editorials, and more. Readers of the *Christian Science Monitor* (*CSM*) will appreciate Our Place, an organized directory of *CSM* articles and related links; you can browse by arts and entertainment, kids resources, travel, poetry, and other categories. Special areas include Mixed Media, where you can find stories about cyberspace, crossword puzzles, e-mail from international bureaus, the Mega Movie Guide, the Bringing Down a Gang series, and a reader forum; a collection of *CSM* Pulitzer Prize-winning stories; and an Internet radio broadcast featuring hourly newscasts and a daily show.

Editor & Publishers Directory of the World's Online Newspapers

http://www.mediainfo.com/ephome/npaper/nphtm/online.htm

Directory of international online newspapers, compiled by the *Editor & Publisher Interactive* research staff. An interesting table of information here is the online newspapers statistics, which provide data on Internet publications by news source type (dailies, weeklies, business, alternatives, etc.) and by continental region. You can also find descriptive listings of links to online newspapers from around the world. If you want to attend journalism industry events, check the Conferences and Calendar of Events section.

The Heritage Foundation

http://www.heritage.org/

The official Web home of this conservative research and educational think tank. Some of the best features of this site include Real Audio samples from Heritage's monthly "Talk of the Town"; the online edition of *Policy Review: The Journal of American Citizenship,* The Heritage Foundation's bimonthly flagship magazine; the 1997 Index of Economic Freedom, a guide to international growth and development; an online edition of *Issues '96: The Candidate's Briefing Book;* and the Tax Reform NOW! news source.

Los Angeles Times

http://www.latimes.com/

The renowned daily news source features continually updated top news stories. Check out the Business Review and Outlook section for entertaining business features, high-tech industry stories, the year in review, and future predictions. Destination L.A. contains a bunch of fun and interesting features for Southern California residents; check out the daily puzzle and information about seismic activity, as well as the guides to local restaurants and coffeehouses, Tinseltown, biking, shopping, and visitor and beach information.

National Public Radio

http://www.npr.org/

A Web complement to National Public Radio. You can listen to new broadcasts of NPR news every hour and find station listings, program information, and transcripts here. Jazz lovers will want to visit NPR's Jazz Profiles page to listen to a weekly one-hour jazz documentary series hosted by Nancy Wilson. You can also listen to other NPR shows, including "All Things Considered," "Morning Edition," "Talk of the Nation," "Making the Music," "Performance Today," and "Seasonings: Food." This is a great companion to the NPR forum on America Online (keyword: NPR).

The New York Times

http://www.nytimes.com/

Web edition of one of the most widely-read newspapers in the world. Some of the features available only on the online New York Times include the "CyberTimes Extra" column, Political Points Internet resource directory, Issues '96 (a joint project with National Public Radio), the Business Digest, the Business Connections financial resources guide, and the Arts & Leisure guide to the week's cultural events in New York. You can also search the real estate database, try your hand at the crossword puzzle and trivia quiz, and explore the Web Specials showcase.

the Onion: Number One in the News

http://www.theonion.com/

Weekly Webzine of satirical news. Nothing is sacred here; the Onion pokes fun at everyone and everything. Read "news" stories about strikes, mergers, and disasters

11

that haven't really happened and are unlikely to occur. The Editorials are even worse—these are fake columns about so-called diseases, holidays, and controversies, among other topics. If you have ever thought the real news was a waste of time, you'll be pleased with this nonsense.

San Jose Mercury News: Mercury Center

http://www.sjmercury.com/

Online newspaper based in Silicon Valley. Go directly to the Breaking News section to read top news stories from the U.S. and around the globe. Mercury Center also offers extensive news and feature articles specifically about Silicon Valley and the high-tech industry. There are tons of useful services available here, including the Free Agent resume database, Family Cyberspace, the NewsHound automatic e-mail news service, and the searchable *San Jose Mercury News* library.

U.S. News and World Report Online

http://www.usnews.com/

A widely-read source of U.S. and international news based on the print magazine. You can view either a straightforward text or multimedia-enhanced version of this online magazine. Special sections include News Watch, Washington Connection, News You Can Use, Colleges and Careers, Town Hall, This Week's Issue, and Corporate Links. Specific highlights are provided with each section.

U.S. Newspapers on the Net

http://www.naa.org/hot/hot.html

Top Internet newspaper picks by the Newspaper Association of America. Newspaper Online Services, Contacts, and URLs is a complete index to every newspaper on the Internet. You can look at the Feature of the Week to immediately see the most recent top choice, or you can find the past winners in the Feature of the Week Hall of Fame. If you're looking for a newspaper in a particular state, click the imagemap graphic of the United States. You can also peruse the Alphabetical Listing of Dailies; a Weeklies, Business Papers, and Alternative Press directory; and Select International Editions.

The Wall Street Journal Interactive Edition

http://www.wsj.com/

Premiere business and financial newspaper on the Web. The main sections are the Front Section, Marketplace, Money and Investing, and Sports. You can use Personal Journal to customize your view of The Wall Street Journal Interactive Edition. Each company listed is linked to a Briefing Book, which provides a complete business profile. The most popular pages include Heard on the Street, Personal Technology, Editorials, U.S. Stocks, and Personal Finance. Be sure not to miss the award-winning Index to Market Data as well as the 14-Day Searchable Archive.

WashingtonPost.com

http://www.washingtonpost.com/

Widely read newspaper based in Washington, D.C. *WashingtonPost.com* consists of three parts: The Post, which presents straightforward news stories in plain text; WashingtonPost.com sections, which feature articles enhanced with related information, discussions, and graphics; and Washington World, which contains news, sports, recreation, restaurant, economy, and entertainment information pertaining to the Washington, D.C. area. Readers around the United States explore the WashingtonPost.com sections to find business, interaction, international, national, sports, and style pages.

TRAVEL

Airlines of the Net

http://w1.itn.net/airlines/

An award-winning, impartial jumpstation of Web-based airline information. Here you can find links to anything relating to air travel, including frequent flyer programs, airline stock quotes, medical airline transports, cargo airlines, manufacturers and suppliers, aviation organizations, airline Usenet newsgroups, airline toll-free numbers, and real-time airline reservations. In addition, there are listings for passenger carriers in all the continents of the world as well as carriers

11

no longer in service (if you still haven't found that lost suitcase). Frequent travelers will appreciate the listings of the best fares, schedules, and travel agents.

AOL travel.com

http://www.aoltravel.com/

The Web site of AOL's Travel Channel. One of the most valuable features here is the interactive imagemap of the United States. Click any state to find information on state parks, museums, colleges, airports, and city sites. You can also learn each state's bird, flower, nickname, motto, and capital. In addition, there is a useful compilation of travel links, including the top ten most useful trip-planning sites, the airline reservations service at Preview Travel, a handy distance calculator, and the Olsen and Associates currency converter. Of course, if you're a member, you can link directly back to the Travel channel itself to get most of the travel-planning resources you need from one place.

Destinations Magazine

http://www.travelersguide.com/destinations/

Elegant publication devoted to vacation travel. You can find important U.S. State Department alerts on overseas travel in the Intelligence section, travel tips and tidbits in FYI, and fun events going on around the country in Happenings. If you're planning a trip soon, check out Travelogue to find Eateries (a dining, café, and bar guide) and Retreats (off-the-beaten-track vacation ideas). The Expressions section offers personal stories, complaints, and recommendations.

Eurolink

http://www.syselog.com/eurolink/

A directory of voluminous travel information about 16 European countries. Simply click the flag of the country you're interested in, and you'll jump to a straightforward list of links on cities, tourism, entertainment, sports, business, government, and other types of information. This site's especially useful for aggregating travel and other information about small countries such as Hungary, Ireland, and Denmark. General European travel resources provide information about Eurail and the European Parliament.

Lonely Planet

http://www.lonelyplanet.com/

Collection of travel ideas from a well-known travel publisher. If you have a specific destination in mind, go to Destinations to access an interactive imagemap of the world or use Text Express, a straightforward index. You can also click Take a Mystery Tour to randomly select a travel guide. Truly unique is the Postcards section where thousands of travelers' reports from every region around the world are compiled into a database of information on visas, border crossings, highlights, scams, and tips and warnings of various sorts.

National Park Services's ParkNet

http://www.nps.gov/

This huge and wonderfully informative site gives you a glimpse into the essential public services provided by the National Park Service, from maintaining the National Registry of historical buildings to acting as steward of our national parks. A search facility lets you plan a trip to national parks. I looked up Antietam National Park and got phone numbers, maps, a copy of the Emancipation Proclamation, local weather conditions, driving instructions, and recommendations for what to wear! From ParkNet you can also link to related resources in the state park systems and the U.S. Fish and Wildlife Service.

Travel & Entertainment Network— Internet Operations (TEN-IO)

http://www.ten-io.com/

A directory of major travel and entertainment organizations and industry trade associations. These organizations are divided into categories such as accommodations, business travel services, cruises, destinations, entertainment, sports and recreation, transportation, travel agents, and travel-related information. If you click the button for any of these categories, you'll view an index of services. Each service offers an image-rich and descriptive catalog; from there, you can get contact information and make your reservations.

Travel Health Online

http://www.tripprep.com/index.html

A central source of travel health information, updated daily. Here you can peruse the alphabetized Directory of Country Summary Profiles to find health precautions, a disease risk summary, official health data, current health concerns, and the recent U.S. Department of State Advisory Consular Information Sheet. In addition, you can locate a travel medicine provider and read information on general travel health concerns, preventive medications and vaccines, and travel illnesses.

Travelocity

http://www.travelocity.com/

Complete information about the places you want to go and the ways you want to get there, with tips for having fun the whole time. Before you go anywhere, check the

Weather page to get the latest travel forecasts and airport reports. Ocean travelers will appreciate Travelocity Cruises by Cruises, Inc. You might be able to save some money by scanning Last Minute Deals. Points of View offers such goodies as the Trivia with Riddler game, a monthly contest, the Travelive chat forum, and the discussion bulletin boards. And don't miss the Spotlight feature or whale-watching column.

TravelWeb

http://www.travelweb.com/

You don't have to leave your home or office to make airline and hotel reservations; simply make a stop at this attractive site. If you're traveling this weekend, click the big button at the top to get the best hotel deals in major U.S. cities. Business travelers should go directly to the Business Traveler Resource Center to find information on special offers, ground transportation, overnight delivery, and computer services. Check the Press Office for recent travel news and features.

TheTrip.com: Flight Tracking

http://sapphire.thetrip.com/

Before leaving for the airport, stop by this site. This is an online real-time flight tracking service. Here you can get immediate data on current flights between major cities within the United States. Simply search for flights by airline, flight number,

11

city, and time, and you'll get up-to-the-minute estimated local takeoff and landing times, status, destination distance, distance to the closest city, altitude (in feet), speed (miles per hour), and airplane equipment.

21st Century Adventures E-zine

http://www.10e-design.com/centadv/

Monthly publication containing a variety of travel features. Travelers on a budget will appreciate PennyWise. World traveler Kaye Madsen provides a valuable tips sheet on saving money while touring the world. You can also take virtual tours via the beautiful photographic galleries of Hawaii, the Rockies, the Grecian Islands, the Alps, Ancient Ephesus, England's Warwick Castle, and Ancient Olympia, as well as a sailing and balloon ride adventure. Don't miss the fun Adventurers Quiz.

USA CityLink

http://usacitylink.com/

The USA CityLink Project is a comprehensive directory of travel, tourism, and relocation information for most U.S. states and cities. You can immediately "visit" a city—or rather its page—to find an organized listing of links to valuable Web sites. The U.S. Information page offers a unique collection of tidbits and features, such as the current approximate census, the Pledge of Allegiance, a sound file of a child singing "The Star Spangled Banner," and the history of the national flag.

Vacations.com

http://www.vacations.com/

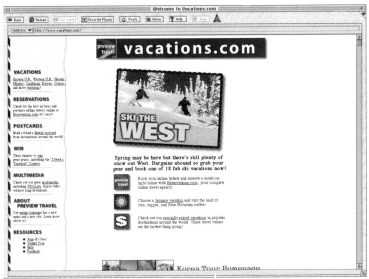

This complete guide to vacation planning comes to you from Preview Travel, an AOL partner and AOL-approved merchant whose vacation-booking service is available on AOL at keyword: Reservations. If you don't have a specific vacation in mind, you can use this Web site's Find-A-Trip to explore vacation types (such as romantic, family, singles, beach, casino, city, cultural, or weekend getaways) or regions (such as North America, Central America, or the Pacific Islands). One benefit of the Web over the forum is that you get video clips such as "Kayaking on Kauai," to help you make your plans (Chapter 6 has a section about Internet video).

11

World Travel Guide

http://www.wtgonline.com/

An encyclopedia-like database of regional information. If you're curious about a particular place, check the A to Z Country Fact Finder to learn about a country's area, population, population density, capital, geography, language, religion, time zone, electricity, communications, history, and government. From each country's fact page, you can access further information on accommodations, addresses, business, climate, essentials, resorts, social, and travel as well as view its map on the Map Page.

Appendix **A**

Your AOL Connection

S o, you got an AOL disk in the mail or packaged with a magazine, or maybe even with this book. What do you do first? How do you get from having a disk to exploring the global Internet? It's a short trip, with three legs:

- *Installing* AOL means putting a copy of the AOL software on your computer's hard disk.

- *Setting up your phone connection* means letting the software figure out your modem speed and type, and your choosing the local telephone numbers you want to use to access the AOL network.

- *Setting up your account* means connecting with AOL and providing the information required to give you full access to AOL and the Internet.

Note   *You can access AOL using a local network or another Internet Service Provider (ISP), instead of by modem connection to AOL's network, as explained in "Using AOL with a Network or Internet Service Provider." However, you must still install the AOL software and register with AOL following the steps in this appendix.*

Once you've installed the AOL software and registered with AOL, it's an easy matter to upgrade your software—get new versions. It's free, and sometimes automatic, and never requires putting another disk into your computer!

For all the "variables" involved—computer types, modem types, software versions, access numbers, service types, and billing plans—AOL has done an amazingly good job providing a simple reliable way of installing and registering. Just in case you do have a question along the way,

- If you have general questions, you'll find useful information in the Help(?) menu, which is available even if you've installed AOL but haven't yet registered.

- If you've registered and have questions about your connection or your account, try keyword: Help and keyword: Quick Answers.

- If you *can't* install or register for some reason, call one of the numbers in the "Numbers to Call if You Have Trouble" box at the end of this appendix.

If you are online and have questions about your connection, go to Member Services (keyword: Help). For help upgrading, go to keyword: Upgrade. For help using AOL, go to the Discover AOL area (keyword: DiscoverAOL) or Member Services (keyword: Help). For help with the Internet, go to keyword Nethelp—or, use this book!

Keywords

Once you're online, the fastest way to get to a specific AOL area or Internet address is using the Keyword window. It's always available from the Go To menu. To use it,

1. Sign onto AOL.

2. From the Go To menu, select Keyword. Enter a keyword in the box.

3. Click GO.

Some keywords you might want to get to know:

■ keyword: Help

■ keyword: Quick Answers

■ keyword: Billing

■ keyword: Access

■ keyword: Nethelp

WHAT YOU NEED

The disk is the key to getting online, but it's not all you need to use AOL. You'll also need:

■ A modem and phone line

■ An amply equipped Macintosh (see the "Recommended System" box)

■ A credit card or other payment means

■ A password and screen name (it's good to think of these things before you start)

A Connection: Dial-up or Network

You can access the America Online service in two ways: using AOL's network (normal dial-up access using a modem); or *not* using AOL's network, which means either:

■ Accessing AOL via a local "TCP/IP" network, such as you find in companies and organizations. If you have any questions about your network or need any help, ask your system administrator. If you can access the Internet over your work network, it's probably a TCP/IP network.

or

■ Running AOL with a dial-up SLIP/PPP connection to an Internet Service Provider.

 Appendix B, this book's glossary, explains terms such as SLIP and TCP/IP.

Dialing into the AOL Network

Dialing into AOL requires a modem. A modem lets your computer send and receive data over the telephone lines, which in turn are connected to AOL's data network. Your modem can be installed inside your computer (internal) or plugged into a jack in the back of the computer (external). And it can be low-speed (9,600 bps or lower) or high-speed (14,400 bps or higher). Unlike ordinary Internet Service Providers, with AOL you will usually never need to worry about the details of your modem: parity, baud, hardware handshaking, and stuff like that. The AOL software figures out what modem you're using.

Tip *If you don't yet have a modem, buy the fastest one you can afford. Once you're online, you can find more information at keyword: Modem. You can always buy a better modem on AOL at keyword: AOL Store (click on the AOL Modem Shop).*

If you'll be using a modem and dialing the AOL network, you'll also need a phone line. In using an Internet service such as AOL, you incur two costs: one is your monthly phone bill from your phone company, which may reflect your calls to AOL if they are toll calls or local calls above "basic" service. The other is the monthly or annual bill from AOL.

Connecting over a TCP/IP Network or ISP

To use AOL over a TCP/IP network or Internet Service Provider (ISP) you must have access to a local TCP/IP network or an account with an Internet Service Provider such as AT&T's WorldNet, Netcom, Mindspring, or any of the hundreds of local ISPs. You'll find a directory of ISPs in Chapter 11 ("Internet Connection").

Recommended System

If you're new to the Mac, welcome to the era of *big software*. Packing a ton of features into a "graphical user interface" (GUI) requires what a few years ago would have been a mainframe computer. Now the "recommended system" for AOL 3.0 is just about average for running a Macintosh application:

- 68030 CPU (68040 recommended)

- 600 x 400, 256-color or greyscale monitor

- System 7.1.0 or later (System 7.5.3 recommended)

- 8 Mb RAM (16 Mb recommended)

- 15 Mb free space on your hard disk

- 9,600 bps modem (14.4 or 28.8 kbps recommended for optimal performance) or a direct TCP/IP Internet connection

Means of Payment

AOL bills you monthly or annually, and you must provide credit-card information (type, number, expiration date) when you register. AOL can also debit your checking account directly, but adds a fee to your bill in order to defray the costs of providing this service. Once you're online you'll find more information about this topic at keyword: Billing. You must provide this information even if you'll be signing on via a network other than AOL's.

A

Way of Identifying Yourself

During registration with AOL, you'll be asked for a screen name and password. Your *screen name* is how other people on AOL and the Internet will recognize you; a *password* is how AOL keeps track of your unique account.

Note   *When you start registration for the very first time, you use the registration number and password provided on the AOL software package; during registration, you choose your own screen name and password.*

SCREEN NAME   A screen name is how AOL members and people on the Internet will know who you are—it forms the personal part of your e-mail address, as you'll see in Chapter 3. You can choose any combination of letters and numbers between three and ten characters, but can't use punctuation marks. Screen names on AOL must be unique. They are not case sensitive, though AOL displays your screen name, in e-mail messages and elsewhere, with an initial capital letter and any other capital letters *you* use during registration. On the Internet you'll see the term *user name* more than *screen name*. It doesn't matter; they're the same thing.

Tip   *When you register, you might not get your first choice, so be prepared with several alternatives. Many people use their first initial plus last name (HHoover) or first name plus last-name initial (FranklinDR).*

PASSWORD   A password ensures that only you can sign onto AOL with your screen name. You enter a password every time you sign on. On AOL you'll need a password that is hard to guess if someone has any *other* information about you. So, it's a good idea to make your password different from your name and the name of anyone in your family. Nor should it contain your birthdate, mother's maiden name, or Social Security number. Creating a password that consists of arbitrary and alternating numbers and letters is a good way of making your password unguessable.

Caution   *Never, in any circumstances, tell anyone your password, even if someone claiming to work for AOL asks for it. As a policy, no one who really works for AOL will **ever** ask you for your password. If someone does ask for your password, say no, then write an e-mail message to AOL's Community Action Team (CAT). Here's how: If the solicitation occurs when you're online (via an Instant Message) go to keyword: GuidePager, then click on Password and follow the instructions. If the solicitation occurs via an e-mail message to you, forward the message as proof of the incident to TOSemail1 or TOSemail2. Display the message, click Forward, type **TOSemail1** or **TOSemail2** in the To box, and click Send Now. In Chapter 3 you'll learn everything you need to know to use e-mail.*

With a modem installed and turned on, with your computer turned on, with the phone line free, with a credit card at hand and a screen name and password in mind, grab that disk and follow the instructions on its package!

SIGNING ON

Once you're registered with AOL, signing on is simple. "Signing on," also known as "logging on," means connecting to the AOL service and from there to the Internet.

Note   *Signing onto AOL is not like flipping a light switch. First of all, you have to open the AOL program. The program itself is large, so it may take a moment or two between the time you double click its icon and AOL displays on your screen. Then, when you sign on, the modem has to be "initialized," the AOL number dialed, a connection established, and your password verified. Things can go wrong: the number can be busy (in which case the second number will be dialed) or your password could be mistyped (you'll be asked to reenter it). If you do have to wait—it'll be worth it.*

An America Online folder is automatically created for you during installation and placed on your hard disk. The folder includes the AOL program itself as well as several folders of tools AOL needs to work.

To sign on to AOL:

1. Open the AOL folder by double-clicking on it, then double click the AOL icon. The AOL program may take a moment to display—it's a big program. When it does display, the Welcome window appears.

2. Type your password in the Enter Password box.

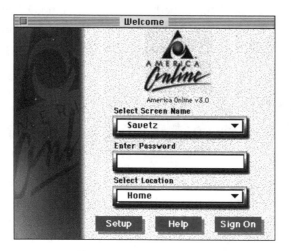

3. Click the Sign On button. AOL now looks for the modem, dials the local phone number you chose during registration, establishes connection with the AOL network, verifies your password, and...you're ready to navigate the Internet!

 *Chapter 2 picks up the story from here: what you do when you sign on, and how you sign off.*

USING AOL WITH A NETWORK OR INTERNET SERVICE PROVIDER

If you already have a SLIP or PPP connection with an Internet Service Provider, you can access AOL via that connection. (SLIP and PPP are defined in Appendix B. In a word, what SLIP or PPP lets you do is connect to the Internet using a modem.)

How do you know if you have such an account? If you have Internet access through a commercial service such as AT&T's WorldNet and pay a monthly fee for dial-in access (using a modem), you probably have a SLIP or PPP connection. If you're using a modem and use a graphical Internet program such as Netscape Navigator or Eudora, you almost certainly have such a connection.

AOL's "bring your own access" pricing plan makes it easy and cost- effective for subscribers of other services to use the content on the America Online service, but dial in through *another* network. The main advantages to this plan are that it's faster to sign onto AOL (at least after you've connected to your ISP) and you're less likely to encounter a busy signal.

To do so:

1. Open the AOL program.

2. Choose "TCP (for LAN or ISP)" from the Select Location menu on the Welcome screen.

3. Choose Preferences from the Members menu. Click on the AOL Link button. Press the Configure button. The AOL software will set up your system for logging in via an ISP. You may be asked to reboot and run the AOL software again.

4. Sign onto your SLIP or PPP connection with your Internet Service Provider. You'll probably have to provide a username and password just as on AOL, and for good measure you should make sure they're different from the ones you use on AOL.

5. Type in your password and sign on to America Online as you normally would.

With TCP/IP selected as your network type, modem information becomes irrelevant to AOL. Even if you're using a modem to access your Internet Service provider, you're still using TCP/IP to access AOL. Any problems with your modem or connection should be pursued with the provider through whom you're getting access.

Caution *You can stay logged onto AOL only as long as your connection is active; if you're disconnected from your ISP, you'll be disconnected from AOL as well. On the other hand, signing on through an ISP won't keep you from getting disconnected from AOL if you are inactive for a long period ("long period" varies with time of day). In that case, getting logged off AOL won't disconnect your underlying ISP connection, and you'll be tying up your phone line (and maybe incurring phone cost or ISP fee, or both) as long as the connection to the ISP is active.*

A

Why Create Special Locations?

If you access AOL from different places or by different methods (a TCP/IP network vs. dialing into AOL's network), you may want to creation different "locations." On the Sign On window, the location you're currently using is shown underneath the password field:

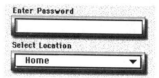

Why create different locations?

■ If you encounter a busy signal (in the evening, say), a different location can make access easier, even if the dial-in number is slower, or further from your house.

■ If you're frequently on the road, you may want to keep a separate location for each place you visit, complete with a local dial-in number.

■ If you use AOL at work or over a SLIP/PPP account from another Internet Service Provider, you might want to create a special location for those occasions.

To create a new location, choose New Location from the Select Location menu.

Signing On as a Guest

From time to time you may find yourself using America Online on someone else's computer. Your computer might be in the shop, or you might be travelling without your own computer. For these times, you start to sign on to your account on another computer that has the AOL software.

At the Select Screen Name box, select Guest, and click Sign On.

You'll be asked for your screen name and password before you connect. The modem will dial normally. Once AOL verifies your information, you'll be able to see your

Buddy List, send and receive e-mail, and use the core AOL features, but you won't be able to do things requiring access to the hard disk of the person whose machine you're using—you won't be able to use Favorite Places, Download Manager, or Personal Filing Cabinet.

Signing On While Travelling

If you take your PowerBook on a business trip or vacation, you can still access AOL even if your ordinary local access number is halfway across the country. Start the AOL program. At the Select Screen Name box, select New Local#, and click Sign On.

As during registration, you'll be asked to supply your current area code and then to select from a list of the access numbers closest to your temporary location. You might want to save the new number as a new location if you'll be in the new place for a while or must return there often.

You can also get a number using the 1-800-827-6364 Customer Service number. Alternatively, you can use AOL's 1-800 access number. For more information, go to keyword: Access.

 If you are on the road, make sure to bring along a phone cable (RJ-11 cord), and make sure to stay in a hotel room with a jack to plug it into!

If you're travelling abroad, you can still sign onto AOL using the AOLGlobalNet network, which carries a variable surcharge depending on the location from which you're calling. The current surcharges are available at keyword: AOLGlobalnet. With this network, AOL is currently available in more than 200 cities in over 80 countries around the world.

Note *AOLGlobalNet is quite a different thing from the new international channels popping up on AOL. Think of AOLGlobalNet as a physical network. Think of the new international channels as communities, in league with AOL's other channels, except that they serve the full range of needs of members in different countries. Currently, there are international channels in Germany, France, England, Italy, and Canada. Each has sports, entertainment, news, and more. These channels are available free to AOL members by going to the Channels menu and clicking International, then clicking World of AOL.*

Information about all of AOL's international services—the International channel and AOLGlobalNet—is available at keyword: International.

MODIFYING YOUR SETTINGS

What if you get a new modem, or change your address, or want to change your screen name? With America Online, it's easy to change the information you provided during registration.

IF YOU WANT TO DIAL IN USING A DIFFERENT PHONE NUMBER. While *offline*, start the AOL program and select New local# from the Select Screen Name drop-down list. Click Sign On. AOL dials a 1-800 number and connects. It prompts you for an area code. Type in an area code and click CONTINUE. Choose two access numbers, as during registration, then confirm your choices. You'll be returned to the Welcome screen. Re-select your actual screen name in the Select Screen Name box, type in your password, and click Sign On.

IF YOU GET A NEW MODEM. While *offline*, start the AOL program and select Setup at the Welcome screen. Choose your modem from the long list under Modem configuration: type. You can also change the modem port and port speed.

TO CHANGE YOUR PERSONAL INFORMATION (NAME, ADDRESS, ETC.). While *online,* go to keyword: Billing. Click on Modify Name or Address, or Modify Billing or Price Plan, and follow the instructions.

IF YOU WANT TO CHANGE YOUR PASSWORD (WHICH YOU SHOULD DO FROM TIME TO TIME). While *online*, go to keyword: Password and enter both your old password and the new one (twice, for verification). Write down your new password.

Tip   *With so many Web sites asking you to register these days, and each of them giving you a separate password, it's easy to forget your password! Find a special place to keep all your passwords.*

IF YOU WANT TO ADD A SCREEN NAME. First of all, you can't delete or change the main screen name on your "master account" (the one you registered with). It's your unique identifier on America Online. Together with your password, it's how AOL knows who you are. But you *can* use up to four additional screen names in your account, and sign on using one of them instead. Each of these additional screen names gets its own password. Keyword: Screen Name has all the details; you can add screen names there too.

Only one screen name for an account can be used online at the same time and screen names must be unique.

Why Would You Want Separate Screen Names?

- If other people in your household use AOL, each person may want a separate screen name, in order to have their own mailboxes. Yes, each screen name gets its own set of mailboxes (described in Chapter 3), and everybody gets their own storage space (2 Mb worth) using AOL's My Place service, as described in Chapter 7.

- If you like to hang out in chat rooms, you may want different screen names for your various online personas.

- If you subscribe to many mailing lists (Chapter 4), you can manage your mailboxes better by subscribing to lists from different screen names. If you ever delete a screen name, make sure to first unsubscribe from any mailing lists.

You'll probably find your own reasons for establishing multiple screen names. Parental Controls—which let parents control their children's access to the Web, e-mail, newsgroups, and other AOL or Internet features—can be set for each screen name on a master account (keyword: Parental).

UPGRADING AOL

Upgrading AOL means getting a new version of the AOL software. Software upgrades used to be a big deal. Now, you will encounter "incremental," more or less automatic upgrades when a single tool or feature gets upgraded.

For big upgrades (such as when the version number changes, like from version 2.5 to version 3.0, or version 3.0 to version 4.0), you must first get yourself a new installation file and run that program. Where do you find this software? Keyword: Upgrade. For lesser upgrades, the process takes place automatically. Let's look at each of these types of upgrade.

A

MAJOR UPGRADES (WITH A NEW VERSION NUMBER)

Making a big upgrade is a two-step process: downloading the installation file and running the file. Since you've already registered with AOL, you needn't provide again information such as your credit card number and street address. Further, the installation program makes note of any preferences you've established for earlier versions (they're stored on your computer) and transfers them automatically to the new version.

 Major upgrades give you a whole new set of AOL files but retain the AOL files you previously had on your system. After you're sure the upgraded version works, you can put the older AOL software in the trash.

You can get the new software online, but must install it while you're offline.

MINOR UPGRADES (SAME VERSION NUMBER, NEW TOOL)

AOL has a powerful new way of giving you "incremental" software releases. When a new service is added or an existing one enhanced, AOL automatically delivers the new software "on the fly" the first time you attempt to use it. Alternatively, when there's new software, you will be asked (in a little window) to update your AOL software automatically when you sign off. For example, if the browser's been spiffed up and you try to go to a Web site, you'll be asked to first wait for the new software to be downloaded, during which time you'll see something like this:

You will not incur any regular hourly charges during this update.

Now Downloading GOODBYE.UTF

61%

Less than a minute remaining

These "tools on the fly" are enhancements to the AOL software.

While the software is downloading (in under a minute or two, usually), you will see a New Features window describing why you are getting the software. After the software has been downloaded, you may be asked to allow the AOL software to restart itself (automatically). Click OK.

Numbers to Call if You Have Trouble

1-888-265-8001	To receive information on AOL Products or Services
1-888-265-8002	Upgrade to the current version or to order an AOL Membership Kit
1-888-265-8003	For billing information or to reactivate a cancelled account
1-888-265-8004	Screen name or password assistance
1-888-265-8005	Obtain a new access number
1-888-265-8007	AOL for Macintosh technical assistance
1-888-265-8006	AOL for Windows technical support
1-888-265-8008	To cancel an account

A

Appendix B

Indispensable Terms

Two excellent glossaries are available on the Internet if you want more detail about any listing in this glossary, or if you want to know about something that's *not* here. *Matisse*, from the Internet Literacy Consultants, has clean and compact definitions of the most important Internet terms (**http://www.matisse.net/ files/glossary.html**). Fuller definitions, are available in the *Webopaedia*, from Sandy Bay Software (**http://www.sandybay. com/pc-web/index.html**). On AOL, Answer- Man's Glossary (keyword: AM Glossary) provides short, crisp definitions of just about anything you'd want to know about the Internet.

address   There are several kinds of addresses on the Internet. An e-mail address, such as **answerman@aol.com**, is used by people to send mail to each other. An Internet address, or *URL*, such as **http://www.aol.com**, is used by people to request information from a computer. An *Internet Protocol (IP)* address, such as **206.139.24.100**, is used by computers on the Internet to send each other data. Gopher, Web, FTP, and e-mail addresses all follow the *domain name* system, and computers are set up on the Internet to "map" domain names to unique *IP addresses*.

address book   On AOL, your Address Book lets you keep track of the people to whom you most frequently send *e-mail* messages. It also lets you assign easy-to-remember names to those hard-to-remember Internet e-mail addresses. With your Address Book you can even maintain simple mailing lists, assigning a single name to a series of e-mail addresses of people you frequently write at the same time.

agent   Software used to perform some task automatically. Currently, many agents are being developed to automate the process of looking for information on the Internet.

Anonymous FTP   *See* **FTP.**

ANS   Stands for Advanced Network & Services, Inc., a company established as a non-profit organization in 1990 to serve as the principle architect of the NSFnet, the U.S. network that was the immediate forerunner of today's Internet. Since 1991,

ANS has been a pioneer in providing commercial access to the Internet. In 1995, AOL acquired ANS in order to provide reliable, fast, and affordable Internet access to a rapidly growing membership. As an AOL company, ANS continues to provide private networking services to hundreds of American companies. For more information, go to keyword: Access.information, go to keyword: ANS.

AOL Link   AOL Link is a part of the AOL software that allows you to use Internet tools that are not built into AOL. For instance, you can use NCSA Telnet, Netscape Navigator, and other Internet software with the help of AOL Link. AOL Link is automatically put in your Extensions folder when you install AOL. For more information, *see* Chapter 10.

AOLnet   America Online's proprietary high-speed, high-capacity data network, which provides access by modem in hundreds of cities in the U.S. For more information, go to keyword: Access.

Archie   An Internet tool used for finding files available via anonymous (publicly accessible) *FTP*. Archie uses a program that regularly visits known anonymous FTP sites, makes a list of files and directories at those sites, and makes the index available to people on the Internet to do searches of the resulting database of files. Searches can be done by e-mail or Telnet, but the easiest way is via the World Wide Web. There are approximately 20 Archie sites around the world; all maintain the same database of files available by anonymous FTP. *See* Chapter 8.

ASCII   Short for American Standard Code for Information Interchange; in practice, simple letters and numbers, unformatted so they can be read by computers on any operating system (Mac, Windows, Unix, etc.). All *HTML* files are available in ASCII format, to make them as widely available as possible.

asynchronous vs. real-time communication   Asynchronous is jargon for "not at the same time." Electronic mail and newsgroups are asynchronous types of communication. You send a message to another person, or to a mailing list, or to a newsgroup for someone else to read later or not at all. "Synchronous" is the opposite of asynchronous, though the more common technical term is "real time." Chat, Instant messages and IRC all take place in real time, that is, with another person reading your message almost instantly after you've typed and sent it. Asynchronous communication is often more "serious" than real-time communication, which is more personal and direct. For more information, *see* Chapter 3 (e-mail), Chapter 5 (newsgroups), and Chapter 10 (IRC).

B

Automatic AOL   America Online gives you many options for quickly and automatically carrying out tasks online, so you can do the reading and composing offline. Many of these tasks can be done using Automatic AOL: reading and posting to newsgroups, reading and sending e-mail, and downloading files. With Automatic AOL (available from the Mail menu), you choose the activities you want to automate, then choose the times when you want these activities to occur (or you can do them "on demand"). With Automatic AOL, for example, you can compose e-mail throughout the day but only go online once a day to *send* all your messages at the same time. Similarly, you can *receive* mail and newsgroup postings either according to some regular schedule or "on demand"—go online once a day, say, and run Automatic AOL, then sign off. Once your mail or newsgroups have been downloaded, you can sign off and read everything offline, at your leisure and without online cost. On the Windows version of AOL, Automatic AOL is known as FlashSessions. For more information, *see* Chapter 4.

bandwidth   The amount of data that can be transmitted over any communications medium (phone line or network) in a period of time, for example bits per second (bps).

BCC (blind carbon copy)   In e-mail, a copy of a message sent to someone without the primary recipient's awareness. The primary recipient is the person whose e-mail address (screen name) is in the To field. Using AOL, to send a BCC to someone, you choose "bcc" from the drop-down menu to the left of the e-mail address. You can send BCCs to any number of people. *See* Chapter 3.

binary   In *FTP*, a mode for transferring any *file* that requires a special program to use it. Basically, all files that aren't text are binary. Some FTP clients require that you indicate whether files you are transferring are text or binary; others detect this information. When in doubt: use binary, since a text file can be transmitted in binary mode but a binary file can't be transmitted as text unless it's been encoded using a technique such as *MIME* (*see* Chapters 3, 6).

bookmark   Hot lists, bookmarks, and Favorite Places all have the same purpose: to give you a means of keeping track of your favorite sites so you can easily return to them. *Bookmark* is Netscape's term for a list of favorite Web sites, while *Favorite Places* is AOL's term for your list of favorites available anywhere—on AOL, on the Web, in newsgroups, etc.

BPS   *See* **bandwidth**.

browser   Software used for displaying an HTML *page*, part of the World Wide Web. A browser takes a plain HTML page, which you download from the Web, and presents any images, formatting, and links contained on that page. The Mac AOL browser is a customized version of the Microsoft Internet Explorer browser. Your browser is always available by clicking the Globe icon of the main AOL tool bar or using keyword: Web or keyword: WWW. In addition, with AOL Link you can run other browsers, such as Netscape Navigator. *See* Chapter 6 on using the integrated browser and Chapter 10 on using the Netscape browser.

button   A small graphic on AOL or the Web that can be clicked to either link to related content or to process something (for example, in Marketplace, a Click Here To Purchase button would process an order if you're buying something). The AOL tool bar consists of buttons.

CAT   AOL's Community Action Team, responsible for enforcing AOL's Terms of Service (available at keyword: TOS).

CC (carbon, sometimes *courtesy,* copy)   In AOL's e-mail program, you send someone a CC if you want to send someone a copy of a message and you want the primary recipient to be aware of the CC. The primary recipient's e-mail address goes in the To field of the Compose Mail window, while people CC'ed go in the CC field. You can send CC's to any number of people by choosing "cc" from the drop-down menu to the left of the recipient's e-mail address. You can send CCs to people on AOL or on the Internet, or both. *See* Chapter 3.

channel   (**1**) On AOL, communities and forums are organized into channels, based on either subject or the actual location of the communities. The subject-based channels are Computers & Software; Entertainment; Games; Health & Fitness; the Hub; the Internet Connection; Kids Only; Learning & Culture; Life, Styles & Interests; MarketPlace; MusicSpace; Newsstand; Today's News; People Connection; Personal Finance; Reference; Sports; Style; Travel. The two place-based channels are Digital Cities (with content about large U.S. metropolitan areas) and International (with content for AOL "affiliates" in foreign countries—Canada, England, France, Germany, and Japan). Within channels, there are clusterings of content as big as some channels—Digital Cities Washington, the International channel affiliates, and Your Business (within Personal Finance), for example. The best way to find content within and across channels is using the Find area (click the Find button in the main window). (**2**) On *IRC*, the equivalent of a chat room, which can be formed by anyone. Unlike a chat room, a channel has an

B

operator, with broad powers to set the channel's topic, name other operators, and kick people out. *See* Chapter 10.

chat   Chat is a form of real-time communication, meaning you communicate with a group of people by sending messages, which they can read almost as soon as you send them. On AOL, chat rooms are available in the People Connection channel and throughout the other channels. The closest thing to chat on the Internet is *Internet Relay Chat (IRC)*. For more information about IRC, *see* Chapter 10.

check box   In Macintosh programs such as AOL, the little square check box gives you the ability to specify a choice (as in the Software Search area shown in Figure 8-5). You can check more than one box (or no boxes). With *radio buttons*, you can (and must) select only one choice. You select a check box by clicking in the little square.

client   The software you run on your computer, such as an e-mail client or FTP client. On the Internet, client software interacts with *server* software. Clients receive, package, and transmit requests for information stored on servers. The whole Internet is built on client/server principles, with applications distributed across a network and many clients accessing the programs and data available on a much smaller number of servers.

compress   *See* **file compression**.

cookie   A small text file created by a Web server and stored on *your* computer to keep track of the sorts of things you do on the server. Web administrators create cookies in order to get information about users' browsing habits and to modify their site accordingly, or to present users with a customized view of the site. The cookie file can trace a user's "click path" through a site, but not between sites. *See* Chapter 6.

CPT file   *See* **SIT file**.

directory   (**1**) The same thing as a folder—a place to keep files together. Your computer has directories, as do FTP sites and Web servers. (**2**) In the context of searching the Internet, a directory is a catalog of resources arranged into subjects such as Business and Medicine. A directory is different from a search *index* in that it is created by people and hence it is selective, more or less subjective, and often

annotated (with site descriptions, ratings, and comparisons). The major directories are Yahoo!, Magellan, and the Virtual Library. Some of the indexes, such as Excite, have their own directories. *See* "Search Terms and What They Mean" in Chapter 9.

domain name A *domain name* is a unique name for a group of computers at one organization on the Internet. People use domain names to identify and communicate with computers connected to the Internet. Domain names consists of several parts, separated by periods ("dots"), proceeding from specific to general. Your domain name is *aol.com*. The general part of the name (*com*, for example) identifies the domain *type*. The main domain types in the U.S. are *edu, com, mil, net, org,* and *gov*. Other countries usually have a "top-level" domain of two characters, such as *ca* for Canada and *nl* for the Netherlands. But you'll see three-letter non-U.S. domains (such as **www.corel.com**) and two-letter U.S. domains (such as **mcps.k12.md.us**). The domain name is the key part of every Internet address (URL). Every domain name can be home to a few or even a few thousand computers.

download To send a file from a generally accessible computer (*server*) to another, usually private computer (*client*), over networks such as AOL and the Internet. You download files from the Internet in many ways: e-mail, FTP, newsgroups, and the Web. AOL's *Download Manager* "queues" files to download when you use e-mail or one of AOL's file libraries. AOL's browser handles Web downloads. *Uploading* is the opposite: it means copying a file from a PC to another computer, where (often) it can be made available to others. On AOL some file libraries allow you to upload files. Chapter 6 (on the Web browser) and Chapter 8 (on FTP) have information about downloading files with AOL.

Download Manager A part of AOL that manages files you download from newsgroups, files attached to e-mail messages, and files you download using FTP and AOL's dozens of software libraries. It *doesn't* keep track of Web site downloads. Using Download Manager you can queue several files for download, automatically decompress files you download, and keep track of when you downloaded them. Download Manager is available from the File menu, even when you are offline, but offline use is limited to decompressing files and keeping track of your downloaded files. Additional information about the Download Manager is available at keyword: Download Info Center and at keyword: Download 101.

electronic mail Or *e-mail* or just *mail*. The main way to communicate with other people on the Internet. E-mail is an example of *asynchronous* communication, meaning it's not instantaneous; the other person may not see the message for days

(or ever). AOL offers choices such as hyperlinks and highly formatted text when you send e-mail to someone else on AOL. Most of these features will be stripped out of mail sent to people on the Internet, however. Using AOL, you can send the same piece of mail to several people on AOL or the Internet at the same time, and you can choose to have one or more indirect recipients (*CCs* and *BCCs*). *Mailing lists* are a way of communicating with a group of people. For more information, *see* Chapter 3.

emoticon   *See* **smiley**.

encryption   A way of scrambling sensitive information to prevent others from accessing it. AOL's browser allows you to encrypt information like your credit-card number when you wish to purchase a product or service from a vendor on the Web. The integrated browser automatically uses an encryption technique called *SSL*, for Secure Sockets Layer, which not only encrypts data but guarantees the authenticity of the other party and ensures the integrity of the data transmitted. *See* Chapter 6.

engine   *See* "Search Terms and What They Mean" in Chapter 9.

Explorer   Internet Explorer is the name of the Microsoft Web browser, which has been customized for AOL and integrated into AOL 3.0. *See* Chapter 6.

extensions   *See* **file extensions**.

e-zine   Also known as a *'zine*, *zine*, and *Webzine*, an e-zine (short for electronic magazine) is a publication that appears exclusively on the Internet, on a more or less regular publishing schedule, with its own editorial staff, writers, purpose, audience, and point of view. E-zines exist for every Internet service, including e-mail (where they're distributed by mailing lists), Gopher, and these days especially the Web (*Webzine*). E-zines have a reputation of being "alternative," but some are devoted to mainstream topics as well. An excellent source of information is John Labovitz's searchable E-zine List at **http://www.meer.net/~johnl/e-zine-list/**.

FAQ   Short for Frequently Asked Questions. Sometimes pronounced as a word ("FAK") and sometimes as F-A-Q. In newsgroups, a classic format for answering questions about the scope of the topic and about the newsgroup itself (what's acceptable and what's not). The original idea was to get everyone up to speed and to keep newcomers from asking the same questions on a newsgroup. Usually, an

individual maintains a FAQ, but everyone in a newsgroup can recommend modifications, giving many FAQs the status of authoritative, community-based documents. A FAQ is usually posted to the newsgroup in question as well as to **news.answers**. The **news.answers** archive, with hundreds of FAQs, is available at the **rtfm.mit.edu** FTP site, which is one of the FTP "Favorite Sites" available on America Online at keyword: FTP (click Go To FTP). The FAQ format has been adopted elsewhere on AOL and the Net. *See* Chapter 5.

Favorite Places An AOL-only feature that allows you to keep track of the "places" you like best, whether they're AOL forums, Web sites, or Internet newsgroups. You add to your Favorite Places folder by clicking the heart in a window's title bar. You access your Favorite Places folder by clicking the Favorite Places icon (the folder with a heart) on your tool bar. With Favorite Places you can easily create folders in order to group related resources for easy access. *See* Chapters 2 and 6.

file Computers use files to keep track of programs and data. A file has a location (a specific folder), a name (its filename), a type (or format, such as GIF), and a size (measured in bytes and kilobytes). The Macintosh Finder lets you view the files on your hard disk. *FTP* is the Internet service you use to *download* (retrieve) files from the Internet. AOL's many file libraries let you download files from AOL, including the programs you need to work with the files you download from the Internet! *See* Chapter 8.

file compression A technique for making a file smaller, so it takes up less space on a disk and can be uploaded and downloaded more quickly. Compressing and decompressing files requires a special program such as StuffIt. AOL's *Download Manager* can be used to automatically decompress some files. *See* Chapter 8.

file extensions The part of a filename that follows the period, as with the **JPEG** in **vertigo.JPEG**. Extensions are not required for Macintosh files, but are common and can be very useful. Extensions can tell you whether a file is compressed (*see* **file compression**), what operating system it's for (Macintosh or Windows), and what program you need to use the file. For more information, *see* Chapter 8.

FileGrabber Only on AOL! Newsgroups can be used to distribute files, such as software and sounds, but the files must first be converted from a *binary* format (computer code) into a text file (*ASCII text*). The text is meaningless to people, but at least it can be inserted into newsgroup postings and distributed across the Internet. To decode the text and turn it back into a computer code (a usable file), the file must

B

be decoded. AOL handles this for you automatically with a program called FileGrabber, which is accessed whenever you try to download a newsgroup posting containing such a file. *See* Chapter 5.

flame   In Internet mailing lists and newsgroups, a heated and unproductive argument. Flaming can be considered a form of hazing on the Internet, or it can serve a rhetorical purpose, or it can be considered merely abusive and rude—a result of not respecting the other person because the communication seems "anonymous." Flaming can be counter-productive insofar as it inhibits others from taking part in the communication. Special newsgroups are devoted to flaming. From the Newsgroups window (keyword: Newsgroups), click Search All Newsgroups and do a search for newsgroups with the word *flame* in their name. *See* Chapter 5.

form   In Web pages, a window giving you the opportunity to state your preferences or indicate a choice, as when you are taking a survey or buying a product. The standard elements of a form are a *text box* (where you type in something), *check boxes* or *radio buttons* (where you select from pre-determined choices), and different kinds of lists. Forms make the Web interactive, not just a means of passively getting information. *See* Chapter 2.

forwarding e-mail   Sending a message you've received to someone else. On America Online, if you select nothing in the original message to you before pressing the Forward button, you automatically forward the entire message. If you select any part of the message, editing and excerpting as you please, you'll forward only what you've selected. In either case, you can precede the message with your own comments as well. When you forward a message on AOL, the Subject line is automatically picked up from the original message; all you have to do is supply an address in the To box. Any files attached to the message you received will be forwarded as well; you can't detach them.

frames   Frames divide a Web browser into several windows, each of which displays a separate page. The benefit of frames is that they allow certain parts of a Web site to remain constant, such as the title, the table of contents, an ad, or the navigation bar. *See* Chapter 6.

freeware and shareware   Freeware is software that doesn't cost anything—as opposed to shareware, which is software you're expected but usually not required to pay for. Freeware may be a "crippled" version of full-blown commercial software, or it may simply be a program made available at no cost by its creator through the goodness of his or her heart. Freeware and shareware are available on AOL (keyword: Software Center), via FTP, and on the Web at sites such as **http://www.shareware.com**. *See* Chapter 8.

FTP   The Internet's File Transfer Protocol service, the most efficient way of moving a file from one computer to another across a *TCP/IP* network. Using FTP is like having access to someone else's computer: you browse directories and you help yourself to (download) files you want, copying them to your own computer. "Anonymous FTP" sites are publicly available. ("Anonymous" means that you automatically log in as **anonymous** and use your e-mail address as a password.) On AOL you can use both the *browser* and the built-in FTP *client* software at keyword: FTP to search and download files. Generally, the browser is better suited to searching, while the built-in client is better for downloading. America Online offers excellent resources for using the files you download via FTP, and many of the files themselves are available on AOL. For more information, *see* Chapter 8.

Fwd: *See* **forwarding e-mail**.

Gopher   An Internet service created in 1991 to permit easy access to Internet resources. Gopher simplified access in several ways. It organized resources in numbered lists, or menus, for easy selection. It provided English names instead of cryptic filenames, for clarity. It provided access to different types of resources, such as images, textual documents, Telnet sites, and FTP sites. The World Wide Web provides these same benefits, with the additional benefits of being able to directly display files of every kind and thus providing a better viewing and publishing platform. You search for Gopher resources using a program called *Veronica*. With AOL's browser you can access Gopher sites, and keyword: Gopher provides all the information and help you need to use Gopher on AOL, with a selection of the best sites. Most Gopher servers are not being maintained any longer, and few new ones are being created. *See* "Gopher's Swan Song" in Chapter 6.

helper app   A small program, or utility, used to present an image or sound or video file. Helper apps can assist the Web browser by displaying data types that the browser itself can't handle.

hierarchy   *See* **newsgroup**.

home page   **(1)** A home page, or personal page, is the creation of an individual, a way of sharing text or images via the World Wide Web. **(2)** A home page is also the

B

first page, or top page, of a Web site, the page from which you begin exploring a site or get an overview of its contents. **(3)** On AOL, your home page is the page your browser opens to automatically when you start it (or go to keyword: www or keyword: Web). You can have the AOL browser open to any home page you wish. For information about the home page your browser opens to, *see* Chapter 6.

host   **(1)** On the Internet, a computer that is "addressable" by (can exchange data with) another computer; it can accept and send *packets*. Sometimes (not quite correctly) used as a synonym for *server*. **(2)** To *host* a Web page means to make disk space available for it and to make it available to others on the Internet.

hot list   *See* **Favorite Places**.

HTML   Short for Hypertext Markup Language. When you use the Web, you download HTML files from Web servers to your computer. HTML files are made up of text that has simple instructions telling a browser how to display formatting (centering, type size and type styles, and so on). HTML is the common language of the World Wide Web: all browsers understand how to read basic HTML, though they vary in their techniques of representing more advanced HTML. The HTML language is regulated in practice by the big software companies, such as Microsoft and Netscape. HTML is simple to learn, especially with editing tools that create the "tags" automatically. AOL's Personal Publisher tool frees you from having to know any HTML to create a page, but for certain effects you may need to learn HTML or use an HTML editor.

http   The *protocol* used on the World Wide Web governing the exchange of messages and files between Web *servers* and *browsers*. When you enter a URL into your AOL browser, you are sending an http message to a Web server asking it to send a specific Web page.

hyperlink   An image or piece of text on a Web page, e-mail message, AOL forum, or elsewhere that is linked to related content. On a Web page, you can tell a textual hyperlink because of its color and underlining. When you pass your mouse over any hyperlink (without clicking), the mouse arrow turns into a pointing finger, meaning you can click on it, and the address (*URL*) of the pointed-to resource appears in the status bar at the bottom of the browser window. You link to that resource by clicking the hyperlink: move the mouse's pointer over the link and click once with the mouse button. The browser lets you return to the place from which you linked using the Back button. However, you cannot go "back" when hyperlinking from an e-mail message or AOL forum.

hypertext   On the Web, a text document in which some phrases and individual words are hyperlinked to enable easy access to information related to the content of the document. Hypertext can function as a glossary linking to definitions of words; as a bibliography linking to related articles about the same subject; and as a way of getting related information that documents, qualifies, or amplifies a particular point. Writing hypertext is an art, requiring selection of the best words and phrases in a way that doesn't intrude on the reading experience.

Hytelnet   A resource, available via Telnet, the Web, and in a stand-alone PC version, that provides access to more than 1,000 *Telnet* sites, particularly library catalogs. Hytelnet can be browsed or searched on the Web. A more detailed discussion can be found in Chapter 10.

icon   A small graphic that stands for, or links to, a program Web page, or forum. Clicking or double-clicking on an icon will open its program, page, or forum.

installation   Preparing a program for use on your computer. Installation usually involves decompressing a file and running a "setup" file. Installing usually means setting up a program for the first time. With AOL, you must also "register"—provide AOL with some personal and billing information—before actually using the software and the service, as explained in Appendix A.

Instant Message   An AOL-only feature that offers direct, one-to-one communication between two members who are signed on at the same time. Similar to *chat*, which allows two or more people to communicate at the same time.

Internet   The world's newest and fastest-growing country, possessing neither borders, nor immigration restrictions, nor formal government, nor regulatory apparatus; a self-governing entity with a strong but benign commercial sector and a disputatious population, yet no standing army or formal legal system. English is the most frequent language, but communication takes place in dozens of other languages. A place to spend a vacation or a lunch hour, a place where privacy is as important as the right to assume another identity. A place to find information and to publish it. Home to millions of chatters and info junkies. Yes, it's also a network of networks. *See* Chapter 1.

B

IP   Short for Internet Protocol, a technical term. IP is the core of *TCP/IP*, the standard that specifies how information is transmitted between computers on the Internet. Every computer on a *TCP/IP* network is identified by a unique *IP address*.

IP address   Every computer on the Internet has a unique IP address. IP addresses provide instructions to packets as they travel to other computers on the Internet. IP addresses consist of four numbers separated by periods ("dots"), each smaller than 255 (for example, 199.4.102.1). When you enter a *domain name* such as **www.aol.com**, it is converted behind the scenes into an IP address.

IRC   Short for Internet Relay Chat. IRC is the Internet's version of chat rooms. IRC is available on America Online through programs such as IRCle, which is available on AOL at keyword: AOL Link. IRC is organized in channels. Communication in IRC channels is informal, as in chat rooms. *See* Chapter 10.

ISP   Short for Internet Service Provider. A company that provides access to the Internet, usually by modem, and provides little or no selection or programming of content. America Online is generally considered to be more than an ISP because it provides not only Internet access, but also its own tools, content, and community.

Java and Javascript   Two different technologies from Sun Microsystems that deliver interactive content over the World Wide Web. Java is a programming language used to create small applications, or "applets," over the Internet. The technology is still experimental but promises a high degree of security and "platform independence" (it runs on any operating system, unlike competing technologies such as ActiveX). Javascript is a computer "scripting" language that can be incorporated into HTML to allow for certain effects such as balloon text and context-sensitive graphics. *See* Chapter 6.

Johnson-Grace   A company bought in 1996 by AOL, and the name of the technology created by the company for compressing (reducing the size of) sound and graphics files for faster distribution across the AOL network. Supported by the AOL browser but not yet widely used on the Internet.

library   On AOL, files and programs are available throughout the service, arranged in software libraries. You can search for files located in any library using keyword: FileSearch. *See* Chapter 8.

listbox   In a window, a box with a list of items that can be selected and linked to: programs, text articles, Web sites, AOL forums, etc. Chapter 2 covers listboxes as well as other things contained inside windows.

listproc   *See* **mailing list**.

LISTSERV   *See* **mailing list**.

mailing list   A group of people who communicate with each other about a shared interest by sending e-mail messages to a single e-mail address. Special list software distributes the message to everyone in the group. Lists range in size from a handful of subscribers to more than 100,000. Joining a list requires a subscription process that consists merely of sending an e-mail message to the software *administering* the list. The major varieties of software used to manage lists include LISTSERV, Listproc, and Majordomo. Lists can be *moderated* or *unmoderated*. Lists can also be distribution-only (newsletters) or true interactive discussion lists. *See* keyword: Nethelp, keyword: Mailing lists; Chapter 5.

Majordomo   *See* **mailing list**.

master account   In AOL, the account belonging to the screen name set up during registration. This screen name has the ability to create up to four additional screen names. It's the screen name responsible for paying bills and restricting the other screen names' access to certain areas and features. *See also* **Parental Controls**.

menu bar   A standard part of a Macintosh program, the menu bar is arranged in a row at the top of the screen. The menu bar consists of a list of "commands" or things you can do. Most programs have File, Edit, Window, and Help menus. In addition, AOL has Format, Go To, Mail, and Members menus. To use a menu, move your mouse over it and press the button; to select from a menu, move the mouse down the menu to the command, and release the button. Many menu commands have keyboard equivalents—shortcuts to the same command using the keyboard. When there are equivalents, the keys are displayed to the right of the command name (for example, the keyboard equivalent of Edit | Copy is COMMAND-C).

message   A message is the unit of *electronic mail*. It originates from one person and is sent to one or more people, or to *mailing list* software, for distribution to a group. The elements of a message are (**1**) the To/CC field, where you specify primary

B

and indirect recipients of the message; (**2**) the Subject field, where you indicate the topic of the message; and (**3**) the body of the message—the content. Messages can contain attached files. In sending e-mail to someone on AOL, you can include clickable hyperlinks and formatted text (bold, centered, text of different sizes, etc.). On AOL, newsgroup postings are called messages, though on the Internet the term for newsgroup term is *article*.

Message board   An AOL-only feature available in many forums throughout the service; the AOL version of newsgroups. A place for members to ask questions and share information with each other and forum leaders. Internet-related message boards are available at keyword: Answerman.

MIME   Short for the Multipurpose Internet Mail Extension, designed to simplify the transfer of files through the "gateways" that separate different e-mail systems. AOL's e-mail program supports MIME. To send someone a file attachment over the Internet, your recipient must also be using an e-mail program that supports MIME. Basically, MIME works by converting your *binary* document (formatted word-processed file, for example) into a text document, then telling the recipient's e-mail program how to handle the attached file.

modem   Short for MOdulator/DEModulator. A piece of hardware that takes your computer's ("digital") signals and converts them into a form that can be sent over ordinary ("analog") phone lines. Modems dial AOL when you want to sign on to the service, and transmit data in both directions when you want to use the service or the Internet. Internal modems go inside your computer; external ones go on your desk. They also differ in speed: a "14.4" modem is capable of sending data at the rate of 14,400 bits per second (a bit is a small unit of data); a "28.8" modem transmits data at twice the speed—or more, if a compression technique is used. Modems are important when you install the AOL software because AOL needs to know exactly what kind of modem you have, but the AOL installation software usually detects this information automatically. More information is available online at keyword: Modem.

moderated   A newsgroup or, more commonly, a mailing list that has a human moderator who keeps track of things. A moderator's responsibilities can range from deciding who can join a mailing list or newsgroup and what can be discussed there, to making sure that the mailing list software is working properly, to breaking up arguments or keeping the discussion on topic. An unmoderated mailing list has no one charged with monitoring people's messages. Most newsgroups are unmoderated.

mouse   Not the rodent that drowns in toilets and gets trapped in heating vents in the winter, but the piece of plastic, molded to fit your hand, attached to the back of your computer with a cable, and used to control your computer. Your basic mouse has one button, which you can press quickly, or *click*. The basic mouse actions are the click, the double click, and the drag. The mouse lets you do everything involved in getting around a Macintosh program: selecting from listboxes and menus; clicking on buttons and tool bars; selecting radio buttons and check boxes; using a scroll bar; dragging things around the desktop; and highlighting (selecting) text in order to cut, copy, and paste it. *See* Chapter 2.

MUD   A multi-dimensional dungeon (or dimension), an electronic place where people assume fictional characters and interact with others to create identities and invent another social world. Some MUDs are peaceable, while others are more warlike. MUDs have applications in business and education as well. Originally available only via *Telnet*, some MUDs are moving to the Web. The Web has also become a good source of information about MUDs, and a way of accessing them. An excellent source of information about MUDs is the MudConnector (**http://www.mudconnect.com**). *See* Chapter 10.

My Place   An FTP-based service, available only on AOL, that allows you to *upload* files from your computer to one of AOL's FTP computers (**members.aol.com**), where they can be referenced by any Web pages you create. Every AOL screen name is allotted two megabytes of space to store uploaded files. For information about My Place, *see* Chapter 7.

Net   *See* **Internet**.

B

AOL's Rules of the Road on the Net

From AOL's Rules of the Road: "The Internet is not owned, or operated by, or in any way affiliated with, AOL, Inc. or any of its affiliates; it is a separate, independent network of computers and is not part of AOL. Your use of the Internet is solely at your own risk. When using the Internet and all of its components, Members must conduct themselves responsibly according to the Internet's own particular code of conduct. Participating successfully on the Internet is really a matter of common sense. Although AOL, Inc. does not control the Internet, your conduct on the Internet when using your AOL account is subject to the AOL Rules."

netiquette   A collection of guidelines for using Internet services and interacting with people on the Internet. Some netiquette guidelines are meant to promote a good civil experience for everyone on the Internet—such as the admonition to avoid humor that could offend or be misunderstood on newsgroups. Other guidelines are meant to protect the physical, networking environment—such as the FTP customs of using nearby servers, logging on after hours, and not browsing or staying logged on too long. Every Internet service—e-mail, newsgroups, FTP, Telnet, and the Web—has netiquette guidelines. Breach of netiquette can have assorted negative consequences, from social disapproval, to getting kicked off your Internet service, to getting included on a "black list." AOL's Terms of Services require members to respect netiquette or risk removal from the service. AOL's Terms of Service are available at keyword: TOS. For a clear and complete Net-centric statement of netiquette guidelines, *see* **ftp://ds.internic.net/ fyi/fyi.28.txt**. For an AOL introduction to the subject, *see* keyword: Netiquette.

Netscape Navigator   A *browser* made by Netscape Communications Corp., and available to AOL members at **http://www.netscape.com**. Currently, Netscape is the world's most popular browser by virtue of its early appearance in the browser market, its great features (summarized in Chapter 10), its pricing (free to non-commercial users!), and its availability on all major platforms (Windows, Macintosh, Unix). Netscape has pioneered or been an early adopter of Internet technologies such as *frames, plug-ins,* and *Java.*

network   A group of computers connected by cabling, telephone wire, radio wave, or other medium, so that they can exchange data. Networks need not be restricted to a specific location, and they can themselves be networked. In a way, the Internet is a radical extension of the idea of networking, because it could ultimately include all computers and enable communication among all people with access to a computer.

newbie Someone new to the Internet or to a specific Internet service, such as FTP or MUDs. With the very rapid growth of the Internet, more than half of all people "on" the Internet in the last year or so have been newbies.

newsgroup An Internet discussion group, organized by topic and intended for broad public access and participation. AOL carries more than 20,000 Internet newsgroups, which are arranged in categories, or *hierarchies*. The whole newsgroup system is called Usenet, which is less a network than a classification scheme. A newsgroup name indicates the category and any subcategories to which it belongs, as well as the specific topic to which it is devoted (for example, **rec.sports.baseball** is about the topic of baseball, available in the sports subcategory, within the main *rec*reational category). You can search for newsgroups at keyword: Newsgroups (click Search All Newsgroups), and you can search for specific newsgroup postings at keyword: DejaNews. *See* Chapter 5.

offline Otherwise know as RL (real life). AOL offers many ways for you to do routine online tasks while you're offline, to keep your online costs down. With *Automatic AOL*, you can read e-mail while you're offline, and compose new messages offline as well. You can also read and write newsgroup postings while you're offline.

online Traditionally, being online meant being signed onto a commercial online service such as America Online, as opposed to *both* offline and "on the Internet." Today, there are plenty of activities that can be done offline as well as online, and, on America Online, going online is required to get onto the Internet. Signing onto AOL makes it possible to use the Internet; nothing else is required, and no additional expense is incurred.

packet The unit of data transmitted over a TCP/IP network such as AOL or the Internet. (Actually, *packet* is the generic term, and the actual *IP* unit is *datagram*.) Files, such as Web pages in the form of HTML files, must be broken up into tiny packets of data before they can be transmitted across networks. Every packet carries information about its source, its place in the sequence of all packets, and its destination. *See* Chapter 6.

B

page   A Web page and the HTML file on which it is based. A collection of pages is a Web site. A *home page* is the top page of a site and also the page your browser automatically opens to. *See* Chapter 6.

Parental Controls   America Online offers many ways for parents to control the experience of children who share their account. (The *master account* is usually in the parents' name, while the associated screen names belong to children in the household.) On the AOL service, parents can restrict kids' access to *chat rooms* and other features, as described throughout the book. Parental Controls vary by Internet service. For *newsgroups,* parents can block access to specific newsgroups and downloads. For *e-mail*, parents can prohibit kids from receiving attachments. For the *Web*, kids can be restricted to sites deemed appropriate for children or teenagers. Using Parental Controls, parents can also restrict children to the Kids Only channel. Parental Controls are available from the Members menu; click on Parental Control.

password   To sign on to AOL you must have a password and screen name, both of which you choose for the *master account* when you first register your AOL account. Once signed on, a master account holder can change, add, and delete up to four screen names, but the screen name used to register can't be changed. Your screen name and password identify you unmistakably to AOL's computers. It is vital to keep your password secret and to choose a password that others won't be able to guess. Tips for choosing a password and a form for actually changing it are available at keyword: Password.

Personal Filing Cabinet   Using your Personal Filing Cabinet (PFC), you can automatically save a copy of every e-mail message you send and receive. You can also save copies of every newsgroup posting you send and receive using *Automatic AOL*. Click the File Cabinet icon for access and more information (and to set your preferences).

Personal Publisher 2   Also known as PP2, a free service available on America Online for creating your own Web *page*. Personal Publisher lets you upload files using My Place, then create a page and link the files without knowing any HTML. Chapter 7 is devoted to PP2, and the service itself is available at keyword: PP2.

plug in   Software that allows a browser to smoothly handle and present multimedia files. Plug-ins were developed for the Netscape Navigator browser, and they're fully supported by AOL's browser (Chapter 10). Some of the major plug-ins you can use with AOL are Real Audio, VDO, and Shockwave. Real Audio and VDO are examples of streaming technology; they allow you to hear sounds and watch little video clips before the files have finished downloading. Other plug-ins can be downloaded from the Web and installed for either the Microsoft or Netscape browser (*see* Table 6-3). Using the older technology of helper applications (*helper apps*), browsers used independent programs and viewers that waited for files to finish downloading before playing them. *See* Chapters 6 and 8.

PPP   Point-to-Point Protocol, a way of accessing the Internet using a modem and the phone lines, preferred by many Internet Service Providers (ISPs). Connecting directly to AOL does not require a PPP connection, but AOL's new Bring Your Own Access pricing plan allows ISP subscribers to run AOL while using another ISP's PPP connection. *See also* **SLIP**.

protocol   A set of rules that computers follow when exchanging data. The Internet is built on widely shared networking protocols called *TCP/IP* and a set of application protocols that underlie the basic Internet services: the Web (*http*), Usenet News (nntp), e-mail (smtp), and FTP (ftp).

quoting   In e-mail and newsgroups, the practice of selectively choosing bits of a person's message to provide context for your response. In responses, by Internet tradition, each line of a quoted passage is preceded by a vertical line (|) or greater-than sign (>). On AOL, you can choose to use this style in your e-mail responses (click on MyAOL and set your e-mail preferences to "Internet"). Unfortunately, you cannot yet automatically quote when responding to a newsgroup article.

radio button   In Mac programs such as AOL, a radio button gives you the ability to specify a single choice (as in the Software Search area shown in Figure 8-5). With radio buttons you *must* click one (and only one) of the buttons. With *check boxes* you can select as many as you want (or no choices). You select a radio button by clicking in the circle, and a check box by clicking in the square.

Re: This tag is automatically tacked onto the beginning of an e-mail or newsgroup message when someone is responding to someone else's message. It can be edited out, but other people won't realize that your message is part of a *thread*—a collection of messages about the same theme.

real time   *See* **asynchronous vs. real-time communication**.

B

Search Terms

Chapter 9 has a text box, "Search Terms and What They Mean," explaining the technical or technical-seeming terms you'll encounter while using search tools, such as *Boolean operator, directory, engine, hits, index, query, relevance,* and *returns.*

server   A computer that makes a program, database, file, or other data available to other computers, called *clients*. The various Internet services—the Web, FTP, Gopher, e-mail—each use their own servers for controlling access to and distributing data to clients.

shareware   *See* **freeware and shareware**.

SIT or CPT file   SIT (StuffIt archives) and CPT (Compact Pro archives) are two common file compression systems on the Macintosh. Several related files can be bundled into one SIT or CPT file, for easy installation and for faster downloading. AOL's Download Manager will decompress SIT and CPT files for you, or you can use a utility such as StuffIt Expander.

SLIP   Short for Serial Line Internet Protocol, SLIP makes it possible for Internet Service Providers' subscribers to access the Internet using their modems. AOL does not provide a SLIP connection, but if you have a SLIP account with an *ISP*, you can log on to it, then run AOL: at the Sign On screen, choose "TCP (for LAN or ISP)" from the "Select Location" menu.

smiley   A way of indicating your intention or emotion by using characters requiring you to tilt your head to the left. Smileys save people the time of expressing their thoughts and feelings intelligibly ;-) If you want a big list of smileys, do a search for **smiley.txt** at keyword: FileSearch.

spam   Unsolicited e-mail or newsgroup postings, generally considered to be a waste of time, *bandwidth*, and disk space.

Spinner, AOL   In both the AOL browser and Netscape Navigator, the logo to the right of the URL box at the top of the browser window. The spinner displays the progress of a page as it's downloading, stopping when a page has been downloaded.

SSL   Short for Secure Sockets Layer, an industry-standard method of securing Internet transactions by encrypting them (scrambling them so they can't be read), authenticating them (making sure the other party is legitimate), and ensuring their integrity (making sure the data doesn't get tampered with).

status bar   In a Web browser, the line of information at the very bottom of the window that gives you information about what you are doing. It indicates whether your mouse is pointing to a hyperlink. If it is, you'll see the URL of that link in the status bar. It also tells you what's going on while the elements of a Web page are downloading one at a time.

surf   To browse the Web or the Net, jumping from link to link, page to page.

TCP/IP   The networking protocols on which the Internet is based. TCP/IP specifies how complex data is broken into pieces (packets) of the same size and structure, sent safely across many networks, then reassembled at the other end. TCP/IP requires several "layers" of protocols to carry out the various tasks of taking an application's data, breaking it into packets, addressing them, passing them off to physical networks, and (at the receiving end) reassembling the packets into a useful form.

Telnet   The protocol, and the applications based on the protocol, that let you access text-based programs, games, and databases on a distant computer. With Telnet, your keyboard and monitor become a "dumb" terminal that allows you to communicate with the distant computer. Telnet makes it possible for people to play real-time simulation and adventure games on the Internet. Telnet also makes it possible to use electronic catalogs of libraries located all over the world. With AOL Link you can use a program such as NCSA Telnet to access Telnet sites. *See* Chapter 10.

text box   An element in which you type some text or numbers to tell a program your preferences, or to order a product, or to register at a Web site, or to enter your keyword when using a search service such as Excite.

thread   In newsgroups, mailing lists, and e-mail, a set of messages about the same subject, or at least with the same Subject line. A thread is like a conversation. AOL's newsreader lets you follow all the messages that comprise a thread, but AOL's e-mail program doesn't let you sort messages in this way. Whenever you see *re*: before a subject, you're looking at a response to another message, and thus part of a thread.

B

TOS   *See* **CAT**.

upload   To send a file from a Mac or any other *client* to a *server*, where it can be used by others or referenced by a Web page. On AOL, the My Place service allows members to upload 2Mb of files per screen name for use in Web pages or for other purposes. *See* Chapter 7. *See also* **download**.

URL   Uniform Resource Locator. The standard Internet scheme for specifying the address, or location, of an Internet resource (such as a Web page or Gopher menu). A typical URL is **http://members.aol.com/jennlt1**. URLs have three parts: the *protocol* (**http**), the *domain name* (**users.aol.com**), and the file name with full directory path (**jennlt1**). File names are sometimes implicit; omitting a file name causes the browser to look for a default page, such as *index.html, main.html,* or something similar. *See* Chapter 6.

Usenet   The organizational scheme for keeping track of *newsgroups*—widely accessible bulletin boards devoted to specific topics. Newsgroups are arranged into categories (or *hierarchies*), and the two major hierarchies are the standard (or traditional) hierarchy and the alternative hierarchy. Usenet is not really a physical network so much as the naming scheme used by Usenet News servers. AOL's Newsgroup feature is available at keyword: Newsgroups. *See* Chapter 5.

Veronica   The search engine used for finding information available by Gopher. Only a handful of Veronica servers are being maintained in the world today, and not all of them are being updated. When you do a Veronica search, you can choose "searching Gopherspace," which means to search an index consisting of all the files pointed-to by all the world's public Gopher servers. You can also choose "search Gopher directories," which is similar to using a directory to find clusters of resources grouped under some subject head such as Business, Humor, or Recipes. On AOL, a Veronica server is available from the search page of the AOL Web site (just click Search on the AOL browser). *See* Chapter 9.

virus   A small program or "macro" intended to create unwanted changes to someone else's computer. Some effects can be destructive, others just annoying. Viruses work by latching onto programs or application templates, then causing programs to act in unexpected ways. The best way to avoid a virus is to scan all files downloaded from the Internet for viruses. Keyword: Virus center has information, current alerts, and anti-virus programs you can use to prevent or eradicate viruses.

All software available from AOL at keyword: FileSearch or any other software library on the service has been virus protected.

WAIS   Short for Wide Area Information System, a technique for indexing large collections of text documents to make them easier to search. WAIS is now rarely used because so few resources have been indexed and because other search tools have taken its place.

Webzine   *See* **e-zine**.

World Wide Web   Millions of *pages* of information, arranged in more or less complex sites, on every subject, connected by *hyperlinks,* and navigated and viewed with a *browser. See* Chapters 6, 7, and 10.

zipped file   A file compression system common on Windows computers, but decodable on a Mac using a program like StuffIt Expander. A file that contains several other files, so the zipped files are simpler to send and receive over a network.

Zine (or 'zine)   *See* **e-zine**.

B

INDEX

N

Start Making the Right Connections with America Online's Special Trial Offer of Fifty Free Hours!

The enclosed CD-ROM includes connection software for Macintosh computers.

How to Install AOL

1. Insert the America Online CD-ROM into your CD-ROM drive.

2. Double-click on the America Online install icon.

3. Follow the simple step-by-step instructions and when prompted, enter the special registration number and password found on the card beneath the CD-ROM.

4. For details on getting connected for the first time, see Appendix A of this book.

**Questions About Connecting? Need a Floppy Disk?
Need a Replacement CD-ROM?**

For any questions about the CD-ROM, call America Online at 1-800-827-6364.

Licensing Agreement

The program contained in this package is proprietary to America Online Inc. (AOL). THIS PROGRAM IS PROVIDED "AS IS" WITHOUT WARRANTY OF ANY KIND, EITHER EXPRESSED OR IMPLIED. THERE IS EXPLICITLY EXCLUDED ANY IMPLIED WARRANTIES OF THE MERCHANTABILITY OR FITNESS FOR A PARTICULAR PURPOSE OR USE. THE ENTIRE RISK AS TO THE QUALITY AND PERFORMANCE OF THE PROGRAM IS ASSUMED BY YOU. IN NO EVENT WILL ANY OF THE McGRAW-HILL COMPANIES, INC., ITS DEALERS AND DISTRIBUTORS, AND/OR AOL BE LIABLE TO YOU FOR ANY LOST PROFITS OR OTHER INCIDENTAL OR CONSEQUENTIAL DAMAGES ARISING OUT OF THE USE OF OR INABILITY TO USE THE PROGRAM, EVEN IF ADVISED AS TO THE POSSIBILITY OF SUCH DAMAGE.

Some states do not allow the disclaimer of certain warranties, so the foregoing may not apply to you.